Language and Style
in
Old English Composite Homilies

Medieval and Renaissance
Texts and Studies

Volume 361

Language and Style
in
Old English Composite Homilies

by

Hiroshi Ogawa

ACMRS
(Arizona Center for Medieval and Renaissance Studies)
Tempe, Arizona
2010

Published by ACMRS (Arizona Center for Medieval and Renaissance Studies)
Tempe, Arizona
© 2010 by the Arizona Board of Regents for Arizona State University
All Rights Reserved.

Library of Congress Cataloging-in-Publication Data

Ogawa, Hiroshi, 1942-
  Language and style in Old English composite homilies / by Hiroshi Ogawa.
      p. cm. -- (Medieval and renaissance texts and studies ; v. 361)
  Includes bibliographical references and index.
  ISBN 978-0-86698-409-6 (alk. paper)
  1. English prose literature--Old English, ca. 450-1100--History and criticism.
  2. Sermons, English (Old)--Style. 3. Sermons, Medieval--England--Style.
  I. Title.
  PR226.O35 2009
  829'.80093823--dc22
                                                                      2009021823

Cover Art:
The Tower of Babel
A scene from a manuscript by Ælfric (11th c.)
The Pentateuch and the Book of Joshua
Image is in the public domain.

This book is made to last. It is set in Adobe Caslon Pro,
smyth-sewn and printed on acid-free paper to library specifications.
Printed in the United States of America.

Table of Contents

Preface

Abbreviations

I.	Introduction	1
II.	Napier XXX: A Wulfstan/Vercelli Composite and its Later History	11
III.	Napier XL and Napier LVIII: Two Other Uses of Wulfstan Homilies and Their Place in the Old English Vernacular Prose Tradition	37
IV.	Late Old English Judgement Day Homilies: The Vercelli Tradition in the Tenth and Eleventh Centuries	63
V.	Napier XXIX: A Homily With a Poetic Source	107
VI.	*In Die Sancto Pasce* and *De Descensu Christi Ad Inferos*: Two Easter Homilies Using Ælfrician Material	139
VII.	Conclusion	173

Appendix — Napier XL (Hatton 114) 183

Bibliography 187

Index 199

Preface

This study of Old English composite homilies had its *fons et origo* more than ten years ago, when I was awarded grants to stay in Oxford in 1992–1993 to pursue research on the Ælfrician and anonymous lives of St Martin, including the one in MSS Junius 85-86 in the Bodleian Library. I owe special thanks to the British Academy, the Japan Society for the Promotion of Science, and the Ministry of Education and Science of Japan for these grants, which enabled me in the first instance to launch a research project that has occupied me during these intervening years, leading to the present study. I published some results of this continuing research several years ago as a monograph, *Studies in the History of Old English Prose* (Tokyo, 2000). The transition to the present study hinges on the anonymous homily known as Napier XXX, which was the subject of the last item of that previous collection and which has since stimulated a different treatment (in the first of the central five chapters of the present book) after a new perspective on the homily was opened to me as a result of studying various other Old English homilies. The other chapters have all been freshly written between 2000 and 2004, in the order in which they now stand, as problems gradually unfolded themselves to my view, so that the draft was completed in March 2004 when I retired from the University of Tokyo. Given its origin, publication in the present form is, I sincerely hope, a fitting acknowledgement of the debts I owe to the countries and institutions which inspired it and rendered it possible; my special thanks are due to Professor Robert Bjork, Director of the Arizona Center for Medieval and Renaissance Studies (ACMRS), and the Editorial Board of the Medieval and Renaissance Texts and Studies (MRTS) of the Center, for agreeing to include my study in this series, and the Center's Managing Editor Mr Roy Rukkila who has overseen publication.

Besides the grants mentioned above, financial assistance has also been received from the Ministry of Education and Science of Japan and later from the Japan Society for the Promotion of Science for five terms of three years since 1994, which has enabled me to pursue my study of Old English homilies and to complete the present book. All these generous forms of support are most gratefully acknowledged. It is also a pleasant duty to acknowledge my indebtedness to the following individuals and institutions who have helped me to complete this study, besides those scholars from whose printed works I have greatly benefited as I acknowledge individually at appropriate places in the following pages: Dr

Bruce Mitchell, who has always been ready with counsel and suggestions ever since I was his student in 1976-77 and kindly answered queries I made on some points of syntax while writing Chapter V of this book; the late Professor Tamotsu Matsunami, who first drew me to Old English and Middle English studies and always encouraged and helped me; Professor Shigeru Ono, for his example as a philologist and continual encouragement, in particular with kind words on a presentation which was to become the basis of Chapter VI; Professor Malcolm Godden, for his generous help with checking the manuscript of Napier XXX as I first began to study this homily and also for his subsequent review of my previous book mentioned above, which has helped me to clarify my own thinking as I was preparing this book; Dr Timothy C. Graham, for valuable criticisms and suggestions concerning my earlier study of Napier XXX and part of Chapter III of this book and for supporting publication of this book; two anonymous Readers for the corrections and suggestions they generously made on the submitted manuscript from which I have benefited much; Mr Clifford Edwards (on behalf of the late Dr Enid M. Edwards [née Raynes]), Professor Donald G. Scragg, Dr Mary Swan, and Professor Jonathan Wilcox, for permission to quote from and make reference to their unpublished dissertations; the staff of the Bodleian Library, Oxford, the British Library, the John Rylands University Library of Manchester, the Showa Women's University Library, Tokyo, and the University Library of Tokyo at Komaba, for valued help in obtaining photographic copies of the dissertations of the scholars just mentioned and other bibliographical materials; the Department of English, University of Tokyo at Komaba, especially Dr Jun Terasawa, for access to the microfilms and facsimiles in the collection of the Centre for Medieval English Studies (Tokyo) and the Miyabe Collection; Dr Kiriko Sato, for the assiduous help she gave, amidst her own engagements as a doctorate student (as she was when I was preparing the draft), with checking the quotations from and references to Old English homilies and their source texts; two of my former colleagues at Komaba, Dr Yoshiko Kobayashi, for providing timely aid with bibliographical material in the Bodleian Library while she was in Oxford in 2001–2002, and Professor Brendan Wilson, to whom I owe the same special thanks as in my previous book, for giving most generously of his time to read all the chapters and related materials in draft, revising my English, and making suggestions both for stylistic improvements and on the structuring of the chapters; and above all my mother, Fumie Ogawa, for support and encouragement, and my family, Teruko, Sumiko, and Fumiko, for support and help with the proofs. To these four and to the memory of my father Kazuo Ogawa who fostered my interest in the English language and its history, I dedicate this book.

Hiroshi Ogawa
Taishido, Tokyo
January 2007

Abbreviations

ASE	*Anglo-Saxon England*
Bosworth-Toller	see below
BT, BTS	*An Anglo-Saxon Dictionary*, ed. Joseph Bosworth and T. Northcote Toller (London, 1898); *Supplement* by Toller (1921), with Revised and Enlarged Addenda by Alistair Campbell (1972)
Clark Hall	John R. Clark Hall (ed.), *A Concise Anglo-Saxon Dictionary*. 4th edn., with a Supplement by Herbert D. Meritt (Cambridge, 1960).
DOE	*The Dictionary of Old English*, ed. Angus F. Cameron *et al.* (Toronto, 1986–)

EETS
  os
  ss
	Early English Text Society
	  Original Series
	  Supplementary Series

JEGP	*Journal of English and Germanic Philology*
LSE	*Leeds Studies in English,* New Series
NM	*Neuphilologische Mitteilungen*
OED	*The Oxford English Dictionary*, ed. J. A. H. Murray *et al.* 2nd edn., Prepared by J. A. Simpson and E. S. C. Weiner (Oxford, 1989)
OES	*Old English Syntax*. 2 vols., by Bruce Mitchell (Oxford, 1985)
PBA	*Proceedings of the British Academy*
PMLA	*Publications of the Modern Language Association of America*

Short titles of Old English texts and the system of reference are, unless otherwise stated in the appropriate notes to the individual items, those adopted in the Dictionary of Old English. The abbreviations and symbols for grammatical terms are used so commonly as to require no explanation.

I.
Introduction

Of the large body of Old English literary works written in prose, homilies (including both *homiliae* and *sermones*[1]) are perhaps the most important genre, both in the number of texts that have survived and the literary quality they achieve. There are some three hundred texts that are so classified by the Toronto Dictionary of Old English. These, together with related genres such as saints' lives and biblical translations, constitute a body of vernacular religious prose which no other European language of the period can rival.[2]

This corpus of homilies represents a vernacular prose tradition extending over several centuries, from the composition of the earliest homilies, possibly in the pre-Alfredian ninth century, to those homilies which are preserved in manuscripts of the early twelfth century. The most important single point in their chronology is the Benedictine Reform for the revival of monasticism in the tenth century, which formed a divide between two traditions of homiletic writing in Anglo-Saxon England. Whereas the homilies that antedate it generally represent the apocryphal tradition of Christian teaching, those coming later, inspired by the ideas of the Reform, are characterized by their deep concern with strict orthodoxy and their dependence on the writings of the Church Fathers to which they often turned as authorities for that purpose. The earlier group of homilies are represented most importantly by the two collections known as the Blickling Homilies and Vercelli Homilies, while the two known authors, Ælfric, an alumnus of the reformer Æthelwold's school at Winchester and later Abbot of Eynsham, and Wulfstan, Archbishop of York and Bishop of Worcester,

---

[1] Milton McC. Gatch defines the distinction as the one 'between *sermo*, a general address on a religious theme, and *homilia*, an exegetical address on a passage of Scripture' ('The Achievement of Aelfric and His Colleagues in European Perspective', *The Old English Homily and its Backgrounds*, ed. Paul E. Szarmach and Bernard F. Huppé (Albany, 1978), pp. 43–73, at p. 45). See also the same author's remark about Archbishop Wulfstan's homilies: 'To make the traditional distinction, [Wulfstan's] writings are in the main not homilies but sermons, not explications of the Gospel pericopes for selected occasions of the liturgical year but public discourses on religious topics' (*Preaching and Theology in Anglo-Saxon England: Ælfric and Wulfstan* (Toronto and Buffalo, 1977), p. 19).

[2] For details see Gatch, 'The Achievement of Aelfric'.

both writing in the decades around the turn of the tenth century, represent the highest achievement of the later group.[3] Ælfric's two series of *Catholic Homilies* and Wulfstan's two dozen homilies now extant demonstrate the possibilities of the homiletic tradition in Anglo-Saxon England, in their orthodox teachings and in the excellence of the prose style they pursued and developed in their different ways.

Another important distinction concerning Old English homilies is whether they are original works or 'composite homilies'—homilies which 'are made up largely of passages drawn with little change from other Old English writings (usually homiletic) and not freshly composed or translated from Latin'.[4] Because of this method of composition, composite homilies have sometimes been called 'scissors and paste' works. But this is a mistake. As Donald Scragg puts it, 'compilers of what are sometimes called scissors and paste homilies don't just cut material from earlier homilies and stick pieces together verbatim'.[5] They produced not unreflective pastiches but compilations, using varying degrees and forms of adaptation to create a new work out of the borrowed passages. Hence the occasional reference to them, in German, as 'Kompilationspredigten' (compilation homilies), which Paul Szarmach explains, from his structural point of view, as 'a collection of religious themes for a hortatory purpose'[6] and further as follows:

> In the genre of the *Kompilationspredigt* there is therefore a form one might label the "concentric homily," which consists of a number of motifs or themes that prepare for a narrative or dramatic center by anticipating the style and content of the center. What source or textual critics might see as a pastiche could very well have a unity obscured by a critic's overconcern with the antecedent parts of the whole. When a homilist uses traditional motifs and themes with rhetorical purpose and design, he is using an author's pen, not "scissors and paste." The kind of critical examination of the structure of the *Kompilationspredigten* undertaken here should bring about a salutary reevaluation of the anonymous tradition.[7]

Seen in this light, composite homilies are important in their own right, in terms of their unity and structure, as Szarmach emphasizes, and further historically. In Malcolm Godden's words:

---

[3] See Gatch, *Preaching and Theology*, pp. 119–28.

[4] M. R. Godden, 'Old English composite homilies from Winchester', *ASE* 4 (1975), 57–65, at 57.

[5] Donald Scragg, *Dating and Style in Old English Composite Homilies* (Cambridge, 1998), p. 11.

[6] Paul E. Szarmach, 'The Vercelli Homilies: Style and Structure', *The Old English Homily and Its Backgrounds*, ed. idem and Bernard F. Huppé (Albany, 1978), pp. 241–67, at p. 241.

[7] Szarmach, 'The Vercelli Homilies', p. 252.

Most of them exist in only one copy, compared with the several surviving copies of most original homilies, and they were probably not given wide circulation. But such homilies can tell us a great deal about the homiletic tradition in England: about attitudes towards homiletic form and content; about the interests of those who read and plundered the homilies of Ælfric and Wulfstan; and about the availability of particular texts in particular areas, and the form in which they were known.[8]

Compilers reveal their 'attitudes' towards preceding works both in 'form and content'—that is, in the language (including style) and substance of the homily, and the adaptations they make in both aspects can tell us much about their own interests and perceptions, thereby defining their places in the tradition of vernacular homilies in which they found themselves and the changing language (again including style) in which the tradition is embodied.

The source writings for compilers are numerous and various. They are usually prose works (mostly homilies), both of known writers (Ælfric and Wulfstan) and anonymous homilists, but occasionally Old English poems provide the source. Some compilers even draw upon Latin homilies from which they translate passages, incorporating them into compilations from Old English writings. Based on these preceding works, Old English composite homilies are, as might be expected, mainly a product of the later period in terms of the division made above, with some of the earliest (such as those in the Vercelli collection) coming probably from not much later than the middle of the tenth century.[9] They are mostly preserved in late tenth- and eleventh-century manuscripts, though compilations continued to be made well into the twelfth century, giving the genre a degree of steady development over the centuries which few others can match. The present study is concerned with the Old English period, as represented by composite homilies that are preserved in tenth- and eleventh-century manuscripts. Later compilations, made as they were after the Norman Conquest in a milieu socially and culturally very different, show signs of forming a distinct phase of the tradition and would be a subject for a separate study.[10]

As our rejection of the 'scissors and paste' theory implies, the idea of the composite homily (or *Kompilationspredigt*) is a new insight gained by recent scholarship in considering the tradition of Old English vernacular homilies. The older view was explicitly inconsistent with it in its treatment of the Wulfstan homilies and works related to them in one way or another. Here the tendency

---

[8] Godden, 'OE composite homilies', 57.

[9] For the date of the homilies in the Vercelli Book, see the following studies by D. G. Scragg: 'The compilation of the Vercelli Book', *ASE* 2 (1973), 189–207; *The Vercelli Homilies and Related Texts*, EETS os 300 (Oxford, 1992), pp. xxxviii-xlii; and *Dating and Style*, p. 5.

[10] For studies of this period, see *Rewriting Old English in the Twelfth Century*, ed. Mary Swan and Elaine M. Treharne (Cambridge, 2000).

was to assume the existence of 'Wulfstan imitators', ever since J. P. Kinard first expressed the idea in 1897, though not in clearly defined terms, to explain those homilies which are not genuine works of Wulfstan but are pastiches of passages from these or are strongly reminiscent of features very characteristic of the Archbishop's renowned prose style.[11] Following half a century of investigation and debate, Karl Jost gave the problem its first comprehensive scholarly treatment. Although the notion has never been clearly stated, there are three ways in which the alleged imitation can be theoretically thought to have been made, but in none of these senses, Jost concluded, should one assume the existence of any imitative practice as a literary movement in the period.[12] This reappraisal, and the views of scholars like Angus McIntosh and Dorothy Whitelock[13] which in the main agree with it, represent the direction in which Wulfstan scholarship has subsequently tended. One has now come to see the uses and influences of Wulfstan's writings not as a special genre but as a particular example of the literary practice common in what J. E. Cross calls a 'period of accepted plagiarism'.[14] Wulfstan might very well have been the most influential figure in the literary world of the day and his works used most frequently by later writers, but only as a result and in the context of a tradition that allowed it.

A recent development of this point of view is Jonathan Wilcox's study of the Wulfstan tradition in the eleventh century, in which he does not speak of 'imitation' at all but of 'use by later sermon writers' of Wulfstan passages.[15] Wilcox identifies fifteen later homilies (including one surviving in a twelfth-century manuscript) as making such use, with full details of the precise extent of their indebtedness to their respective Wulfstanian sources.[16] These results, together with his method of approach to Wulfstan composite homilies, are now generally

---

[11] James Pinckney Kinard, *A Study of Wulfstan's Homilies* (Johns Hopkins University diss., 1897), p. 44. See Karl Jost, *Wulfstanstudien* (Bern, 1950), p. 111.

[12] Jost, *Wulfstanstudien*, pp. 110–5.

[13] Angus McIntosh, 'Wulfstan's Prose', *PBA* 34 (1948), 109–42, at 126, and Dorothy Whitelock (ed.), *Sermo Lupi ad Anglos*. 3rd edn. (London, 1963), p. 19; Whitelock's view here is based upon and expands her statements in the first edition (p. 14 n. 1) and the second (pp. 26–7).

[14] J. E. Cross, 'The Literate Anglo-Saxon — On Sources and Disseminations', *PBA* 58 (1972), 3–36, at 7.

[15] Jonathan Wilcox, 'The Dissemination of Wulfstan's Homilies: The Wulfstan Tradition in Eleventh-Century Vernacular Preaching', *England in the Eleventh Century*, ed. Carola Hicks (Stamford, 1992), pp. 199–217. Wilcox's Wulfstan corpus includes fifteen 'additional undeveloped homiletic pieces' (p. 200) not printed in Bethurum's edition (see n. 23), such as Napier XXIV. Further, he assumes some lost Wulfstan homilies, and his list of extracts includes indirect borrowings (via earlier borrowings) from Wulfstan's originals.

[16] For details, see Wilcox, 'The Dissemination', pp. 206–13.

accepted, and they provide a useful point of departure for my examination of relevant composite homilies in this study.

The study of the Ælfric tradition in Old English also has a long history, though there does not seem to have been any theory of 'Ælfric imitators' developed for passages drawn from Ælfric's writings by later compilers.[17] Borrowed passages have been identified and compared with Ælfrician sources by generations of scholars, among them Jost, N. R. Ker, D. G. Scragg, and Godden.[18] But it was Mary Swan who was the first to provide in 1993 a systematic account of 'Ælfric as source', identifying all composite homilies drawing on his homilies in the *Catholic Homilies*;[19] she shows that there are twenty-six of these (including eight in twelfth-century manuscripts) and describes them in comparison with the sources. Swan's comprehensive treatment provides the essential groundwork for the future study of the use of Ælfric in later compilations, and I am indebted to it in what follows (see Chapter VI).

Swan herself, and other scholars like Clare A. Lees, Mary P. Richards, and Joyce Hill,[20] have already carried the matter further, by making detailed accounts of some of the compilations in the eleventh and twelfth centuries. In one of these, Swan characteristically interprets her composite homilies in terms of reception theory:

> An Old English text which draws from vernacular rather than Latin sources may be performing cultural translations — of register, context and audience — and not linguistic ones, but the possibilities for interpretative dialogue with sources and influences are just as great. Concepts of and attitudes to source material, and adaptation of its ideas, are manifested in Old English texts which use Old English sources, and which themselves constitute documented instances of Anglo-Saxon reader-response. Copies of Old English texts almost always show differences from the detail of the 'original', and no matter how small and apparently careless, such differences give access to the method and purpose of these reuses of vernacular materials,

---

[17] See Jost, *Wulfstanstudien*, p. 114.

[18] See Jost, *Wulfstanstudien*; N. R. Ker, *Catalogue of Manuscripts Containing Anglo-Saxon* (Oxford, 1957); D. G. Scragg, 'The corpus of vernacular homilies and prose saints' lives before Ælfric', *ASE* 8 (1979), 223–77; Godden, 'OE composite homilies'.

[19] Mary Swan, 'Ælfric as Source: The Exploitation of Ælfric's *Catholic Homilies* from the Late Tenth to Twelfth Centuries' (Ph.D. thesis, University of Leeds, 1993).

[20] See Clare A. Lees, 'Theme and Echo in an Anonymous Old English Homily for Easter', *Traditio* 42 (1986), 115–42; Mary P. Richards, 'MS Cotton Vespasian A. XXII: The Vespasian Homilies', *Manuscripta* 22 (1978), 97–103; Mary P. Richards, 'Innovations in Ælfrician Homiletic Manuscripts at Rochester', *Annuale Mediaevale* 19 (1979), 13–26. For Joyce Hill, see below.

and allow speculation about the form in which earlier Old English texts were available to later compilers.[21]

Swan's 'reader-response', as I understand it, means in effect what Godden refers to in traditional terms as 'attitudes' shown by compilers to their homiletic materials, and her argument from a theorist's point of view confirms the importance of seeing, as Godden does, composite homilies not as mere targets of source studies but for what they are—historical records of the way in which earlier homiletic works are understood and accepted by later writers of the period who transmit them in their own ways. Joyce Hill pleads persuasively for traditional scholarship in this new context thus:

> It will be clear from my comments so far that I think reader-response criticism and perceptions of the eventful text have much to offer medieval scholars. But I would go on to argue that, in taking advantage of these insights and means of articulation, we need to continue to deploy the concepts and techniques of traditional scholarship, although we might do so with a slight shift of emphasis. Source-study is a case in point. Traditionally, this has most commonly concerned itself with ultimate sources, but if we pay more attention to immediate sources, we will come closer to the reality of the text itself by uncovering the way in which it comes into existence already in dialogue with its own past and implicitly or explicitly defines its position in its own present. It is this kind of investigation which I have attempted in studying Ælfric's use of Smaragdus as an intermediary for patristic authorities, and it is what those scholars have done who have studied homilies which in turn use Ælfric, Wulfstan, or anonymous Old English homilies as sources.[22]

As Hill notes in the last sentence above, work from this point of view has also been done for composite homilies drawing upon anonymous homilies, as notably in Scragg's studies of the Vercelli homilies and their later developments.

While recent studies have greatly advanced our understanding of Old English composite homilies in these ways, they have concerned themselves mostly

---

[21] Mary Swan, 'Old English Made New: One Catholic Homily and its Reuses', *LSE* 28 (1997), 1–18, at 1; see also Swan's article, 'Memorialised Readings: Manuscript Evidence for Old English Homily Composition', *Anglo-Saxon Manuscripts and their Heritage*, ed. Phillip Pulsiano and Elaine M. Treharne (Aldershot, 1998), pp. 205–17, esp. pp. 206–7, where she refers to similar theorists' terms used in Clare A. Lees, 'Working with Patristic Sources: Language and Context in Old English Homilies', *Speaking Two Languages: Traditional Disciplines and Contemporary Theory in Medieval Studies*, ed. Allen J. Frantzen (Albany, 1991), pp. 157–80.

[22] Joyce Hill, 'Reform and Resistance: Preaching Styles in Late Anglo-Saxon England', *De l'Homélie au Sermon: Histoire de la Prédication Médiévale*, ed. Jacqueline Hamesse and Xavier Hermand (Louvain-la-Neuve, 1993), pp. 15–46, at p. 45.

with ideas and substance and the way these are subjected to change as earlier homiletic materials are used by later homilists. Much excellent work has been done to uncover details of textual differences between sources and their later adaptations or between layers of reuse, and to establish the history of relevant homilies and the relationship of manuscripts which transmit them, but little attention seems to have been paid to linguistic aspects of transmission. The present study is intended to be a contribution to this area of study by examining compilers' language, syntax and style in particular, in comparison with the source texts. The importance of these differences of linguistic usage in characterizing compilers can be shown by a preview of passages from some composite works drawing upon Wulfstan's homilies.[23] A case in point is an eschatological passage from Wulfstan's Homily XIII:

> *WHom* 13.8 Of eorðan gewurdan ærest geworhte þa ðe we ealle of coman, ⁊ to eorðan we sculan ealle geweorðan ⁊ syððan habban swa ece wite a butan ende, swa ece blisse, swa hwæðer swa we on life ær geearnedon. Eala, lytel is se fyrst þyses lifes, ⁊ lyðre is, þæt we lufiað ⁊ on wuniað, ⁊ for oft hit wyrð raðost forloren þonne hit wære leofost gehealden.

The first half of this (down to *geearnedon* in the third line) is borrowed verbatim into Lambeth 489, fol. 37r/3–10, except for a short sentence (*⁊ of eorðan we sceolon ealle arisan on domes dæg*) which is added (after *we sculan ealle geweorðan* in the second line). On the other hand, the second sentence of the same passage (beginning with *Eala*) is changed into something stylistically very different in:

> Napier XL 189.3 and uton gecnawan, hu læne and hu lyðre þis lif is on to getruwianne, and hu oft hit wurð raðost forloren and forlæten, þonne hit wære leofost gehealden.

Longer passages drawn upon in Napier LV and Napier LVIII (*WHom* 6.3–24 and 5–20, respectively) demonstrate the point more clearly. While the former work (Napier 282.22–283.18) uses the passage almost verbatim, with only three minor changes (substituting *hi* for *hit* to refer to *folc*, deleting *on domesdæg*, and reversing the word order of *eow nu*), the latter (Napier 303.24–304.14) is a mass of changes, with a lot of addition and an expansion at one point of Wulfstan's fourteen words into a sentence more than three times as long. Moreover, these two contrasts in borrowing from the same homilies show how, even among those compilers who introduce substantial alterations, the style of prose in which they do this can vary considerably. As I shall argue in detail in a later chapter, the compiler of Napier XL usually writes in terse, controlled prose with precise syntax, as witness the continued use of *hu*-clauses in the above passage, accommodating a loosely

---

[23] Citation is made from Bethurum's and Napier's editions of Wulfstan's and the anonymous homilies, respectively. For details of these editions, see Chapter II, n. 6.

inserted parenthesis (⁊ *lyðre is* . . .) in Wulfstan's original passage neatly into a long but well-ordered sentence—a style which might well be expected of a compiler who is sometimes called the 'pedantic' adapter on other grounds. On the other hand, the changes the compiler of Napier LVIII introduces in the passage being discussed point to a style which is expansive and explanatory, sometimes to the point of verbosity, so much so that Jost refers to their effect as a 'Wortschwall' (flood of words) and their author as 'das genaue Gegenteil eines Wulfstannachahmers' (the exact antithesis of a Wulfstan imitator).[24] For further details of the two homilies, see Chapter III.

It is important to add that such distinct methods of rewriting—verbatim borrowings versus substantial changes and stylistic variations—are not limited to special passages from particular sources but are a constant feature of many, if not all, compilations. An example may be taken again from the piece in Lambeth 489 and Napier LVIII. The former draws, for its ending (fols. 36v/15–37v/1), upon four extracts made directly and indirectly from Wulfstan, which the compiler simply links together with little change of any sort, as we have seen above. This ending is preceded by the body of the homily (fols. 31r/3–36v/15) which draws upon Ælfric's *De Dominica Oratione* (*Catholic Homilies*, First Series, item XIX), where the compiler again follows the source verbatim, apart from occasional omissions and additions from other pieces by Ælfric. The resultant composition retains accordingly, among other things, different preferences for vocabulary items, such as *hælend* 'Saviour' and *gylt* 'sin' (neither of which Wulfstan ever uses) in the body but *drihten* (rather than *hælend*) meaning Christ in the ending; no attempt has apparently been made to bring details of Ælfric's and Wulfstan's language in the two parts into line with each other or to rewrite the whole piece in the compiler's own language. A different sort of consistency is shown by Napier LVIII. As we have seen earlier, this work makes substantial changes to the material drawn from Wulfstan's Homily VI, and this method of rewriting is carried into the rest of the eleven extracts (made from Wulfstan's and anonymous homilies) which make up the homily (see again Chapter III)—a situation which is also seen in Napier XL, whose compiler rewrites his sources, Wulfstanian and anonymous alike, in the way outlined above. Such methodical differences indicate methods of rewriting which vary from compiler to compiler, not from passage to passage within single compilations, and confirm the necessity of examining the full details of language and style for individual compilers.

This preliminary look at a selection of passages, then, confirms what Angus McIntosh assumed for the Wulfstan tradition, as exemplifying the situation for composite homilies of the period generally:

> Though I should regard Wulfstan as the one man of his generation likely to have produced a definite school, its members would scarcely have as their

---

[24] Jost, *Wulfstanstudien*, pp. 264–5.

main ambition a desire to pass off their work as his. And even if they had, it is probable that in such a situation, where they would be following what was not an age-old tradition, their own personal characteristics would appear in what they wrote, in rhythmical details as well as in matters of syntax and vocabulary.[25]

The purpose of the following chapters is to attempt to uncover details of these 'personal characteristics' in language and style in a wide selection of composite homilies and consider their significance in the history of the vernacular homiletic literature of the period. I begin, in Chapter II, with Napier XXX as a good example of Old English composite homilies, seeing it not as a product of 'Wulfstan imitation' but as a work which uses Wulfstanian sources and anonymous sources of the Vercelli homilies with its own design and purpose. I also look in detail at the later use of this homily appearing in two homilies, themselves composite. The use of Wulfstan's writings by later homilists is further explored in Chapter III, where I discuss in detail two homilies (Napier XL and Napier LVIII) which were seen above to show different attitudes towards their respective sources. I argue that the compilers of the two homilies revised their materials in quite different ways, producing stylistically distinct prose. I then consider how the differences might be viewed in relation to the tradition of vernacular homiletic prose, putting them in their 'manuscript context'. One of the major sources for Napier XL just discussed is the eschatological homily Vercelli II, which is adapted for use in two more composite homilies, Vercelli XXI and Fadda X. These latter, and the variant texts of Napier XL itself, are the subject of study in Chapter IV, forming what may be termed the Vercelli tradition of Old English Judgement Day homilies. I discuss the tradition by examining how passages, often identical, from the ultimate Vercelli II source are adapted differently by homilists of varying stylistic inclinations and also how, in the case of the different Napier XL texts, the homily was subject to further variation and development as it was transmitted in different manuscripts. The theme of Judgement Day also inspired part of the Napier XXIX homily, which I discuss in Chapter V. However, I do not discuss it in relation to another Old English tradition of Judgement Day homilies which it might have represented but as a unique composite homily with a poetic source. I examine in particular how far it is a poetic homily as has been previously thought and argue that the homily is unique in showing diverse treatments, rather than the usual method of consistent adaptation, of four major sources as widely different as a Judgement Day poem and directions for confessors. In Chapter VI, I consider another important strand of Old English composite homilies—with Ælfric as source, an aspect which Napier XXIX in the preceding chapter represents only marginally. I discuss the problem in detail in relation to two Easter homilies (*HomS* 27 and *HomS* 28) and argue that despite this shared feature, the homilies

---

[25] McIntosh, 'Wulfstan's Prose', 126.

differ significantly from each other in content and the treatment they give their respective Ælfrician passages, as well as in style and other linguistic matters and the way they make biblical references. Finally, Chapter VII is a conclusion, in which I summarize some of the more important results of my study and consider what implications we may draw from these for the variety and history, in matters of language and style and (possibly) content, of vernacular prose in the homiletic literature of the late tenth to eleventh centuries.

One final point should be made briefly about the term 'source' as used in the following chapters. When I speak of 'addition', 'omission', and other changes made in a composite homily in comparison with its source, it is not my intention to claim direct manuscript acquaintance between the two texts. The extant form of the source text may be the nearest one can get to the compiler's manuscript source, which may well have been lost in many cases.[26] The gap is inevitable and does not affect the essential point of comparison, since textual variation itself is the concern of the present study. Another related problem concerns the way Old English compilers worked. It has recently been argued that they often worked not directly from written text but from memory, altering, for instance, an Ælfric homily by introducing portions of other texts which they have memorised, or indeed recopy[ing] the Ælfric homily itself from memory, introducing conscious and unconscious changes as they write'; variation in precise verbal detail 'could be signs of memorised reproduction in some earlier version or versions rather than an indication that one surviving copy has directly deviated from another'.[27] This is too large a problem to open here. But one may perhaps say that in whatever way textual variation may be created—consciously or unconsciously and through borrowing from written text or reproduction from memory —, it is there all the same, indicating the compilers' own habits of linguistic usage, and revealing consistent patterns of variation which tell something about their attitudes towards precedent works and the way they express those attitudes.

---

[26] See, for example, the case of Vercelli homilies used in Napier XXX, discussed in Chapter II.

[27] Swan, 'Memorialised Readings', pp. 211 and 213. Another case for the theory of transmission by memory is made in Loredana Teresi, 'Mnemonic transmission of Old English texts in the post-Conquest period', *Rewriting Old English*, ed. Swan and Treharne, pp. 98–116. For some evidence of biblical quotation from memory, see Chapter VI.

II.
Napier XXX: A Wulfstan/Vercelli Composite and its Later History[1]

I

Of all the Old English composite homilies, one of the best-known is the one classified by the DOE as *HomU* 27 (Cameron No. B3.4.27), which is in print as the thirtieth item in Arthur Napier's collection of 'Wulfstan' homilies (including some which are no longer accepted as the Archbishop's genuine works),[2] hence commonly known as Napier XXX or pseudo-Wulfstan XXX. It is a work of general admonition regarding the true Christian life, titled *Be rihtan cristendome* in the manuscript in which it is uniquely preserved complete (Bodleian Library, Hatton 113, s. xi 3rd quarter).[3] It is a good example of the genre in that it is 'a curiously complicated pastiche',[4] and as such, has attracted the attention of generations of scholars ever since the earliest days of Wulfstan scholarship. It is now generally accepted that this complicated pastiche draws upon two great strands of the homiletic tradition of the period: Wulfstan's writings (the *Institutes of Polity* and its associated materials, and Homilies VI, XIII and Napier

---

[1] Sections I to IV of the present chapter are a complete revision of my previous study of the homily, 'A "Wulfstan Imitator" at Work: Linguistic Features of Napier XXX' (*Studies in the History of Old English Prose* (Tokyo, 2000), pp. 263–85). I take this opportunity to acknowledge once again the special debts I owe to Professor Malcolm Godden and Dr Timothy C. Graham, for their generous help with that study, from which I have benefited greatly in this revision, too.

[2] For details of this edition, see n. 6 below.

[3] For details of the manuscript, see N. R. Ker, *Catalogue of Manuscripts Containing Anglo-Saxon* (Oxford, 1957), pp. 391–9. From circumstantial evidence, D. G. Scragg puts the composition in the second quarter of the eleventh century; see his 'Napier's "Wulfstan" homily xxx: its sources, its relationship to the Vercelli Book and its style', *ASE* 6 (1977), 197–211, esp. 210.

[4] Angus McIntosh, 'Wulfstan's Prose', *PBA* 34 (1948), 109–42, at 141 n. 29.

XXIV[5]) for the opening and concluding sections but four anonymous homilies in the Vercelli Book (Homilies IV, IX, X and XXI) for the middle section.[6] This unparalleled range of source texts makes the homily a particularly interesting case-study of the Old English compiler at work, thoughtfully editing his materials to create a new homily.

The close association Napier XXX has with Wulfstan in its opening and concluding sections, reinforced by Wulfstanian features of style observable throughout, has sometimes caused the homily to be referred to as the work of a 'Wulfstan imitator'—a position which finds recent expression in D. G. Scragg's study of the homily, which established its sources as above. Scragg argues that '[o]ne of the most noticeable stylistic features throughout N[apier XXX] is the use of pairs of near synonyms'[7] and further as follows:

> Intensifying pairs and empty phrases which add to the rhetorical effect are associated stylistically in late Old English with Wulfstan, and the compiler of N is a good example of a Wulfstan imitator. He even 'Wulfstanizes' Wulfstan's authentic work when he borrows it: for example in section *a* the 'weorþan [*sic*] *and* werian' of *Polity* is replaced by 'griðian and friðian', a couplet Wulfstan uses frequently in legal writings, and the phrases 'wordes ne weorces' and 'Godes lagum fyligean', both of which are common in Wulfstan's writings, are added to the source material. Wulfstan's 'Understande,

---

[5] This homily is generally accepted as a work by Wulfstan, though it is not included in Bethurum's edition of the Archbishop's homilies (see n. 6 below). See her edition, pp. 36–41, esp. p. 36; Jonathan Wilcox, 'The Dissemination of Wulfstan's Homilies: The Wulfstan Tradition in Eleventh-Century Vernacular Preaching', *England in the Eleventh Century*, ed. Carola Hicks (Stamford, 1992), pp. 199–217, esp. pp. 200–1.

[6] For details see Scragg, 'Napier's "Wulfstan" homily xxx', 197–207. References to the text of Napier XXX are to Scragg's edition appended to his EETS edition of the Vercelli homilies (*The Vercelli Homilies and Related Texts* (EETS os 300. Oxford, 1992)). This edition is also used for the four Vercelli sources of our homily, as well as for the other Vercelli homilies studied in this book. References to the other source texts are made to the following editions: *Die 'Institutes of Polity, Civil and Ecclesiastical'*, ed. Karl Jost (Bern, 1959); *The Homilies of Wulfstan*, ed. Dorothy Bethurum (Oxford, 1957); and *Wulfstan: Sammlung der ihm zugeschriebenen Homilien nebst Untersuchungen über ihre Echtheit*, ed. Arthur Napier (Berlin, 1883; 2nd edn. with a bibliographical appendix by K. Ostheeren. Dublin and Zürich, 1967). In citing from Napier's edition, I substitute *i* for Napier's *j* before a vowel, and follow the DOE text in capitalization. Abbreviations for the texts and the system of reference thereto are those adopted in the DOE, except that (i) the texts in Napier's collection are referred to by page and line and (ii) that part of the material associated with *Polity* which is not by Wulfstan (printed in Jost, pp. 242–61) is also referred to as *Polity* with page and section numbering, e.g. *Polity* 242.53. The last three sentences of this note also apply to citations in the other chapters of this book.

[7] Scragg, 'Napier's "Wulfstan" homily xxx', 207.

se ðe wylle' is used in a transitional passage between extracts from two Vercelli homilies at the beginning of section *f*, and the typically Wulfstanian superlative 'hit is ealra wundra mæst' is also used to move from one Vercelli source to another at the beginning of section *k*. The old-fashioned words 'oferhygednesse' and 'oferhydge [*sic*]' in Vercelli xxi are replaced by the Wulfstanian 'ofermodignys' three times, and the adverb 'witod', favoured by Wulfstan in the sense 'clearly' normally expressed by 'witodlice', occurs once in a linking passage which has no known source in section *h*.[8]

This list of 'Wulfstanian' features is impressive. However, it does not explain a different set of evidence of 'non-Wulfstanian' features found both in the Wulfstan and anonymous sections of the homily—including the use of the verbs *oncnawan* and *forgifan* (in the sense 'to give') rather than the typically Wulfstanian *gecnawan* and *gifan*, respectively—which led Karl Jost to assert of the homily: 'Von einer Nachahmung des Wulfstanstils vermag ich aber rein nichts zu sehen'.[9] As I have argued in the Introduction and shall show in more detail below,[10] the homily should be described not so much as a work of imitation but rather as a compilation made out of Wulfstanian and anonymous materials, using and rearranging them in its own way; its frequent reminiscences of the Archbishop's prose style may again not be directly imitative but reflective of the tradition of homiletic writing in which it exists, though the Archbishop was certainly an outstanding figure in that tradition. In fact, Scragg himself seems to imply as much in a more recent study. He re-conceptualizes, with particular reference to Napier XXX, what he had previously described as one of the most noticeable features of the 'Wulfstan imitator', in these terms:

> The general pattern that emerges from these examples is that this type of verbal expansion, repetition of an idea in slightly different words, is a feature of the passing down of homiletic material from one generation to another. Compilers of what are sometimes called scissors and paste homilies don't just cut material from earlier homilies and stick pieces together verbatim, as the term scissors and paste rather unfortunately implies. Throughout the history of the vernacular homily, from the tenth century to beyond the end of the Anglo-Saxon period, they adapt, they re-order, they re-word. And when they expand, they do so usually, as here, in very insignificant ways in terms of overall meaning, but in ways which they felt were highly

---

[8] Scragg, 'Napier's "Wulfstan" homily xxx', 208. This assessment is accepted in Wilcox, 'The Dissemination', pp. 211 and 216.

[9] Karl Jost, *Wulfstanstudien* (Bern, 1950), p. 210.

[10] See also my article 'Aspects of "Wulfstan imitators" in Late Old English sermon writing', *Studies in English Historical Linguistics and Philology: A Festschrift for Akio Oizumi*, ed. Jacek Fisiak (Frankfurt am Main, 2002), pp. 389–403, esp. pp. 395–6.

significant in terms of impact on their audience, in other words they alter style but not substance.[11]

If this represents a view now generally accepted for Napier XXX, we may do well to seek to redefine the process of 'Wulfstan imitation' from that point of view, by looking in the first instance at specific details of how such 're-ordering' and 're-wording' is achieved in our compiler's usage of word pairs.

For one thing, the evidence of the synonymous pair 'griðian and friðian' may not be as decisive as Scragg implies in his earlier study, for his assertion about it occurring 'frequently in legal writings' of Wulfstan needs qualification. With the aid of the Toronto Microfiche Concordance and the computerized Dictionary of Old English Corpus,[12] one can see now that the word pair is rather infrequent in Old English generally, used only three times each in Wulfstan's legal writings (*LawVI-Atr* 42.3, *LawICn* 2, *LawICn* 4) and in some late anonymous homilies in Napier's collection (*HomU* 48 (Napier LIX)[13] 308.28, *HomU* 59 (Napier XXXVII) 179.24 and our example in Napier XXX, line 2),[14] besides the one in the Chronicle (*ChronE* 227.23 (1093)). For Wulfstan, 'weorðian and werian' is apparently the more familiar pair, which he uses at least twice in the *Polity* (*WPol* 2.1.1.87, 203 or 2.1.2.59, 98 in the shorter version), once in *LawVIAtr* 45 (with reversed order of the verbs) and twice in homilies (*WHom* 10c.57, 151). The pair 'griðian and friðian' is thus hardly Wulfstanian, and whether use of it by the Napier XXX compiler is a case of 'Wulfstanization' or not is, to say the least, arguable.

Of greater importance as evidence are those frequent word pairs which the compiler adds or into which he expands single words in his sources, Wulfstanian or anonymous. He does this, for example, in extracts from Vercelli IX as he links them with his original sentences:

---

[11] D. G. Scragg, *Dating and Style in Old English Composite Homilies* (Cambridge, 1998), p. 11.

[12] Richard L. Venezky and Antonette diPaolo Healey, *A Microfiche Concordance to Old English* (Toronto, 1980); Angus Cameron, Ashley Crandell Amos, Sharon Butler, and Antonette diPaolo Healey, *The Dictionary of Old English Corpus in Electronic Form* (Toronto, 1981; now available as TEI-P3 conformant version, 2000 Release, on CD-ROM).

[13] Bethurum does not include this piece in her Wulfstan edition but thinks that 'it may have been Wulfstan's own summary of statements of Christian duty' (*The Homilies*, p. 38). If it is, it does not affect my argument that the synonymous pair in question is not particularly Wulfstanian.

[14] Christiane Berger (*Altenglische Paarformeln und ihre Varianten* (Frankfurt am Main, 1993), p. 89) gives the same list of examples, though she does not clearly distinguish genuine Wulfstanian texts and spurious ones. The last example but one is not to be found in the Microfiche Concordance, since *HomU* 59 (Napier XXXVII 178.19–179.32) in which it occurs is a later addition to the DOE Corpus.

Napier XXX 100 Understande se ðe wylle his agene *neode ⁊ ðearfe*. Ealle þa tungon þe æfre *clypedon ⁊ spræcon* syððan Adam, se forma mann þe Crist ærest gescop, þeah hi gyt on þysum life wæron ⁊ ða þe nu gyt syndon ⁊ ða þe towerde syndon ær domes dæg cume, ealle hi ne mihton *asecgan ⁊ areccan* hu wa þam sawlum byð þe on helle beon sceolon. Uton us warnian symble wið þa hellican witu ⁊ geþeodan us to ðam uplican rice, for ðam þe þær ys *seo bliss* ⁊ þæt wuldor þæt nan eorðlic mann *ne can ne* ne mæg mid his wordum *areccan ⁊ asecgan* þa wynsumnysse ⁊ *blisse* þæs heofonlican lifes. Þa geongan men hopiað þæt hi moton lange on þissere worulde libban, ac se hopa hi *bepæcð ⁊ beswicð*, þonne him leofost wære þæt hi lybban moston. Se ealda man him mæg gewislice witod witan þæt him se deað genealæcð for ðære oferylde þe him on sihð, for ðam ðe he mæg *oncnawan ⁊ ongytan* be manegum þingum þe him þonne deriað.

(Italics indicate only expansion using word pairs.) In such expansions, word pairs used are often ones which never occur in Wulfstan's homilies, as *areccan ⁊ asecgan* here (in the fourth and eighth lines),[15] or are at any rate different from Wulfstan's own phraseology, like *seo bliss ⁊ þæt wuldor* here (in the seventh line; cf. *lof ⁊ wuldor* or *ece lif ⁊ ece bliss*, frequent in Wulfstan's homilies) and *oncnawan ⁊ ongytan* (in the last line but one, while Wulfstan has the exact pair *ongitan ⁊ oncnawan* once (*WHom* 8b.63) but never otherwise uses the verb *oncnawan*[16]). Examples of these kinds from other parts of the homily include two more uses of *areccan ⁊ asecgan* (lines 98 and 181; on the latter see the next section), and *prowian ⁊ ðolian* (line 156, expanding *VercHom* 4.65 *prowian*, and line 208; on the latter see the next section), *gesyne ⁊ opene* (line 161) and *worhte ⁊ dyde* (line 170). None of the last three pairs occurs in Wulfstan's homilies;[17] Wulfstan's own equivalent for the last is *gescop ⁊ geworhte*, as in *WHom* 6.30 and elsewhere. These departures from Wulfstan's own phraseologies seem to suggest distinct levels of Wulfstan imitation—the habit of using word pairs itself and the choice of specific pairs. On the first level, the compiler of Napier XXX may be said to be a 'Wulfstan imitator', but not on the second. The number of 'non-Wulfstanian' pairs of synonyms throws doubt on the idea that the compiler of Napier XXX is borrowing

---

[15] This has been pointed out by Jost (*Wulfstanstudien*, p. 210). But the two examples of *areccan and asecgan* and one of *oncnawan and ongytan* in the passage quoted are all he gives of the 'non-Wulfstanian' word pairs in the homily.

[16] For Wulfstan's use of *gecnawan* to the exclusion of *oncnawan* and *tocnawan*, see Jost, *Wulfstanstudien*, p. 137 n. 4; Shigeru Ono, 'The Old English Equivalents of Latin *cognoscere* and *intelligere*—The Dialectal and Temporal Distribution of Vocabulary', *On Early English Syntax and Vocabulary* (Tokyo, 1989), pp. 169–207, esp. pp. 186–9.

[17] The one other example of *gesyne ⁊ opene* that I know of occurs in *LS* 34 (Seven-Sleepers), line 86. For a slightly varied form *gesewene ⁊ geopenode* which occurs in Pope XXVII, see Scragg, 'Napier's "Wulfstan" homily xxx', 204–5.

for his own use a stock of Wulfstanian phrases with which he has familiarized himself.

The distinction of levels may also be helpful in thinking of some of the other Wulfstanian examples given by Scragg (see the first quotation). The superlative may well be a characteristic element of Wulfstan's rhetorical prose, but the exact phrase 'ealra wundra mæst' is not.[18] Nor are some 'empty phrases' such as 'on þysum life' (used by our compiler at lines 122, 154, 162 and 208), though 'her on life' (used at lines 50, 125 and 155) is one Wulfstan himself uses commonly in homilies. Intensifying adverbs such as *georne* and *eall* (inflected as adjective or adverb), both favourite words of the compiler (added in lines 51, 155 and 179, and in 34, 123, 180, 187, 189 and 206, respectively),[19] could hardly have been imitated from Wulfstan; they are a common stylistic feature throughout a wide range of vernacular homiletic prose of the period of which Wulfstan was only a part, however important and influential.

To return to word pairs, the compiler of Napier XXX's independence of Wulfstan's exact practice and other precedents in his sources has further manifestations. Scragg in his later study gives an interesting case.[20] In

> Napier XXX 164 Ðær þonne ne mæg ænig man oðres gehelpan, se fæder þam suna ne se sunu þam fæder ne seo modor þære dehter ne seo dohtor þære meder, ne nan mæg oðrum,

the compiler has expanded the wording in his source at this point (*VercHom* 4.69 *Þær þonne ne mæg se fæder helpan þam suna, ne se sunu þam fæder, ne nan mæg oðrum*) to a greater extent than this latter itself has expanded the antecedent source text in the Macarius homily (*Ne mæg þær þonne gefultumian se fæder þæm suna, ne se sunu þæm fæder*).[21] More interesting, Scragg notes, is the verb *gehelpan* taking a genitive

---

[18] Wulfstan uses the form *wundra* (gen. pl.) only twice in his homilies (*WHom* 4.44, 5.59), without the superlative *mæst* on either occasion; see Mabel Falberg Dobyns, 'Wulfstan's Vocabulary: A Glossary of the "Homilies" with Commentary' (Ph. D. dissertation, University of Illinois at Urbana-Champaign, 1973), s.v. *wundor*. On stylistic features of Wulfstan's prose, see Bethurum, *The Homilies*, pp. 87–98; Dorothy Bethurum, 'Wulfstan', *Continuations and Beginnings: Studies in Old English Literature*, ed. Eric Gerald Stanley (London, 1966), pp. 210–46, esp. pp. 229–35; Dorothy Whitelock, *Sermo Lupi ad Anglos* (3rd edn. London, 1963), pp. 17–28; A. P. McD. Orchard, 'Crying wolf: oral style and the *Sermones Lupi*', *ASE* 21 (1992), 239–64; and James P. Kinard, *A Study of Wulfstan's Homilies: Their Style and Sources* (Johns Hopkins University diss., 1897), pp. 19–32.

[19] For these two words and the phrases *on þysum life* and *her on life*, see Scragg, 'Napier's "Wulfstan" homily xxx', 208.

[20] Scragg, *Dating and Style*, pp. 10–11.

[21] Patrizia Lendinara ('"*frater non redimit, redimet homo* ...": A Homiletic Motif and its Variants in Old English', *Early Medieval English Texts and Interpretations: Studies Presented to Donald G. Scragg*, ed. Elaine Treharne and Susan Rosser (Tempe, Arizona,

object in the opening expansion in the Napier XXX text; this was presumably the normal practice of whoever made the expansion, someone who 'failed to notice that in the material that he was copying, *helpan* was followed by a dative'.[22]

Another point of interest in the compiler's practice is the way he deals with a word pair where there is already one in his source text. He seldom uses it as it is, but expands it into a phrase with three members (e.g. *þas caseras oððe rice cyningas oððe ænige oðre wlance men* (line 131), expanding *VercHom* 10.224 *þa strengestan ⁊ þa ricestan*) or a pair of paired phrases (e.g. *ealle helle gryras ⁊ yrmða ⁊ þara synfulra sawla tintregan ⁊ susla* (80), expanding *VercHom* 9.145 *ealle helle geryne ⁊ þara sawla tintrega*). But most often he, for no clear reason, reverses the words in pairs: *on wuldre ⁊ on blisse* (line 68, from *VercHom* 21.155), *afeallað ⁊ ahreosað* (145, from *VercHom* 10.218), *sorhlic ⁊ earmlic* (202, from *Polity* 245.70), and *embe Cristes þrowunge ⁊ embe his hidercyme* (203, from *Polity* 245.70), the last change being made at the cost of the incongruous order of events that has resulted.

These various aspects of usage will be sufficient to show word pairs as a hallmark of the compiler's prose and indicate how far he is from being a 'Wulfstan imitator' in practicing it. This being so, we shall now have to see how this independence of mind has guided the compiler in other aspects of his work of adapting his sources and making out of them a text of his own.

II

As the examples above partly show, the word pairs the compiler of Napier XXX adds (including those where he expands a single word in the sources) are not distributed evenly throughout the homily. The opening section in which 'griðian and friðian' occurs has no other added word pair and few substantial alterations of other kinds either, apart from several linking sentences that are added. Examples of new word pairs multiply as the compiler proceeds to draw upon the anonymous sources in the Vercelli Book and continue to be fairly common in the concluding section where he turns again to Wulfstanian materials. Thus, while he retains in the last section Wulfstan's word pairs such as *magon ⁊ motan* (line 174) and *mage ⁊ mote* (178), the compiler adds *gestrangie ⁊ getrymme* (line 182, expanding *WPol* 2.2.2.169 *getrymme*; cf. *WHom* 8b.86 *getrymme ⁊ gestrongige*),

---

2002), pp. 67–80) discusses the Napier XXX passage and its variants (including the one in Bazire and Cross 7) as examples of what she calls 'the motif of "no aid from kin"' in Old English homilies and poetry. The Bazire and Cross 7 passage will be discussed in section V below. On the anonymous Macarius homily, see Chapter V.

[22] Scragg, *Dating and Style*, p. 11. Napier emends *oðres* to *oðrum*. See also Scragg, 'Napier's "Wulfstan" homily xxx', 203–4. The compiler again uses the verb with a genitive object in line 178 (*Helpe gehwa his sylfes georne þa hwile þe he mage ⁊ mote*), but here he may be following the usage in the source (*WPol* 2.1.1.167).

and four 'non-Wulfstanian' word pairs—*worhte ⁊ dyde* (see section I) and *totwæmað ⁊ todælað* (195, expanding Napier XXIV 122.6 *todælað*),[23] and two others he has used in the middle section: *asæd ⁊ areht* (line 181) and *prowode ⁊ ðolode* (208), expanding *WPol* 2.1.1.169 *asæd* and *WHom* 6.196 *polode*, respectively.[24] He also insists, as in the middle section, on his own practice, reversing the order of paired words and phrases as in the source, in *sorhlic ⁊ earmlic* and the pair of *embe*-phrases, both already mentioned (see section I). Here may be included his use of the non-Wulfstanian verb *oncnawen* (line 209) in place of Wulfstan's *gecnawen*. There are numerous other alterations, including those affecting the syntax of lines 171–2 and 180–2, in the concluding section; on these see the next section of this chapter. All in all, as Scragg discussing lines 184–97 notes in his later study, 'the compiler who added tautological words and phrases for stylistic effect to material drawn from Vercelli homilies IX and IV . . . has done the same thing to Wulfstan'.[25]

The difference in attitudes towards Wulfstanian material between the opening and concluding sections is striking. It looks as if the compiler, starting as a faithful reviser of his sources, gradually reconciles himself to the idea of touching up his sources and becomes less shy about making his own contribution to the homily as he continues with his task of compiling. The initial impetus was apparently given by the Vercelli sources which are probably more than half a century earlier and had to be retouched anyway to incorporate in the new composition—an impetus which lasted into the last section whose sources of material are nearly contemporary with the compilation. One simple observation about verb forms strengthens this impression. The verb *uton* 'let us' occurs very often throughout the homily, in two forms. It occurs as *utan* in the opening section (lines 9 (twice), 27 and 28), as it does in its source *Polity*, in particular in the longer version in MS Junius 121; it then becomes *uton* in the middle section (lines 33, 42, 50, 52, 63, 64 and 105),[26] in agreement with the forms in the Vercelli sources except for line 105, and continues to take that form even in the concluding section (lines 174, 176 and 193), despite the fact that its sources use the form *utan*; the only exception to this apparent development is *utan* occurring at the very end of the homily (line 212), which agrees with the form in its source sentence (*WHom* 6.214).[27] *Uton* is apparently the compiler's own form, which he also uses in sentences he adds.

---

[23] In fact, this exact pair seems to be distinctive of the compiler of Napier XXX; see Scragg, *Dating and Style*, p. 20 n. 41. See further Chapter III.

[24] See Scragg, 'Napier's "Wulfstan" homily xxx', 207.

[25] Scragg, *Dating and Style*, p. 15.

[26] The EETS edition misprints the manuscript form on lines 50 and 52 as *utan*.

[27] A similar observation is made by Richard Becher, *Wulfstans Homilien* (Leipzig diss., 1910), pp. 69–70. I do not mean to claim that it is specifically MS Junius 121 that was the source of our homilist's knowledge of the *Polity*, any more than that the base manuscripts of the standard editions were the actual manuscript sources for the compiler

Compared with these alterations in the concluding section, those in the opening section are not particularly striking. But the few alterations that are made prove to be of significance for the subsequent construction of the composite homily, setting its general tone, as it were. For example, the opening sentence *Mycel is nydþearf cristenum mannum þæt hi heora cristendom rihtlice healdan* is a reworking of *WPol* 2.1.1.203 *Riht is, ðæt cristene men cristendom georne healdan mid rihte*. Here the transposition of *cristene men* into the main clause emphasizes the nature of the audience for whom this new homily is delivered — 'for both sexes, perhaps even for seculars', as Scragg assumes.[28] The universality of this reference to Christians in the third person is immediately paraphrased in the next sentence by the first person *we* (*Ealle we habbað ænne heofonlicne fæder þæt is God sylfa*), which then determines the form of the homily. The compiler subsequently uses *we* as the only regular form of personal reference, transforming what was originally an admonitory address from the pulpit into something in which he identifies himself with those he is addressing — a transformation which renders the recurrent vocative *men ða leofestan/leofan men* in the Vercelli and Wulfstanian sources (*VercHom* 21.87, 94, 158, *WHom* 6.214) out of place for the compiler.[29] Other points of interest in the opening sentence, such as *rihtlice* replacing *mid rihte* and *heora* added to *cristendom*, will be discussed below; see section IV. As in the use of word pairs, our compiler is here not merely copying extracts from his sources mechanically but has his own ideas and designs to work by, however warily and gradually, making the compilation his own text.

III

Changes to the sources begin to be frequent, as I pointed out above, in the middle section of the homily where the compiler draws on the anonymous homilies of about half a century earlier which he may well have felt in need of revising according to the linguistic usage of his day. This aspect of the compilation of Napier XXX can be seen clearly in its vocabulary. The compiler shuns poetic words and those expressions that are apparently obsolete or archaic. Examples of the former are *folde* 'earth, land, world' and *dreosan* 'to fall, perish', both discussed

---

for the materials in the middle and concluding sections. The whole comparison is only meant to highlight the changing forms of *utan/uton* within the homily and the possible influences of sources on them. Manuscript variation of the *Polity* and other source texts in relation to our homily requires more work.

[28] Scragg, *Dating and Style*, pp. 10–11.

[29] Scragg ('Napier's "Wulfstan" homily xxx', 210) mentions these omissions as part of his argument against a theory of common authorship for Napier XXIX and Napier XXX. On this theory and details of Napier XXIX, see Chapter V.

by Roberta Frank.[30] As she notes, these poetic words occur in one of our Vercelli sources (*VercHom* 10.240 *foldan*) and its variant text (*HomU* 3 (Belfour XII) 130.16 *drosæð*, replacing *VercHom* 10.218 *hreosaþ*), but they are shunned in our homily in favour of *eorðan* (line 144) and *ahreosað* (146), respectively. Equally revealing, since it presents an analogue to what M. S. Griffith argues with respect to the decay of the Old English poetic tradition in the *Paris Psalter*,[31] is the absence in our homily of the poetic formulas ending in *-end* that are used in the Vercelli sources meaning the Christian God (*VercHom* 9.141 *scyppendes*, 21.144 *heofona wealdend ⁊ sigora syllend*); instead, our homilist has *drihten*, with a qualifying adjective on both occasions (lines 57, 76 (quoted below)).[32] Similar, if not strictly poetic, examples include *on worulda woruld* (*VercHom* 21.143) and *reste* in the sense 'resting place, grave' (*VercHom* 10.225),[33] which are, judging from the examples given in Bosworth-Toller, apparently archaic and are altered in our homily to *ecelice* (line 56) and *byrgen* (133), respectively. In the light of these alterations, *ofermodignes* (lines 52, 53, 54) (described by Scragg as a Wulfstanian feature, in place of *oferhygd/oferhygedness* in the Vercelli source (see section I)) and the compiler's addition *ofermodig* (140), might rather be a consequence of the chronological and dialectal distribution of the words, for the *ofermod*-type of the *superbia* vocabulary is in general use in late West-Saxon texts as against the Anglian *oferhygd*-type, as Hans Schabram has established.[34]

Updating can be seen no less clearly in syntax, the best illustration being change in word order. Examples occur, as will be seen below, not only in the middle section of the homily but in the concluding one which draws on Wulfstanian materials, though not in the opening section whose source is similarly Wulfstanian. Thus, initial verb-subject order in statements in *VercHom* 9.144 *Sægeð hit eac*

---

[30] Roberta Frank, 'Poetic Words in Late Old English Prose', *From Anglo-Saxon to Early Middle English: Studies Presented to E. G. Stanley*, ed. Malcolm Godden, Douglas Gray, and Terry Hoad (Oxford, 1994), pp. 87–107, at pp. 96–7 and 102–3.

[31] M. S. Griffith, 'Poetic language and the Paris Psalter: the decay of the Old English tradition', *ASE* 20 (1991), 167–86, at 179.

[32] The compiler also adds the adjective *eallwealdenda* with *se* before *drihten* when he takes this head word over from the source, at lines 33 and 70; see Jost, *Wulfstanstudien*, p. 210; Scragg, 'Napier's "Wulfstan" homily xxx', 208.

[33] For poetic usage in this sense, see, for example, *Beowulf*, line 747 and other examples in the poem.

[34] Hans Schabram, *Superbia: Studien zum altenglischen Wortschatz. Teil I. Die dialektale und zeitliche Verbreitung des Wortguts* (Munich, 1965). Scragg himself seems to imply this when he speaks of the two *oferhygd*-words as 'old-fashioned'. There are other special preferences the compiler shows for particular vocabulary items, such as *lif* (lines 50, 122, 125, 154, 156, 162, 208) and *eorðe* (157) rather than *woruld* in the phrase 'on (þyssum) . . .' and its variants (see section I above); and *æfre* (174) and *symble* (194) in place of *a* used in the Wulfstanian and anonymous sources. These are apparently not related to chronology and are presumably stylistic choices.

on bocum þæt . . .[35] becomes SV *Hit segð . . .* (line 79). More frequent are changes affecting the arrangement of a verb or adjective in relation to its object or modifier, in favour of the following four order patterns: verb-object (*ætywan eall* (line 46), *gewyrcan heora byrgene* (132), and *man deð unlybban* (171), replacing object-verb in *VercHom* 21.130, *VercHom* 10.225 and *WPol* 2.2.2.8, respectively[36]); *beon*-adjective-genitive object (*sy gemyndig drihtenes ælmihtiges* (line 76), reversing the order genitive object-adjective of *VercHom* 9.141); auxiliary-infinitive (*sceal habban* (line 180), altered from *WPol* 2.1.1.168 *habban sceal*); and non-final verb in subordinate clauses, as in line 37 and in the last clause of Napier XXX 75 quoted below, where the verb has been moved from the final position of *VercHom* 21.90 and 9.142, respectively. Changes are occasionally made into orders that are contrary to those just illustrated; see, e.g. the order object-verb in lines 123 and 184. However, the overall movement towards 'modern' word order is obvious.

Other syntactical alterations include the use of verbal periphrasis by adding an auxiliary verb—of tense, in *forgyfen hafað* (line 130), or mood, in *geearnian wyllað* (50), *mihte oððe moste libban* (125), and *wyle . . . manian* (131); in all these the source sentences in the Vercelli homilies have a simple verb form. *Willan* in the attitudinal nuance—'to choose to', as *OED* (s.v. *Will* 7) paraphrases it—in collocation with the verb *geearnian*, as in the second example above, is attested further in a *gif*-clause (line 41) which the compiler adds, though the collocation itself also occurs in the Vercelli homilies as well as Wulfstan's homilies.[37] These uses of auxiliary verbs obviously point to a tendency towards 'modern' periphrastic or analytic constructions. So perhaps might the use of the preposition *fram* in the last sentence of the following passage in comparison with the case form in the source text:

> Napier XXX 75 ⁊ nys þær ænig man þe þær sy gemyndig drihtenes ælmihtiges for ðam sare þe he on wunað. Þær beoð þa sawla forgytene fram eallum þam ðe hi ær cuðon on eorðan.

---

[35] On this word order, see Bruce Mitchell, *Old English Syntax*, 2 vols. (Oxford, 1985), §§3930–6, and my study of it in some Vercelli Homilies and associated Old English prose in 'Initial Verb-Subject Inversion in Some Late Old English Homilies', *Studies in the History*, pp. 235–62.

[36] See further *hreowe don ure synna* (line 155), where part of the object is moved to post-verbal position, from *VercHom* 4.64 *ure synna hreowe don*.

[37] For details, see Hiroshi Ogawa, *Old English Modal Verbs: A Syntactical Study* (Copenhagen, 1989), pp. 116 and 303 n. 10. On the other hand, *sceal beon* in the Vercelli source (*VercHom* 4.70) is replaced by the futuric *bið* in Napier XXX 166 *Ac anra gehwylcum men byð gedemed æfter his agenum gewyrhtum*, presumably because the compiler wanted to make it parallel to the simple verb forms that are used in the two immediately preceding sentences with the same reference to Judgement Day.

VercHom 9.140 nis þær nænig man þæt þær sy his scyppendes gemyndig for ðam sare þe him onsiteð. ⁊ þær beoð þa sawle forgytene ealra þæra þe hi ær on eorðan gemetton.

Here, however, the addition of *fram* entails a grammatical 'reanalysis' and hence a change of meaning—from gen. pl. *ealra þæra* qualifying *þa sawle* ('the souls of all their earthly acquaintances being forgotten (by them)') in the Vercelli text to the agentive *fram eallum* qualifying the passive construction ('the souls (of the dead) being forgotten by all their earthly acquaintances') in our compilation; the compiler is more likely to have introduced his own reading than merely updating syntax. It is interesting to observe that the compiler has made another 'reanalysis' in the opening sentence of the passage being discussed, rewriting *for ðam sare þe him onsiteð* (where the sorrow oppresses the man), as *for ðam sare þe he on wunað* (where the man lives in sorrow), thereby making the clause parallel to the preceding one referring to life in hell (*Wa byð þam þe . . . ðær symble wunian sceal*); on this passage see further the next section. But it is also possible that the compiler shunned the word *onsittan* because at least in the sense 'to oppress', it was no longer a common word when he was writing. See BT, s.v. *onsittan*, III.

IV

Another area of syntax where the compiler makes frequent changes concerns relative pronouns. While his use of *þe* in *nys þær ænig man þe þær sy gemyndig* (line 75) in place of the 'conjunction-relative' *þæt* in the source (*VercHom* 9.141)[38] might be another case of updated syntax, the other examples, mostly of the compound relative replacing the simple *þe* or *se*, seem to suggest other considerations. That he uses the compound form *se þe* both in a factual statement (line 84, *þone mycelan garsecg, se ðe . . . ealle ðas eorðan utan emblið*, replacing *se* in the Vercelli source) and the final doxology (214 *mid drihtene sylfum, se ðe leofað ⁊ rixað a butan ende on ecnesse, amen*, replacing Wulfstan's *þe*) shows that they are probably not replaced for meaning but stylistic effect.[39] This is seen more clearly in the alternation between the compound *se þe* and simple *þe* as the compiler shows it in a passage describing a variety of bodily infirmities which come upon us with old age:

---

[38] The Vercelli Book has lost a leaf for this part, and the text is supplied from the version in MS E (Bodley 340 and 342), as in Scragg's edition. On the 'conjunction-relative' *þæt*, see *OES*, §§2139–44, and Kirsti Kivimaa, Þe *and* Pat *as Clause Connectives in Early Middle English with Especial Consideration of the Emergence of the Pleonastic* Pat (Helsinki, 1966), pp. 43–4.

[39] For Ælfric's use of the compound and simple relative pronouns, see Chapter VI.

> Napier XXX 113 Him amolsniað ⁊ adimmiað þa eagan,[40] þe ær wæron beorhte ⁊ gleawe on gesihðe. And seo tunge awistlað, þe ær hæfde getinge spræce ⁊ gerade. ⁊ ða earan aslawiað, þa þe ær wæron ful swifte ⁊ hræde to gehyrenne fægere dreamas ⁊ sangas. And þa handa awindað, þa ðe ær hæfdon ful hwæte fingras. And þæt feax afeallað, þe ær wæs fæger on hiwe ⁊ on fulre wæstme. And þa teð ageolwiað, þa ðe wæron ær hwite on hiwe. ⁊ þæt oreð stingð ⁊ afulað, þe ær wæs swete on stence.

The corresponding passage in the source (*VercHom* 9.90–7) also has both relatives but chooses between them apparently indiscriminately for each clause. Of these, the compiler rewrites two, one each of the simple and compound forms, in such a way that his choice is the simple form when the antecedent is a singular noun with the demonstrative *se* or *þæt* but the compound relative for any plural antecedent preceded by *þa*; the only exception, *þa eagan, þe* . . . (in the first line), rewriting the compound form in the source, is allowed to stand, one supposes, to avoid what would otherwise have become a rather clumsy succession of two *þa*'s without any intervening verb as in the rest of the series.[41] The compiler's handling of the relative pronouns is thus at once more methodical and rhetorical, with its rhetorical effects deriving from the repetitive figures of sound (*þa . . . þa*), which are reinforced by the originally demonstrative function of the second *þa*; here *þa* (or any form of *se* as a constituent of the compound relative) 'is probably emphatic "thóse (who)" and so part of the principal clause, thereby giving us what is in effect the *se'þe* relative'.[42] It is perhaps significant to note that all this alteration is made in a passage which is highly rhetorical as a whole, with its long succession of balanced clauses, and numerous additions (*adimmiað . . . beorhte . . . getinge . . . dreamas . . . fæger on hiwe . . . stingð*), expanding single words into word pairs and sustaining that balance.

    The passage just discussed is only one of the many rhetorical passages characteristic of the middle section as opposed to the opening and concluding sections of the homily. Another, some six lines in the EETS edition following the *ubi sunt* formulas ('Hwær syndon/ys . . .? Hwær com/comon . . .?'), illustrates another aspect of the compiler's wish to match language to emotive content:

> Napier XXX 145 Ðas hean mihta her on worulde afeallað ⁊ ahreosað ⁊ to lore wurþað. Swa læne ys seo oferlufu eorða gestreona, efnes hit bið gelice rena scurum þonne hi nyðer of heofonum swyðost dreoseð ⁊ eft raðe eall

---

[40] The misprint in the EETS edition (*amolsniað ⁊ dimmiað eagan*) is corrected in Scragg, *Dating and Style*, pp. 8–9.

[41] The compiler omits the reference to feet between tongue and hands (*VercHom* 9.93 ⁊ þa [fet] aslapað þe ær wæron ful swifte [⁊ hræde] to [gange])—an omission which is also witnessed in the E version; see Scragg, *The Vercelli Homilies*, p. 166, apparatus.

[42] *OES*, §2170.

toglideð,[43] þonne bið fæger weder ⁊ beorht sunne. Swa tealte syndon eorðan welan, swa todæleð se lichoma ⁊ seo sawul. Ðissere worulde wela wurðeþ to nahte, ⁊ ðas eorðlican þing wurðaþ to sorge, eallum þam þe hy to swyðe lufiað.

What is striking here is neither sound nor tautological words and phrases, but the words *swa* and *þonne*, which combine to create unusually involved syntax. The first *swa* starts a distinct sentence, comparing the transience of earthly riches both to the vulnerability of earthly powers, as described in the preceding sentence, and to showers of rain which soon pass away ('efnes hit bið gelice . . .'). This is recapitulated by the second *swa*-clause, which evidently continues the sense of the preceding clauses, with *eorðan welan* as a variation of *eorða gestreona*, but at the same time points forwards to the third *swa*-clause; this last, then, translates all the departure of earthly things to the departure of the body from the soul. In other words, the second *swa* is used *apo koinou*. So is apparently the first of the two *þonne*-clauses, which as a temporal clause at once points backwards to raining ('just as it is like rain showers when they fall . . . and soon pass away') and forwards to fine weather following it ('when they fall . . . and soon pass away, then there will be fine weather and bright sun'). The resultant correlative *þonne . . . þonne*, incorporated into the sequence of *swa*-clauses, gives a tightly-knit prose-paragraph, whose stylistic effect modern punctuation, either as above or in Napier's edition ('swa læne . . .; efnes hit bið . . . scurum, þonne hy . . . toglidað, þonne bið . . .; swa tealte . . ., swa todæleð . . .'), can hardly succeed in capturing.[44] It is given a force appropriate to its content, if not logical clarity in terms of the main and subordinate clauses of modern grammatical analysis. The effect may be seen more easily by comparison with the Vercelli text of the corresponding passage, which has only one *þonne*-clause but an extra *and* ('⁊' between the second and third *swa*-clauses) instead of the compiler's second *þonne*:

> *VercHom* 10.241 Swa læne is sio oferlufu eorðan gestreona, emne hit bið gelice rena scurum, þonne he of heofenum swiðost dreoseð ⁊ eft hraðe eal toglideð—bið fæger weder ⁊ beorht sunne. Swa tealte syndon eorðan dreamas, ⁊ swa todæleð lic ⁊ sawle.

---

[43] Napier emends the last two verb forms as *dreosað* and *toglidað* as appropriate for the plural subject *hi*. See Frank, 'Poetic Words', p. 102.

[44] The manuscript text (fols. 77v/18–78r/3), with its distinctive use of punctus and capitalization, reads: Ðas hean mihta her on worulde afeallað. ⁊ ahreosað. ⁊ to lore wurþað. Swa læne ys seo oferlufu eorða gestreona. efnes hit bið gelice rena scurum þonne hi nyðer of heofonum swyðost dreoseð. ⁊ eft raðe eall toglideð. þonne bið fæger weder. ⁊ beorht sunne. swa tealte syndon eorðan welan. Swa todæleð se lichoma ⁊ seo sawul. For more details of the manuscript text of this passage and others, see my previous study of the homily ('A "Wulfstan Imitator" at Work', pp. 263–85, esp. pp. 272–6).

This omission of *and* in favour of *þonne* leads us to the compiler's treatment of the conjunction vis-à-vis the usage in his sources. He makes four additions of *and* (lines 47, 52 (the first one), 60, 129) and three omissions (lines 77, 178, 179). These conflicting cases make it difficult to say with certainty why alteration is made where it is in one way rather than the other. But the distribution of the examples — all occurring in the middle, anonymous section of the homily apart from two omissions (see below) — may not be coincidence. They suggest that the alteration, like the two features shown above and the additions of intensifying words frequent in the middle section (see section I), is for stylistic effect, attuned to the emotive content of the section, as distinct from the surrounding Wulfstanian ones. Three of the additions of *and* occur in a passage (lines 44–71) which draws on an extract from Vercelli XXI,[45] itself derived in part from the Old English poem *An Exhortation to Christian Living*. This suggests the compiler's sense of prose rhythm as a consideration in adding the conjunction. For example, the first addition, resulting in '⁊ beoð þonne mid urum sawlum ece symle earme oððe eadige' (line 47), occurs in the flow shaped by these immediately preceding lines:

> Napier XXX 44 We syndon deadlice menn and to duste sceolon on worulde wurðan wurmum to æte ⁊ of eorðan we sceolon eft ealle arisan on domes dæge ⁊ drihtene sylfum ætywan eall þæt we ær dydon.

By rearranging these as metrical lines, Angus McIntosh refers to them as 'something which with the slight revision of one line reveals itself clearly as a fragment of a genuine Old English poem'.[46] However, the one line — '⁊ of eorðan we sceolon eft ealle arisan' rather than McIntosh's strictly metrical 'and of eorðan eft ealle arisan' — itself, one would argue, demonstrates the compiler's own sense of prose rhythm, and this rhythm probably goes on to prompt the compiler, in the following line in question (line 47), to avoid asyndesis but add the conjunction before *beoð*; the subject of this verb is in any case to be supplied from the preceding portion.[47] Similarly, one of the omissions of *and* results in a sentence beginning with *Þær beoð*, making it parallel to the preceding *Đær ne byð* ... in yet another rhythmical and rhetorical pattern:

---

[45] On Vercelli XXI, see Chapter IV.

[46] McIntosh, 'Wulfstan's Prose', 141 n. 29. McIntosh's italics indicating alliteration are not reproduced.

[47] Another example of *and*, added in the form of Tironian nota writ large before *ealle* in line 58 (*ac se stiðmoda cyning, drihten ælmihtig, awearp of ðam setle þone modigan feond ⁊ of ðam wuldre eac þæs heofonlican rices. ⁊ ealle þa ðe mid him æt ðam ræde wæron, hi wiston þe geornor, witum besette on þære byrnendan helle, wið hwæne hi winnon ongunnon*) presents a problem of interpretation. For discussion, see Ogawa, 'A "Wulfstan Imitator" at Work', pp. 284–5.

Napier XXX 74 Wa byð þam þe þær bið geteohhod to ⁊ ðær symble wunian sceal. Ðær ne byð sybbes lufu to oðrum, ⁊ nys þær ænig man þe þær sy gemyndig drihtenes ælmihtiges for ðam sare þe he on wunað. Þær beoð þa sawla forgytene fram eallum þam ðe hi ær cuðon on eorðan.

When he turns from the anonymous sources to the Wulfstanian ones for his concluding section, the compiler no longer adds any *and* but omits two examples in the source (*WPol* 2.1.1.167–8 *and gebuge ælc man . . . And eac se . . .*)[48] in succeeding sentences (lines 178–9, after omitting the initial *ac* in the preceding sentence). What is more characteristic of his sentences in this section is hypotaxis introduced in place of parataxis in the source, as seen in *Ne mæg se preost ænigum synfullum men wel dædbote tæcan . . ., þe ma þe ænig læce mæg ænigne untrumne mann wel lacnian . . .* (line 171, where Wulfstan says: *WPol* 2.2.2.8 *Ne mæg ænig lace well lacnian . . .; ne ænig man ne mæg eac dædbote wel tæcan . . .*) and two other sentences in rapid succession in the final passage of the homily:

Napier XXX 204 *we syndon swa heardre heortan þæt we ne magon ongytan þa godcundan lare þe us man lærð ⁊ laþað to urum drihtne fram deofles anwealde.* Us ys eallum swyðe micel þearf þæt we understandon þæt hit to ðam dome nu georne genealæcð, þe drihten sylf to cymð, *þonne he wyle æt us witan hu we him geleanod habbon eall þæt he for us prowode ⁊ ðolode on þisum life.*

The italicized parts are adapted, respectively, from 'and he bið swa heard swa stan, and he ne mæg ongytan ða godcundan lare, þe hine lærð and laþað to urum drihtne . . .' (*Polity* 245.70) and 'forðam þonne he wile æt us witan . . .' (*WHom* 6.194). Here again, the compiler seems to have his language attuned to the content, which is more discursive and reasoned than in the anonymous section and would demand logical rather than emotional treatment. By making these adaptations according to the general tone of the different sections, the compiler makes his own sense of the tripartite structure of the homily—the anonymous middle section surrounded by orthodox teachings and exhortations from the Wulfstanian sources—the more meaningful and effective.

These cases of distinction in style between the anonymous and Wulfstanian sections should not make us blind to the fact that the compiler usually writes in a straightforward and readable style in all sections. He obviously shuns the preposition *mid* with a noun of abstract idea, using the adverb *rihtlice* (line 1) in place of Wulfstan's *mid rihte* and an *on*-phrase in *on urum mode* (33) in place of *VercHom* 21.87 *mid arfæstum ⁊ mid wellwillendum mode.*[49] It may also be this taste for the matter-of-fact style of a practical mind that makes the compiler say *Eal*

---

[48] In the version in CCCC 201, item 168 reads *And witod se . . .*, lacking the word *eac*, used in Junius 121 and our homily.

[49] He also prefers *on* in a local sense, in *on moldan bepeaht ⁊ on witum gecyrred* (line 142), where the Vercelli source has *mid* and *in* (*VercHom* 10.236).

man sceal aspiwan synna þurh abryrde andetnysse (line 170, in place of *WPol* 2.2.2.8 *þurh gode lare*) and *Þonne geearnige we us ece blisse on heofona rice mid drihtene sylfum* (213, where Wulfstan says: *WHom* 6.216 *æt ðam sylfum Gode*) and prefer an animate instead of inanimate subject for the verb *læran* in the above-quoted passage (Napier XXX 204, reading *þa godcundan lare þe us man lærð*, in place of ... *lare þe hine lærð*). For another thing, the compiler adds a noun to an adjective used as noun in the source (saying the more explicitly *þa rican men* and *earmre sawle*[50] in lines 138 and 159, respectively) and also a number of grammatical words: the demonstrative *se* (in inflected forms) before nouns of various meanings on seven occasions (including the pattern possessive + demonstrative in line 38, *mid his þam deorwurðan blode*[51]) and the genitive *þisse/þissere* before *worlde* and *eorðan* (143, 144). He even adds a possessive adjective before a noun on a few occasions, reinforcing its coreferential relation to the subject of the clause, as in *hi heora cristendom rihtlice healdan* (line 1) and *Uton ... geþencan on urum mode* (33). All these additions of small words make for clarity of sense, though at the risk of being occasionally redundant.

The clarity the compiler achieves through his rewriting sometimes characterizes his clause syntax, as best seen in an extended sentence in the anchorite and devil story,[52] where the latter relates the terror of hell:

> Napier XXX 85 And he, se deofol, þa gyt cwæð to þam ancran: 'Gyf ænig mann wære ane niht on helle ⁊ he eft wære æfter þam ofalædd, ⁊ ðeah man þone garsecg mid isene utan ymbtynde, ⁊ þonne ealne gefylde mid fyres lige up oþ ðone heofonas hrof, ⁊ utan embsette hine þonne ealne mid byligeon ⁊ heora æghwylc oðres æthrinan mihte, ⁊ to æghwylcum þæra byligea wære man geset ⁊ se hæfde Samsones strengðe (se wæs ealra eorðwarena strengst þe ær oððe syððan æfre gewurde) ⁊ þeah man þonne gesette an brad isen þell ofer þæs fyres hrof, ⁊ þeah hit wære eall mid mannum afylled ⁊ ðæra æghwylc hæfde ænne hamor on handa, ⁊ þeah man bleowe mid eallum þam byligeon ⁊ mid þam hameron beote on þæt isene þell ⁊ se lig

---

[50] The word *sawle* is squeezed in later at the end of the line, and Napier omits it from his text. On this addition, see further the next section.

[51] Scragg calls this construction 'slightly archaic syntax' ('Napier's "Wulfstan" homily xxx', 205). For examples in other homilies, see, e.g. Napier XL 187.10 based on *VercHom* 2.56 (Chapter III, p. 45), and *VercHom* 2.15 and *VercHom* 21.185 (Chapter IV, pp. 67 and 66 n. 17, respectively). The other examples of the added demonstrative *se* occur in lines 54, 69 (before *drihten*; see n. 32), 150 (twice), 187 and 188. On the last two examples, see Scragg, *Dating and Style*, p. 14.

[52] Fred C. Robinson has named the story 'The Devil's Account of the Next World' in an article which bears this title (*NM* 73 (1972), 362–71). For the history of this story, formerly known as the Theban Legend, in Old English, see Robinson's article just mentioned and Scragg, *The Vercelli Homilies*, pp. 153–7.

brastlode, ne awacode he næfre for eallum þisum, to ðam werig he wære for þære anre nihthwile.

The sentence consists of a *gif*-clause, in which are embedded some ten subordinate clauses (depending on how one defines a clause) and which is then followed by a rather short main clause. The length and complexity of the subordinate matter, however, is balanced by the arrangement of its constituent clauses which is logical and clear, particularly in three respects: (1) the conjunction *þeah* repeated four times following the initial *gif*, (2) the use of relative *se . . . þe* to set off the explanation about Samson as parenthetical, and (3) the appropriate form of subordination *Gyf. . ., ne awacode he næfre for eallum þisum.* The significance of this arrangement is brought out very clearly by comparison with the three variant texts of the passage that survive, though comparison is impossible with the Vercelli source, which has lost a leaf for this part.[53] The variant texts all fail in at least one of the respects just specified. The Corpus version (CCCC 303, p. 202), failing in (1), has the initial *Gif* introducing five sequences of expressed subject and verb or verbs which are simply coordinated by *and* ('ꞇ') without any further subordinating conjunction (and lacking any clause about Samson). Failure in (1) is no less characteristic of the Hatton version (Hatton 115, fol. 145), with *Þeah* instead of *Gif* in the Corpus introducing a long sequence of clauses which are simply conjoined by *and* ('ꞇ'); even the explanatory clauses about Samson which are here added are treated in this way (*Þeah . . . ꞇ ælc þara manna hæbbe Samsones strenge ꞇ se Samson . . . ꞇ he hæfde twelf loccas ꞇ on ælcum locce he hæfde . . .*).[54] The last point is set right by the use of the relative *se þe* in the other version (Cotton Tiberius A. iii, fols. 87v-88r). However, this version in its turn fails in (3), with the main clause beginning with *ꞇ þeahhwepere* rather than the grammatically required *þeahhwepere*, as if the author had lost his sense of the subordinating conjunction with which he had started the passage.[55] Compared with these three, our compiler's version of the sentence shows a control over his prose which gives it clarity of sense and ease of style. It is perhaps this quality among others for which Jost describes the anchorite and devil story in Napier XXX as written 'in stilistisch überarbeiteter Form' as compared with the Tiberius version and 'lesbarer gestaltet' than the latter.[56]

---

[53] For studies of the relationship between the different versions, see Robinson, 'The Devil's Account', 362–5. Scragg questions some of Robinson's views in '"The Devil's Account of the Next World" Revisited', *American Notes and Queries* 24 (1986), 104–10, and Robinson replies to this in the *Afterword 1993* to a reprint of his 1972 article (*The Editing of Old English* (Oxford, 1994), pp. 204–5).

[54] For more details of this Hatton version as part of the anonymous homily known as Fadda X, see the section on this homily in Chapter IV.

[55] For similar examples of 'ungrammatical' subordination in anonymous homilies, see, e.g. *VercHom* 9.108–13, 18.28 and 18.32–5, all involving *þeah*.

[56] Jost, *Wulfstanstudien*, pp. 208 and 210.

This fundamental merit of style links other distinctive features of the homily we have seen earlier, such as a desire for force expressed by word pairs, updated vocabulary and syntax, and a basic contrast between the constituent sections with different emphases of adaptation according to the nature of their source materials, and makes them all contribute effectively to the unity of the homily. The resultant homily Napier XXX is not a work of mere imitation but a good example of the composite homily, showing a well-thought-out design and execution.

V

We do not know how Napier XXX was seen by contemporary and later homilists and audiences. But we have evidence to suggest that 'the piece quickly became widely distributed',[57] since extracts from it are re-used in homilies contained in different manuscripts—CUL Ii. 4.6 (s. xi med., made at Winchester) and Cotton Otho B. x (s. xi[1], place of origin unknown), while the extant Napier XXX itself is written in a Worcester manuscript after the homily was originally composed, probably at Canterbury.[58] This circulation indicates a remarkable popularity, when most composite homilies of the period exist in only one copy.

The homily in CUL Ii. 4.6 is the one now edited by Joyce Bazire and J. E. Cross as item 7 of their collection of Rogationtide homilies (*HomS* 41; Cameron No. B3.2.41).[59] This is a composite penitential homily which is made up mainly of extracts from various homilies of Ælfric, all in the *Catholic Homilies* and *Lives of Saints*.[60] Towards the beginning of this compilation, the compiler interpolated the last third of Napier XXX (line 154, beginning half way through a passage lifted from Vercelli IV, to the end of the last Wulfstanian concluding section), with four omissions: lines 168–73 ('God wyle . . . oninnan bið'), 174–5 ('⁊ æfre . . . magon'), 176–82 ('Uton lufian . . . þearf ys') and 200–1 ('Ne us . . . forðsiðe').[61] One may well suppose that these omissions 'may have been made partly because these include ideas to be presented later, and partly to excise ideas which are

---

[57] Scragg, *The Vercelli Homilies*, p. 395.

[58] See Scragg, *The Vercelli Homilies*, p. 395; id., 'The corpus of vernacular homilies and prose saints' lives before Ælfric', *ASE* 8 (1979), 223–77, esp. 254 and n. 9. For details of the manuscripts, see Ker, *Catalogue*, pp. 31–5 and 224–9; on Cotton Otho B. x, see further below and Chapter III, where I discuss its item 18 (Napier LVIII).

[59] Joyce Bazire and James E. Cross (eds.), *Eleven Old English Rogationtide Homilies* (Toronto, 1982), pp. 90–100.

[60] For details of the sources and construction of the homily, see M. R. Godden, 'Old English composite homilies from Winchester', *ASE* 4 (1975), 57–65, esp. 59–62; Bazire and Cross, *Rogationtide Homilies*, pp. 90–3.

[61] Godden counts these as three omissions ('OE composite homilies', 59–60). See also Bazire and Cross, *Rogationtide Homilies*, pp. 90 and 93 n. 3.

irrelevant to the exhortation of a penitent'.[62] Whatever the reasons, these omissions, and substitution of the concluding sentences (Napier XXX 212–4) by one expanded by a passage from Wulfstan's homily (*WHom* 13.53–5),[63] are the major work of the compiler in the part where he draws on Napier XXX. Here, as elsewhere in the homily, according to Malcolm Godden, '[h]is treatment of [the] sources was fairly conservative. . . . The shorter extracts sometimes show more change, but there is no radical rewriting, and in some cases sources have been copied verbatim'.[64] Godden goes on to conclude:

> The passages are skilfully woven together on a rather superficial level by inserting frequent connectives and using verbal associations, but there is rather less concern with an underlying thread of thought or argument. There is, though, a certain amount of independence in organizing the material. The homilies do not follow the structure of any one source but have their own organization and character.[65]

What Godden refers to above as 'a rather superficial level' of adaptation may be seen in details of wording of the Napier XXX part. Here again, omission is a major feature of the compiler's method. He omits some of the distinctive wording of the source text—*georne* (line 17 before *alysan*, from Napier XXX 155)[66] and one out of two or more members of repetitive phrases, as in *Nis nan mann on eorðan swa mære ne swa mihtig* (line 19; Napier XXX 156 *Nis nan man swa rice on eorðan ꝼ swa mihtig ꝼ mære*) and *us eallum to ðearfe* (line 24; Napier XXX 163 *Gode to willan ꝼ us sylfum to þearfe*); this latter feature is also found in a later part drawing upon another anonymous homily, in *he his agene þearfe gehyre seggan* (line 66; Napier LVIII 306.16 *he his agene þearfe gehyre secgan and embe godes mærð smeage*). Apart from these occasions, the compiler never tampers with word pairs used in Napier XXX but has once used *oþþe* in *þa gyltas þe we æfre gefremedon oþþe dydon* (line 23) instead of *and* in Napier XXX 162, perhaps changing the combination of verbs into something more than a rhetorical flourish. A special case of shorter text is the compiler's passage (lines 25–7, quoted later) to the effect that no one can be helped by relatives at doomsday, corresponding to the one discussed by Scragg (Napier XXX 164–6; see section I). Of the four clauses (with or without

---

[62] Bazire and Cross, *Rogationtide Homilies*, p. 90.
[63] See Godden, 'OE composite homilies', 60; Bazire and Cross, *Rogationtide Homilies*, p. 90; Wilcox, 'The Dissemination', p. 209.
[64] Godden, 'OE composite homilies', 64. Godden says this, and concludes as quoted below, with respect to Bazire and Cross 7 and another item in CUL Ii. 4.6, which he argues persuasively to be composed by the same Winchester compiler as Bazire and Cross 7; see 'OE composite homilies', 62–5.
[65] Godden, 'OE composite homilies', 65.
[66] The compiler prefers not to use the word *georne* again in 'hit to þam dome nu geornlice genealæcð' (line 55), against Napier XXX, line 206.

an expressed verb) in this latter text, two (*ne seo modor þære dehter ne seo dohtor þære meder*) are lacking in this compilation. In this difference and similar evidence, Godden sees 'signs that the text of Napier XXX used by the Ii. 4.6 compiler was slightly different from the extant one', particularly because the two clauses in question do not appear in the antecedent source for this part, Vercelli IV (for the text, see section I), either.[67] Likewise, *Wa bið hire þonne earmre* (line 20) agrees (apart from the form of the verb *beon*) with the Vercelli antecedent source (*Verc-Hom* 4.67) against Napier XXX 159 *Wa byð hyre þonne, earmre sawle*. In this case, the agreement makes it possible to argue that the word *sawle* in the Napier XXX text, treated in the EETS edition as proper to the text, may not be an addition by the compiler but by a later corrector, since the word is squeezed in later at the end of the line.[68] These special cases apart, the general effect of this compiler's style in the examples of omission listed seems obvious, weakening rather than reinforcing the rhetorical force characteristic of Napier XXX as a whole.

Compared with omissions, the additions made by the compiler are few and contribute nothing of substance. The additions are mostly of small, if not entirely empty, words, such as *þær* and *her*, or of grammatical words, the demonstrative *þæt* added before *ece wite* (line 29) and examples of 'frequent connectives' (as Godden puts it)—the causal conjunction *forðan þe* (25) and adverb *forði* (63) and *ac* added twice. This last is added on one occasion (line 28) as a linking word immediately after the first long omission, but on the other (47) it does not appear congruous with the sense, used to link sentences which are made parallel by the

---

[67] Godden, 'OE composite homilies', 60. The other evidence Godden gives of Bazire and Cross 7 agreeing with the antecedent source against Napier XXX is *ure ealra* (line 32 and Napier XXIV 121.6) and *ealra cristenra manna* (Napier XXX 184).

[68] The word is included in the text of the EETS edition with an editorial sign which 'indicates a letter or letters squeezed in later or added in the margin' (p. lxxxii), but nothing more specific is said in the editorial apparatus. Napier does not include the word in his text. I have only consulted the manuscript on microfilm. But Professor Malcolm Godden, who very kindly took the trouble to check the manuscript for me, says (private communication) regarding the punctuation on the manuscript in the part of Napier XXX, as follows: 'Much of the punctuation is clearly original—same ink, well-spaced, etc. But quite a lot is rather cramped, as if it might have been squeezed in subsequently, and sometimes these more cramped marks are in a slightly lighter ink and/or finer pen (or occasionally thicker pen). A few instances were pretty definitely added subsequent to the writing, because of the way they are squeezed in, but the rest of the more cramped instances could just reflect the scribe's way of writing. Apart from 2 or 3 instances of a colon shaped mark (:) that are obviously in the hand and ink of the tremulous hand, none of the punctuation marks is necessarily by a different scribe: the ink colours are not substantially different, and the occasional differences of shape or position or weight could be explained by the need to fit the mark into a small space. What I think I see in the MS is compatible with the notion of the same scribe, or an early corrector, adding some punctuation marks after the text was written, but with this MS it seems a rather subjective business to decide.'

accompanying alteration of a verb but which are not really adversative: *Geþence gehwa him sylf hu sceort and hu earmlic þis læne lif is. Ac ne þence we na fram dæge to dæge þæt we to Gode ne gecyrron* (Napier XXX 197 *Geþence gehwa . . . Ne yldon we na . . .*). The rest of the examples referred to above do not affect meaning, either, but show stylistic, often rhythmical choices, as we shall see below.

There are two other additions. One, of *deaþ* in *Crist ðrowode deaþ* (line 39), seems redundant rather than clarifying, repeating as it does the same phrase used just a few lines earlier. The other addition, of several words (including *mann* and *gehelpan*) in the last of the parallel clauses about no one being able to be helped by relatives at doomsday (see below), is another part of the problem of textual history pointed out by Godden; see above.[69]

Mention was made above of connectives that are added by the compiler. To these should be added use of *and*, whereby he changes the subordinate *ponne*-clause (Napier XXX 206 *hit to ðam dome nu georne genealæcð, þe drihten sylf to cymð, þonne he wyle æt us witan hu we him geleanod habbon*) into a coordinate clause (line 56, *Drihten sylf to cymð and wile þonne æt us witan . . .*). This might reflect what Godden calls 'the loose style characteristic of the compiler'.[70] What may be shown more definitely is preference for word order shown in the resultant *and*-clause, for there the compiler places the adverb *þonne* after the finite verb, as he also does in the other relevant sentence *Ðær beoð þonne on us sylfum gesyne and opene ealle þa gyltas* (line 22), as opposed to Napier XXX 162 *Ðær þonne beoð . . .* Here consideration for prose rhythm is obviously involved and this might have made itself felt more widely as the compiler made an adaptation of extracts from Ælfric's works in the subsequent part of his homily. There is perhaps room for future work here. But it will suffice for the moment to add another indication of the compiler's prose rhythm from the Napier XXX part: *þær* and *her*, when added by the compiler (see above), are placed invariably before the finite verb (lines 26, 27, 59). The other change of position of adverbs—of *ær* in *buton hi beon her on worulde ær gebette* (line 24; Napier XXX 163 *buton hi beon ær her on worulde gebette*)—might be interpreted similarly.[71]

But the most striking of the features of the compiler's style in comparison with that of his source text is the double negative introduced by adding *ne* or *nan*. This was seen earlier in a case of omission (at line 19, *Nis nan mann . . . swa mære ne swa mihtig*), making good the loss of one part of a tautological phrase.

---

[69] Another thing to notice about the textual difference in this passage is the use in Bazire and Cross 7 of the dative *oþran* as the object of *gehelpan*, where the Napier XXX compiler has the genitive *oðres*, as pointed out by Scragg; see n. 22.

[70] Godden, 'OE composite homilies', 60.

[71] The short passage adapted from Napier LVIII which immediately follows the Napier XXX part provides another example: line 66, *Ne sceal næfre nanum cristenum menn to langsum þincan . . .*; Napier LVIII 306.15 *Ne sceal nanum cristenum men æfre to langsum þincean . . .* On the alteration of *næfre* and *æfre* here, see immediately below.

Further, it occurs characteristically in the 'no one can be helped by relatives' passage (lines 25–7): *þær ne mæg nan mann opran gehelpan — ne se fæder þam sunu ne se sunu þam fæder — ne nan mann þær ne mæg oprum gehelpan* (using the first *nan* in place of *ænig* and adding *ne* before *se fæder* and the last *mæg* in the Napier XXX passage).[72] However, unlike other differences between the two versions of the passage, double as opposed to single negative here is not likely to be a result of the textual transmission Godden speculates for Napier XXX itself (see above). It is more probably a personal preference of the compiler, who has it again in a passage based on Napier LVIII, in *næfre* (line 66) against the latter's *æfre*.

None of the changes to the Napier XXX text so far examined suggests any attempt on the compiler's part to update the language of his source — not unexpectedly, since he is writing supposedly not long after the source homily was written.[73] Nor is there conflicting evidence in the vocabulary of the compilation, except possibly for the replacement of verbs with the prefix *ge-* by *dydon* (line 23) and *abidan* (50), for 'there seems to be a trend towards a decline of the prefix [*ge-*] from eOE to lOE', as Risto Hiltunen observes.[74] But he adds:

> we must not forget that the prefix is a conspicuous feature of OE, early or late. That we are only dealing with tendencies will become apparent from any lOE text, where verbs with *ge-* abound. It is not until eME texts, such as *Ancr[ene Riwle]*, that the consequences of the above tendencies become manifest.[75]

Among the vocabulary items that would indicate more clearly the compiler's personal preferences are the Wulfstanian adverb *witod* shunned in favour of *witodlice* (line 48), single word expressions rather than composite forms, seen in *behreowsian* (line 17; Napier XXX 155 *hreowe don*) and *gemyndige* (43; Napier XXX 194 *on gemynde*),[76] and *ne wearð* (61) in place of *nes* (Napier XXX 211). On rare occasions the compiler also introduces a slight change of meaning by his own choice of prepositions: *þurh his micclan mildheortnysse* (line 40, instead of *for* in the source) and *lif oð æfen* (48, instead of *æt*).

---

[72] The first *ne* is printed as *he* in Bazire and Cross's edition; the misprint has remained uncorrected in the second edition (published as *King's College London Medieval Studies* IV, 1989). It should be added that Napier XXX has the word *ne* added before the last *mæg* above the line in the manuscript, as noted in the EETS edition. Napier incorporates the addition into the text.

[73] See n. 3.

[74] Risto Hiltunen, *The Decline of the Prefixes and the Beginnings of the English Phrasal Verb* (Turku, 1983), p. 65.

[75] Hiltunen, *The Decline of the Prefixes*, p. 65.

[76] This latter single word expression is in fact the distinctive feature of the Bazire and Cross 7 version in comparison with the other four versions of the passage. See below and Chapter III.

Another later homily to lift a passage from Napier XXX is Napier LVIII, preserved in Cotton Otho B. x. The passage used is Napier XXX, lines 193–7, which 'was extremely popular among Old English homilists',[77] used in Bazire and Cross 7 (lines 43–6) as well as Napier LVIII and with parallels in two more homilies (Napier XXIV and Lambeth 489, item 5). As in Bazire and Cross 7, the passage is supplemented here with an earlier line (line 182) from the same source attached at the end, to read:

> Napier LVIII 306.8 and uton habban us symle on urum gemynde þone timan, þe us eallum towerd is. Ðonne se lichama and seo saul hi totwæmað and todælað, þonne us forlætað ealle ure woruldfrind, ne magon hi us þonne ænigum gode, ac bið æt gode anum gelang eall, hwæt we gefaran sceolon. God us gestrangige and getrymme to ure agenre þearfe.

This is an almost verbatim re-use, with only the addition of two words (*and* and *urum*) and the transposition of *habban* and *us* in the opening sentence and an omission (of *werige* before *saul*) in the second. The passage has been claimed to be borrowed directly from Napier XXIV,[78] the ultimate source of all the parallels. But there is good reason to believe that it is not; the wording is much closer to Napier XXX than to Napier XXIV, as we shall see in detail in discussing Napier LVIII in the next chapter.[79]

Napier LVIII is preserved incomplete both at the beginning and ending, because of the fire of 1731 in which Cotton Otho B. x was badly damaged. Consequently much uncertainty remains about what the manuscript contained. But it seems from Wanley's accounts made before the fire that it contained another homily, item 16, using an extract from Napier XXX, 'end[ing] as Napier 1883, 152/2–6 (end of no. 30)'[80] — or perhaps more than one extract, since the anchorite and devil story, reported by a seventeenth-century scholar to form a subsequent part of the manuscript, 'seems likely [to have been] in art. 16', as N. R. Ker says.[81] Ker further thinks that '[f]f. 26, 23, 24, 25 (pr. Napier 1883, no. 58) probably belong here [art. 18], but possibly to art. 16',[82] implying that there may possibly have been not two but one homily drawing upon Napier XXX in Otho B. x. Whichever may be the case, use in a manuscript of at least three extracts from

---

[77] M. R. Godden, 'An Old English penitential motif', *ASE* 2 (1973), 221–39, at 229.

[78] See Wilcox, 'The Dissemination', p. 208.

[79] See Chapter III, pp. 58-9 and n. 59. The relation of Napier XXX and Napier LVIII was pointed out by Scragg, 'The corpus', 254. See also Scragg, *The Vercelli Homilies*, p. 395 and n. 2 on the same page.

[80] Ker, *Catalogue*, p. 226.

[81] Ker, *Catalogue*, p. 226. See also Scragg, *The Vercelli Homilies*, p. 395.

[82] Ker, *Catalogue*, p. 227.

Napier XXX seems a good testimony of its popularity soon after it was written (probably in the second quarter of the eleventh century).[83]

The popularity of Napier XXX may not only reflect the homilist's successful adaptation of his sources but also tell its own tale of the popularity which these sources—Wulfstan's writings and the anonymous homilies in the Vercelli Book—seem to have enjoyed among the writers of composite homilies of the period at large. Further aspects of these two strands of the Old English tradition of homiletic literature are explored in the following two chapters—first, in the next chapter, with respect to two homilies which use passages from Wulfstan, and then in Chapter IV, with respect to a Vercelli homily used in one of these two as it is used and re-used in different homilies and different manuscripts.

---

[83] Scragg ('The corpus', 254) notes that parallels with Napier XXX also occur in Pope XXVII and Napier XLVI. They are Pope XXVII, lines 121–3 (parallel to Napier XXX, lines 161–3) and Napier XLVI, 241.20–242.1 (parallel to Napier XXX, lines 202–5). But these 'are too short to be certain which way the borrowing went' ('The corpus', 254) and are not considered in this chapter.

III.
Napier XL and Napier LVIII: Two Other Uses of Wulfstan Homilies and Their Place in the Old English Vernacular Prose Tradition

In the introductory chapter we took a preliminary look at a selection of passages from Wulfstan's homilies, and saw briefly how they are given different treatments by later compilers. Napier XL and Napier LVIII emerged there as a point of focus in considering the linguistic aspects of the tradition of Wulfstan homilies. These two composite homilies, unlike the other two compared with them, adapt the Wulfstan passages substantially both in syntax and through the addition and omission of material, and they do this in different ways, rewriting them in prose of distinct styles. It was further suggested that such treatments and their stylistic consequences are not restricted to special passages from particular homilies but can be seen more generally. The present chapter proposes to pursue these points by examining the two homilies in full detail in comparison with their sources. As homilies on different topics, Napier XL and Napier LVIII do not share any passage from the same source. But the wide range of their sources—Wulfstan and anonymous homilies for Napier XL and some ten passages from Wulfstan's homiletic and legal writings for Napier LVIII—will provide us with adequate materials for studying details of the different prose styles that are used to rewrite them and which might have formed an important part of the Wulfstan tradition and the vernacular prose tradition generally.

Napier XL

Napier XL (*HomU* 32; Cameron No. B3.4.32.3), titled *In die iudicii*, is a compilation consisting of three parts—the introduction (drawn in one version probably from Wulfstan), the main body, which adapts the first half of an anonymous homily in the Vercelli Collection (Vercelli II, lines 1–66), and the conclusion, drawing again on Wulfstan's homilies.[1] The homily survives in four eleventh-century

---

[1] For details, see the studies mentioned below in n. 2.

manuscripts, and their textual relationship has been studied recently by D. G. Scragg and Jonathan Wilcox.[2] Wilcox demonstrates that the manuscripts are witnesses to three distinct stages of composition, represented by a common core, surrounded by two versions of the introduction and conclusion respectively. The version I propose to examine below is the one in British Library, Cotton Cleopatra B. xiii (s. xi 3rd quarter), edited by Arthur Napier. It represents in the introduction a later development, but is on the whole relatively close to what is postulated to be the earliest form of composition, written by a single homilist called the 'pedantic' adapter[3] (on this byname see below). In the shared main body, the Cleopatra version is, as it happens, 'furthest from [Vercelli] homily II'[4] but contains many readings which may be important witnesses to the compiler's perception of style and sense as he rewrote the material from Vercelli II, as we shall see. I shall first focus on this part.

The most noticeable feature of the compiler's language is, as Wilcox notes,[5] his choice of prepositions, particularly of *in* where *on* might equally have been used. Thus, the compiler often has *in*, to replace *on* in the Vercelli source, both in referring to the Day of Judgement (e.g. Napier XL 183.15 *In þam dæge ure drihten cymð*, in place of *VercHom* 2.15 *On þam dæge*[6]) and in describing various conditions in which human beings find themselves in this world and on Judgement Day (e.g. 188.7–10, where Vercelli II lacks a corresponding passage but another variant text definitely prefers *on*; see p. 41); though, as this last passage suggests, our compiler occasionally uses *on*; see further 187.3 *On þam dæge* (*VercHom* 2.51 ⁊ *þonne*) and 183.3.[7]

---

[2] D. G. Scragg (ed.), *The Vercelli Homilies and Related Texts*, EETS os 300 (Oxford, 1992); Jonathan Wilcox, 'Napier's "Wulfstan" Homilies XL and XLII: Two Anonymous Works from Winchester?', *JEGP* 90 (1991), 1–19. The variation and development shown by the four manuscripts will be discussed in Chapter IV.

[3] See Wilcox, 'Napier XL and XLII', 5–11. For Karl Jost's different view on the authorship, see below and n. 27.

[4] Scragg, *The Vercelli Homilies*, p. 49.

[5] Wilcox, 'Napier XL and XLII', 6–8. This feature is shared by the introduction and conclusion; see p. 47. In Old English generally, *on* is far more common than *in*, though poetry seems to use the latter comparatively commonly, while *in* remains in the Anglian dialect but *on* predominates in West-Saxon. For details, see Bruce Mitchell, *Old English Syntax*, 2 vols. (Oxford, 1985), §§1191–3. In this sense, the compiler's preference for *in* may support my argument below that his style tends to be conservative rather than 'modern'.

[6] For the editions from which citation is made in this chapter, see Chapter II, n. 6. For Napier XL, the editor occasionally emends his base manuscript with readings from the other manuscripts. Where the edited text differs significantly from the manuscript text, I give the latter in square brackets.

[7] In a few other places (e.g. Napier XL 182.10, corresponding to *VercHom* 2.2), he and the Vercelli homilist agree in using *in*.

Other grammatical changes are few. In the main body of the homily, the compiler makes slight and inconsistent changes in word order in a few sentences (e.g. preposing the predicate verb in Napier XL 185.13 *sceolon lætan*, from *VercHom* 2.28 *lætan sculon*, but postposing one in 184.18 *þam synfullum þinceð*, from *VercHom* 2.20 *þinceð þam synfullan*); replaces an expanded form in *VercHom* 2.12 by a simple verb form in 183.10; and replaces a demonstrative by a demonstrative plus noun, as antecedent of a relative pronoun (182.12 *þæt mancyn, þe nu is . . .*, for *VercHom* 2.3 *þa þe nu her syndon . . .*), while preferring *þe* (188.10) to *se þe* (in a variant text in Fadda X 132) as the relative pronoun itself. But he goes no further; on changes in verb forms and personal pronouns see below. There is no evidence that the compiler, unlike that of Napier XXX for example, made it part of his aim to modernize the language of a work of at least half a century earlier, according to the linguistic usage of his own day.[8]

What we do find frequently is addition, and much less frequently omission, of words and longer elements of sentences which seem to reveal our compiler's concerns. The most renowned are those additions which earned him the byname 'pedantic adapter' and which are detailed by Wilcox[9]— additions of biblical quotations in Latin (Napier XL 182.8, 184.7–8), an account of the Last Judgement derived from Matthew 25 (184.10–18), and a detail about the heavenly host that will come with the Lord on the Day of Judgement (183.15–184.2).

Other additions, such as those in Napier XL 184.4 *þa Judeas magon swutele geseon* (*VercHom* 2.18 *Judeas magon geseon*), 185.7 *ða earman synfullan sceolon þonne sare aswæman* (*VercHom* 2.25 *. . . sculon sarige aswæman*),[10] and 182.15 *þæt earme mancynn and þæt synfulle ofer him sylfum heofiað and wepað and waniað and hi þonne swyðe feorhtiað* (*VercHom* 2.10 *þa synfullan heofiaþ ⁊ wepaþ*), show slighter changes which are nevertheless as characteristic. Particularly noteworthy is the last example. Here, the initial four words are an addition made to link the sentence to the preceding phrase *þæt mancyn* (Napier XL 182.12; see below), and further to supplement the meaning of *þæt synfulle*, forming with it a synonymous pair—an aim which is carried further by the longer addition at the end (*and waniað and . . . feorhtiað*), effecting an enhanced pairing of paired expressions linked by alliteration (*heofiað . . . wepað . . . waniað . . . feorhtiað*); the additions are at once semantic and rhythmical. It is this latter aspect which comes to the foreground as the homily gradually develops. Thus, the compiler's rhythmical style has produced alliterative pairs like Napier XL 184.5 *ahengon and acwealdon* (with alliteration on minor syllables;[11] *VercHom* 2.18 *cwealdon ⁊ hengon*) and 185.9 *fram*

---

[8] On the other hand, Scragg (*The Vercelli Homilies*, p. 48) finds evidence that archaic vocabulary is avoided in our compilation and the others based on Vercelli II.

[9] Wilcox, 'Napier XL and XLII', 5–6.

[10] For the addition of *þonne*, see further Napier XL 183.2 and 185.3.

[11] On alliteration on minor syllables, see John C. Pope (ed.), *Homilies of Ælfric: A Supplementary Collection*, 2 vols. (EETS os 259 and 260, London, 1967–68), Vol. I, pp. 126–7.

wlite and fram wuldre (VercHom 2.26 fram þam wuldre). Even in the more complicated structure with multiple phrases of Napier XL 182.12 *þæt mancyn, þe nu is in idelum gylpe and on synnlustum and in þam wohgestreonum goldes and seolfres beswicen*, his preferred mode is unmistakable, compared with the simple accumulation of words and phrases in the source (VercHom 2.3 *þa þe nu her syndon on myclum gylpe ⁊ on unnyttre gesyhðe goldes ⁊ seolfres ⁊ godwebbes ⁊ woggestreona*); the compiler's *beswicen* at the end completes his rhythm based on two-stress phrases linked by *and* and, possibly, paraphrases *on unnyttre gesyhðe* in the Vercelli text, in a way which is in keeping with the force of that rhythm. The compiler later gives this passage a further development, as we shall see below.

This predilection for paired expressions[12] becomes most pronounced when the compiler reaches the section of the Vercelli source which describes the terrors of Judgement Day and the pains of hell which await those who do not dread it (VercHom 2.25–68). This section is composed in rhythmical style, coming to its height in what an earlier editor prints as alliterative verse.[13] Our compiler adapts details of this whole section according to his own rhythmical practice, sometimes reducing the material in the source (e.g. Napier XL 185.19 *Se is yrmða dæg and ealra earfoða dæg*, in place of eight *dæg*-phrases in VercHom 2.37–9), but more often replacing and expanding it. The pattern, seen at its clearest in the 'metrical passage', is of two-stress phrases paired by *and* and often reinforced by alliteration, which form the basic units and are then juxtaposed one after another, entirely omitting the inter-phrasal *and* used in the source:

> Napier XL 186.7 . . . þæra beorga geberst and þæra bymena sang, se brada bryne ofer ealle woruld and se bitera dæg, se micla cwealm and þæra manna man, seo sare sorh and þæra sawla gedal, se sara sið and se sorhfulla dæg, þæt brade bealo and se byrnenda grund, þæt bitere wite and se blodiga stream, feonda fyrhto and se fyrena ren, hæðenra granung and reafera wanung. Heofonwara fulmægen and heora hlafordes þrym, þæt ongrislice gemot and seo egesfulle fyrd, se reða wealdend and se rihta dom, ure fyrena edwit and þæra feonda gestal, þa blacan andwlitan and þæt bifiende wered, se forhta cearm and þæra folca wop, þæra feonda grimnes and

---

[12] The compiler, though, occasionally uses tripartite expressions for expansion, as in Napier XL 185.11 *manna mod syndon earmlice apystrode and adysgode and gedwealde* (VercHom 2.28 *earmlice apist[r]ode*). See Max Förster (ed.), *Die Vercelli-Homilien. I.–VIII. Homilie* (Hamburg, 1932; repr. Darmstadt, 1964), p. 46 n. 15.

[13] Förster, *Die Vercelli-Homilien*, pp. 47–9 (lines 47–72). For the 'metrical passage', see also Wilcox, 'Napier XL and XLII', 4–5; Scragg, *The Vercelli Homilies*, p. 50; and, for the version in CCCC 201, E. G. Stanley, '*The Judgement of the Damned* (from Cambridge, Corpus Christi College 201 and other manuscripts), and the definition of Old English verse', *Learning and Literature in Anglo-Saxon England: Studies Presented to Peter Clemoes on the Occasion of His Sixty-Fifth Birthday*, ed. Michael Lapidge and Helmut Gneuss (Cambridge, 1985), pp. 363–91, esp. pp. 365–9.

> se hluda heof, þæt sarige mancynn and se synniga heap. Seo graniende ne-
> owelnys and seo forglendrede hell, þæra wyrma ongrype and þæra sorhwita
> mæst, se niðfulla here and se teonfulla dæg.

(The underlined words are the compiler's additions, and those with a wavy line his replacements.) The rhythm that is thus effected is brisk and pungent, in clear contrast to the endless series of *and*-coordination in the Vercelli text:

> *VercHom* 2.43 . . . ⁊ þara bymena sang ⁊ se brada bryne ⁊ se bitera dæg ⁊ þara sawla gedal ⁊ se deaðberenda draca ⁊ diofla forwyrd ⁊ se nearwa seaþ ⁊ se swearta deaþ ⁊ se byrnenda grund ⁊ se blodiga stream ⁊ mycel fionda fyrhto ⁊ se fyrena ren ⁊ hæðenra granung ⁊ hira heriga fyll, heofonwarena mengo ⁊ hiora hlafordes miht, ⁊ þæt mycle gemot ⁊ sio reðe rod ⁊ se rihta dom ⁊ þara feonda gestal ⁊ þa blacan ondwlitan ⁊ bifiendan word ⁊ þara folca wop ond se scamienda here ⁊ sio forglendrede hell ⁊ þara wyrma gryre.

What appears in the 'metrical passage' to be almost the compiler's passion for regular rhythm is no less clear in other passages for which there is no parallel sentence in the Vercelli Homily: Napier XL 182.8 *in þam dæge heofene and eorðe cwaciað and heofiað and ealle þa ðing, þe on him syndon*, and 188.3–10. For this latter passage, a variant text (Fadda X) may provide a clue for comparison with the lost original of what we now have as Vercelli II.[14] Thus, Napier XL 188.7 *on hæte and in earfoðnesse, in neowlum attre and in ecere forwyrde, in arleasnysse* [MS *in arl.* om.] *and in mislicum wita cynne, on muðe and on fæðme þæs deaðberendan dracan*, repeats the pattern seen in the 'metrical passage'; it adds alliteration (*attre ... ecere*; *deaðberendan dracan*) and omits the *and* (the last one) linking paired phrases in the 'source': Fadda X 130 *on hæto and on nacodnesse, on nearnesse and on ecre forwyrde, on arleasnesse and on missenlicum cynna witum, and in fæpme þæs beornendan dracan*. The comparison also reveals another feature of our compiler's rhythmical style—use of rhyme (*in arleasnysse and in ... cynne*). This again is shared by the 'metrical passage' above: *hæðenra granung and reafera wanung* (in the fifth line) and *se niðfulla ... and se teonfulla* (end of the passage).[15]

I have referred above to omission of *and* as a feature of the compiler's 'metrical passage' by which he has regularized the rhythm in it. There are passages elsewhere which reveal other aspects of his treatment of this conjunction. In the

---

[14] See Wilcox, 'Napier XL and XLII', 5 n. 18. Reference to the work is to A.M. Luiselli Fadda (ed.), *Nuove Omelie Anglosassoni della Rinascenza Benedettina* (Florence, 1977).

[15] The Vercelli version itself contains an instance: *se nearwa seaþ ⁊ se swearta deaþ* (in the second line of the quotation above). On the rhythmical style of Vercelli II, see Otto Funke, 'Studien zur alliterierenden und rhythmisierenden Prosa in der älteren altenglischen Homiletik', *Anglia* 80 (1962), 9–36, esp. 33–6; D. R. Letson, 'The Poetic Content of the Revival Homily', *The Old English Homily and Its Backgrounds*, ed. Paul E. Szarmach and Bernard F. Huppé (Albany, 1978), pp. 139–56, esp. pp. 140–1.

source text of the main body of Napier XL, the account of Judgement Day is developed along a series of *in/on þam dæge*, with its eight occurrences occasionally preceded by *and* ('⁊') but mostly not:

> *VercHom* 2.2–51 In þam dæge þa hleoðriendan ligeas forbærnaþ ... ⁊ on þam dæge gewit sunnan leoht ... ⁊ on þam dæge bið dryhtnes rod blode flowende betweox wolcnum, ⁊ in þam dæge bið dryhtnes onsyn swiðe egeslicu ... In þam dæge þa synfullan heofiaþ ⁊ wepaþ ... In þam dæge beoð blawende þa byman ... On þam dæge [siteð] ure dryhten in his þam myclan mægenþrymme ... On þam dæge us bið æteowed se opena heofon ...

The conjunction occurs only towards the beginning, and there it is apparently used on no clear principle. Our compiler restructures all this, omitting two uses of the temporal phrase but adding two new ones and, more importantly, adding *and* at several places, effecting a division into three subsections or 'scenes': (1) the terrors of the Day and man's lamentation at them (Napier XL 182.8–183.15); (2) the coming of the Lord and His Judgement, and how men ought to consider it (183.15–185.19); and (3) what will be revealed on this 'yrmða dæg and ealra earfoða dæg' (185.19–187.3):

> Napier XL 182.8 In þam dæge heofene and eorðe cwaciað and heofiað ... And in þam dæge þa hleoðriendan ligettas forglendriað ... And [*MS* Ac] in þam dæge þæt earme mancynn and þæt synfulle ofer him sylfum heofiað and wepað ... And on þam dæge on þam fyrenan wylme sæ forhwyrfeð ... And in þam dæge singað þa byman ... (183.15) In þam dæge ure drihten cymð in his þam micclan mægenþrymme ... And in þam dæge ures drihtnes ansyn byð ... (185.19) Se is yrmða dæg and ealra earfoða dæg. In þam dæge us byð æteowed seo geopenung ...

As can be seen, each subsection begins with the temporal phrase without *and*, while this conjunction precedes every use of the temporal phrase within the first and second subsections. The last subsection, which is the 'metrical passage' described above, contains only one *In þam dæge* which introduces it, and when this part, 'probably an interpolation or, at least, an afterthought',[16] ends, the compiler adds again the temporal phrase, in place of *VercHom* 2.51 *⁊ þonne ...*, to move into the final portion of the main body; here again, the initial sentence, itself without *and*, is followed by an *and*-clause, replacing a *þær*-sentence in the Vercelli source: Napier XL 187.3 *On þam dæge us byð eall þyllic egsa æteowed, and þa synfullan þonne woldon geswican georne, gif hig mihton*. The restructuring that has resulted depends on the compiler's treatment of *and*, which is thus far from fortuitous; it reflects his sense of the 'prose paragraphs' into which he undertakes to mould his source. A similar use is made of this conjunction in the concluding part, as we shall see.

---

[16] Wilcox, 'Napier XL and XLII', 5.

If the compiler's use of *and* in the passage just examined indicates his emphasis on a structured account, other passages suggest no less strongly his concern with this conjunction on the level of sentence syntax. This is shown most clearly by the insertion of one (together with the preceding *men* after *ealle*) after the first clause in:

> Napier XL 183.11 and þonne ealle men arisað of deaðe; and, swa hwæt manncynnes swa eorðe ær forswealh oððe fyr forbærnde and sæ besencte and wilde deor fræton and fugelas tobæron, eall þy dæge arised [*MS* ealle on þam dæge arisað of deaðe].

By this means, the compiler avoids what would otherwise have been an awkward sequence of *ealle* (pl.) . . . *eall þæt* (sg.) in asyndetic clauses as in the source, particularly as Scragg punctuates them: *VercHom* 2.13 ⁊ *þonne ealle arisaþ, swa hwæt swa . . ., eall þæt þy dæge arised*.[17] Somewhat different is *VercHom* 2.58 ⁊ *þonne þa[m] lichoman bið laðlic leger gegyrwed, in þære cealdan foldan gebrosnod*, where *and* is grammatically not required before *in*. But the compiler apparently prefers the balanced structure of coordination which he achieves by substituting a finite verb for a past participle at the end: Napier XL 187.11 *And þonne sona þam lichaman bið laðlic legerbed gegyrwed, and in þære cealdan foldan gebrosnað*. In still another example, the compiler commits 'hypercorrection', introducing a superfluous *and* before the *gif*-clause and making the latter dependent on a main clause which never actually appears:

> Napier XL 187.14 Þonne bið sorhlic sar and earmlic gedal lices and sawle. And, gif þonne seo sawl huru slidan sceal in þa ecan wita mid þam werian and awyrgedan gaste and þar þonne mid deoflum drohtnoð habban . . . on fæðme þæs deaðberendan dracan, þe is deofol genemned.

Still, his sense of clear structure is not entirely lost even here, compared with the clumsy series of *þæt*-clauses within the *gif*-clause in the source, as Max Förster concludes: 'Der Satz würde glätter, wenn man *þæt hio þonne* striche'[18]—that is, from *VercHom* 2.61 *gif þonne se earma innera man, þæt is seo werige sawl þe her forwyrht bið ⁊ agimeleasedu Godes beboda, þæt hio þonne æfter þan gedale aslidan scile in þa ecean helle witu . . .* The compiler aims at a meticulous, well-ordered sentence in

---

[17] Förster (*Die Vercelli-Homilien*, p. 45) reads with a semicolon after *arisaþ* (his line 15), though the awkwardness still seems to remain. There is no punctuation mark either after *arisaþ* or before *eall* in the Vercelli manuscript. In the manuscript text of Napier XL (Cotton Cleopatra B. xiii), on the other hand, the compiler (or the scribe) reverts after the *swa hwæt swa*-clause to the pl. *ealle*. But he at least avoids the awkward sequence of *ealle . . . eall* in asyndesis. The other three manuscripts (CCCC 419, CCCC 201, and Hatton 114) share, with some spelling variation, a reading closer to the Vercelli text.

[18] Förster, *Die Vercelli-Homilien*, p. 50 n. 47.

all these examples, as he also does in Napier XL 189.3–5 in the concluding part; see below. Examples from other areas of syntax are discussed below.

The compiler carefully uses verb forms to achieve logical sentences of clear structure. This aspect comes out very clearly when in the following two sentences he adds an indicative in accord with the following verb and changes a finite verb to an infinitive, respectively, within what he thereby restructures as single units of successive clauses:

> Napier XL 185.11 manna mod . . . æfre sceolon lætan þæt deaðberende deofol mid ungemætre costnunge hig to þan gedwellan, þæt hy swa mycele synna fremman, swa hy nu doð, and nellað þæs willan gewyrcan, þe hyg of eorðan lame geworhte (*VercHom* 2.30 . . . þæt hie synne fremmen ⁊ þæs willan ne wyrceaþ, . . .)[19]

> Napier XL 185.7 ða earman synfullan sceolon þonne sare aswæman . . . and þanon gewitan in þa ecan tintregu helle wites (where *VercHom* 2.27 has a separate indicative clause ⁊ *þonne gewitað hie* coordinate to *sculon . . . aswæman*).

Similarly, the compiler is meticulous about personal pronouns. He sets right an evidently incorrectly repeated *hie* (Napier XL 185.13 for *VercHom* 2.29);[20] replaces a pronominal form to solve the confusion of the first and third person found in the Vercelli source (thus 182.12 *þæt mancyn . . . and þæs him naht ne ondrædað*, from *VercHom* 2.3 *þa þe nu her syndon . . . ac we sint nu þam geliccost fortruwode*); and corrects false concords of number as well as person:

> Napier XL 184.18 þonne þam synfullum þinceð, þæt nan wiht ne sy þæs hates ne þæs cealdes . . . þæt hig þonne mihte fram ures drihtnes lufan asceadan, gif hi þonne þæs wealdan mihton; and þa ungesæligan yrmingas nellað nu þæt geþencan ne his willan be sumon dæle wyrcan, nu hig eaðe magon (where *VercHom* 2.20 has: 'þam synfullan . . . þæt hine þonne mæge . . ., ⁊ nu nellaþ . . . nu we eaðe magon!').

The last example, accompanied as it is by the change of *mæge* to *mihte* in the presence of an hypothetical *gif*-clause with the preterite subjunctive, brings us to rhetorical aspects of the compiler's style. He aims to clarify his point as precisely and soberly as possible, as he also does with a similar use of the *gif*-clause in:

> Napier XL 187.4 þa synfullan þonne woldon geswican georne, gif hig mihton; and him þonne wære leofre, þonne eall middaneard to æhte geseald, þæt hy næfre acennede ne wæron fram fæder and meder.

---

[19] On this sentence, see Stanley, '*The Judgement of the Damned*', p. 372, note to lines 10–11. This note will be considered in Chapter IV.

[20] See Förster, *Die Vercelli-Homilien*, p. 46 n. 16.

Here one might note with Förster and Scragg[21] that the compiler deviates from the Vercelli source, where the first verb is *gewiscan*: *VercHom* 2.51 *Þær þa fyrenfullan þonne meahton gewiscan þæt hie næfre ne wæren acennede fram hiora fædrum ⁊ modrum . . . Hwæt, him þonne [þæt] wære leofre þonne eal middangeard . . .* Still, by rewriting the subsequent portion drastically as above, the compiler reaches a solution which is sensible and better than that of the scribe of the CCCC 419 version;[22] this latter is inconsistent in having the verb *geswican* but otherwise agreeing with the source text: N 76 *þa synfullan þonne woldan gewi[s]can* [MS *geswican*] *georne gif hy mihton þæt hy næfre acennede ne wæron . . . And him þonne wære leofre …*).

More revealing perhaps are the changes the compiler makes to the statement to the effect that people do not dread (*ne ondrædað*) the Day of Judgement sufficiently, which recurs in the Vercelli text (lines 32, 34, 36 and 56). For the third occurrence, for example, the compiler attaches a new main clause to which the original statement is now made subordinate, introduced by *þæt*: Napier XL 185.17 *La hwæt, þence we þæt we us ne ondrædað þone toweardan dæg þæs micclan domes.*[23] By this addition, the compiler implicitly passes judgement on people's negligence ('it is our illusion to think that we can afford not to dread . . .'). The same effect is achieved in another passage by adding clauses to the effect that we do not learn sufficiently from others' examples to dread the Day:

Napier XL 187.7 *La hwæt, we nu ungesælige syndon þæt we us bet ne warniað and* [*MS* a. *om.*] *þæt we ne ondrædað us þe swyðor, þe we dæghwamlice geseoð beforan urum eagum ure þa nehstan feallan and sweltan;*

VercHom 2.56 *La [hw]æt, we us ne ondrædaþ þæt we dæghwamlice geseoð . . ., nu we þam oðrum ne gelyfaþ, ure þa neahstan swelta[n].*

It appears as if the compiler was not sure that the original statement would be interpreted as it should be — as a warning rather than a boast, a scrupulousness

---

[21] Förster, *Die Vercelli-Homilien*, p. 49 n. 40, and Scragg, *The Vercelli Homilies*, pp. 67–8, note to line 52.

[22] See Scragg, *The Vercelli Homilies*, pp. 67–8, note to line 52. Reference to the CCCC 419 version (Scragg's siglum N) is to the line of his edition printed in the EETS volume of the Vercelli homilies. For more details of manuscript variation of this passage, see Chapter IV, p. 90.

[23] Here and in Napier XL 187.7 (see below) I follow Scragg's reading and punctuation of the parallel sentence in N. Napier construes the initial *hwæt* as interrogative. But this is not very likely in the light of the evidently exclamatory *(ea)la hwæt* in three preceding sentences (Napier XL 184.18, 185.5, and 185.11, though *hwæt* in 185.5 is editorial) to which the present one is probably parallel. In any event, the fact remains that the compiler has chosen to add a clause to the downright *we (us) ne ondrædað* to make the meaning clearer.

which might have been justified by the presence of *nu* 'now that, since' in the source, which could have implied acceptance of the statement as such and which is consequently paraphrased by an unequivocally negative *ne... þe swyðor, þe...* The danger at any rate might have existed for both examples to the extent that the subject *we* was open to different interpretations, inclusive of the author himself or not; the compiler might have been again fastidious about the use of personal pronouns. It is also interesting to observe that he entirely omits the other two examples of *ne ondrædað* in the Vercelli source, both with *men* as subject, together with the surrounding few lines.[24]

Other examples of the compiler's rhetorical use of language include chiasmus developed over a long stretch of sentences in Napier XL 184.2–13 *and þonne bið he þam synfullum swiðe wrað æteowed, and þam soðfæstum he byð bliðe gesewen. ... And in þam dæge ures drihtnes ansyn byð ... reðe and egesfull þam synfullum gesewen, and he byð bliðe and milde þam soðfæstum æteowed* (where the order of adjectives and dative nouns as well as that of the two participles is reversed in the second hemistich), and an expansion, with verbal echoes, of an earlier theme of the man steeped in sin (182.12; see p. 39) into 183.3–10 *And on þam dæge ... ealle þa wohgeornan woruldrican mid heora golde and seolfre and godwebbum and eallum ungestreonum þonne forweorðað.*[25] On the other hand, in Napier XL 182.15–183.3, which is based on *VercHom* 2.10 *In þam dæge þa synfullan heofiaþ ꝫ wepaþ, for þan hie ær noldon hira synna betan, ac hie sarige aswæmaþ ꝫ in susle afeallað*, the latter's last clause beginning with *ac* is entirely omitted. This is presumably because it blurs rather than clarifying the causal relationship established by the preceding *for þan*; one is obliged to wonder for a moment, as the compiler might have done, how the adversative sense of *ac* can fit in with the preceding statement which is self-contained. These examples again argue for the compiler's continuous concern with a coherent account and clarity of sense and a form that is appropriate for it.

I have so far focussed on the main body of Napier XL, because it is, of the three parts of which the homily consists, by far the longest and contains by far the largest number of changes made to the earlier homiletic sources. Furthermore, the introductory and concluding parts are less amenable to comparative analysis in reference to the material they draw on. The introduction is very short and is written in Wulfstan's style but its exact source is not known.[26] Nor is the source for the two passages in the conclusion (Napier 189.8–11 and 189.15 to end, which might well both be the compiler's additions), while in the rest of the

---

[24] For a different use of *ne ondrædað* in Napier XL 182.14, see p. 44.

[25] Wilcox thinks that this portion 'is probably from the original homily despite its absence from A [Vercelli II]' ('Napier XL and XLII', 5 n. 18). However, the word *mancyn*, used here and elsewhere in the compilation but never in that part of Vercelli II on which it draws, suggests that in any case the compiler had a hand in this portion of text as it stands.

[26] See Wilcox, 'Napier XL and XLII', 6.

conclusion the Wulfstanian sources are at one point rearranged but are mostly closely followed. These circumstances perhaps lie behind the conclusion reached by Karl Jost that the introduction and the conclusion (as in Napier's edition) are the work of a second reviser, distinct from the compiler of the main body, who knows no better than 'aus fertigen Wulfstansätzen einen neuen Anfang und Schluss anzubringen'.[27]

Jost is probably right as far as the introduction goes. For, as Wilcox has demonstrated,[28] it represents a later substitution for the original introduction (presumably by the 'pedantic adapter'). In fact, this latter, preserved in the version in CCCC 419, shares a feature with the main body of our version, the use of *in* rather than *on* (N 2 *in urum life*). The conclusion to our version, too, despite Jost's assertion, does share a few features with the main body, such as again the use, though not exclusively, of *in*, as in Napier XL 190.5 *in ealra worulda woruld* (where the CCCC 201 version has *on*),[29] and alliterative pairs of words and phrases in, e.g. 188.14 *man and morðor*, 189.2 *eallum mode and eallum mægne* (both probably going back to Wulfstan) and in what might well be an original passage by the compiler: 190.3 . . . *wuniað on wlite and on wuldre and on wynsumnesse æfre. Þar byð mærð and myrhð* . . .[30] Again, the compiler certainly uses Wulfstan sentences almost verbatim, as in Napier XL 189.11–15 drawn from *WHom* 2.65 *And on þam dome, þe ealle men to sculan, ure Drihten sylf eowað us sona his blodigan sidan ⁊ his þyrlan handa ⁊ ða sylfan rode þe he for ure neode on ahangen wæs, ⁊ wile þonne anrædlice witan hu we him þæt geleanedan*, but not without a touch of his usual adaptation. He deletes Wulfstan's initial *and* and, more importantly, incorporates the following *þe ealle men to sculan* into the preceding sentence which might well be his own: Napier XL 189.9 *ac lufian we georne þæne hehstan cyning and þæt upplice rice, and ondrædon we us symle þæne toweardan dom, þe we ealle to sceolon*; he changes again Wulfstan's third person *ealle men* to *we ealle*. Another thing to notice here is the admonition to dread the Last Judgement *ondrædon we us* . . . The compiler asserts this with an appropriate brevity, in a way which emphasizes his inclination not to use the negative *we (us) ne ondrædaþ* without expanding it in one way or another to ensure the intended disapproval, as detailed earlier.

All this agrees with the compiler's usage of language in the main body of the homily. But most revealing perhaps is the tendency towards a neat, orderly sentence structure, seen, as in the main body, in the conclusion, in the sentence looked at briefly in the introductory chapter (p. 7):

---

[27] Karl Jost, *Wulfstanstudien* (Bern, 1950), p. 218.

[28] Wilcox, 'Napier XL and XLII', 6–7.

[29] In fact, this feature constitutes the main linguistic evidence for Wilcox's assumption about single authorship for what he defines as the first stage in the development of Napier XL; see Wilcox, 'Napier XL and XLII', 6–8.

[30] The phrase *mærð and myrhð* also occurs in Wulfstan. For the implication of this, see Scragg's note to Vercelli II, lines O.114–17 (*The Vercelli Homilies*, p. 69).

> Napier XL 189.3 and uton gecnawan, hu læne and hu lyðre þis lif is on to getruwianne, and hu oft hit wurð raðost forloren and forlæten, þonne hit wære leofost gehealden.

The compiler uses a succession of indirect questions and an infinitive (*hu læne . . . on to truwianne, and hu oft . . .*), to replace what might be called a loose construction, with a parenthesis (⁊ *lyðre is*), in the source: *WHom* 13.12 *Eala, lytel is se fyrst þyses lifes, ⁊ lyðre is, þæt we lufiað ⁊ on wuniað, ⁊ for oft hit wyrð raðost forloren þonne hit wære leofost gehealden.* The sentence is immediately followed by another twist the compiler gives to the Wulfstan source, bringing into focus causal relationship out of the latter's coordination:

> Napier XL 189.5 Ðeos woruld is sorhful and fram dæge to dæge a swa leng swa wyrse, forþam ðe heo is on ofstum, and hit nealæcð þam ende,
>
> *WHom* 20(EI).7 ðeos worold is on ofste, ⁊ hit nealæcð þam ende, ⁊ þy hit is on worolde aa swa leng swa wyrse.

If this hypotaxis represents sophistication of thought and style, it is a quality which, like the other features shared by the different parts of the homily, argues that the compiler's is a style that is conservative rather than 'modern' and 'bookish' rather than colloquial, in line with his accepted character as the 'pedantic adapter'.

Napier LVIII

Napier LVIII (*HomU* 47; Cameron No. B3.4.47) is a homily which survives in a single manuscript (British Library, Cotton Otho B. x, s. xi[1]) in an imperfect condition, with the beginning and ending lost because of the Cottonian fire of 1731.[31] What has survived comprises various doctrines of the Christian faith, 'draw[ing] on a broad range of vernacular sources, mostly by Wulfstan but also by other writers'.[32] The exact sources of the passages from these other writers — Napier LVIII 302.11–303.19, 305.7–17, 305.26–306.8, and two others in 304.15 and 306.15–17 — have not been identified; the second of these 'may derive from a revised lost Wulfstan source', according to Wilcox,[33] while Jost refers

---

[31] For details of the manuscript, see N. R. Ker, *Catalogue of Manuscripts Containing Anglo-Saxon* (Oxford, 1957), pp. 224–9.

[32] Jonathan Wilcox, 'The Dissemination of Wulfstan's Homilies: The Wulfstan Tradition in Eleventh-Century Vernacular Preaching', *England in the Eleventh Century*, ed. Carola Hicks (Stamford, 1992), pp. 199–217, at 208–9. See also Jost, *Wulfsanstudien*, p. 265.

[33] Wilcox, 'The Dissemination', p. 208. Wilcox follows the suggestion made by Jost (*Wulfstanstudien*, pp. 264–5).

to the third as not dissimilar to Ælfric's prose;[34] the last two might even be the compiler's original sentences. For obvious reasons, I shall defer discussion of the non-Wulfstanian parts until after I have examined the compiler's language in the rest, collating it with its Wulfstanian sources as identified by Wilcox.[35] But for a new, more likely identification, different from Wilcox's, for one of the Wulfstanian passages (Napier LVIII 306.8–14), see the end of this section.

Like Napier XL, Napier LVIII makes innumerable changes to the original sentences in the sources, but, as was suggested earlier, it differs remarkably from the former in the way it actually does this, even in areas which are shared by the two homilies. Thus, Napier LVIII uses word pairs far less often; the compiler's additions, of which there are only nine clear examples, scarcely make this rhetorical device more prominent in the homily. Moreover, the compiler's additions of word pairs are usually not alliterative, e.g. Napier LVIII 306.18 *rædað and syngað* (*WHom* 6.23 *rædað*) and 303.29 *fram synnum and gyltum gecyrron . . . and . . . eallra þæra sawla gescead witan and agildan* (*WHom* 6.10 *fram synnum gecyrre . . . ealra þæra sawla . . . gescead agyldan*); those that are alliterative are 301.22 *wealdend and wyrhta* (with no equivalent in Wulfstan) and 303.22 *manian and mingian sceolon* (*WHom* 8b.5 *myngian ⁊ læran*).[36] It should also be noted that this last is a non-Wulfstanian pair in that its first element is a word Wulfstan never uses in his homilies. Together with the first pair in Napier LVIII 303.29 above, because *gylt* is a 'Winchester word' which Wulfstan avoids using,[37] this shows that the compiler does deviate from Wulfstan's usage of the language, even in vocabulary items; he is not a mere imitator.

Similarly, the compiler of Napier LVIII, like that of Napier XL, adds and omits *and*, but the effect seems different. His omissions, occurring as they do both where he turns to a new source (e.g. Napier LVIII 305.17; see below) and where he goes on with the source in hand (e.g. 306.27; see below), are apparently not related to what he might have thought of as discrete units of discourse. In fact, the omissions are all but one made when the word was immediately followed by a subordinate conjunction in the source: *þeah* (Napier LVIII 301.10,

---

[34] Jost, *Wulfstanstudien*, p. 265.

[35] These include one of what Wilcox calls 'additional undeveloped homiletic pieces' ('The Dissemination', p. 200), Napier XXIV; see Chapter II, n. 5.

[36] There are two other additions where alliteration falls on minor syllables: Napier LVIII 306.20 *asecgan and areccean* (*WHom* 6.24 *asecgan*) and 306.10 *totwæmað and todælað*. But this latter might not be the compiler's addition, if one assumes, as I shall argue later, that the sentence which contains this derives from Napier XXX, not from Napier XXIV 122.6 (with *todælað* alone), as Wilcox thinks; see pp. 58–9.

[37] See, for *manian*, Jost, *Wulfstanstudien*, p. 264; and, for *gylt*, Helmut Gneuss, 'The origin of Standard Old English and Æthelwold's school at Winchester', *ASE* 1 (1972), 63–83, esp. 76–8. For more details of this latter word, see Walter Hofstetter, *Winchester und der spätaltenglische Sprachgebrauch* (Munich, 1987), pp. 6–7.

from *WHom* 8c.126; and 305.17 *Þeah læwedum mannum wif si alyfed*, from *WPol* 2.1.1.196 *And þeah . . .*) and *sona swa* (306.27 *Sona swa he þæt þohte þurh ofermodignysse*, from *WHom* 6.30 *and sona swa he . . . þæt geðohte*); the omissions are probably syntactical. The exception, in which *and* did not precede another conjunction but was dropped, contains a further ironing out of Wulfstan's rhetorical rephrasing introduced by *þæt is*:

> Napier LVIII 306.20 An is ece ælmihtig god, þe gesceop heofenas and eorðan and ealle gesceafta. On frumon he gelogode on heofena rice engla weredu micele and mære.

> *WHom* 6.25 . . ., ⁊ on fruman he gelogode on þære heofonlican gesceafte, þæt is, on heofona rice, engla weredu mycle ⁊ mære.

More often, the compiler adds *and*. Again, where he does so is independent of where he changes sources, nor is it marked in any clear way by a continuous train of thought which would demand it. For example, he adds one in Napier LVIII 300.2 *and hlaforda gehwylc eac ah swyþe micele þearfe, þæt he his men rihtlice healde. And hit bið his agen þearf* . . . (the second *and*), and 300.8 *Us ealle he gebohte mid gelicum wurðe, þæt is, mid his agenum blode; and ealle we syndon godes agene neadþeowan*, besides 299.28, where he uses *and* in place of Napier XXIV 119.16 *forðam* (conj.). The result is that the passage which contains these three sentences (Napier LVIII 299.27–300.15), which is the opening passage of the homily (as it now imperfectly begins) and printed by Napier as one paragraph, has all its constituent sentences but two begin with either this conjunction (including two uses taken over from the Wulfstan source) or some other conjunction or connective adverb (*eallswa*, *þi* and *þonne*, all taken over from the source); the two exceptions instead both begin with an anaphoric form (*Eall . . . hit*; *Us ealle*). The impression one gets from all this is of a monotonousness which is by no means atypical of the prose of the homily as a whole.

While examples of change in the two areas so far discussed are relatively few in Napier LVIII, there is ample evidence for the compiler's concern with word order as he revises Wulfstan's sentences. Here, however, the evidence is largely conflicting. Thus, the compiler changes VS to SV, as in Napier LVIII 300.2 (see above, from Napier XXIV 119.18 *and eac ah hlaforda gehwilc*), but goes the other way as often, as in 304.4 *and eac ah þæt folc swiðe micele þearfe* (from *WHom* 6.16 *⁊ folc ah eac myccle þearfe*). He shows the same fluctuation with respect to other sentence elements—V and O (with VO, e.g. Napier LVIII 301.6 *gif we sceolon us wið deofol gescyldan*, from *WHom* 8c.117 *gyf we us sculan . . .*, but OV, e.g. 301.21 *Swyþe micele þearfe gehwylc man ah*, from *WHom* 8c.138 . . . *gehwylc ah swyðe mycle þearfe*), Aux and Inf (with AuxInf, e.g. 301.25 *þæt cild mage sprecan*, from *WHom* 8c.142 . . . *specan mæge*, but InfAux, e.g. 303.22 (see p. 49)), and O and Adv (with OAdv, e.g. 302.7 *þe ðæt on life geleornian nele*, from *WHom* 8c.152 . . . *on life þæt* *geleornian nele*, but AdvO, e.g. 301.24 *georne his gingran tihte*, from *WHom* 8c.141 *his gingran georne tihte*). From these examples it is hardly possible to discern any clear tendency in the compiler's usage of word order. However, the presence of four examples in which he brings forward the verb (finite verb or infinitive) away from the clause final position—Napier LVIII 301.22, 303.31, and 306.27 (see p. 50), besides 301.25 above—suggests that he tends towards 'modern' orders, rather slightly perhaps but at least more clearly than the compiler of Napier XL.

Other examples of revised word order in Napier LVIII include two which are rather contrastive in the effect the revision produces:

> Napier LVIII 302.6 ne he rihtlice ne bið husles wyrðe, þe ðæt on life geleornian nele, ne furðon clænes legeres æfter his forðside (*WHom* 8c.151 ne he rihtlice ne bið husles wyrðe ne clænes legeres, se ðe on life þæt geleornian nele, huru on Englisc, buton he on Læden mæge).

> Napier LVIII 300.8 Us ealle he gebohte mid gelicum wurðe, þæt is, mid his agenum blode (*WHom* 8b.61 Mid gelicum wurðe Crist bohte þone kasere ⁊ þone rican kyning ⁊ þone earming; þæt wæs mid his agenum blode).

In the first, the postposing of one object (*clænes legeres*) of *wyrðe* seems to balance the omission of material (*huru . . . mæge*) at the end. On the other hand, the second change all but destroys the rhetorical effect of the *mid*-phrase Wulfstan placed both at the beginning and end; with the first *mid*-phrase moved to its 'normal' position, the compiler's use of *þæt is* is very pedestrian.

The features I have examined so far have much to tell about what the prose of Napier LVIII is *not*, but little about what it is, though it was pointed out above that it tends to lose much of the rhetorical elaboration of the Wulfstan sources and to be flat and monotonous. For further assessment of the compiler's prose, one has to move on to the rest of his revisions, which largely comprise additions (including expansions) and omissions. More numerous and telling are the additions. These reveal, on the most obvious level, his fondness for hyperbole, using a range of intensifiers—most frequently *swyþe (micele)* (with eight examples, as in Napier LVIII 300.12 *swyðe micele þearfe*, for *LawEpisc* 15 *þearfe*) but also *georne* (302.3, for *WHom* 8c.148), *micele* (305.18, for *WPol* 2.1.1.196), *deope* (304.17; see n. 51), and *eall* (306.9, for Napier XXIV 122.5; 306.17, for *WHom* 6.22) and *mid ealle* (301.14 *hit mot mid ealle forwurðan*, for *WHom* 8c.130).[38] Other recurrent patterns include a noun or personal pronoun added to (and, in one instance, replaced for) a demonstrative pronoun used as antecedent of a relative pronoun (e.g. Napier LVIII 300.11 *þam mannum, þe . . .*, for *LawEpisc* 14 *þam þe . . .*;

---

[38] Occasionally the compiler omits these words from the sources, e.g. *eal* (in Napier LVIII 301.12, from *WHom* 8c.128) and *æfre* (in 301.22, from *WHom* 8c.140). For *deope*, see also Napier LVIII 300.25 *swiðe deope gebete*, where this adverb is taken over from the source (Napier XXIV 120.14)

300.23 *he, se þe* . . ., for Napier XXIV 120.12 *se, ðe* . . .; and 306.25 . . . *godes euengelica, þe* . . . for *WHom* 6.29 *þæs efengelica ðe* . . .);[39] what might be called 'reflexive' and hence pleonastic use of the possessive pronoun (e.g. 301.26, for *WHom* 8c.143 (see p. 55), and 306.8 *uton habban us symle on urum gemynde*, for Napier XXIV 122.4 or Napier XXX 193, both without *urum*); doubly qualified nouns (306.21 *ece ælmihtig god* and 302.1 *ænegum cristenum men*, with *ælmihtig* and *cristenum* added); and additions of expressions of place (e.g. *her* in 300.11 *her on eorþan*, and 300.14 *on þisum life*) and time (e.g. 300.10 *on domes dæg*), and of a wide range of adverbial phrases. The last category includes longer additions (and expansions) which, like some of those enumerated above, come close to verbosity, as in Napier LVIII 300.22 *þurh fæder and modar oððe æniges mæges gemeleaste* (Napier XXIV 120.12 *þurh maga gemeleaste*), 300.29 *cildes onfon æt fulluhte oððe æt bisceopes handum* (Napier XXIV 120.16 *cildes onfon*), and 305.23 *sunnannihtum ne mæssenihtum ne wodnesnihtum ne frigenihtum ne næfre on lenctentide ne næfre, þonne fæsten aboden sy* (*WPol* 2.1.1.197 *freolstidum ne fæstentidum*).

The effect of all this addition and expansion may be seen more clearly in context. Take, for instance, a passage described by Jost as a 'Wortschwall' (flood of words);[40] the revised portions are underlined.

> Napier LVIII 303.24 Se cwyde is swiþe egeslic, þe <u>drihten</u> þurh þone witegan be þam cwæð, þe godes folce bodian sceolan, þæt syndon bisceopas and mæssepreostas. <u>He cwæð se witega</u>: 'clypiað hlude and ahebbað up <u>eowre</u> stemne and cyþað minum folce, þæt <u>hi</u> georne <u>fram synnum and gyltum</u> gecyrron. <u>And</u>, gif <u>ge</u> þonne þæt ne doð, ac forsuwiað hit and nyllað folce <u>heora</u> þearfe gecyðan, þonne sceole <u>ge eallra þæra sawla gescead witan and agildan on domes dæg</u>, þe þurh ðæt losiað, <u>þæt</u> hi nabbað þa lare and þa mingunge, þe hi beþorfton.' Þes cwyde mæg beon swyþe gemindelic <u>eallum gehadedum mannum</u>, þe to þam gesette <u>syndon</u>, þæt hi godes folce riht bodian sceolon; and <u>eac ah þæt folc</u> swiðe micele þearfe, þæt hi wære beon þæs cwydes, þe ðæræfter gecweden is. He cwæð se witega æfter þam: 'gif <u>þa gehadedan men</u> riht bodiað and <u>hi þæt folc</u> gebigean ne magon to rihte <u>and to heora agenre þearfe and neode</u>, þonne gebeorgað <u>hi him sylfum swaþeah and heora</u> agenum sawlum <u>on domes dæg</u>. And <u>þa</u>, þe <u>him hlystan nellað and þæra þinga geman and hlystan, þe man heom bodað and segð</u>, ac willað <u>forð on</u> woh <u>and gewill</u> drifan and geswican nyllað, <u>hi</u> sceolon <u>þæs habban</u> ece wite, <u>and hi næfre cuman ne motan to godes rice</u>.'

---

[39] A similar alteration was also seen in Napier XL but is more pronounced in the present homily. In its usage of the relative pronoun itself, Napier LVIII shares with Napier XL a preference for the simple *þe* (Napier LVIII 302.7, for *WHom* 8c.152 *se ðe*), and uses *þæt* (301.18) for *WHom* 8c.136 *þæt ðe*. For Napier XL, see above (p. 39).

[40] Jost, *Wulfstanstudien*, p. 264.

One notes, in particular, some of the features illustrated in the last paragraph repeated here—*eallum gehadedum mannum þe* in the eighth line, in place of Wulfstan's *eallum þam þe* (*WHom* 6.14), *swiðe* added to *micele þearfe* in the tenth line, and *on domes dæg* added in the fourteenth line—and the tautology *He cwæð se witega* towards the beginning. It should also be noticed here that the compiler occasionally uses a 'non-Wulfstanian' vocabulary item or form as an addition to or replacement for Wulfstan's original: *gyltum* (on this word see p. 49) and *syndon* (in place of the typically Wulfstanian indicative *syn*).[41] He further prefers *drihten* (in the first line) and *þurh þæt ..., þæt ...* (in the seventh line), to Wulfstan's original *God* (*WHom* 6.5) and *þurh þæt ..., þe* (6.14), respectively.[42] All this makes it difficult again to believe that the compiler is particularly intent on imitating a stock of Wulfstanian phrases and forms with which he has familiarized himself.[43]

But most revealing in the passage being discussed is the quotation of Ezekiel 3:18–19 (which is taken over from Wulfstan), introduced by the second *He cwæð se witega* (in the eleventh line). Here the compiler first spells out pronominal reference in the opening *gif*-clause (*þa gehadedan men ... and hi þæt folc ...*, in place of Wulfstan's *ðu Godes folca ... ꝥ ðu hit ...*),[44] then adds a *to*-phrase to the preceding parallel one (*to rihte and to heora agenre þearfe and neode*) and a reflexive dative in parallel to the dative noun object to reinforce a single notion (*him sylfum ... and heora agenum sawlum*), and, to crown it all, comes to the lengthy last sentence (*And þa, þe ...* to end). The sentence is not only clumsily constructed in the first

---

[41] The form *syndon* also occurs elsewhere, at Napier LVIII 300.5 and 304.28. The earlier parts of the homily contain another 'non-Wulfstanian' *gehwilc man* (Napier LVIII 301.21, 302.9) in place of Wulfstan's partitive *manna gehwilc*. For the Wulfstanian *syn* and partitive type, see, respectively, Dorothy Whitelock (ed.), *Sermo Lupi ad Anglos*, 3rd edn. (London, 1963), pp. 43–4; Pope, *Homilies of Ælfric*, Vol. I, pp. 101–2; *OES*, §651; and Jost, *Wulfstanstudien*, pp. 165 and 263.

[42] On *þurh þæt ..., þæt/þe ...*, see *OES*, §§2426 and 3093. For the compiler's other preferred conjunctions, see Napier LVIII 301.25 *swa raðe swa*, in place of *WHom* 8c.142 *æfre swa ... raðost*, and 300.27 *þe læste* (see p. 55) instead of the usual *þy læs þe*. According to A. Adams, *swa hraþe swa* 'is almost peculiar to the works of Ælfric', while Wulfstan's superlative form is 'rare' in Old English prose (*The Syntax of the Temporal Clause in Old English Prose* (New York, 1907), pp. 69–71). For *þe læste*, H. G. Shearin finds only three instances in Old English prose, with the other two from the *Benedictine Rule* (*The Expression of Purpose in Old English Prose* (New York, 1903), p. 98); see also *OES*, §2931.

[43] See Jost, *Wulfstanstudien*, pp. 265–6, where he asserts: 'Er [the compiler] ist das genaue Gegenteil eines Wulfstannachahmers. Wenn ihm ein Wulfstantext in die Hände fällt, so entstellt er ihn dermassen mit seiner Salbaderei, dass von Wulfstans stilistischer Eigenart ein guter Teil verloren geht.'

[44] The use of *þa gehadedan men* in place of Wulfstan's *ðu* is, of course, accompanied throughout this passage by the replacement of *ge* or *we* for the original singular forms, with concomitant plural forms of verbs and demonstratives.

half, with the infinitive *hlystan* repeated in coordinate phrases and *him*, referring to the definite *þa gehadedan men*, continued by the indefinite *man*. But it is a mass of accretions based on Wulfstan's terse sentence of just fourteen words: *WHom* 6.19 *⁊ se ðe woh drifð ⁊ geswican nele, he sceal habban ðæs ece wite*. As can be seen, each of the revisions adds little that is new or that supplements Wulfstan's statement in significant ways; they are repetitive, almost to the point of verbosity.[45]

Additions (again including expansions) of clauses tend to sustain this quality of the compiler's prose. Of a wide range of subordinate clauses that are added, one of the most common is clauses of condition. In Napier LVIII 303.20 *Gehadedum mannum gebyrað, gif hi ænige miltse habban sceolan æt gode, þæt* . . . and 305.21 *Nagan læwede men þurh hæmedþingc, gif hi godes miltse habban willað, wifes gemanan* . . ., the compiler exploits the *gif*-clause significantly by using *sculan* and *willan* for different nuances appropriate to ordained men and laity, as he also does in other parts of the homily.[46] But he definitely does not do so, in what Jost refers to as 'ein reichlich unklares' *buton*-clause in Napier LVIII 300.16 *ælc cild sceall beon binnon pryttigum nihtum gefullod mid rihte, buton hit ær beo*, 'womit vermutlich gemeint sein soll, die Frist von 30 Tagen könnte noch verkürzt werden'.[47] But this is exactly what is implied in the word *binnon* 'within', and any expansion of its meaning would not have been deemed necessary or even desirable by a writer of a different style (like the compiler of Napier XL, for example); here the compiler of Napier LVIII talks perhaps too much.

The same can be said of the *swa*-clauses he adds in Napier LVIII 300.12 and 300.20 *ða dædbote betan georne æfre swa lange, swa he libbe, swa se bisceop him wissige* (both *swa*-clauses), and a relative clause in 301.22 *on god ælmihtigne, þe is wealdend and wyrhta eallra gesceafta*. In this latter, reference in an alliterative phrase to God the Ruler and Creator is presumably occasioned by the preceding addition of *ælmihtig*, but it stands in sharp contrast to Wulfstan's terse *ænne God* (*WHom* 8c.140) and might even seem rather unnecessarily eloquent in this context of instruction on the importance of the baptismal vow. Even more superfluous perhaps is the relative clause in Napier LVIII 304.32 *Be þam man mæg swiðe eaðe witan, se þe hit underniman wile, þæt* . . ., where the restrictive *se þe*-clause is not quite congruous with the preceding generic *man*, particularly in its collocation with *mæg eaðe* 'can easily'. Similarly, in Napier LVIII 305.19 *gehadede men hit sceolon him asecgan, undernimð se, þe wile*, the addition of the hortative *se, þe wile*

---

[45] Ezekiel 3:18–19 is again quoted in the *Catholic Homilies*, First Series, Praefatio 111–16, where Ælfric translates even more tersely and closely than Wulfstan, emphasizing the verbosity of Napier LVIII.

[46] *Sculan* is used further at Napier LVIII 301.6 and 302.13, and *willan* at 303.7 and 303.17; only the first definitely follows Wulfstan's usage. For the use of modal verbs in *gif*-clauses in Old English, see Hiroshi Ogawa, *Old English Modal Verbs: A Syntactical Study* (Copenhagen, 1989), *passim*.

[47] Jost, *Wulfstanstudien*, p. 263.

'he who wishes' destroys, if anything, the emphasis on Christian duties underlying the passage and is in a sense anticlimactic—an incongruity which is alien to Wulfstan's frequent use of the phrase as a 'challenger' to the audience.[48] It should be added that in this last example, as in Napier LVIII 305.35 (see below p. 58), the compiler's hortative construction has the initial verb in the indicative mood, not subjunctive as is regular in Wulfstan's usage.[49]

Other examples include additions and expansions of noun clauses, as in Napier LVIII 301.26 *tæce man him . . . his paternoster and his credan, and þæt hit cunne hit sylf bletsian rihtlice* (*WHom* 8c.143 *tæce man him . . . pater noster Ꝑ credan*), 303.21(expanding *WHom* 8b.5 *myngian Ꝑ læran þæt hi geornlice to Gode Ꝑ to his halgum gebugan* into a main clause with three verbs followed by an object noun and two indirect questions) and 301.30 (repeating *þæt . . . he hit leornige* after *WHom* 8c.146 *leornige hit georne; Ꝑ ne sceamige . . . for his ylde*), and addition of a purpose clause, itself made up of three constituent clauses: 300.26 *Ne nænne man man ne læte unbisceopod to lange, þe læste him forðsið getimige, and he næbbe þa gerihtu, þe him to gebyredon* (for Napier XXIV 120.15). In all these, as before, the compiler is verbose—a tendency which culminates in a passage about how often a man is allowed to be married. The source (*WPol* 2.1.1.195) stops at 'more than three times', but our compiler still goes on: Napier LVIII 305.5 *. . . mid ealle misdon, gewurðe hit feorðan siðe; and, gif hit oftur gewyrð, nyte we, hu þæt faran mæg.*

I have referred above to noun clauses that are the compiler's additions. There are also noun clauses that exemplify the process of expansion of a phrase in the source, as for example, of *WPol* 2.1.1.190 *be ðæs apostoles leafe læwede man mot . . .* into Napier LVIII 304.24 *Sanctus Paulus se mæra godes apostol cwæð, þæt se læweda man moste . . .* and *WPol* 2.1.1.191 *Ac þa canones forbeodaþ þa bletsunge þærto* into 304.26 *hit is forboden swyþe, þæt man þa bletsunge þærto ne do*; in both, the abstract nouns in the source (*leafe, bletsunge*) are paraphrased in a clausal form.[50]

---

[48] See, for example: *WHom* 10c.111 *Eac ic lære georne manna gehwilcne þæt he his synna andette gelome . . .; forðam, understande se ðe wille, eal hit mæg to ðearfe*; and 5.23 *And gecnawe se ðe cunne, nu is se tima þæt ðeos woruld is gemæncged mid mænigfealdan mane . . .*

[49] Randolph Quirk (*The Concessive Relation in Old English Poetry* (New Haven, 1954), p. 99) quotes two examples (*Met* 19.1, 20.26) of the 'challenge pattern' with the indicative, though Mitchell (*OES*, §3455) thinks that 'they may be independent [clauses]'. In any event, the indicative is rare in this type of construction in Old English.

[50] At one point the compiler does not use an expanded clause but a *to*-infinitive, in a way which is not dissimilar to the usage in Napier XL 189.3 (see p. 48): Napier LVIII 306.28 *þa worhte Crist helle him on to wunienne and eallum ðam oðrum englum, þe mid him æt þam ræde* (end of the extant text). But his method is otherwise to paraphrase rather than condense in the passage in which this sentence occurs as a whole; see Wilcox, 'The Dissemination', pp. 208–9. The sentence marks, according to Wilcox, the compiler deviating, in the middle of a complex sentence (after a *sona swa*-clause; see p. 50), from the Wulfstanian source; Wulfstan's counterpart (*WHom* 6.31–3) comprises a series of *and*-clauses but shows a lot of alliteration.

An apparently contradictory kind of alteration is shown by a few sentences, in which the compiler chooses not to use verbs of commanding and the like followed by a noun clause. For example, in

> Napier LVIII 300.16 *Eac we secgað eow to soðan, þæt ælc cild sceall beon binnon þryttigum nihtum gefullod . . . (300.22) Gif hit þonne . . . dead wurðe, þonne þolige he, se þe hit on gelang sy . . . Ne nænne man man ne læte unbisceopod to lange*,

> Napier XXIV 120.8 *And we biddað and beodað, þæt ælc cild sy binnan þrittigum nihtum gefullad . . . Eac we læराð, þæt man ænig ne læte unbiscopod to lange*,

he abandons the two uses of the construction in the source, in favour first of a plain verb of saying (*secgað*) and then of a simple clause with the hortative subjunctive (*Ne . . . man ne læte . . .*).[51] This latter expression may have been preferred in accord with the preceding *þonne þolige he* (taken over from the source) to which it is parallel, and to that degree the compiler impresses the flow of the sentences. However, he does so at the cost of the logical structure of the source, for Wulfstan might well have repeated the complex construction where he does as a signal that he was introducing different topics (baptizing an infant, and confirmation). In comparison, our compiler makes more of simple structure and plain expression. In this sense, the passage just quoted, as much as the expansions into clauses, is indicative of the compiler's preference for a mode of expression which is less abstract and more direct and, perhaps, closer to natural speech.

The remaining alterations made in the Wulfstanian parts of Napier LVIII consist largely of omissions of material provided by the sources. Particularly noteworthy in this respect is the fact that, quite contrary to the 'pedantic adapter' of Napier XL, our compiler omits a biblical quotation in Latin at Napier LVIII 303.27 (where the Latin precedes the Old English text in *WHom* 6.7) and translates a biblical name *Lucifer* (*WHom* 6.28) into *Leohtberend* (306.24). He further chooses to omit a clause in favour of a simplified sentence structure, e.g. Napier LVIII 300.6 *Eallswa bealdlice clipað se þeowa . . ., eallswa se hlaford* (where he condenses two comparisons with two verbs in *WHom* 8b.59–61 into one with one), and to iron out theological niceties, e.g. 302.6 *ne he rihtlice ne bið husles wyrðe . . . æfter his forðsiðe* (where he dismisses a *buton*-clause together with a noun phrase at the end; see p. 51). Again, in Napier LVIII 301.12 *butan hit gelæste, þonne hit ylde hæfð, eall, þæt on his geoguðe gode wæs behaten, hit mot mid ealle forwurðan*, he omits a *gif*-clause (and the temporal clause embedded in it) which immediately followed in *WHom* 8c.130: *gyf hit Godes lage forgymde, syððan hit ða ylde ꝗ þæt*

---

[51] For once the compiler uses *is beboden þæt . . .* (Napier LVIII 304.16) in place of *WPol* 2.1.2.187 *gebirað eac, þæt . . .*, but then it is qualified by *deope*.

andgyt hæfde þæt hit Godes lage gyman mihte; here long clauses of condition both before and after the main clause might have seemed cumbersome to the compiler. In any event, these examples agree in pointing to a matter-of-fact style as a basic quality of the prose of Napier LVIII. So does the unrhetorical treatment of *þæt is* discussed earlier (see pp. 50, 51), and two sentences in which the compiler 'reanalyzes' the personal pronoun as he finds it in his sources, viz. Napier LVIII 300.22 *Gif hit* [sc. *ælc cild*] . . . *dead wurðe*, from Napier XXIV 120.11 *gif hit . . . gewyrðe* (where *hit*, referring to the death of a child, might not have been very gratifying to the literal mind of the compiler) and 300.5 *hi syndon gode gelice leofe se hlaford and se þeowa*, with a tautological subject, from *LawEpisc* 13 *hy* [sc. *nydþeowas*] *syn Gode efen leofe ⁊ þa ðe syndon freolse*.

For the rest of the homily for which sources are not known, it is not possible to continue analysis in the same way. But we do find the relevant passages interspersed with those details of language and style which were seen to be characteristic of the compiler. Take, for instance, a passage which may derive from a revised lost Wulfstan source:

> Napier LVIII 305.7 Hit is fullic and fracodlic þingc and gode ælmihtigum and eallum his halgum lað, þæt hi ne gymað heora sylfra æt þam unþeawe, þe dysige men on ungewunan healdað, þæt hi ne gymað heora sylfra, swa hi beþorfton, ac befylað fracodlice hi selfe and eac geunwurðiað ge wið god ge wið men, þæt hi farað fram wife to wife, eallswa stunte nytenu doð, þe nan andgyt nabbað. Deah þa dysegan and þa ungeradan his gelyfan nyllan, eall hit byð þæs deofles lar and tihting, þæt hi swa farað. Ac swa hwilc man, swa ðæne unðeaw ær beeode, he geswice.

As Jost aptly points out,[52] the passage is stylistically the compiler's own. The words *fullic* and *tihting* (both used in word pairs) are never used by Wulfstan in his homilies, nor is *geunwurðiað*; *eall hit* in the seventh line, referring back to men's '*fullic and . . . lað*' way of life as described in the preceding clauses, makes the following *þæt hi swa farað* redundant; and, above all, the second clause, *þæt hi ne gymað heora sylfra*, is made to recapitulate itself in the next *þæt*-clause, in a way which is far from elegant—though usual with the compiler. It is perhaps with respect to this inelegant syntax that Jost accuses the compiler of 'Geschwätz' (idle talk) in this particular passage, saying: 'Einen Satz wie [Napier 305.8–10] möchte ich jedenfalls nicht Wulfstan zur Last legen'.[53]

Other features which might well have been the outcome of the compiler's revision include mixing up of first and third person pronouns, ending up with *hi* with reference to the generic *man* (Napier LVIII 306.2 *Ne þurfon we na to urum mægum ne nan man to his wife ðencean . . ., þæt him man . . ., þæt hi hine . . .*); the

---

[52] Jost, *Wulfstanstudien*, p. 265.
[53] Jost, *Wulfstanstudien*, p. 265.

hortative *se þe* clause with the indicative main verb (305.35 *understent se, þe gesælig bið*);[54] the intensifying *swyþe* (303.6, 303.12); the 'reflexive' possessive (302.12, 302.20 *se, þe nele . . . his cyricean secean and his mæssan þærinne gestandan and gehyran*); and 303.5 *her on life*.[55] These examples show sufficiently clearly that the compiler revised what are now lost sources, Wulfstanian or not, in essentially the same way as he did for the rest of the homily, though exactly to what degree we cannot know.

My final issue concerns the source of a passage in Napier LVIII which 'was extremely popular among Old English homilists':[56]

> Napier LVIII 306.8 and uton habban us symle on urum gemynde þone timan, þe us eallum towerd is. Ðonne se lichama and seo saul hi totwæmað and todælað, þonne us forlætað ealle ure woruldfrind, ne magon hi us þonne ænigum gode, ac bið æt gode anum gelang eall, hwæt we gefaran sceolon. God us gestrangige and getrymme to ure agenre þearfe.

This is one of the five versions of the passage which survive, the other four being in Napier XXIV, Napier XXX, Bazire and Cross 7, and the homily in Lambeth 489, fols. 31–38, as I have mentioned in an earlier chapter.[57] The one assumed by Wilcox to be the source for our passage is that in Napier XXIV.[58] There are, however, four important points on which the two versions do not agree:

(1) *totwæmað and todælað* (2nd line); Napier XXIV 122.6 *todælað*;

(2) *þonne us forlætað ealle ure woruldfrind* (3rd line); Napier XXIV 122.6 *þonne us forlætað ealle ure weoruldfreond and nede scylon*;

(3) *ænigum* (dative; 4th line); Napier XXIV 122.8 *ænige* (instrumental); and

(4) *God us gestrangige and getrymme to ure agenre þearfe* (5th line); lacking in Napier XXIV.

A far more likely immediate source of our passage, then, is the version in Napier XXX (lines 193–7, plus line 182 for the ending), which agrees with it in all the four points above, and even to the spellings of some words, such as *eall* (against Napier XXIV *eal*) and *woruldfrind* (against Napier XXIV as in (2) above). It is,

---

[54] See Jost, *Wulfstanstudien*, p. 265 n. 3.

[55] In the last two respects, Wulfstan's own usage varies. In his homilies, for example, he uses the 'reflexive' possessive with *cyrican secan* (*WHom* 14.18), but never uses it with the noun *mæsse*, to the best of my knowledge; see Mabel Falberg Dobyns, 'Wulfstan's Vocabulary: A Glossary of the "Homilies" with Commentary' (Ph. D. dissertation, University of Illinois at Urbana-Champaign, 1973), s.vv. *cyrce, cyrice*, and *mæsse*.

[56] M. R. Godden, 'An Old English penitential motif', *ASE* 2 (1973), 221–39, at 229.

[57] See Chapter II, p. 34.

[58] Wilcox, 'The Dissemination', p. 208.

I would argue, this homily which represents the earliest adaptation (as far as we can know) from the ultimate source, Napier XXIV.[59] The Napier LVIII and Napier XXX versions are so nearly identical (apart from the positioning of the sentence 'God us . . . þearfe' and editorial punctuation) that it is hardly possible to think that they are independent adaptations of the same source, while a borrowing from the other direction is very unlikely, given the textual history and make-up of Napier XXX.[60] The Napier XXX version reads:

> Napier XXX 182 God us ealle gestrangie ⁊ getrymme to ure agenre þearfe . . . (193) Uton us habban symble on gemynde þone timan þe us toweard ys þonne se earma lichama ⁊ seo werige sawul hi totwæmað ⁊ todælað. Þonne us forlætað ealle ure woruldfrynd, ne magon hi us þonne ænigum gode, ac bið æt Gode anum gelang eall hwæt we gefaran sceolon.

The Two Homilies and the Vernacular Prose Tradition

The compilers of Napier XL and Napier LVIII both draw very heavily upon Wulfstan and other preceding Old English homiletic works. But they revised these earlier materials in quite different ways, producing stylistically distinct prose. The 'pedantic adapter' of Napier XL writes in terse, controlled prose with precise syntax and poetic rhythm, whereas the prose of Napier LVIII is above all a product of fussy additions and prolix expansions. The one looks backward to the old style in the vernacular prose tradition; the other comes close to the natural, if not literally colloquial, speech of everyday life with all its diffuseness. These products represent two diametrically different styles out of the many which might well have been available to the 'Wulfstan imitators', as Angus McIntosh has aptly pointed out.[61]

The differences between Napier XL and Napier LVIII might be a matter of individual styles. But one feels inclined to ask if they might possibly be viewed

---

[59] I had come to this conclusion in August 2000, before I became aware that the same view had long been expressed, though in different contexts, by D. G. Scragg; see his article 'The corpus of vernacular homilies and prose saints' lives before Ælfric', *ASE* 8 (1979), 223–77, at 254, and *The Vercelli Homilies*, pp. 395–403. As for the other two versions, the one in Lambeth 489 agrees with Napier XXIV in the four points mentioned above (though not in others), while the version in Bazire and Cross 7 shows complete agreement, apart from spelling variations, with Napier XXX, except at line 43, *gemyndige* (against the latter's *habban . . . on gemynde*; see Chapter II, n. 76). Scragg gives no details of the four versions in comparison.

[60] For details, see D. G. Scragg, 'Napier's "Wulfstan" homily xxx: its sources, its relationship to the Vercelli Book and its style', *ASE* 6 (1977), 197–211.

[61] Angus McIntosh, 'Wulfstan's Prose', *PBA* 34 (1949), 109–42, at 126. The passage is quoted in Chapter I (pp. 8-9).

in the context of the tradition of vernacular homilies of which those two works are a part. Concerning CCCC 419, which preserves a revised text of Napier XL, Wilcox says:

> No manuscript of the period survives which contains a collection analogous with that in N [CCCC 419 and its companion volume CCCC 421], where a broad range of anonymous homilies are apparently afforded equal status with homilies by Ælfric and Wulfstan. The range of contents and its textual independence make N a unique and valuable witness to the homiletic tradition of the eleventh century, comparable in importance to the more famous late tenth-century collections, the Vercelli Book and the Blickling Homilies.[62]

One might wonder if these anonymous homilies are 'afforded equal status' because some of them at least are what might be called 'standard pieces' of the genre as much as Ælfric's and Wulfstan's homilies — an assumption which is in accord with the fact that Napier XL survives in multiple copies (as detailed at the beginning of this chapter), as do all except one of the anonymous homilies in CCCC 419.[63] It is also in accord with the likelihood discussed by Wilcox that Napier XL shares an exemplar with the Wulfstan homilies surrounding it (Ker's items 4–7 and 9–10) in CCCC 419.[64] Stylistically, as we have seen above, Napier XL looks, if anything, backward to the earlier tradition of vernacular homilies. With regard to its content, it should also be noted that Judgement Day, which is its theme, is a typical theme of the homilies of pre-Conquest England.[65] All this leads us to infer that Napier XL is a traditional homily on a very important theme and as such is an 'established' example of the genre. This seems to be at least part of what Scragg implies when he discusses the 'independence' of CCCC 419 (and CCCC 421):

> Throughout the anonymous pieces N shows a textual independence in the intelligent addition or omission of words or phrases. This freedom and the range of items included suggest that the collection was put together with care and authority.[66]

---

[62] Jonathan Wilcox, 'The Compilation of Old English Homilies in MSS Cambridge, Corpus Christi College, 419 and 421' (Ph.D. dissertation, University of Cambridge, 1987), p. 242.

[63] For details, see Scragg, 'The corpus', 249–51.

[64] Wilcox, 'The Compilation', p. 223.

[65] See Kathleen Greenfield, 'Changing emphases in English vernacular homiletic literature, 960–1225', *Journal of Medieval History* 7 (1981), 283–97, at 284–5.

[66] Scragg, 'The corpus', 252–3.

It is more difficult to consider the evidence of Napier LVIII by placing it in its 'manuscript context', because of the badly damaged condition of its manuscript, Cotton Otho B. x. Perhaps the only clue is provided by the description made of the manuscript by Wanley before the fire. Based on this, Ker reports that the manuscript, particularly its A part, is a volume of lives of saints, mostly by Ælfric.[67] It is almost as if Napier LVIII, distinct from these surrounding Ælfrician works both in content and style, has somehow found its way into the volume as a 'casual' additional item. In this, the homily may be an example of the tendency for '[a]nonymous homilies recorded at this time . . . to occur in the environment of collections predominantly of Ælfric homilies'.[68] But it is in remarkable contrast to Napier XL, particularly as preserved in CCCC 419. Moreover, again in contrast to this latter homily, Napier LVIII is preserved in a single manuscript; it even 'ended imperfectly according to Wanley'.[69] From all this, it seems fairly obvious that Napier LVIII, far from being an established part, such as Napier XL is, of Old English homiletic prose, is perhaps a later accretion to it, at least in matters of syntax and style. It may well be a typical example of the 'preaching' rather than the 'quasi-literary' homilies which Godden assumes Old English composite homilies generally are:

> it seems likely that such composite homilies were individually designed for preaching use (in contrast to the more general, quasi-literary role that might be assumed for the work of Ælfric and Wulfstan) and might therefore bring us closer to spoken Old English.[70]

There is another point of contact with the Napier LVIII manuscript. Its place of origin is not known, but is 'possibly the same place' as that of Cotton Vitellius C. v.[71] This latter manuscript contains an Ælfrician item (Pope XXVII), with flanking passages not Ælfric's own, and one of these, lines 1–11, is an addition adapted from Wulfstan passages (*WHom* 13.80–4, 103–6) and particularly close to the version of this Wulfstan homily which was preserved in Cotton Otho B. x (though now lost, except for the incipit and explicit recorded by Wanley).[72]

---

[67] Ker, *Catalogue*, pp. 224–7.

[68] Wilcox, 'The Compilation', p. 242. See further what Malcom Godden says about the two composite homilies contained in Cambridge, University Library, Ii. 4.6: 'They occur side by side as the only non-Ælfrician homilies in the manuscript . . . No doubt he [the compiler] added his own two homilies to the collection too and perhaps used it as a source book, for it contains three of the Ælfric homilies from which he borrowed' ('Old English composite homilies from Winchester', *ASE* 4 (1975), 57–65, at 62).

[69] Ker, *Catalogue*, p. 227.

[70] Malcolm Godden, 'Review of *Studies in the History of Old English Prose*, by Hiroshi Ogawa', *Studies in English Literature* (Tokyo), English Number 42 (2001), 111–17, at 116.

[71] Wilcox, 'The Dissemination', p. 214.

[72] See Wilcox, 'The Dissemination', p. 209 n. 46.

Perhaps more significant for our problem, this prefixed passage to Pope XXVII as it survives starts with what John C. Pope calls 'a prolix expansion' at lines 1–6,[73] and the rest is also stylistically not unlike Napier LVIII.[74]

There is further evidence of the currency of such an 'unskilful' style, beyond the two manuscripts being discussed. Pope says:

> Thus it appears that the author of the flanking passages [Pope XXVII 1–14, 107–23] was neither Ælfric nor Wulfstan but someone who made rather unskilful use of both. It is conceivable that he was the same person as the author of Napier XLVI. The style of the last passage quoted above [Napier XLVI 238.10–18, with which Pope XXVII, 114–21 is 'almost identical'] is far more in accord with the rest of Napier XLVI than with anything in Ælfric. It is also in accord with the style of Napier XXIX, in which some of the same ideas occur.[75]

(Napier XLVI survives in CCCC 419 (s. xi[1]; south-eastern?) and Bodley 343 (s. xii[2]; West-Midlands?), and Napier XXIX in Hatton 113 (s. xi 3rd quarter; Worcester).) Whether this similarity of style among works of such diverse places of composition or copying implies anything more than an accident—common authorship for some of the relevant homilies, as Pope infers, or 'a change in taste', such as Ian A. Gordon detects in the late Anglo-Saxon period,[76] remains an outstanding and perhaps insoluble problem.

---

[73] Pope, *Homilies of Ælfric*, Vol. II, p. 773. For example, the adapter adds two subordinate clauses in the middle ('þeah hit huru wære eall on urum anwealde þa hwile þe we her on life wæron'), and expands '... ðam þonne þe ær geearnode' in the Wulfstan source into '... þonne þam menn þe her on þisum life geearnað'.

[74] See, e.g., the addition of *forþi* (line 6).

[75] Pope, *Homilies of Ælfric*, Vol. II, p. 774. On Napier XXIX see Chapter V.

[76] Ian A. Gordon, *The Movement of English Prose* (London, 1966), p. 43. For another aspect of this 'change in taste', see Jonathan Wilcox, 'Wulfstan and the twelfth century', *Rewriting Old English in the Twelfth Century*, ed. Mary Swan and Elaine M. Treharne (Cambridge, 2000), pp. 83–97.

IV.
Late Old English Judgement Day Homilies: The Vercelli Tradition in the Tenth and Eleventh Centuries

Discussing the changes which set homilies in the period 960–1100 apart from those in the immediately following century or so (1100–1225), Kathleen Greenfield sees the most distinctive feature of the former period as the 'sense of the imminence of the last judgement' and the 'substantial portion of the homiletic literature' which that sense permeates.[1] Greenfield illustrates this with a few examples both from Ælfric and Wulfstan and from anonymous homilies.[2] But how in fact the sense is pervasive throughout the Old English period can be seen more clearly, for example, by looking at a 'Theme' index compiled for the homilies by Ælfric and Wulfstan and those in the anonymous Blickling and Vercelli Collections. The compiler identifies some ninety passages that are built upon the 'theme and image' of 'the Day of Judgement', as well as five homilies which are entirely concerned with it.[3] The ramifications of this wide use of the theme in this compiler's corpus and elsewhere in Old English makes it an issue of supreme importance in the history of vernacular homilies in the period. Particularly important here are the homilies in the Vercelli Collection, which include four that are entirely or largely homilies on the Day of Judgement. Two of these, Vercelli II and Vercelli XXI, and two other anonymous homilies that use extracts from the first of these, represent what might be called the Vercelli tradition of Judgement Day homilies, which is the subject of the present chapter.[4]

---

[1] Kathleen Greenfield, 'Changing emphases in English vernacular homiletic literature, 960–1225', *Journal of Medieval History* 7 (1981), 283–97, at 284.

[2] Greenfield, 'Changing emphases', 284–5.

[3] Robert DiNapoli, *An Index of Theme and Image to the Homilies of the Anglo-Saxon Church: Comprising the Homilies of Ælfric, Wulfstan, and the Blickling and Vercelli Codices* (Hockwold cum Wilton, 1995), pp. 31–2. On the Judgement Day theme in the Blickling and Vercelli homilies, see Milton McC. Gatch, 'Eschatology in the Anonymous Old English Homilies', *Traditio* 21 (1965), 117–65, esp. 128–34 and 151–8.

[4] Extracts which are made ultimately from Vercelli II are also used in Napier XLII (*HomU* 34) and Tristram III (*HomS* 45), but they are too brief to merit examination here.

The available evidence helps to establish that the four homilies just mentioned may be considered as three blocks of material: (1) the ultimate source, now represented by Vercelli II, which was produced presumably in the later tenth century;[5] (2) Vercelli XXI and a version of Vercelli IX (Fadda X), which use different extracts from Vercelli II but can both be shown, from internal evidence, to have used its earlier form as their source; and (3) Napier XL, which rewrites the first half of Vercelli II, while drawing, in some versions of the introductory and concluding portions, upon known and presumably lost works by Wulfstan; it in turn has four versions of its own.[6] The chronological order of Vercelli XXI, Fadda X, and Napier XL is not certain, though the last-mentioned homily, with its use of Wulfstan material, might be considered relatively late.[7] Since much is already known about the make-up, language, and style of Vercelli II,[8] my concern in the following pages is to see how the subsequent homilies rewrite it and how they differ from each other in the way they do so.

Vercelli XXI, Fadda X, and Napier XL are all composite homilies, each with its own variety of sources to draw upon. But their chief interest for the present study lies in their shared use of Vercelli II and the diversity which may be found in them in the way selection and adaptation is made from that common source. Seen in this light, they will reveal much about the homiletic tradition in Anglo-Saxon England, rewriting Vercelli II and other earlier materials into a succession of works which testify to a development of the Judgement Day theme and of the linguistic medium in which it was transmitted.

So is the extract from Vercelli XXI used in *HomU* 12.3; see D. G. Scragg, *The Vercelli Homilies and Related Texts*, EETS os 300 (Oxford, 1992), pp. 50, 364, note to lines 219–20, and 365, note to lines 239–44. See further the last section of this chapter.

[5] The manuscript (Vercelli, Biblioteca Capitolare CXVII) is usually dated s. x^2; see N. R. Ker, *Catalogue of Manuscripts Containing Anglo-Saxon* (Oxford, 1957), p. 460. The date of composition is difficult to establish. Jonathan Wilcox thinks that Vercelli II 'predates the second half of the tenth century' ('The Compilation of Old English Homilies in MSS Cambridge, Corpus Christi College, 419 and 421' (Ph.D. dissertation, University of Cambridge, 1987), p. 94), but Scragg is very cautious, saying with respect to the Vercelli collection of homilies as a whole: 'My own view is that until we have greater understanding of the context for which the items were composed, the possibility of composition within a range from the later ninth to the later tenth centuries must remain open' (*The Vercelli Homilies*, p. xxxix).

[6] For full discussion of the relationship between these blocks, see Scragg, *The Vercelli Homilies*, pp. 48–51; Jonathan Wilcox, 'Napier's "Wulfstan" Homilies XL and XLII: Two Anonymous Works from Winchester?', *JEGP* 90 (1991), 1–19, esp. 1–11.

[7] Wilcox suggests 'a date after 1014' for the second stage of the homily, when the introduction and conclusion drawn from Wulfstan's works are added ('The Compilation', p. 94).

[8] See Scragg, *The Vercelli Homilies*, pp. 48–69; Max Förster, *Die Vercelli-Homilien: I.-VIII. Homilie* (Hamburg, 1932; repr. Darmstadt, 1964), pp. 44–53.

Vercelli XXI

Vercelli XXI is a composite homily consisting in terms of sources of three sections, the last of which (lines 158 to end) is for the most part an adaptation of the first half (lines 1–81) and some other portions of a homily preserved as the second item of the Collection of which it is itself a part.[9] As D. G. Scragg has argued,[10] though, it is clear from the occasional textual divergences that this item, Vercelli II, is not itself the source upon which the compiler of Vercelli XXI worked; rather, the two texts seem to 'hav[e] a common ancestor at no great distance'.[11] The adaptation is of the passages describing the terror of the Last Judgement, which were also found attractive to the compilers of Napier XL and, on a much lesser scale, Fadda X. However, the compiler of our homily's method of adapting his source and the style in which the resultant work is written are very distinct from those of the latter works, as we shall see.[12]

The alterations made in Vercelli XXI to the text of Vercelli II are numerous but are described by Scragg as 'generally insignificant':

> The changes he [the compiler] made to the text of homily II are generally insignificant. There are some simple linguistic alterations, presumably representing modernization. The occasional brief passages omitted are either those felt to be unintelligible in the source, or those missed in error or because of change of fashion. The most obvious change, however, is the addition of phrases which he has already used. But in substance homily XXI is remarkably faithful to homily II, much closer to it than either is to any of the later versions of homily II recorded in conjunction with Wulfstan material (Napier XL).[13]

Scragg obviously means that the changes are 'insignificant' in terms of the 'substance' of the homiletic text. But the rewritten text's deviation from the source text in linguistic usage and style is a different matter. Here Scragg speaks of 'modernization'. But one wonders how far in fact any modernization is made, particularly when one further reads that 'the language of *a* [Vercelli XXI] is heavily modernized' and that 'lines 158-end are drawn, with only the slightest

---

[9] For details, see Scragg, *The Vercelli Homilies*, pp. 347–50. The last section of the homily draws briefly for its conclusion upon portions from the St Père Latin homiliary, as does the first half as a whole. The compiler's language in these translated parts will be discussed later.

[10] Scragg, *The Vercelli Homilies*, p. 349. Examples of inclusion of the material in Vercelli XXI which is omitted in Vercelli II will be discussed below.

[11] Scragg, *The Vercelli Homilies*, p. 349.

[12] On the language and style of Napier XL, see Chapter III and a later section of this chapter.

[13] Scragg, *The Vercelli Homilies*, p. 349.

modification of language, from homily II'.[14] These statements, apparently not consistent with each other, leave the problem still open to investigation. I shall also contend that the changes made in Vercelli XXI include a few which might not be wholly insignificant even in terms of substance and hence of the development of the Vercelli tradition of Judgement Day homilies.

But I start with the language. Of the alterations made in Vercelli XXI presumably for modernization, Scragg cites one example each from grammar and vocabulary: *VercHom* 21.174 *on ðam dæge* replacing the instrumental *þy dæge* (*VercHom* 2.15) and 21.201 *byrnende* replacing 'a perhaps archaic *forglendrede*' (2.50).[15] There are quite a number of other examples of this kind in the area of grammar. In word order, for example, one finds the 'modern' SV instead of VS order after a sentence-initial adverbial phrase in the source in *VercHom* 21.165 *On ðam dæge dryhtnes rod byð blode flowende* (*VercHom* 2.7 *ꝫ on þam dæge bið dryhtnes rod flowende*) and in 21.171 (though not in 21.174); this 'modern' tendency might also explain, though somewhat remotely, the change in *VercHom* 21.211 *þæt bið þonne sarlic sar* (from *VercHom* 2.60 *þæt þonne, la, bið sarlic sar*) and 21.231 *þe læs him þæt yrre God witnie* (from 2.80 *þe læs him God þæt yrre witnige*), where the verb is moved immediately next to the subject, reinforcing the SV order. A different aspect of word order is shown by the post-posed genitive in *VercHom* 21.197 *seo mycle fyrhto þara feonda*, replacing a genitive in pre-position in the source (*VercHom* 2.46 *mycel fionda fyrhto*). Here the addition of the preceding demonstrative may have brought with it the change;[16] on this addition, see below.

Again, one might perhaps see modernization in the use of *uton* + infinitive in place of the hortative subjunctive in a long series (*VercHom* 21.219–39 for *VercHom* 2.69–79 and 107–13, where the latter uses the *uton* construction once and twice in the two segments, respectively), and the addition of the demonstrative before a noun, as in *VercHom* 21.186 *þone toweardan ege þæs domes dæges* (*VercHom* 2.37 *ege domes dæges*), 21.197 (see above) and 21.206 *mid þam gestreonum þe heofon behwylfeð* (2.55 *mid gestreonum*); both changes are at any rate in line with what were to be regular patterns in the history of the language. In *VercHom* 21.174 *sitt ure dryhten on his myclan mægenþrymme*, the demonstrative is omitted from what is often referred to as an 'archaic' construction with the possessive and demonstrative before a noun,[17]

---

[14] Scragg, *The Vercelli Homilies*, pp. 48 and 347. Elsewhere Scragg speaks of 'a slightly modernized version of Vercelli II' in describing Vercelli XXI ('The corpus of vernacular homilies and prose saints' lives before Ælfric', *ASE* 8 (1979), 223–77, at 232).

[15] Scragg, *The Vercelli Homilies*, p. 349 n. 2.

[16] Paul E. Szarmach thinks that this arrangement of modifiers in comparison with those in Vercelli II and Napier XL (186.12 *feonda fyrhto*) 'demonstrate[s] the "prose dilution" of the poetic half-line in its varying stages' (*Vercelli Homilies IX-XXIII* (Toronto, 1981), p. 90, note to line 162).

[17] See D. G. Scragg, 'Napier's "Wulfstan" homily xxx: its sources, its relationship to the Vercelli Book and its style', *ASE* 6 (1977), 197–211, at 205; see also Rudolf

seen in *VercHom* 2.15 *in his þam myclan mægenþrymme*. This is not only in line again with the later development in the language but might also involve dialectal difference. The pattern 'possessive + demonstrative + noun' is sometimes held to be an Anglian feature,[18] and the example in Vercelli II above may be one of those small number of non-West Saxon forms that have survived from the exemplars, in the Vercelli collection of homilies which are generally written in late West Saxon.[19] So may the first person possessive *ussa, usse* in the source (*VercHom* 2.69, 76) replaced by *urra, ure* in our compilation (*VercHom* 21.219, 226),[20] *ne wæren* (*VercHom* 2.52) replaced by the contracted *næron* in *VercHom* 21.203, and the preposition *in* replaced invariably and widely by *on*, either in the phrase *in/on þam dæge* referring to Judgement Day (*VercHom* 21.160, 166, 168 and 171, for *VercHom* 2.2, 8, 10, and 12), or in other phrases expressing place (*VercHom* 21.170 *on susle afeallan*, 174, 180, 214–5 (three examples), for *VercHom* 2.12 *in susle afeallað*, 15, 27, 63–4, respectively). In these last two alterations, one has more certainly to do with dialectal difference and modernization, since the compiler's usage in both cases represents what is by common consent a late West-Saxon feature as opposed to the Anglian.[21] That *on* in the last alteration represents modernization may be further borne out by the fact that the corresponding forms in a version (Cotton Cleopatra B. xiii)[22] of another

---

Vleeskruyer (ed.), *The Life of St. Chad: An Old English Homily* (Amsterdam, 1953), p. 140. But Bruce Mitchell calls this description into question on the grounds that the pattern is found in Ælfric and is not always eliminated in the later version of *Gregory's Dialogues* (MS H); see his *Old English Syntax*, 2 vols. (Oxford, 1985), §§103–12. The compiler of Vercelli XXI himself retains the 'archaic' pattern in *VercHom* 21.185.

[18] See Vleeskruyer, *The Life*, p. 48; M. Grünberg, *The West-Saxon Gospels: A Study of the Gospel of St. Matthew with Text of the Four Gospels* (Amsterdam, 1967), p. 317.

[19] For the dialect of the Vercelli Homilies, see Scragg, *The Vercelli Homilies*, p. xliii; id., 'The compilation of the Vercelli Book', *ASE* 2 (1973), 189–207; Paul W. Peterson, 'Dialect Grouping in the Unpublished Vercelli Homilies', *Studies in Philology* 50 (1953), 559–65. Peterson assumes the language of Vercelli XXI to be 'Late West Saxon with Anglian and Kentish features' (565).

[20] On the formation of *ure, urra* and the etymologically earlier forms in *us(s)*- and their dialectal distribution, see *OED*, s.v. *Our*; Karl Brunner, *Die englische Sprache: Ihre geschichtliche Entwicklung*, 2 vols. (Tübingen, 1960–62), Vol. 2, p. 126; id., *Altenglische Grammatik nach der angelsächsischen Grammatik von Eduard Sievers*, 3rd, revised edn. (Tübingen, 1965), §§335–6; Alistair Campbell, *Old English Grammar* (Oxford, 1959), §§701 and 706; and Scragg, *The Vercelli Homilies*, p. lxv. Campbell also notes that '-*ss* forms occur in many lW-S texts' (p. 290 n. 3).

[21] See *OES*, §1130, and §§1191–3, respectively. For *in* as an Anglian feature, see also Scragg, 'The compilation', 207; Vleeskruyer, *The Life*, p. 30; Peterson, 'Dialect Grouping', 564; and Richard Jordan, *Eigentümlichkeiten des anglischen Wortschatzes* (Heidelberg, 1906), pp. 42–4. For the distribution of *in/on* in the Vercelli Homilies as a whole, see D. G. Scragg, 'The Language of the Vercelli Homilies' (Ph.D. thesis, Manchester University, 1970), pp. 327–30, esp. p. 328.

[22] See the section on Napier XL.

homily derived from Vercelli II, Napier XL, are mostly *in* but sometimes are underlined and have *on* added over them 'in diff[erent] ink'.[23] It should also be added that the compiler of Vercelli XXI's preference for *on* extends to alteration of other expressions in the source, as in *VercHom* 21.171 *on feower healfa* (*VercHom* 2.12 *of*), 21.202 *On þam dæge* (2.51 *⁊ þonne*), and 21.255 *se leofað . . . on wuldre ⁊ on wyrðmynde aa butan ende on ecnesse* (2.117 *þam is wuldor ⁊ wyrðmynd þurh ealra worulda woruld aa butan ende*), while he uses *innan* (*VercHom* 21.209 *innan þære cealdan eorðan*, *VercHom* 2.58 *in*) for the distinct sense of 'in'.

Other grammatical changes of interest include those relating to gender and inflectional endings of nouns (*VercHom* 21.184 *þone deofol*, from *VercHom* 2.34 *þæt mycle dioful*,[24] and the expected genitive form of the feminine *sorg* in 21.188 *sorge dæg*, from 2.39 *sorges dæg*), a simple verb form in place of an expanded form (21.171 *blawað*, from 2.12 *beoð blawende*), the relative *se* (21.255) rather than *se ðe* (2.117), and the preference for a correlative form of conjunction over a single conjunction (*oððe . . . oððe* and *ne . . . ne* in 21.229–30 and 21.247–8, from *oððe* and *ne* in 2.80 and 2.114, respectively). It is doubtful that these changes were also made for modernization. In the genitive *sorge/sorges*, for example, the uncommon form in the source is more likely to be intended to rhyme with the immediately preceding *sares dæg*, and the compiler perhaps disregarded this rhythmical consideration of his source.[25] A similar tendency on the part of the compiler of Vercelli XXI can be seen in his treatment of word pairs; see below.

But there is evidence for modernization in Vercelli XXI in vocabulary, too. Besides the one given by Scragg (see above), one notes two clear examples of updating by a prosaic word: *eorðe* (*VercHom* 21.209) for the poetic *folde* (*VercHom*

---

[23] E. G. Stanley, '*The Judgement of the Damned* (from Cambridge, Corpus Christi College 201 and other manuscripts), and the definition of Old English verse', *Learning and Literature in Anglo-Saxon England: Studies Presented to Peter Clemoes on the Occasion of His Sixty-Fifth Birthday*, ed. Michael Lapidge and Helmut Gneuss (Cambridge, 1985), pp. 363–91, at p. 382, apparatus. Enid M. Raynes says that it is 'in later hand' ('Unpublished Old English Homilies: Mainly from MSS. CCCC 188, Hatton 114, 115, and Junius 121, together with Vercelli Homily IX' (D.Phil. thesis, Oxford, 1955), pp. 64–6, apparatus). For the preference of *in* over *on* in Napier XL in comparison with Vercelli II, see Chapter III. Variations within the four versions of Napier XL will be discussed in a section on this homily later in this chapter.

[24] In *VercHom* 21.182, the compiler uses the plural *ða deoflu* in place of the neuter singular form in the source (*VercHom* 2.32).

[25] Clark Hall (*A Concise Anglo-Saxon Dictionary*, 4th edn., with a Supplement by Herbert D. Meritt (Cambridge, 1960), s.v. *sorg*) attributes 'occ[asiona]l g[enitive] s[ingular] in -es' to the word. As a matter of fact, one sees with the aid of the Toronto Microfiche Concordance and the DOE Corpus of Old English (see Chapter II, n. 12) that the form *sorges* occurs only twice in Old English, and it is interesting to observe that the other example, *Bo* 16.18 *to tacnunge sorges ⁊ anfealdes sares*, occurs in an almost identical rhythmical context. See Stanley, '*The Judgement of the Damned*', p. 386.

2.59), and *gebrasl* (a variant form of *gebrastl*, in 21.191) in place of 'the unique' and 'perhaps no longer comprehensible *blæstm*'²⁶ in *VercHom* 2.42. Less certain, but perhaps to be understood in the same way, are *VercHom* 21.239 *(þa hwile þe we) her beon moton*, replacing what is a *hapax legomenon* and apparently poetic *ura wega wealdan* meaning literally 'to control the ways of our lives' (*VercHom* 2.112),²⁷ and *earfoðness* and *ælc* (*VercHom* 21.187 and 204) used respectively in place of *earfoðe* and *æghwilc* (*VercHom* 2.37 and 53). The last two replacements seem to be more common words than their counterparts in the source in late Old English at any rate. Bosworth-Toller demonstrates that *earfoðe* is more common in poetry and *earfoþnes* in late Old English prose, while, with respect to the other alteration, Leena Kahlas-Tarkka and Karl Jost show that *ælc* is the commonest word for the meaning 'every, each' in Old English generally and is so in Wulfstan in late Old English.²⁸ It might also be added that the compiler of Vercelli XXI clearly prefers verb forms with the *a*-prefix to the simplexes in the source, thus *VercHom* 21.176 *ahengon*, 185 *agolden*, and 230 *agylte* (and 232 *agylt* (p.p.), in his original sentence). But whether this preference reflects a significant tendency or not is unclear. It is worth noting, however, that the compiler also shows 'a particular fondness for the prefix [*fore-*]' over the corresponding unprefixed forms.²⁹

The compiler of Vercelli XXI also changes, consciously or unconsciously, the sense of sentences by his own choice of particular vocabulary items. Thus, he replaces the word *tintreg* 'torment' in *VercHom* 2.27 *in þa tintrego þære ecean helle* by *trega* (*VercHom* 21.181); if virtually synonymous with it, the word may retain

---

²⁶ Roberta Frank, 'Poetic Words in Late Old English Prose', *From Anglo-Saxon to Early Middle English: Studies Presented to E. G. Stanley*, ed. Malcolm Godden, Douglas Gray, and Terry Hoad (Oxford, 1994), pp. 87–107, at pp. 95–6. By contrast, as Frank notes, all the four manuscripts except one (CCCC 201) of Napier XL use the poetic *blæst*; see below, p. 96.

²⁷ This may be compared with *PPs* 90:11 . . ./ *þæt þu wilwega wealdan mostest*, for which there is no exact counterpart in the Vulgate Latin. The noun *wilweg* 'a pleasant way, a desirable way' (BT, s.v.) occurs twice more in the genitive as object of *forwyrnan* in Vercelli X, line 41 and its variant text, Napier XLIX 252.17.

²⁸ Leena Kahlas-Tarkka, *The Uses and Shades of Meaning of Words for* Every *and* Each *in Old English* (Helsinki, 1987), p. 72; Karl Jost, *Wulfstanstudien* (Bern, 1950), p. 166. On *earfoþnes* see also *DOE* (s.v.), where the word is described as 'freq[uent] in Ælfric'. On the other hand, the word *totwæmaþ*, by which the compiler of Vercelli XXI (21.247) replaces *gedalaþ* in the source (*VercHom* 2.114), is never used by Wulfstan, who always has *todælan*. For examples of these two words in contrast, see Chapter II, pp. 18 and 34; see further Scragg, *The Vercelli Homilies*, p. 69, note to O.114–17.

²⁹ D. G. Scragg, 'An Old English Homilist of Archbishop Dunstan's Day', *Words, Texts and Manuscripts: Studies in Anglo-Saxon Culture Presented to Helmut Gneuss*, ed. Michael Korhammer, with Karl Reichl and Hans Sauer (Cambridge, 1992), pp. 181–92, at p. 187. This preference is shared by Vercelli XIX, XX and Tristram III, and partly on this evidence Scragg (pp. 182–8) assumes single authorship for the four pieces.

something of its etymological sense 'grief, pain'.[30] More suggestive is the change made to *VercHom* 2.76 *mid eallre usse heortan ⁊ hygdo* 'with all our heart and mind', whereby our compilation reads *VercHom* 21.225 *mid eallre heortan hyldo* 'with all loyalty of heart'—a change of which the compiler might have been reminded by the same phraseology used in Vercelli XIX as a translation of Latin *contrito corde* (and which would hence be another piece of evidence for the common authorship for Vercelli XIX and XXI and two other homilies), as Scragg argues.[31]

However, such examples are rare in Vercelli XXI. The majority, if not all, of the changes of vocabulary items made in it suggest an attempt on the part of its compiler to update the language of the homily he is adapting. Taken together with the changes in grammar discussed earlier, they demonstrate sufficiently clearly that, far from being interspersed with only slight changes, the language of the homily is heavily modernized. In this respect, Vercelli XXI points to a distinct development from its 'sister' homily Napier XL within the Vercelli tradition of Judgement Day homilies.

On the other hand, Vercelli XXI, quite unlike Napier XL again, makes few changes that might be considered stylistic rather than grammatical. When the compiler does choose to make one, he does so differently from the compiler of Napier XL. For example, in adapting the account of Judgement Day as it is developed over a long stretch of sentences in the source (*VercHom* 2.2–51), the compiler of Napier XL was seen to omit and add the conjunction *and* at several points according to his metrical scheme and sense of 'prose paragraph'.[32] By contrast, the compiler of Vercelli XXI simply omits the conjunction, twice before the sentence-initial *on ðam dæge* (21.164, 165) and twice more in different contexts (21.166 and 21.216, where in this last case the preposition *on* is added instead, rectifying the apparently erroneous second *and* ('⁊') in the manuscript reading of *VercHom* 2.65 *betweox deadum ⁊ dioflum, ⁊ bryne ⁊ on biternesse*).

Another sphere for revision shared by the two homilies is the 'broken construction' in *VercHom* 2.25 *þa earman fyrenfullan sculon sarige aswæman fram ansyne ures drihtnes* . . . *⁊ þonne gewitaþ hie in þa tintrego þære ecean helle*, where Vercelli XXI (line 178) and Napier XL (185.7) happen to agree, replacing the semi-independent coordinate clause (*⁊ þonne gewitaþ* . . .) with a continued use of infinitive (*⁊ þanon gewiton* . . .). On the other hand, the two later versions proceed separately in adapting the source, in:

---

[30] See Clark Hall, s.v.; F. Holthausen, *Altenglisches etymologisches Wörterbuch*, 2nd edn. (Heidelberg, 1963), s.v. On the other hand, the Glossary to the EETS edition explains this use of the word as 'torment'. Förster thinks that the word (here in the form *tregan* (acc. pl.)) is an error for *tintregan* (*Die Vercelli-Homilien*, p. 46, apparatus). For *tintreg*, see Gatch, 'Eschatology', 150 and 162–3.

[31] Scragg, 'An OE Homilist', pp. 183–4; see n. 29 above.

[32] See Chapter III, p. 42.

Late Old English Judgement Day Homilies 71

> *VercHom* 21.169 for ðan þe hie ær noldan hyra synna betan, ac hie þonne sceolon sarie aswæman ⁊ on susle afeallan (*VercHom* 2.11 . . ., ac hie sarige aswæmaþ ⁊ in susle afeallað, *where Napier XL (183.3) omits the* ac-*clause entirely*).

> *VercHom* 21.207 we us ne ondrædað þæt we dæghwamlice geseoð beforan urum eagum ure neahstan sweltan (*omitting* nu we þam oðrum ne gelyfaþ *inserted between* urum eagum *and* ure þa neahstan *in the Vercelli II text*); *while Napier XL adapts more freely*: 187.8 we nu ungesælige syndon, þæt we us bet ne warniað, and þæt we ne ondrædað us þe swyðor, þe we dæghwamlice geseoð beforan urum eagum ure þa nehstan feallan and sweltan.

As I have argued earlier,[33] the Vercelli II text poses a slight difficulty of meaning in both sentences—in understanding how the *ac*-clause relates to the preceding causal relationship in the first sentence, and the possibly misleading *nu*-clause as giving the reason for not fearing the Last Judgement (*VercHom* 2.36 *we us ne ondrædaþ*) in the second. Perhaps to clarify these points, each of the two adaptations omits the relevant clause from one sentence or the other. But the other change each version makes—one making the slightest modification of tense in the first sentence and the other rewriting the second completely—suggests the different attitudes of the two compilers and the nature of their changes as a whole. On the whole, the revision in Napier XL would seem to be more severe and thoroughgoing; it suggests the compiler's concern with subtle points of sense and his own conscious style. The compiler of Vercelli XXI sought a different clarification; his revision is aimed at making simpler and better sense of the source text in so far as this can be done without changing its arrangement of words and clauses radically.

In addition to this comparative evidence, the stylistic character of the compiler of Vercelli XXI can be seen in the way he reacts to the rhythmical prose of the source text. Apart from the changes in syntax (*VercHom* 21.197) and vocabulary items (21.191, 201) already mentioned, he leaves almost intact the 'metrical passage' describing the pains and miseries that await those who do not dread Judgement Day (*VercHom* 21.188–202, corresponding to *VercHom* 2.39–51). But when he later reaches a passage of exhortation, he rearranges the list of sins people must shun from:

> *VercHom* 2.72 dysinessa ⁊ gedwollcræftas, gitsunga ⁊ gifernessa, leasunga ⁊ licettunga, tælnessa ⁊ twyspræcnessa, niðas ⁊ nearoþancas, ⁊ heamolscipas ⁊ eall[e] þa þeawa[s] þe dioflu on him sylfum onstealdon

into

---

[33] See Chapter III, pp. 46 and 45, respectively .

VercHom 21.222 disignessa ⁊ gifernessa, gytsunga ⁊ leasunga, liccettunga ⁊ talnessa, niðas nearuþancas ⁊ gedwollcræftas ⁊ twyspræcnessa ⁊ ealle þa þeawas þe deoflu on him astealdon.

It is not possible to say with certainty on what principle he rearranges them the way he does, but by doing so he certainly disrupts the tightly-knit structure of alliterating word pairs and rhyme which characterizes this part of the original prose[34]—a modification which is made once again in the same way in the sentence immediately following the cited list, where our compiler repeats the preposition *mid* for each of the four noun phrases, thereby discarding the original poetic rhythm of three alliterating word pairs, with *mid* governing each of them.[35] In fact, quite unlike many anonymous homilists of the period, the compiler seems to show no real interest in using word pairs as a device of any importance for his adaptation, adding very few of them to those he found in his source. He adds just two in the homily as a whole, one *geræd . . . ⁊ geleornod* in a sentence original to him (*VercHom* 21.158; on this sentence, see further below) and the other *biddað ⁊ myndgiað ⁊ eac halsiað* (21.107), expanding Latin *rogo . . . et . . . ammoneo*, both perhaps from memory of the stock of homiletic commonplaces. Otherwise, he reverses the order of words used in a pair (*VercHom* 21.176 *ahengon ⁊ cwealdon*, from *VercHom* 2.18), and even omits a word pair here and there, reducing *VercHom* 2.24 *to sceawigenne ⁊ to smægenne* to *VercHom* 21.178 *to smeagenne* and 2.108 *snotre ⁊ soðfæste ⁊ mildheorte* to 21.234 *soðfæste ⁊ mildheorte*; cf. the changes made in the list of sins cited above. These examples, added to those discussed in the previous paragraph, point strongly to plain simplicity as a guiding principle of the style of Vercelli XXI's compiler. It is not his concern to exploit rhetorical devices and stylistic embellishments to elaborate and expand the prose of the source, but he writes in a style which tends 'towards relatively unadorned and straightforward expression', as Paul E. Szarmach puts it,[36] in adapting Vercelli II as well as Latin and other material in the earlier parts of the homily, as we shall see.[37]

---

[34] See Wilcox, 'Napier XL and XLII', 4–5.

[35] In another passage, the compiler does not repeat but omits the preposition *mid*: *VercHom* 21.184 *Antecrist mid helle witum ⁊ his yrmðum ⁊ his ðam sarum suslum* (*VercHom* 2.35 *Antecrist mid his helle witum ⁊ mid his yrmþum ⁊ his þam saran suslum*). The reason is again difficult to know. The change could have been dictated by the compiler's own sense of prose rhythm. But it seems at any rate important to notice that the compiler simplifies rather than elaborating the sentence structure here, too.

[36] Paul E. Szarmach, 'The Vercelli Homilies: Style and Structure', *The Old English Homily and Its Backgrounds*, ed. idem and Bernard F. Huppé (Albany, 1978), pp. 241–67, at p. 250.

[37] Still, we seem to have a crux in what he writes in *VercHom* 21.217 *on eallum þam witum þe deof[l]um wæs geearwod fram þære þe hie on forwurdon ⁊ hie sylfe geearnodon*. In particular, *fram þære þe* . . . does not make good sense any more than the corresponding

But before that, it remains to see, with respect to that part of the homily which is based on Vercelli II, how omissions and additions are made by the compiler of a kind not covered by grammatical and stylistic changes discussed above. They are mostly omissions from and additions to the original material of the homily, and some of these are described and illustrated by Scragg in the passage quoted at the beginning of this section and the footnotes to it. Omissions occur, Scragg says, because the sentences were 'felt to be unintelligible', e.g. *VercHom* 2.28–32 (containing slight confusion of syntax[38] and omitted at *VercHom* 21.181), or 'missed in error or because of change of fashion', e.g. *VercHom* 2.16–17 . . . *⁊ his lichoman; þonne bið seo wund gesewen þam firenfullum, ⁊ þam soðfæstan he bið hal gesewen*[39] (omitted at *VercHom* 21.175), and 2.19–23 (omitted after 21.177).[40] Another example of the first type might be the omission of *dæge* in *VercHom* 21.219 *uton wyrcan god on þam þe we þurhteon magon*, as compared with *VercHom* 2.70 . . . *on þam dæge þe we ðurhteon mægen*; the phrase *on þam dæge* makes poor sense in this context. Otherwise, omission is mostly of single small words, e.g. *þæt* (in *VercHom* 21.230 from *VercHom* 2.80), *þonne* (in 21.214, from 2.64) and *þær* (in 21.210, from 2.59), and these are generally not very significant, though they could possibly suggest the compiler's own prose rhythm according to which he rewrote his source text.

Nor, generally, are additions. In one instance, *VercHom* 21.194 *se bitera dæg ⁊ se micla cwyld ⁊ þara manna dream ⁊ seo sarie sorh ⁊ þara sawla gedal*, as compared with *VercHom* 2.44 *se bitera dæg ⁊ þara sawla gedal*, the addition may well be only apparent, since it is evident from the variant texts of Napier XL that 'some phrases are omitted here'[41] in the source text as it survives in Vercelli II. Addition is probably genuine in *VercHom* 21.235 *godfyrhte ⁊ gesybbsume ⁊ geþwære ⁊ geþyldige ⁊ eaðmode ⁊ þeawfæste*, where the four adjectives between the first and the last make up for the 'avoidance of the unique *larsume*'[42] used at this point in the source (*VercHom* 2.110)—more probably so because it is surrounded by a few sentences (*VercHom* 21.231–4, 237–8) which seem to be original to the compiler, or at least

---

phrase in the source (*VercHom* 2.67 *fram þære frymþe, þe . . .*). For discussion, see Scragg, *The Vercelli Homilies*, pp. 68–9 (note to lines 66–8) and 364 (note to lines 217–8).

[38] See *VercHom* 2.27 and 2.30 (Chapter III, p. 44).

[39] The sentence is followed by another *þonne* in the next sentence, which makes one inclined to think that this might be a case of homoeoteleuton.

[40] Scragg, *The Vercelli Homilies*, p. 349 nn. 3 and 4. The three line references to Vercelli II are as in Scragg's footnotes.

[41] Scragg, *The Vercelli Homilies*, p. 67, note to line 44. Scragg thinks that 'there is no certainty about what they were', though Förster supplies those 'omitted' words from Vercelli XXI and Napier XL, to read '⁊ se micla cwyld ⁊ þara manna man ⁊ seo sarie sorh' between *se bitera dæg* and *⁊ þara sawla gedal* (*Die Vercelli-Homilien*, p. 48, lines 57–8).

[42] Scragg, *The Vercelli Homilies*, p. 69, note to lines 108–10.

to expand the source text.[43] However, these surrounding sentences all begin with *uto(n)* exhorting men to act as true Christians should do; they represent mere homiletic commonplaces and are not substantial to the content of the homily, any more than the four adjectives added in between.

However, some other examples are more important. When the compiler of Vercelli XXI says *uton lufian ure neahstan, þæt syndon ealle cristene menn, swa swa us sylfe* (line 226, based on *VercHom* 2.77), he is repeating the parenthetic explanatory phrase which he has already used at the beginning of the homily (in line 2), in a way described by Scragg in the passage cited at the beginning of this section. It is a phrase of his own and its continued use is an indication that drawing as he does very heavily on earlier homiletic materials, he never forgets to rewrite them in the prose he feels most at home with, as long as he can easily achieve this without changing the sentence structures and words of his source very drastically. So is the repeated use of *be his (agenum) gewyrhtum* (as against *VercHom* 2.20 *æfter his sylfes gewyrhtum* which he uses it to replace) in *VercHom* 21.157 and 177,[44] and, in the earlier part based on Latin homilies, of the clausal *awriten is on halgum gewritum/Cristes bocum* (with varied word order) in 21.13 (for Latin *scriptum est*) and 21.20 and 21.35 (both with no Latin equivalent). This last phraseology is paralleled later in the homily by a change — the very first one the compiler introduces after turning to Vercelli II to start describing Judgement Day — where he adds: *VercHom* 21.158 *þæs ðe we geræd habbað ⁊ geleornod on haligum bocum*. These last two additions seem particularly important. They show the compiler laying emphasis on authority and the authenticity it gives to his homily, in much the same way as Malcolm Godden shows that another anonymous writer of a composite homily does to record his respect for Ælfric as a 'learned authority'.[45] In a somewhat different context, Milton McC. Gatch explains the point thus:

> It is often difficult to determine in the Blickling and Vercelli collections whether it was the translator himself or some predecessor working in Latin who selected the items to be used for a given homily, but it is clear that very little original material went into the sermons. In choosing their sources, then, the homilists were concerned not to speculate or to innovate but to transmit that which the authorities ('these holy books' or some 'noble teacher') had vouchsafed is the Gospel. It is the tradition as it has been received which is the basis of all the teaching and exhortation in these codices.[46]

---

[43] See Scragg, *The Vercelli Homilies*, pp. 364–5, note to lines 231–3.

[44] See Scragg, *The Vercelli Homilies*, p. 349 n. 5.

[45] M. R. Godden, 'Old English composite homilies from Winchester', *ASE* 4 (1975), 57–65, at 64.

[46] Gatch, 'Eschatology', 163.

For the compiler of Vercelli XXI, the authority to be emphasized to authenticate his Judgement Day homily as Christian writing is not any of his predecessors but Scripture itself ('Cristes bocum', 'halgum gewritum'). This reliance takes a more direct form in what would seem to be the one addition the compiler makes in substance to the homily, in the biblical reference to four angels standing at the four corners of the earth before the Doom (Revelation 7:1): *VercHom* 21.171 *On ðam dæge, feower englas blawað feower byman on feower healfa þysses middangeardes*[47] (where the Vercelli source (2.12) has just *In þam dæge beoð blawende þa byman of .iiii. sceattum þyses middangeardes*). This addition, then, and the general emphasis on the Scriptures in which it occurs, may suggest a shift, albeit slight, introduced by the compiler of Vercelli XXI in the Vercelli tradition towards a more 'learned' type of Judgement Day homilies, from what its ultimate source was found to be, a 'mit wenig Gelehrsamkeit befrachtete Predigt'[48] using 'mostly apocryphal sources'.[49]

In the examination above of the language of that section of Vercelli XXI which draws on the text of Vercelli II, I have emphasized in several places its 'relatively unadorned and straightforward' style and some other features as common to the compilation as a whole, including the other two sections. It is not my intention to go into the full detail of this sustained piece of writing, but it will be useful, for our understanding of the nature of this composite homily and its position in the Vercelli tradition of Judgement Day homilies, to illustrate some of its aspects with reference to a couple of passages from each of the earlier sections.

The first section, lines 1–125, is a translation of extracts from Latin homilies in the St Père homiliary.[50] The compiler translates them very closely, omitting and changing nothing of substance, but not too literally. His method is generally that of paraphrasing into idiomatic English, with even occasional brief additions and omissions of words and phrases, rather than an over-literal imitation of Latin sentence constructions. A good example is the final passage of the section which contains a series of *gif*-clauses:

VercHom 21.116 Witodlice we cumað orsorge on domes dæge toforan Cristes þrymsetle, ⁊ beoð rihtwise þonne on ecum gemynde. ⁊ we beoð fram him forð gecigede to þam heofonlican gebeorscipe mid þam mærum

---

[47] An analogue to this description occurs in Blickling Homily VII, which is based on the Apocalypse of Thomas: *BlHom* 95.13 (ed. Morris) *& þonne hateþ Sanctus Michahel se heahengl blawan þa feower beman æt þissum feower endum middangeardes*. For Morris's edition, see Chapter VI, n. 55.

[48] Jost, *Wulfstanstudien*, p. 218.

[49] Wilcox, 'Napier XL and XLII', 5.

[50] For details, see Scragg, *The Vercelli Homilies*, p. 347; James E. Cross, *Cambridge Pembroke College MS. 25: A Carolingian Sermonary Used by Anglo-Saxon Preachers* (London, 1987), pp. 143–73.

heahfæderum Abrahame ⁊ Isace ⁊ Iacobe ⁊ eallum haligum werude. He us gegearwað þa heofonlican for ðam eorðlicum ⁊ þa ecan þing for þam hwilendlicum þingum þysse worulde, gif we ælmyssan don willað on urum life, ⁊ gif we dædbote don willaþ urra misfenga, ⁊ gif we þa hingriendan fedaþ ⁊ him drinc gesyllað, ⁊ gif [we] þa nacodan be urum mihtum scrydað, ⁊ gif we þa elðeodigan onfoð þonne hie ure be[ð]urfen.

In the Latin the conditional clauses come first. The translator-compiler postpones them all, and adds, in his first and second *gif*-clauses, the modal verb *willan* (*don willað . . . don willaþ*) to translate the Latin simple verb forms (*facimus . . . agimus*),[51] as well as *on urum life* and *urra misfenga* in the first and second of the same clauses respectively; in one of the foregoing independent clauses, too, he expands a phrase, adding *þam mærum heahfæderum . . . ⁊ eallum haligum werude* to *Abraham et Isaac et Iacob* in the Latin. The number of conditional clauses is also reduced, from seven *si*-clauses to five *gif*-clauses, partly as a result of the omission of the last *si*-clause: *et si haec omnia diligenter agimus*. This is merely 'resumptive', recapitulating the six preceding ones, and by omitting it, the Old English translator-compiler obviously chose to shun rhetorical embellishment in favour of plain prose. This attitude to rhetorical elements in the Latin source is again manifested in a passage which enumerates the 'holy offerings' we must bring and offer to God (*VercHom* 21.100–5). In listing the twelve Christian qualities as the offerings, the Latin homilist makes an interruption after the third (*caritatem perfectam*) and then continues, again by way of resumption: *et post haec humilitatem, . . .*; the Old English translator-compiler dispenses with this sophistication but links all the qualities, simply and mechanically, by the conjunction *and* ('⁊'). Here he is following one of the 'main patterns' for linking words and phrases in Old English prose ('A and B and C and . . .'),[52] as he regularly does in similar listings elsewhere in his translation, viz. lines 20–5 (with twelve *and*'s), 43–4, 49–54 (with nineteen *and*'s), 88–94 and, later in the last section, 243–5 and 249–52 (with thirteen *and*'s).

Another illustration comes from the passage on the twelve virtues of the spirit (*VercHom* 21.61–82), in which each virtue is named and explained. Here the translator-compiler does not use *and* but allots an independent sentence, with or without the initial adverb *þonne*, to each virtue, following the sentence divisions in the Latin: *Þæt fyrmeste mægen þære sawle ys . . . Þonne ys þæt oðer mægen . . . Þæt eahtoðe mægen ys . . .* (Latin *Prima enim uirtus animae est . . . Secunda est . . .*

---

[51] I cite the Latin from Cross's texts (*Cambridge Pembroke College 25*, pp. 156–72).

[52] For details, see Mary Blockley, *Aspects of Old English Poetic Syntax: Where Clauses Begin* (Urbana and Chicago, 2001), pp. 47–71, esp. p. 58. Blockley adds that this particular pattern 'appears only occasionally in Old English prose' (p. 58); but see also her Appendix, at p. 217, where she notes: 'The conjunction of prose phrasal coordination tends to appear between each of a series of three or more items: A and B and C and D and . . .'.

Octaua est . . .). But he again makes additions in details of the wording, first of the phrase *of eallre ure heortan ⁊ of eallre sawle ⁊ of eallum mægene* in explaining the first virtue, which he has used earlier at the beginning of the homily, translating Latin *ex toto corde tuo et ex tota anima tua et ex tota uirtute tua*,[53] and then of *mægen (. . .) þære sawle* to the ordinal numeral quite mechanically from the second virtue on throughout the passage. Syntactically, he translates all the twelve Latin predicative infinitives defining each virtue into *þæt*-clauses (e.g. Latin *Undecima est auaritiam spernere . . .* into *Þæt endlyfte mægen þære sawle ys þæt man forhycge gytsunge . . .*), with the invariable word order SVO regardless of the Latin order. The result is simple but idiomatic Old English prose;[54] if it is monotonous and unsophisticated, it is because it is intended to be so in accordance with the Latin. The translator-compiler also uses finite clauses to expand Latin participial constructions and noun phrases, with similar results.[55]

The second section (*VercHom* 21.126–57) is, as is generally agreed, a 'prose dilution' of two vernacular poems[56] — one an unknown poem which has left its

---

[53] See Scragg, *The Vercelli Homilies*, p. 348 n. 4.

[54] An exception to this general tendency of the compiler's style occurs in *VercHom* 21.246 *on þam synt engla weredu ⁊ rihtwisra togeladung þær symle wuniendra*, translating almost word-for-word the Latin construction: *in quo sunt agmina angelorum et congregatio iustorum ibi semper manentium*; see further *VercHom* 21.98–9. But such examples are very rare. The compiler's concern is evidently to write in straightforward Old English prose rather than follow the Latin wording slavishly, so much so that at one point he writes rather loosely, mixing up two types of expression for requesting: *VercHom* 21.107 *Ðig we eow biddað . . . þæt we gehealden ealle ðas foresædan þing on urum mode of eallum urum mihtum.* Strict logic would require *ge*, not *we*, as the subject of the dependent clause, since the sentence concerns asking somebody else to do something, not asking permission to do something. The 'error' is made presumably because in the compiler's mind the pronoun *we* usually meant 'we Christians (inclusive of himself)' and was used more often than not in exhortations; cf. the *uton* construction which immediately follows the sentence.

[55] See *VercHom* 21.83 *of þam hie scinað beforan Godes gesyhðe* (Latin *fulgentes ante conspectum domini*), 21.55 *þam þe hine her on worulde lufiað ⁊ his willan wyrcað oð hira endedæg* (Latin *diligentibus se*), and 21.97 *ongean ealle þa god þe he us forgifen hæfð* (Latin *beneficiis suis uicem*).

[56] The phrase is Angus McIntosh's ('Wulfstan's Prose', *PBE* 34 (1949), 109–42, at 127–8 n. 7). On the poetic sources, see Szarmach, *Vercelli Homilies*, p. 89, note to lines 67–75; Scragg, *The Vercelli Homilies*, pp. 347–8. The problem has recently been given a new turn in Charles D. Wright, 'More Old English Poetry in Vercelli Homily XXI', *Early Medieval English Texts and Interpretations: Studies Presented to Donald G. Scragg*, ed. Elaine Treharne and Susan Rosser (Tempe, Arizona, 2002), pp. 245–62, where the author argues that we can 'recognize poetic form and intent' in a third passage (lines 141–9, 'between the loosely alliterative passage . . . and the prose dilution of *Exhortation*'), which 'may be a remnant of a lost Old English poem' (p. 253). For a view contrary to these that the prose version preceded the verse, see Cross, *Cambridge Pembroke College 25*, pp. 149–50.

obvious marks in frequent alliteration, word pairing and poetic diction in lines 128–41 (e.g. lines 132 *earme oððe eadige* and 133 *þone uplican eðel secan*[57]), and the other the poem known as *An Exhortation to Christian Living*. The 'dilution' is clearly in evidence in this latter passage (*VercHom* 21.149–57). The imperative verbs in the poem are replaced by the hortative *uton* construction in accordance with usage in the other sections, while lines 4–6 of the poem are rearranged into a prose order, to the detriment of their alliterative two-stress phrases:

> *Exhort* 4 . . ., and wæccan lufa
> on hyge halgum   on þas hwilwendan tid,
> bliðe mode,   and gebedum filige
> . . .

VercHom 21.150 ⁊ uton bliðum mode on haligum hige wæccan lufian ⁊ gebedum fylgian on þisse hwilwendan tide.

It should also be noted that the dative *bliðum mode* replaces the instrumental *bliðe mode* of the poem; this could be another case of modernization.[58] What follows these lines is characterized by additions the compiler made to the poetic text, so that three poetic lines are expanded into nearly three times as many words in prose:

> *Exhort* 13 . . . glengað and bringað
> þa soðfæstan   sauwle to reste
> on þa uplican   eadignesse,

VercHom 21.154 . . . geglengaþ ⁊ gebringað þa soðfæstan sawla on blisse ⁊ on wuldre on þære uplican eadignesse on þam ytemestan dæge þysses woruldrices, þe dryhten on demeð æghwylcum menn be his gewyrhtum.

In this expansion, the compiler again uses words and phrases which he is to repeat later—*on þam ytemestan dæge* (cf. *VercHom* 21.159 *se ytemesta dæg*),[59] *be his gewyrhtum* (cf. 21.177 *be his agenum gewyrhtum*), and prefixed verbs *geglengað and gebringað* (cf. 21.176 *ahengon*, 185 *agolden*, 230 *agylte*, 232 *agylt*; see further n.

---

[57] DOE describes the word *epel* as 'disproportionately freq[uent] in poetry' (s.v.); see, for example, *Creed* 32 *uplicne eðel secan* and 37 *þone uplican eðel secan* and *Exhort* 74 *swincan / wið þæs uplican eþelrices*. Another example of poetic diction in the second section of Vercelli XXI occurs a little later in line 144 *heofona wealdend ⁊ sigora syllend*, which is in fact part of the evidence for Wright's argument mentioned above in n. 56. On *-end* nouns as poeticism and the decay of their use, see M. S. Griffith, 'Poetic language and the Paris Psalter: the decay of the Old English tradition', *ASE* 20 (1991), 167–86.

[58] See Scragg, *The Vercelli Homilies*, p. 348 n. 3.

[59] See *OED*, s.v. *Day* 8b. This phrase in the sense 'Judgement Day' is not recorded in *A Thesaurus of Old English*, ed. Jane Roberts and Christian Kay with Lynne Grundy (London, 1995), s.v. 16.02.01.08.03, but it is common in prose.

29). Finally, by adding a reference to the Last Judgement at the end of the section, the compiler prepares himself and the audience for the subject he is now to treat in the last section. The 'diluted' section, then, no less than the 'Latin section', argues strongly that the compiler is in control of his materials, widely different as they are, and the alterations he made in the two sections reinforce some of the features of his linguistic usage—modernization and straightforward prose style, in particular—as a step in the development of the Vercelli tradition of Judgement Day homilies.

Fadda X

While Vercelli XXI discussed above and Napier XL to be discussed later both draw very heavily upon Vercelli II, much briefer extracts from it (lines 56–66, 34–5, and 69–73)[60] are used in an anonymous homily traditionally known as Fadda X (*HomU* 15; Cameron No. B3.4.15),[61] re-edited more recently by Scragg as a variant text preserved in MS L (Hatton 115, fols. 140r-7r; s. xi²) of the ninth item in the Vercelli Collection of homilies.[62] Vercelli IX is called an eschatological homily,[63] but in fact it is far less concerned with the approaching end of the world or the Day of Judgement as such than either of the two other homilies derived from Vercelli II, let alone Vercelli II itself. It is more of 'a collection of religious themes for a hortatory purpose' and 'exhibits a series of linked themes',[64] particularly the torments and miseries of hell and the joys of heaven which are more often depicted in general terms.

This absence of effective reference to eschatological crisis as the unifying theme of the homily becomes even more marked in the revised version represented by Fadda X. Vercelli IX refers explicitly to Judgement Day twice, in the introduction in a not entirely unequivocal way[65] (*VercHom* 9.4 *læten we us singallice bion on gemyndum ⁊ on geþancum þæs egesfullican dæges tocyme, on ðam we sculon Gode riht agifan for ealles ures lifes dædum*) and the conclusion (9.206 *þencen*

---

[60] For details, see Scragg, *The Vercelli Homilies*, pp. 49–50 and 152–3.
[61] A. M. Luiselli Fadda (ed.), *Nuove Omelie Anglosassoni della Rinascenza Benedettina* (Florence, 1977), pp. 186–211. For convenience of reference, I use Fadda X as a short title for the homily, but citations from the work will be made from Scragg's recent edition; see below, n. 62.
[62] Scragg, *The Vercelli Homilies*, pp. 159–83.
[63] See Scragg, *The Vercelli Homilies*, p. 151.
[64] Szarmach, 'The Vercelli Homilies', p. 241.
[65] The equivocal nature of the first few lines of Vercelli IX is discussed in Gatch, 'Eschatology', 149–50.

*we togeanes his tocyme, þæt is se egesfullica dæg*⁶⁶ . . . *For þan þæt bið mycel scamu þæt man his sylfes scamige on þam myclan gemote*), but both references no longer appear in Fadda X, as it is provided with a new introduction and conclusion. Fadda X in turn has two references to Antichrist, both equating him with the devil, added in the expanded description of the horror of hell, which runs as below following the opening of the interpolated passage:

> Fadda X 110 Hwæt, þæt þonne bið sarlic sar ⁊ earmlic gedal lices ⁊ saule gif se earma innera mon, seo sawul, sceal slidan in þa ecean helle ⁊ in þa ecean witu mid ðone awergdan gast Antecrist, ⁊ þær mid deofle drohtnaþ habban, in morþre ⁊ in mane, in susle ⁊ in sare, on wean ⁊ on wyrmum, betweonan deaþum ⁊ deoflum, in bryne ⁊ on biternesse, in balwum ⁊ on bradum lege, in earmþum ⁊ on earfeþum, ⁊ on sweartum bryne ⁊ on swiltcwale . . . on arleasnesse ⁊ on missenlicum cynna witum, ⁊ in fæþme þæs beornendan dracan se þe is deoful cweden. Uton us for þon bewarnian þæt micle deoful Antecrist mid helle witum, . . .

These references to Antichrist are presumably prompted by the usage of the term in Vercelli II (though in its earlier part) on which the homily draws at this point. However, the idea is never developed, either for its significance as a sign of the coming end of the world or in any other way which would reflect the medieval tradition that has come to form around this figure.⁶⁷ Concomitantly, in what is the one explicit reference to Judgement Day in it, which is an addition made in an interesting passage to which I shall return, Fadda X speaks of the day as nothing imminent to the homilist and his audience, but something remote and conceived rather vaguely as part of an hypothetical comparison that is only posed to point up the horror of hell:

> Fadda X 91 þeah . . . ⁊ þonne [mon] gebinde þa fet þæs monnes to ufewardum þæm treo þe wære ane niht on helle, ⁊ him þonne læte hangian þæt heafod adun . . ., þonne wile he þis eall lustlice geþafian, þeah he scyle syx

---

⁶⁶ The word *domes* is inserted before *dæg* by a later hand; see Scragg, *The Vercelli Homilies*, p. 182, apparatus.

⁶⁷ On the history of the medieval Antichrist tradition, see Richard Kenneth Emmerson, *Antichrist in the Middle Ages: A Study of Medieval Apocalypticism, Art, and Literature* (Manchester, 1981); Bernard McGinn, *Antichrist: Two Thousand Years of the Human Fascination with Evil* (New York, 2000), pp. 79–142. The position that Antichrist is an incarnation of the devil is particularly evident in vernacular anonymous homilies in Old English, including Vercelli II and Vercelli XXI, according to Emmerson (pp. 82, 151, and 289 n. 11). Emmerson also notes that '[e]ven Ælfric and Wulfstan, more careful theologians, may have conceived of Antichrist as the devil incarnate' (p. 82), but adds that they held the standard exegetical position on the problem (pp. 150–5 and p. 268 n. 27). For a distinctive and more meaningful treatment of Antichrist in the concluding part of Napier XL based on Wulfstan's homily, see the next section of this chapter.

þusen[da] wintra ⁊ eac þæt ðusend þe domes dæg on gewyrþ, wið þon þe he næfre ma þa helle ne gesece.

These alterations made in Fadda X emphasize the fact that the homily has moved even more decisively than Vercelli IX away from the specific contexts of apocalypticism and the Last Judgement.

What gives Vercelli IX effective unity as a homily is, as has been pointed out repeatedly,[68] enumeration—enumeration of three kinds of death contrasted with three of life (lines 32–40), the inescapability and other qualities of death that awaits us all (lines 41–58), four levels of separation imposed by death (lines 68–83), five *onlicnessa* of hell (lines 84–113), and the terrors and miseries of hell (lines 131–7) which are balanced with the joys of heaven (lines 173–82). It is important to note that this reliance on lists, numbered and unnumbered, is more than a peculiarity of style of the prose of Vercelli IX. It shapes the structure of the homily and is itself functional to its theme and contents, as Szarmach has persuasively argued:

> The homilist's heavy reliance on the list as a rhetorical device to structure much of the first half of this work looks at first glance like mere mechanical schematizing. . . . But this particular double list of three [levels of death and life] is more than an aid to memory or an indication of monastic provenance. With this dichotomous list that opposes the undesirable to the desirable the homilist has begun to prepare his audience for the contrasting visions of the Theban legend [as told in the second half of the homily]. The audience will be ready to see things in terms of only two alternatives, the unspeakably horrible one and the inexpressibly joyful one, because the homilist arranges his materials, whenever he can, so that rhetorical order reflects moral choice. To give his audience the habit of thinking in extremes the homilist orders his paragraph on dreading death by using antithetical adjectives. . . . The play on subjective and objective senses of adjectives creates an antithetical point of view in the audience. Earning heaven and *gesæliglice* fleeing hell, the exhortation in the opening, are becoming a way of thinking as well as a subject of thought.[69]

As was suggested above, the compiler of Fadda X departed farther from the Judgement Day theme itself in favour of the lists which seem to have attracted him very much in Vercelli IX.[70] He retains all the lists, adding ones of deadly sins (lines 8–11) and seven *helle witu* (lines 14–17) in a new introduction of his own. It is also in his extended description of the torments of hell that he interpolates, in

---

[68] See Szarmach, 'The Vercelli Homilies', pp. 242–3; Scragg, *The Vercelli Homilies*, pp. 151–2; Gatch, 'Eschatology', 148–9.

[69] Szarmach, 'The Vercelli Homilies', pp. 242–3.

[70] See Scragg, *The Vercelli Homilies*, p. 153.

lines 106–33, a revised passage of extracts drawn from Vercelli II, which 'again consists largely of formulaic and repetitive lists'.[71]

The first half of the interpolated passage (lines 106–22) gives a list of the torments of hell which in fact represents a 'longer version' than the one surviving in Vercelli II (and its derivative Vercelli XXI); the latter's last portion of the list (*VercHom* 2.66 . . . *⁊ on fulnesse ⁊ on eallum þam witum þe dioflu gearwedon fram þære frymþe, þe hie to gesceapene wæron ⁊ hie sylfe geearnedon*) is replaced by a continued list. It is essentially the same version as the one in Napier XL,[72] in the continued list of torments as a whole (quoted for the most part as Fadda X 110 above) and in the details of its wording, such as *þæt læne lic þær weorþeð to fylnesse* (line 109, immediately preceding the quotation; *VercHom* 2.59 *gerotaþ to fulnesse*), *earmlic gedal lices ⁊ saule* (in the first line of the quotation; *VercHom* 2.61 *þæs lichaman ⁊ þære sawle*), *drohtnaþ habban*[73] (in the third line; *VercHom* 2.64 *drohtigan*), and the *gif*-clause (in the second line) to be discussed below, which is much shortened and simplified from *VercHom* 2.61. In all these, Fadda X agrees with Napier XL against Vercelli II.[74] On the other hand, Fadda X differs both from Napier XL and Vercelli II in other details of wording and grammar, including lines 108 *þenne þæm lænan lichoman bið laðlic legerbed gegearwod ⁊ in þære caldan foldan lið gebrosnod* (with its alliterative *lænan* and *lið* lacking in the other two but itself lacking the adverb *sona*, which is used in Napier XL 187.11), 110 *grimmum gylstre ⁊ þæm wælslitendan wyrmum to mete*[75] (Napier XL 187.13 *þam wælslitendum wyrmum weorðed to æte*; *VercHom* 2.60 *þam wælslitendan wyrmum to æte*) and, in the second line of the long quotation above, *in þa ecean helle ⁊ in þa ecean witu* (followed by a unique reference to Antichrist, as mentioned above), in contrast to a single *in*-phrase both in Napier XL and Vercelli II, and most notably the initial sentence of the interpolated passage (line 106); here, as we shall see later, Fadda X is close to Vercelli II but simplifies its syntax, while Napier XL rewrites it considerably. In the expanded list of torments itself, Fadda X contains a few additional words not in Napier XL and displays a different pattern of alternation

---

[71] Scragg, *The Vercelli Homilies*, p. 153.

[72] For Napier XL, I cite here from the P (Cotton Cleopatra B. xiii) version as edited by Napier (see n. 91), for convenience of reference. On the other three versions, see the next section of this chapter.

[73] The word *drohtnoþ*, as distinct from *drohtað* (as in the O (Hatton 114) version of Napier XL), seems to be a rare form in Old English. It is recorded in the Toronto Microfiche Concordance only three more times: in Napier XL (187.16, in a variant text of the passage being discussed), *GD* 2(C).1.98.3 and the poem *Andreas*, line 1402. Raynes thinks that it 'may be Anglian' ('Unpublished Homilies', p. clvii).

[74] But the O version of Napier XL agrees with the Vercelli text in the second example. See further the next section of this chapter (p. 97).

[75] The alliterative phrase *grimmum geolstre* occurs elsewhere only once, in another Vercelli homily (*VercHom* 4.126).

between *in* and *on*, using the latter preposition definitely more often than Napier XL. These differences would seem too substantial to be described as occasional departures on the part of Fadda X from Napier XL to which it otherwise kept fairly closely. On the contrary, Fadda X and Napier XL are probably derived independently from the original version of Vercelli II which contained the continued portion of the list omitted from Vercelli II and Vercelli XXI as they survive, as Scragg argues.[76] Scragg also notes that apart from the 'extra lines', Fadda X is 'verbally closer' to Vercelli II than to Napier XL.[77]

The process of transmission assumed above would also seem to be corroborated by the rest of the interpolated passage in Fadda X (lines 123–33) and its counterparts in the other versions. After a brief linking passage in which all three versions have a phraseology in common (*don/wyrcan god*) in slightly different constructions, they return to enumerating. But Napier XL becomes radically different from this point,[78] starting with 188.14 *Uton man and morðor æghwar forbugan*, against *Forlætan we morþor ⁊ man* (Fadda X *mæne aþas*) in the others, and going directly into the conclusion; one version of this homily (the N version in CCCC 419)[79] has three more words in the list in common with Fadda X and/or Vercelli II, but it uses them in different constructions and to different purposes, using one (*gifernes*) in a list of its own of the devil's eight crimes. By contrast, Vercelli II continues with a list of undesirable qualities starting with *morþor ⁊ man* as shown above. It is shorter than the one in Fadda X but is essentially the same list, on which Fadda X has obviously expanded, as in the earlier list, with its characteristic fondness for elaborate enumeration, even at the cost of a single word used twice (*oferfylle* in lines 127 and 128). Vercelli II and Fadda X again both conclude the list with a reference to other possible vices not included in it. In doing so, however, Fadda X does not refer to the *þeawas* imposed on men by the devil as in Vercelli II, but to the *synne* to which human flesh is very likely to succumb (Fadda X 131 *æghwylce synne þissum gelice þa þæm lichoman bið eaþe in to slidenne*), with the word *slidenne* perhaps echoing the earlier reference in the interpolated passage about the soul falling into hell (111 *gif se earma innera mon, seo sawul, sceal*

---

[76] Scragg, *The Vercelli Homilies*, pp. 49–50.

[77] Scragg, *The Vercelli Homilies*, p. 49. But the problem of the ultimate line of transmission might go even deeper, as Scragg himself suggests in an earlier study: 'The interpolation in L [Fadda X] is parallel to Napier XL, 187.7–188.10. A[the Vercelli Book]'s Vercelli II parallel with Napier XL ends at 188.2 . . . But after leaving Napier XL, L's interpolation continues briefly with A's Vercelli II (equivalent to Förster, lines 95–9). In other words L's text appears to derive either from a fuller version of Vercelli II than survives in A or from a version of Napier XL which had more of the original Vercelli II homily in it than surviving copies show' ('The corpus', 247 n. 8).

[78] See Förster, *Die Vercelli-Homilien*, p. 51, apparatus.

[79] For details of this and other manuscripts of Napier XL and their variant texts, see the next section of this chapter.

slidan in þa ecean helle). Finally, it has an extra sentence at the very end: Fadda X 132 *Þær bið ofergyten ealle þa god þa ðe men on eorþan ær lufedon*.

What is more striking stylistically is the way the essentially identical list just examined is presented in Vercelli II and Fadda X. Both versions of the list consist of alliterative words and phrases used in pairs, and here, if not elsewhere, Vercelli II emphasizes this arrangement by using these pairs as units, which are then, with few exceptions, juxtaposed one after another without a linking *and* between them (e.g. *VercHom* 2.72 *ærætas ⁊ ealogalnesse, dysinessa ⁊ gedweollcræftas, gitsunga ⁊ gifernessa*).[80] Fadda X's list is more discursive, with no attempt at grouping the words and phrases into such regular patterns but using *and* ('⁊') at almost every point between two words and phrases throughout the list. Napier XL (the N version) is very different from these. Its list of the devil's eight crimes is purely enumerative and hence not alliterative except by chance, and it simply repeats *and* for enumeration.

I referred above briefly to two sentences in Fadda X which simplify the syntax of their sources. One of them, Fadda X 111 (quoted in the last paragraph but one) does this by removing what is a clumsy repetition in the source text:

VercHom 2.61 gif þonne se earma innera man, þæt is seo werige sawl þe her forwyrht bið ⁊ agimeleasedu Godes beboda, þæt hio þonne æfter þan gedale aslidan scile in þa ecean helle witu, . . .

The source of the clumsiness is *þæt hio þonne* in the last clause, which recapitulates the subjects of the preceding clauses, as Max Förster points out.[81] Fadda X omits this recapitulating and hence pleonastic *þæt hio*, as well as the whole of the immediately preceding clause, except *seo sawul* in it, which now stands in apposition; it omits concomitantly both the first and second *þonne* in the source, which are perhaps rhythmical rather than logical. Here Napier XL goes along almost identical lines, omitting even the appositive construction while retaining *þonne* at the beginning of the *gif*-clause (187.15 *gif þonne seo sawl huru slidan sceal* . . .); for more details of this revision, see Chapter III (pp. 43-4).

In the other example, however, based on *VercHom* 2.56 *we us ne ondrædaþ þæt we dæghwamlice geseoð beforan urum eagum, nu we þam oðrum ne gelyfaþ, ure neahstan swelta[n]*, Napier XL (187.8–11; see Chapter III, p. 45) and Fadda X (106–7) proceed quite differently. As I have argued in Chapter III, this Vercelli II sentence might have been open to misinterpretation as a boast ('We do not dread; why should we?'), not warning ('We do not dread as much as we should'), given

---

[80] Vercelli II does not always show as much regularity in following this pattern but often simply repeats the conjunction *and*, as in the 'metrical' passage. It is Napier XL which adheres to the pattern rigidly in rewriting this passage. See Chapter III, p. 42.

[81] Förster says: 'Der Satz würde glätter, wenn man *þæt hio þonne* striche. Vielleicht hat aber der Übersetzer nach dem Zwischensatze damit das Subjekt wieder aufnehmen wollen. Das *þæt* möchte man aber demnach jedenfalls entbehren' (*Die Vercelli-Homilien*, p. 50 n. 47).

the unqualified statement *we us ne ondrædaþ* and the causal *nu*-clause which increases, if anything, the ambiguity. Perhaps with a view to alleviating this problem, the compiler of Napier XL rewrites the sentence wholesale in his logical way.[82] In comparison with this, the compiler of Fadda X contents himself with a simple and easy way out; he omits the troublesome *nu*-clause entirely, while adding the adverb *huruþinga* 'especially', presumably to emphasize negation. It looks as if he was insensitive to the ambiguity that might have still remained in the phrase *we us ne ondrædaþ* itself. In rewriting syntax, as in frequent enumeration, he is practical-minded, and his concern is always with simple, straightforward statements regardless of subtleties and nuances of meaning or style.

In fact, simplifying syntax, both on the sentence level and beyond it, is a feature of the compiler's style which can be seen more widely in Fadda X as it modifies the original homily represented by Vercelli IX. Scragg has noted 'the simplification of A[Vercelli IX].27–30 in L[Fadda X].31–2 and of A.59–82 in L.56–66'.[83] Other examples in long stretches of clauses may be studied with respect to the compiler's use of the syntactic pattern 'þeah . . ., þeah *or* hwæðere . . .', with this invariable order of subordinate and main clauses, of which there are five examples, viz. Fadda X 84–8 and 160–70, besides the three discussed below. They are all derived, with different degrees of modification, from sentences in Vercelli IX, apart from one for which this latter homily happens to offer no parallel text, because of a missing leaf in the codex. I have referred in an earlier chapter to this last example,[84] comparing it with the Napier XXX version and other renderings of this passage of the anchorite and devil story (also known as 'The Devil's Account of the Next World'[85]) in which it occurs. As I showed there, in making the devil tell how the horror of a single night in hell so oppresses the soul that no din surrounding it, however great, can awaken it, our Hatton 115 version arrives at a less readable sentence structure[86] than the rendering in Napier XXX, not least because of an extended sequence of *and*-clauses piled up for about ten lines within the *þeah*-clause before it reaches the main clause. Even the explanatory clauses about Samson (who is introduced abruptly as a prototype of a man of great strength) are treated in this way:

---

[82] See Chapter III, pp. 45-6. See also the previous section of this chapter, where Vercelli XXI's treatment of the sentence in question was considered.

[83] Scragg, *The Vercelli Homilies*, p. 152 n. 6.

[84] See Chapter II, pp. 27–28.

[85] See Chapter II, n. 52.

[86] For a similar quality of the original prose of Vercelli IX, see further lines 114–15, where Förster detects a possibility of 'eine plumpe Nachahmung einer lateinischen Periode' ('Der Vercelli–Codex CXVII nebst Abdruck einiger altenglischer Homilien der Handschrift', *Studien zur englischen Philologie* 50 (1913), 20–179, at 109).

Fadda X 140 Þeah mon þone garsecg mid isernum weallum utan betyne, . . . ꝥ sy to ælcum þara man togeset ꝥ ælc þara manna hæbbe Samsones strenge (ꝥ se Samson ealle F[i]llestina þeode gererde ꝥ heora duguþe afylde, ꝥ he hæfde twelf loccas ꝥ on ælcum locce he hæfde twelf manna mægen) ꝥ man þonne sette . . ., hweþere for eallum þyssum gedyne ne mæg seo sawl awacian seo þe wæs ær ane niht on helle.

Here Napier XXX and the Tiberius A. iii version are more structured, using relative clauses for the description of Samson.[87] Our compiler, more than those of these latter two versions, simplifies the syntax of the passage, focussing upon the rhetoric of the 'þeah . . ., hwæþere' pattern, which the piled-up *and*–clauses within it are made to enhance.

Another example illustrates the compiler's use of the concessive pattern in a different way:

Fadda X 42 ꝥ se deaþ is to ondrædanne for þon nænig mon nis þæt hine mæge befleon. Þeah se mon eardige on middum burgum ꝥ on middan his mægþe betweoh hundteontigum þusenda manna mid wepnes ecgum, ꝥ þeah he si hundteontig þusenda fæþma under eorþan in iserne cyste belocen, hwæþere he sceal sweltan.

Instead of piling up *and*–clauses within the *þeah*-clause, the compiler condenses the corresponding passage in Vercelli IX (lines 41–50) by, *inter alia*, combining into a single unit of concession (*þeah . . . ꝥ þeah . . ., hwæþere . . .*) what are separate sentences in the original homily:

VercHom 9.42 ꝥ he is for þan nyðerlic, se deað, þeah se man gewite in ða neowelestan scrafa ꝥ on þa deoppestan dene þe on middangearde sy, þonne sceal he þeahhwæðere sweltan. . . . ꝥ he is for þan mænigfealdlic, þeah se man eardige in middum burgum ꝥ on midre his mægðe ꝥ betweox hundteontegum þusenda manna, þonne sceal he hwæðere sweltan.

It may also be noted that in the process the compiler not only omits the intervening sentences in Vercelli IX (lines 45–7)[88] but simplifies the structure of the two retained sentences themselves, doing without the anacoluthic *he is forþan* . . . in both, with the total effect of emphasizing the simple logic of the inescapability of death.

But perhaps most revealing is the other example describing the horror of hell, in which the two features illustrated above come together. The compiler first

---

[87] The Corpus version omits the description about Samson; see Chapter II, p. 28.

[88] Scragg (*The Vercelli Homilies*, p. 152 n. 6) speaks of the entire omission of Vercelli IX, lines 42–8 (including the first sentence (ꝥ *he is. . . sweltan*) of *VercHom* 9.42 quoted above) here. This last sentence is admittedly not very close verbally to the second *þeah*-clause in Fadda X. But the idea seems similar in both renderings.

simplifies the narrative, as Scragg notes,[89] by omitting about the same length (*VercHom* 9.115–22) from the passage, and then goes on:

> Fadda X 90 ⁊ þeah þæt lengost treow stonde on middangearde on þæm hehstan clife oððe munte, ⁊ þonne [mon] gebinde þa fet þæs monnes to ufewardum þæm treo þe wære ane niht on helle, ⁊ him þonne læte hangian þæt heafod adun þæt him sige þæt blod on syx healfa ut þurh þone muþ, ⁊ hine þær sece elc þara yfla þe æfre on eorþan fram [anginne secgean gehyrde] ⁊ hine þonne þa sæyþa cnyson ⁊ beaten þe heo mid hire brogan forþbringæþ, þonne wile he þis eall lustlice geþafian, þeah he scyle syx þusen[da] wintra ⁊ eac þæt ðusend þe domes dæg on gewyrþ, wið þon þe he næfre ma þa helle ne gesece.

As in the example from the 'Devil's Account', the opening *þeah*-clause has a long sequence of *and*-clauses embedded in it, most of them derived from the original passage in Vercelli IX. But the compiler makes it longer by combining into this prolonged single concessive relationship what are two sets of subordinate and main clauses (*gif. . ., þonne . . .*; and *þeah . . ., þonne . . .*) in Vercelli IX; the first of these in fact expresses what is a concession in our passage (*þeah . . . him þonne læte hangian . . .*) in a different kind of subordination, not as something to be endured but something more desirable (*þonne bið him leofre . . . þæt he hangie . . .*):

> *VercHom* 9.122 For þan gif hwylc man bið on helle ane niht, þonne bið him leofre, gif he þanon mot, þæt he hangie siofon þusend wintra on þam lengestan treowe ufeweardum þe ofer sæ standeð on þam hyhstan sæclife,[90] ⁊ syn þa fet gebundene to ðam hehstan telgan . . . ⁊ þeah hine ælc tor gesece þe on eallum clyfum syndon, þonne wile he eall þis luflice þrowian wið ðan þe he næfre eft helle ne gesece.

By telescoping the original passage in this way, the compiler simplifies not only its syntax but also its sense. To reinforce the telescoping, he inserts a second *þeah*-clause (*þeah he scyle . . .*) after the main clause. But central to his rearrangement of the Vercelli IX material is the concessive pattern (here varied as 'þeah . . ., þonne . . .'), which structures his rhetoric; it is almost a habit of mind for him. It is in this fundamental sense an important part of his style, as much as his fondness for enumeration.

The concessive pattern and enumeration may be syntactically very different. But both show the compiler's habit of thinking in formulaic terms. It is this habit which gives his composition at once a unity and a distinctness of style not shared by any of the other homilies in the Vercelli tradition of the Judgement

---

[89] Scragg, *The Vercelli Homilies*, p. 152 n. 6.
[90] The Vercelli Book lacks a leaf after *sæclife*; the text after this is supplied from Bodley 340, as in Scragg's edition.

Day theme. And it may be precisely this habit of mind which led the compiler to turn where he did for material for interpolation—passages from Vercelli II which consist largely of enumeration and enabled him to deploy the quality of the prose style so characteristic of him.

Napier XL — Variation and Development

A third ramification of the Vercelli tradition of Judgement Day homilies is the anonymous homily usually referred to as Napier XL (*HomU* 32; Cameron No. B3.4.32.3), which is preserved in four manuscripts: British Library, Cotton Cleopatra B. xiii (P, s. xi 3rd quarter), CCCC 419 (N, s. xi[1]), CCCC 201 (X[d], s. xi[med]), and Bodleian Library, Hatton 114 (O, s. xi 3rd quarter).[91] The first of these versions as the base text of the homily was discussed in full detail in comparison with its sources in an earlier chapter of this book, and how Napier XL rewrites Vercelli II where it draws upon it need not be our main concern here. It suffices to say that Napier XL is a revision by a 'pedantic adapter' who has left his mark first in the 'pedantic' additions of two biblical quotations in Latin and of a biblical account of Judgement Day, and, linguistically, in a style which uses terse, controlled prose with precise syntax and poetic rhythm and which looks backward to the old style in the Old English vernacular prose tradition. It is my concern in this section to examine how these developments from Vercelli II were subject to further variation and developments as the homily came to survive in its present four versions.

Textual relationships among the four versions are complicated. There are two introductions and conclusions respectively, shared by different groupings of manuscripts: one introduction is shared by O and P and the other by N and X[d], while OPX[d] have in common a conclusion. Within the common core of the homily drawing upon Vercelli II, the four versions contain about seventy variant readings, which collectively show that the relationship is not one of immediate

---

[91] The editions used are: Arthur Napier, *Wulfstan: Sammlung der ihm zugeschriebenen Homilien nebst Untersuchungen über ihre Echtheit* (Berlin, 1883; 2nd edn. with a bibliographical appendix by Klaus Ostheeren, Dublin and Zurich, 1967), pp. 182–90 (P, emended on the evidence of the other manuscripts); Scragg, *The Vercelli Homilies*, pp. 53–65 (N); Stanley, '*The Judgement of the Damned*', pp. 370–8 (X[d]). References to these editions are to page and/or line, as appropriate, preceded by the manuscript siglum; citation for the X[d] version will be made with reference to the line number on the printed page and not to the editor's own marginal line numbering, since this refers to each fifth manuscript line and is difficult to make out for any words that come in between. The Hatton version (O) is unedited, and for reference I use my own transcription made from the manuscript on microfilm; see Appendix. The sigla for the manuscripts are Scragg's ('The corpus', 225–64).

dependence between the manuscripts. The variant readings are alterations as well as errors and apparent omissions which are sometimes unique to single manuscripts but are often shared by different combinations of manuscripts, either in agreement with or against the Vercelli II text. On the evidence of these variant readings, Jonathan Wilcox assumes the following stemma for the four manuscripts:[92]

N   X^d O   P

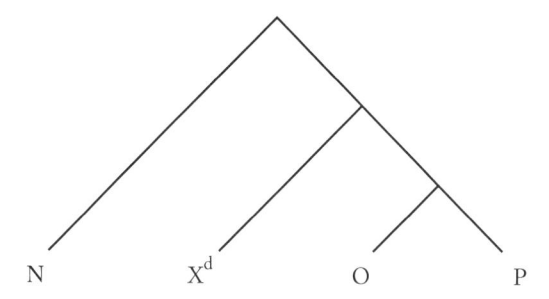

These complicated relationships determine the nature of the examination to be made in this section. One can hardly hope to compare the four manuscripts with each other to see how the text of one manuscript rewrites another, since none of them is immediately related to another, nor do we know the texts of the shared exemplars which are assumed to have existed at some points in the stemma above. Instead, I shall mainly examine the N version in comparison with P, with observations where appropriate on the others, because N is evidently a later adaptation. Still, the adaptation is mostly of the introduction and conclusion; in the main body of the homily N does not always show readings which are later, as Scragg aptly reminds us:

> OPX^d have in their conclusion a sentence from the end of [Vercelli] homily II, and it is therefore likely that they represent the earlier composite piece, N being a later adaptation of it. But in the main body of material derived from homily II, NX^d are closer to the anonymous homily than are OP in two readings.[93]

What we have before us in the four versions of Napier XL is thus mostly variation, not a record of successive stages of revising the homily. What little evidence we may have of the development of the homily is to be found in the later

---

[92] Wilcox, 'The Compilation', p. 85. For an older hypothesis in which the three versions NOX^d are assumed to share an exemplar, see Richard Becher, *Wulfstans Homilien* (Leipzig diss., 1910), p. 78.

[93] Scragg, *The Vercelli Homilies*, pp. 48–9.

substitutions for the original introduction and conclusion (as represented by OP and N, respectively). One might also expect to find in a few fortunate cases evidence for peculiarities of linguistic usage on the part of any of the revisers, and these might be of importance in the history of the language and the tradition of vernacular prose writing of the period.

We may begin with variant readings in the main body of the homily. There are about fifty of these between N and P. In some, N's reading is confirmed by OX[d], suggesting that P probably represents errors which arose in transmission, as in N 80 *we nu ungesælige synd þæt we us bet ne warniað ⁊ þæt we ne ondrædað us* ... (P 187.8 *we us bet ne warniað þæt we ne ondrædað us* ...), and N 10 *⁊ þæs hym naht ne ondrædað ac hym orsorh lætað* (where P 182.14 lacks the *ac*-clause). Scragg sees homoeoteleuton in P in this last example.[94] The same reason might explain the omission in P of *ne þæs eaðes ne þæs earfoðes*, which occurs as a member of five alliterating antitheses in NOX[d]: N 43 *ne* ... *þæs hates ne þæs cealdes, ne þæs heardes ne þæs hnesces, ne þæs wraðes ne þæs wynsumes, ne þæs eaðes ne þæs earfoðes, ne þæs leofes ne þæs laðes*. Neither reading is confirmed by the Vercelli text which has three antitheses (the first two and the last of N). But it would seem more likely to have been a case of original expansion into five followed by omission, perhaps by homoeoteleuton, by the P scribe, than a later addition to the original series of four antitheses. In all three cases Arthur Napier restores the readings of NOX[d] in his edition of the homily based on P (at 187.8, 182.14, and 185.1, respectively).

Napier also emends, on the evidence of NOX[d], the manuscript reading of P *ealle on þam dæge arisað of deaðe* as 183.14 *eall þy dæge ariseð*. However, P's reading here might be a result of revision on the part of its compiler, particularly because it echoes the preceding sentence (183.11 *þonne ealle men arisað of deaðe*) to which the clause in question might have been intended to be parallel. At all events the source sentence in Vercelli II (lines 13–15) — an asyndesis of three clauses whose relation to each other is not clarified by a confusing alternation of sg. *eal* and pl. *ealle* within them — might have been a problem, as I have argued in Chapter III, which the original compiler of the homily as well as later revisers felt they should sort out in their own ways.[95]

One may assume a similar process of revision for what is perhaps the most substantial difference between N and P in the common main body of the homily, involving transposition of whole sentences:

> P 187.4 and þa synfullan þonne woldon geswican georne, gif hig mihton; and him þonne wære leofre, þonne eall middaneard to æhte geseald, þæt hy næfre acennede wæron fram fæder and meder.

---

[94] Scragg, *The Vercelli Homilies*, p. 53, apparatus.
[95] For details, see Chapter III, p. 43 and n. 17.

N 76 ⁊ þa synfullan þonne woldan [X^d woldon þonne] gewi[s]can [*MS* geswican; O gewiscean, X^d gewiscan, *corrected from* geswican[96]] georne gif hy mihton þæt hy næfre acennede ne wæron [O næron, X^d ne wurdon] fram fæder ne meder [OX^d ne fram meder]. And him þæt þonne wære leofre þonne eall middaneard to æhte geseald.

The revision on the part of P seems to have originated from a confusion (witnessed by the forms in N and X^d) between *geswican* and *gewiscan*, as Scragg explains:

> *gewiscan* is confirmed by A[Vercelli II]a[Vercelli XXI], though the ancestor of NOPX^d almost certainly had *geswican*, and in O an intelligent copyist has presumably substituted *gewiscean*. P solves the problem posed by *gewiscan* be [*sic*] rewriting this and the following sentence.[97]

As a product of this complicated process, the revision in P 187.4 may be a good example showing how substantial changes could have been made in transmission to the homily.

Other possible examples of later revisions made in P to the original text of Napier XL include 184.8 *Þæt is on englisc* (NOX^d *on ure gepeode*) and 184.17 *þæt ece fyr, þe wæs deofle gegearwod and eallum his geferum*, where N as well as OX^d has a rather striking wording: N 41 . . . *þe wæs deoflum gegearwod ⁊ his gegencgum eallum*. The use of *eall* in post-nominal position is unusual in Old English.[98] So is the word *gegenge*, particularly in reference to Satan's troop of fallen angels; it is recorded in this sense only twice elsewhere, once, it is interesting to observe, by Wulfstan (*WHom* 5.112).[99] P also has sg. *deofle* agreeing with the following *his*, where NOX^d have pl. *deoflum*, despite *his* being left unaltered. The P reviser might have wanted to change all these details of wording in line with a more normal usage of his day, though it is not possible in the absence of further evidence to be certain of this. Similarly, P has *to* in post-position in 184.16 *heom to cwyð* against NOX^d *to heom cwyð*, and the relative pronoun *þe* (188.10) in place of NOX^d *se*. But again, it is not possible to say with certainty whether or not these alternatives in P indicate its reviser's own preference and what significance if any they have in the development of these details of grammar of the language.

---

[96] I owe this information to Stanley, '*The Judgement of the Damned*', p. 374, apparatus.

[97] Scragg, *The Vercelli Homilies*, pp. 67–8. See Chapter III, p. 45.

[98] See *OES*, §453. N has another example of postposed *eall*, in a sentence based upon Wulfstan: ⁊ [*mid*] þam unwrencan eallan (line 115); on this sentence, see n. 140.

[99] The other example occurs in the Benedictine Office (*LitBen* 7.1 (Ure) 82.10), a work in which Wulfstan is generally thought to have had a hand. But whether the use of this Wulfstanian item of vocabulary in our anonymous homily is anything more than an accident is uncertain. The word is rare in other uses too, with four examples, mostly from late prose. I owe all this information about the word to the DOE Electronic Corpus and its Microfiche Concordance.

The second, and most frequent, kind of variation between N and P is represented by those examples in which N's reading is shared by X^d against OP—an important pattern which speaks very positively for the relationship of the four manuscripts as summarized by Wilcox in the stemma shown earlier. Here it is often difficult to see what the difference would mean in the textual history of the homily, unless supported by other evidence. In one case, N 46 *þæt hy þonne mæge fram ures drihtnes lufan asceadan* and P 185.2 *þæt hig þonne mihte . . .*, the former reading, paralleled in X^d, is confirmed by the Vercelli II text, as Scragg has pointed out.[100] The evidence goes to the contrary with regard to preposition usage in N 24 *singað þa byman on þam feower sceatum middaneardes* and P 183.11 *of þam feower sceatum middaneardes* (*VercHom* 2.12 *of*). Scragg argues that here OP represents one of the two 'coincidental changes' made to the original version of the homily, not a direct derivation from the Vercelli text, since 'A [Vercelli II] *of* is in a slightly different syntactic context from OP *of*'.[101] This might well be so. One might wonder, however, whether the syntactic difference apparently being referred to—concerning usage of the demonstratives within the *of*-phrase, between Vercelli *of .iiii. sceattum þyses middangeardes* and OP as above—would be directly relevant; addition of a demonstrative before a noun, for example, might have been made independently of preposition usage in OP, as in P 184.4 *þa Judeas*. One would rather feel inclined to ask if OP *of* does not come from the Vercelli text and NX^d *on* is a revision, perhaps as a result of a general preference for that preposition in these versions. But the revision would seem more likely to have been made independently,[102] since N and X^d differ in the extent to which they consistently prefer the preposition, as we shall see shortly.

One might think that the same process of transmission accounts for the other example where the reading in OP agrees with that in the Vercelli source against NX^d: P 184.18 *þonne þam synfullum pinceð* (*VercHom* 2.20 *þam synfullan*) and N 43 *firenfullan*/X^d *firenfullum*. Here, however, it is perhaps more likely that the agreement may be 'coincidental', as Scragg argues, noting that '*synful* and *firenful* alternate throughout the homily in all versions'.[103] The point is explained in greater detail by Wilcox:

---

[100] Scragg, *The Vercelli Homilies*, p. 49 n. 1; id., 'The corpus', 251 n. 2.

[101] Scragg, *The Vercelli Homilies*, p. 49 n. 1.

[102] One might perhaps argue alternatively that N and X^d share an exemplar from which the use of *on* here, if not always elsewhere, derives, supposing a line of transmission similar in part to the one proposed by Becher; see n. 92. However, this would definitely contradict the fact that N alone has sentences which are omitted from X^d as well as from OP; for some such examples see below. For another reading shared by N and X^d, one involving an apparent 'error' in inflectional ending (*ða(m) ece hellewitu*), see below, p. 94.

[103] Scragg, *The Vercelli Homilies*, p. 49 n. 1.

However, an examination of the other uses of words for 'sinful' in this homily indicates that N and X^d may not share a revision at this point. There are three other such occurrences in those parts of Napier XL drawn from Vercelli II. In each case Vercelli II (contained at the relevant places in two manuscripts) has the word *fyrenful-*, while all four manuscripts of Napier XL have *synful-* (Nap. XL, 184/2, Verc. II, 20; Nap. XL, 185/8, Verc. II, 30; Nap. XL, 187/4, Verc. II, 74). It seems that the compiler of Napier XL felt free to vary these synonyms almost at random. Napier XL does not always reject *fyrenful-*: it is used in a passage not based on Vercelli II at 184/14. The freedom with which this word was altered in copying is indicated also by the variation between *fyren* in N, X^d, and P and *synn* in O at Napier XL 186/16. Hence it is probable that at 184/18 the author of Napier XL altered Vercelli II's *synfullan* to *fyrenfullan* and that O and P share in *synfullum* a variant which happens to coincide with the original reading of Vercelli II.[104]

Turning back to variants where NX^d are closer to the Vercelli source text than OP, there are two other occurrences that have been discussed as such. But a closer examination seems to suggest that these do not go back directly to the Vercelli text, either. This may be seen more readily in the alleged relationship[105] between *VercHom* 2.28 *[manna] mod . . . æfre lætan sculon þæt deaþberende dioful . . . hie to þam gedwellan þæt hie synne fremmen 7 þæs willan ne wyrceaþ*, and:

N 55 . . . hy to ðam gedwellan þæt hy swa micle synna gefremmen swa hy nu doð 7 þæs willan ne gewyrcan,

X^d 372.24 . . . hi to ðam gedwelle,[106] þæt hi swa micle sinne fremman swa hi nu doð 7 þæs willan ne wyrcan,

---

[104] Wilcox, 'The Compilation', p. 85. The last sentence but one has the following footnote: '[106] It may also explain the nonsensical error in X^d at 188/4, where the word *fyrenum* in N and OP (here in the sense 'fiery') has been copied as *syrenum* in X^d, perhaps because the scribe at first intended to write *synnum*.' Wilcox's references to Vercelli II are to Förster's edition.

[105] See Scragg, *The Vercelli Homilies*, p. 49 n. 1; id., 'The corpus', 251 n. 2.

[106] This is Stanley's emendation from MS *gedwellan*, as in the other manuscripts. Discussing the syntax of the clause leading to this manuscript form of the verb (*hi æfre sculon læton þæt deaðberende deofol mid ungemættre costnunge hi to ðam gedwellan*), Stanley says: 'The construction is mixed, confusing *þæt hi . . . sculon lætan deaðberende deofol . . . hi to ðam gedwellan, þæt . . .* , "that they must suffer the mortiferous devil to seduce them to this, that", with *þæt hi . . . sculon lætan þæt deaðberende deofol . . . hi to ðam gedwelle, þæt . . .* , "that they must suffer that the mortiferous devil seduce them to this, that"; the latter is easier syntax, and a stage of subj. sg. with *-en* for *-e* may underlie *-an* of *gedwellan* in the extant manuscripts' ('*The Judgement of the Damned*', p. 372, note to his lines 10–11). Stanley apparently takes the *þæt* immediately preceding *deaðberende deofol* to be a conjunction. But it might well be a demonstrative; *deofol* as a neuter noun is not uncommon (see BT

where the other versions read:

> P 185.14 . . . hig to þan gedwellan, þæt hy swa mycele synna fremman, swa hy nu doð, and nellað þæs willan gewyrcan,

> O 44 . . . hy to ðan gedwellan. þæt hy swa mycle synna fremmen swa swa hi nu doð. ⁊ nellað þæs willan gewyrcan . . .

It might be argued that NX^d are closer than OP to the Vercelli text in that they lack *nellað* on which the verb *(ge)wyrcan* depends in OP. But what seems to be more important is the fact that where the Vercelli source has discontinuous verb forms in the *þæt*-clause (*fremmen* (subj.) . . . *wyrceað* (ind.)), Napier XL corrects this in all versions, though in two different ways, represented respectively by NX^d (where *(ge)wyrcan* is parallel to *gefremmen/fremman*, not to *doð*, and should be subjunctive) and OP (where *nellað . . . gewyrcan* is parallel to *doð* as part of the *swa (swa)*-clause). NX^d may therefore be no closer to the Vercelli text than OP. The two groups may both represent a revision of the source text, and the variation they show between them is probably part of the history of the Napier XL homily itself, though which of them represents its original reading remains uncertain.

The other example is a case of varying vocabulary items, as between NX^d *hellewitu* (N 86 *in ða ece helle witu*, X^d 376.8 *in ðam ece hellewitu*), confirmed by the Vercelli source (*VercHom* 2.63 *in þa ecean helle witu*), and OP *witu/wita*, as Wilcox notes.[107] What Wilcox does not note is the fact that there is still a sense in which NX^d are not closer to the Vercelli homily here. The adjective modifying the relevant noun in NX^d is in an irregular, uninflected form after the demonstrative *ða(m)* as above, as against the expected *ecan* in OP. The form *ece* has passed unnoticed by the editors of the N and X^d versions, but it might well be an error for the weak plural *ecan* (acc. in N) or *ecum* (dat. in X^d).[108] Whether error

---

and Clark Hall, s.v.). Under this interpretation, there would be no need to assume confusion in syntax nor emendation of the MS form, for which a rather complicated process of alternating inflectional endings would have to be posited.

[107] Wilcox, 'The Compilation', p. 84.

[108] And, in X^d, *hellewitu* might be an error for *hellewitum*, unless it were an insignificant variant spelling for *hellewite* (sg. dat.), in which case *ecan* would be the appropriate form of the adjective. But this is unlikely, since there is no example of such confusion of inflectional vowels in the manuscript, as far as I am aware. As for the adjective itself, no uninflected form is recorded in *DOE* (s.v *ece* Adj., Att. sp.) as neut. acc. or dat. pl., either weak or strong. In any event, there seems to be some confusion which might have arisen in transmission. On the other hand, P *wita* of course represents a form for the neut. acc. pl. ending in -*u*, which is not uncommon in late Old English manuscripts. For another aspect of irregular morphology in late Old English, see examples of a strong adjective after a demonstrative, such as *ÆCHom* i. 2.44 *on þisum dæigþerlicum dæge*, 2.55 *þam heofenlicum cyninge*, and 2.194 *þam ælmihtigum scyppende*. On this problem, see *OES*,

or not, it is hard to imagine that this irregular form was used independently in N and X[d], all the more so because in an earlier line of almost identical wording, N and X[d] both have the regular weak form *ecan*, in common with OP: N 52/X[d] 372.20 *in þa ecan tintregu helle wites*. One would have to assume that the 'ancestor' of the present four versions contained this 'error', which was later corrected in OP, or alternatively that despite Wilcox's stemma of manuscripts shown earlier and the evidence that supports it, N and X[d] might share an exemplar which contained that irregularity. The latter possibility is as yet very slight. But it might be worth considering together with some other material of possible relevance.[109]

While in the previous groups of examples N shares with at least one other version a reading which differs from that of P, N also contains errors and other kinds of reading of its own. The force of these unique readings is summarized in Wilcox's stemma given earlier, showing N representing a line of transmission in which OPX[d] do not share. Thus, N (lines 66 and 95) alone lacks a phrase and a word, *seo sare sorh* and *on*, as in P 186.9 and 188.9, which are required metrically in the 'metrical passage' describing the horror of Judgement Day and which are confirmed by Vercelli II. It also has two sentences which are omitted, perhaps by homoeoteleuton, from the other versions[110] but which again go back to Vercelli II:

> N 11 In ðam dæge gewiteð sunnan leoht ⁊ monan leoht ⁊ þæt leoht eallra tungla, ⁊ ures drihtnes rod bið blode beurnen betwux weolcnum ⁊ middanearde. On þam dæge ures drihtnes andwlita bið on wunderlicum hiwe, ⁊ wundor bið æteowed eallum mannum on þam andwlitan, and þa Iudeas magon geseon þonne þæne ðe hy ær swungon ⁊ heora spatlum on spiwon.

> *VercHom* 2.6 ⁊ on þam dæge gewit sunnan leoht ⁊ monan leoht ⁊ þa leoht ealra tungla. ⁊ on þam dæge bið drihtnes rod blode flowende betweox wolcnum, ⁊ in þam dæge bið dryhtnes onsyn swiðe egeslicu ⁊ ondryslicu ⁊ on þam hiwe þe he wæs þa hine Iudeas swungon ⁊ ahengon ⁊ hiora spatlum him on spiwon.

The sentences are thus probably an original part of the Napier XL homily.[111] If so, they are important as a unique addition to the evidence showing how the original compiler of the homily modified his source text. Most important are the word order SV used from the second clause onwards (where the Vercelli text consistently has VS), and the preposition *in* in place of Vercelli *on* and vice versa once

---

§118; Susan Irvine, 'Linguistic Peculiarities in Late Copies of Ælfric and their Editorial Implications', *Essays on Anglo-Saxon and Related Themes in Memory of Lynne Grundy*, ed. Jane Roberts and Janet Nelson (London, 2000), pp. 237–57, esp. p. 243.

[109] There are other sets of readings which Scragg finds would not agree with the assumed relationship of the manuscripts; see n. 121.

[110] See Scragg, *The Vercelli Homilies*, p. 49.

[111] See Wilcox, 'The Compilation', p. 84.

each; rewriting the preposition is also seen in P.[112] In the linkage of the three sentences marked by the initial *on/in þam dæge* in the source, N omits the temporal phrase itself (before *ures drihtnes rod* in the second line) and *and* ('ꝛ') preceding the temporal phrase (after *middanearde* in the third line). In this, it again parallels P in making revisions beyond the sentence level, though the way it does this in this short stretch of clauses seems to differ from P's revision, which is apparently made in terms of distinct scenes.[113] Variation in these grammatical details, particularly in the use of *and* and *in/on*, will be given further consideration as we compare other passages in all versions with respect to these features later. It should also be noted that in place of the antepenultimate clause in the Vercelli passage above (ꝛ *in þam dæge bið dryhtnes onsyn . . . on þam hiwe*), the compiler has two clauses expanding it (*On þam dæge ures drihtnes andwlita bið on wunderlicum hiwe,* ꝛ *wundor bið . . . on þam andwlitan*), with *andwlita* and *wundor/wunderlic* as the key words linking them and moulding them as a meaningful expansion. Here, as elsewhere in the homily, the compiler shows his sense of methodical rewriting in terse, well-controlled prose.

Other minor examples of unique readings in N include three vocabulary items (N 29 *bocum*, OX^d/P 184.7 *halgum gewritum*; N 37 *cwædon*, OX^d/P 184.11 *sædon*; and N 43 *nan þing*, OX^d/P 184.19 *nan wiht*, the latter confirmed by VercHom 2.21 *noht*) and a regular dative form (N 40 *on dæge*) in place of the endingless one or 'endingless locative', as Alistair Campbell calls it,[114] in OX^d/P 184.15 *on dæg*. In all these, N presumably represents a revision of the reading preserved in the other versions, as the agreement of these latter with the Vercelli text in the third example suggests. So probably, for the same reason, does the omission of *eaðe* in N 48 *nu hy magon*, from OX^d/P 185.5 *nu hi* [O *hy*] *eaðe magon* (*VercHom* 2.23 *nu we eaðe magon*), though whether the omission is by error or not is impossible to tell.[115]

So the comparison of N (often reinforced by either one or both of O and X^d) and P reveals much variation in the precise wording of the text which has arisen

---

[112] For details, see Chapter III, p. 38.

[113] See Chapter III, p. 42.

[114] Alistair Campbell, *Old English Grammar* (Oxford, 1959), §572. See also Ashley Crandell Amos and Antonette diPaolo Healey, 'The Dictionary of Old English: The Letter "D"', *Problems of Old English Lexicography: Studies in Memory of Angus Cameron*, ed. Alfred Bammesberger (Regensburg, 1985), pp. 13–38, esp. p. 15 and n. 34; *DOE* s.v. *dæg*. But the form in question could be an example of the accusative after *on*. Cf. *ÆCHom* i. 4.248 *Nu on sunnandæg mines æristes dæge*; on this alternation of *dæg* and *dæge*, see Frederic G. Cassidy and Richard N. Ringler, *Bright's Old English Grammar and Reader*, 3rd edn. (New York, 1971), p. 237, note to lines 288f.

[115] See Wilcox, 'The Compilation', p. 84. In the immediately preceding clause, N and X^d lack the phrase *be sumon dæle*, which is probably an addition made in O/P 185.4 *nellað nu þæt geþencan ne his willan be sumon dæle wyrcan*; cf. *VercHom* 2.23 *nu nellaþ his willan wyrcean*.

through transmission either by error or as revision, but very little change of substance, and still less that would tell us about changing linguistic usage and different styles which could have been embodied in the four versions as they represent different stages of the Vercelli tradition of Judgement Day homilies and of the Old English tradition of vernacular prose.

If we turn to the versions in O and X^d as the primary texts for comparison, we seem to find some evidence for the last category of difference just mentioned. For example, O uses the Wulfstanian indicative *syn* (line 67)[116] (NX^d *synd/sind*, P 187.8 *syndon*) and *lichoman* (line 79) instead of NX^d/P 187.15 *lices*, and adds *swyðe* (line 5) to modify *egesfull* (NX^d/P 182.6 *Ðæs dæges weorc byð egesfull eallum gesceaftum*), though exactly what these differences may mean may not be possible to determine. On the other hand, one reads *gebrastl* in X^d (374.7) — a word shared by the parallel passsage in Vercelli XXI as we saw in an earlier section — along with the 'poetic' *blæst* in NO/P 186.5 — a difference which presumably occurred as part of the tendency for all the versions to modernize the source text of Vercelli II at this point, for, as Roberta Frank argues, '[b]oth poetic *blæst* and prosaic *gebrastl* . . . appear to be separate "updatings" of a perhaps no longer comprehensible *blæstm*'.[117] Similarly, X^d 376.2 reads *moldan* (along with the 'prosaic' *eorðan* in N 83) in place of the 'poetic' *foldan* used in O/P 187.12 and in *VercHom* 2.59,[118] while X^d 370.24 *swutollice* is more likely than not a new word in comparison with *swutele* used in the other versions (e.g. P 184.4 *þa Judeas magon swutele geseon*), judging from the texts each of the synonyms tends to occur in.[119] Quite different from the three examples above is X^d *leger* (376.1 *bið þam lichaman laðlic leger gired*), where NOP all have *legerbed* (e.g. P 187.11 *þam lichaman bið laðlic legerbed gegyrwed*), for here X^d agrees with Vercelli II (line 58) and Vercelli XXI (line 209). But in the use of the past participle *gired* (where NOP and the two Vercelli versions all read *gegyr(w)ed*),[120] X^d is again unique.[121]

---

[116] For discussion of this form, see the studies referred to in Chapter III, n. 41.

[117] Frank, 'Poetic Words', p. 96.

[118] Poetic and prosaic are again Frank's descriptions of the words ('Poetic Words', p. 97). Here Vercelli XXI (line 209) does not agree with X^d but with N.

[119] Bosworth-Toller, for example, cites examples of *sweotole* mostly from the prose of the earlier period and poetry but those of *sweotollice* from the earlier and later periods, including Ælfric's works. Poetry seems to use *sweotole* almost exclusively, with thirteen occurrences (including one comparative form) as against three of *sweotollice/swutollice* recorded in the Concordance (J. B. Bessinger, Jr. and Philip H. Smith, Jr. (eds.), *A Concordance to the Anglo-Saxon Poetic Records* (Ithaca and London, 1978)).

[120] For the loss and re-formation of the consonant *w* in the conjugation of *gegierwan*, see Campbell, *Old English Grammar*, §753(5).

[121] For two other forms unique to X^d agreeing with Vercelli II and Vercelli XXI, *storm* (NOP *prosm*) and *ealwihtna* (NOP *hel(l)wihta*), see Scragg, *The Vercelli Homilies*, p. 49 n. 4; Stanley, '*The Judgement of the Damned*', pp. 386–7, notes to his lines 8 and 10; Wilcox, 'The Compilation', p. 85. Scragg finds them 'difficult to reconcile with the omis-

The last citation from X^d above also contains a unique word order VS with an intervening dative noun (against 'dative + VS' in the other versions). A more notable case of difference in syntax is the use of *hig* in X^d beside the dative *him* (or lack of any relevant form) in the other versions:

> P 184.12 he byð bliðe and milde þam soðfæstum æteowed, þæt is, þam ðe [X^d þe hig, NO þe him] to [X^d in to] ðære swiðran healfe þonne beoð gelædde. Þa fyrenfullan witodlice him [X^d hig] beoð þonne on dæg on þære wynstran healfe gehwyrfede, . . .

E. G. Stanley emends the first *hig* followed by *in to* in the manuscript of X^d into *him to in*.[122] This sounds plausible. On the other hand, one could perhaps argue that *hig* might equally well be a 'tautological' personal pronoun forming a relative combination with *þe* (*þe hig* 'who'),[123] as the second occurrence of the same form, which Stanley retains, evidently is tautological in the following sentence; one might wonder if the common pattern of difference between X^d and the rest in the two consecutive sentences might not favour this view. In that event, the first *hig* would not be an error any more than the second but a revision, either by the addition of *hig* (if the exemplar was of the P type) or 'reinterpretation' of the *him* in the exemplar (if it was of the NO type).[124]

I have discussed above two sentences that are uniquely contained in N (lines 11–16), where I noted, together with a feature to be discussed immediately below, a slight difference from the usage of the conjunction *and* as shown in P. The two sentences occur in the middle of the series of *in/on þam dæge* (with or without *and* or *ac* before it) referring to the Day of the Last Judgement, and the difference from P becomes more conspicuous in the rest of the series; so much so that N omits all five instances of *and* or *ac* as used in P. As I have argued earlier,[125] these instances (at P 182.10, 182.15, 183.3, 183.10, and 184.10) are functional, occurring as they do to link clauses within each of the three 'scenes' into which the whole account of the terror of the Day may be divided. If the distinction between this usage and the omission of the conjunction when going over to a new 'scene' (as at P 182.8, 183.15, and 185.19) is part of the original compiler's design for his adaptation, as I would take it, it was to all appearance no longer appreciated

---

sion in OPX^d of N.11–16 which is clearly derived from homily II'. This problem might be relevant in considering the common 'error' *ece* in NX^d against OP *ecan* discussed earlier.

[122] Stanley, '*The Judgement of the Damned*', p. 372, apparatus.

[123] For this use of personal pronoun, see *OES*, §§2180–90.

[124] The dative *him* in NO might well refer to Christ on Judgement Day, forming with the following noun *healfe* the 'possessive dative' construction. But the X^d reviser might possibly have taken it in his exemplar (if it was of the NO type) as a 'reflexive' dative, which he might not have liked to use with verbs of motion (*gelædan* and *gehweorfan*) in the past participle.

[125] See Chapter III, p. 42.

when the homily reached the compiler of the N version. On the other hand, the integrity of the usage in P is retained much better in the other versions; O omits 'scene'-internal *and* twice (at points corresponding to P 182.10 and 183.10)[126] and X^d just once (corresponding to P 184.10). But no version adds the conjunction where P does not have one.

The other feature contained in N 11–16, alternation between the prepositions *in* and *on*, is also subject to variation but shows a very different picture in the four versions as it occurs in the rest of the homily. There are two main contexts in which the alternation occurs, i.e. the series of *in/on þam dæge* considered above and the word pairs that are piled up in describing the misery and horror of the Last Judgement in what is printed as the second 'metrical passage' in Stanley's edition of the X^d version (376.1–30). As I have shown elsewhere,[127] the P version often prefers *in* for *on* (favoured in Vercelli II) in both contexts. Now N and O share a slightly different tendency, adding one example each of *on* when P holds to *in* as in Vercelli II where they go parallel (P 188.7 *on hæte and in earfoðnesse*, N 93 . . . *on earfoðnesse*; and P 183.10 *And in þam dæge* (*VercHom* 2.12 *In*), O 16 *On*). But both N and O occasionally use *in* even where P has *on* (P 183.3 *And on þam dæge*, N 19 *In*, O 12 *in*; P 188.6 *on cyle and on wanunge*, N 92 *in . . . in*, O 78 *On . . . in*),[128] and to that degree they, like P, tolerate both prepositions. Quite distinct is X^d, which with no single exception has *on*, in both of the two contexts mentioned above and elsewhere, e.g. 370.8 *þæt mancyn þe nu is on idelum gilpe ⁊ on sinlustum* (NO/P 182.12 *in . . . in*).[129] This range of variation, and the general tendency to prefer *in* which is nevertheless clear in comparison with the source text, is perhaps the most remarkable case of changing linguistic usage to be found in Napier XL as it is transmitted in the four versions, for it is generally held that the use of *in* is an Anglian feature which was gradually replaced by late West-Saxon *on*. The variation in the four versions, all in eleventh-century manuscripts, probably demonstrates what are at once chronological (and concomitantly geographical) and stylistic aspects of this development; the exclusive use of *on* in X^d shows how the development has run its course at least in one mid-eleventh-century manuscript, though not in the others, including two later ones (OP, both s. xi 3rd quarter).[130]

---

[126] Wilcox, perhaps following Napier's critical apparatus, says mistakenly that 'O share[s] a slight revision in the addition of "and" at 183/10' ('The Compilation', p. 84).

[127] Chapter III, p. 38.

[128] The clauses and phrases containing these examples are independent of Vercelli II.

[129] This contrast is carried into the introduction shared by N and X^d: N 2 *in urum life*, X^d 370.2 *on*. Wilcox ('Napier XL and XLII', 6 n. 21) also notes this, saying: 'X^d always has *on*', but he does not seem to have considered my second type of context, which gives fifteen examples of *on* used in X^d alone.

[130] A different alteration of prepositions occurs in P 187.9 *we dæghwamlice geseoð beforan* [N *beforan*, O *ætforan*, X^d *for*] *urum eagum*.

If the alteration *in/on* represents the clearest case of changing linguistic usage in the four versions of Napier XL, we find change of substance in the conclusion of the version N, which is evidently a substitution for the original one as in OPX^d.[131] The conclusion in N is wholly Wulfstanian, drawing, after two short sentences held in common with OPX^d, upon Wulfstan's free-standing pieces 'De Uitis Principalibus' and 'De Uirtutibus' and extracts from his Homilies III and IX.[132] In both parts, the compiler of N follows his source very closely, with only a small number of minor changes in the wording of the text, as we shall see shortly. What is really significant is the magnitude of this substituted conclusion itself, with its new focus and relation to the main body of the homily. While the original conclusion as in OPX^d is also largely Wulfstanian but is a concatenation of general admonitions to love God and do his will and fear the Day of Judgement, the conclusion in N brings in Antichrist as the focus, thereby creating a closer unity with the rest of the homily, reinforcing its Judgement Day theme through this added emphasis on apocalypticism. This change in emphasis is summarized very succinctly by Scragg:

> The result of the changed ending in N is that, against other versions of Napier XL which end with a series of disjointed injunctions and warnings, we have an organized passage contaning a severe reminder of the wiles of Antichrist, an appropriate conclusion to the eschatalogical [*sic*] material of Vercelli II.[133]

As Scragg's last clause above implies, the changed conclusion represents a development of Napier XL and of the Vercelli tradition of Judgement Day homilies as a whole. It is a development which perhaps reflects the age when, with a growing sense of eschatological crisis around the millennial year, the Last Judgement and the coming of Antichrist as its forerunner were believed and expected to be imminent.[134] Responding to this, the compiler of N made the warning of the homily more urgent by his choice of a new conclusion; the conclusion, and concomi-

---

[131] See Scragg, *The Vercelli Homilies*, pp. 48–9; Wilcox, 'Napier XL and XLII', 7–8.

[132] For details, see Wilcox, 'The Compilation', pp. 91–3; id., 'Napier XL and XLII', 8–11. In these studies, Wilcox establishes the two free-standing pieces, not the related passages in *WHom* Xc, as the immediate sources of the first part of the conclusion.

[133] Scragg, 'The corpus', 251.

[134] See Emmerson, *Antichrist*, pp. 51–4. For the view that there was not any particularly stronger sense of imminent Doomsday in the tenth century than in other medieval periods, see McGinn, *Antichrist*, p. 100. Another thing to notice about the treatment of Antichrist in the Wulfstan passage (*WHom* 9.107–50) used almost verbatim in N's conclusion is that the author, unlike the compiler of Fadda X (discussed in an earlier section of this chapter), does not equate the devil and Antichrist, but calls the latter *se earmsceapena man* 'the wretchedly-created man' as well as *þeodlicetere* 'arch-hypocrite' and *þeodfeond* 'arch-enemy'. Emmerson shows in detail that Wulfstan, and Ælfric, generally

tantly the general tone of the homily, has been rendered closer to the thought of the age and the orthodoxy of the Church which shaped it, promoting Antichrist into an important element of the eschatological homily.

Another feature of the Wulfstan material on which the N version draws in its conclusion is the list of vices and virtues, which is based on Alcuin's *De virtutibus et vitiis liber*, a popular and influential theological treatise of the day which owes much to authors like Cassian, Gregory, and Isidore.[135] Use of such material again represents a shift away from the mostly apocryphal material of Vercelli II upon which the main body of our homily draws, in favour of the doctrine of the Church and standard theological works to which homilies at that time seem to have increasingly come to turn as their learned authorities.[136] This appeal to authorities is to be seen clearly, if not very abundantly, elsewhere in Napier XL. The N version refers to the Scriptures in the conclusion (136 *gyman . . . þæs ðe bec beodað*, though this is borrowed verbatim from *WHom* 9.136–7), while it adds a sentence, shared by X[d], containing a similar reference at the very beginning of the homily before it begins to draw on Vercelli II: N 1 *ure drihten, ælmihtig God, us þus singallice manað ꝺ lǣreð þurh his ða halgan bec þæt we riht ꝺ soð don* . . . These references to the Scriptures are lacking in the other versions, with a different introduction and/or conclusion. But all four versions share another aspect of the feature being discussed which in the first instance separates Napier XL from Vercelli II: the 'pedantic' additions of *swa se apostol cwæð: 'In quo omnis creatura congemescit'* (e.g. P 182.7, N 5) and other Latin texts of biblical quotations and of a biblical account of Judgement Day, as we have seen in an earlier chapter.[137] All this is furthermore paralleled by what was seen earlier to occur in Vercelli XXI in comparison with Vercelli II. As such, the appeal to authorities, together with the feature discussed in the previous paragraph, represents a changing emphasis in the Vercelli tradition of Judgement Day homilies and perhaps a new direction in homiletic writing of the time in general.

One might ask if this attitude to scriptural authority and authoritative works might explain the limited number of changes made to the Wulfstan material in the

---

held the standard patristic position on the problem (*Antichrist*, pp. 149–55); see further n. 67 of this chapter.

[135] See Roland Torkar, *Eine altenglische Übersetzung von Alcuins De Virtutibus et Vitiis, Kap. 20* (Munich, 1981), pp. 9–15. For the use of Alcuin's tract in Old English, see pp. 22–35 of that book, and *Sources of Anglo-Saxon Literary Culture: A Trial Version*, ed. Frederick M. Biggs, Thomas D. Hill, and Paul E. Szarmach, with the assistance of Karen Hammond (Binghamton, New York, 1990), pp. 20–1; Clare A. Lees, 'The Dissemination of Alcuin's *De Virtutibus et Vitiis Liber* in Old English: A Preliminary Survey', *LSE* 16 (1985), 174–89.

[136] Scragg makes a similar point: 'We may postulate a gradual reduction in the dependence of the conclusion of Napier XL on [Vercelli] homily II' (*The Vercelli Homilies*, p. 50).

[137] See Chapter III, p. 39.

conclusion in the N version. In the part drawn from Wulfstan's tracts on vices and virtues, N is almost identical with them, with two slight adjustments. It changes, with the addition of initial *and* and the object *us* in the middle, the original third person statement into the first person *utan* exhortation (N 99 *And utan wið deofolscin scildan us georne* . . . ; where Wulfstan says: *Micel is eac neodpearf. manna gehwilcum þæt he wið deofolscin. scilde him georne* . . .), while making the list of vices and virtues run smoothly through the use of *and* rather than giving them as numbered items (e.g. N 101 *ðæt is modignes 7 gifernes* . . ., rendering Wulfstan's *þæt is .i. modignes. .ii. gifernes.* . . .); and finally ends this part with a substituted sentence.[138]

The rest of the conclusion, too, uses the Wulfstan material almost verbatim, including the homilist's habitual use of synonymous pairs of words and other phraseologies typical of him, such as N 143 *soð is þæt ic sæcge* (*WHom* 9.143) and 146 *a swa nyr ende þyssere worulde swa wyrð fyrenlusta* . . . (*WHom* 9.147), and the phrase *beon geþuht(e)* in N 116 *His word 7 weorc beoð gode geþuhte* (*WHom* 9.114), which is commonly used by Ælfric and Wulfstan but is rare in anonymous homilies.[139] The few changes that do occur are all in minor details and often inconsistent. For example, the conjunction *and* is omitted in N 115 from *WHom* 9.112 *And þa beoð rihtliceteras þe to ðam gewuniað*, but is added in N 124 *7 eall þæt cymð of deofle*, replacing the *ac* in the source (*WHom* 9.123).[140] *Eall* is omitted and added once: N 143 *mid swilcan laran Antecrist cwemeð* (*WHom* 9.144 *mid eal swylcan laran*) and 150 *beorgan us georne wið ealle unþeawas* (*WHom* 3.75 *wið þæne egesan*). The last example involves change of the head noun, suggesting an attempt on the compiler's part to 'improve' the text. So might the following changes, whereby the word *swicol/swicolnes* is omitted from Wulfstan's original: N 121 *And to fela manna eac is nu on þyssere worulde* (*WHom* 9.120 *on ðissere swicelan worulde*) and N 131 *7 Antecrist lærð unsoðfæstnesse* (*WHom* 9.130 *unsoðfæstnysse 7 swicolnesse*). It might be that the literal mind of the compiler liked to think that the original 'deceitful world' is too much of a 'transferred epithet' and that 'swicolnes' should be an attribute of 'unsoðfæstnes' as an item of Antichrist's teaching, not an item of his teaching in its own right.[141]

---

[138] For the text of Wulfstan's tracts and full details of comparison, see Wilcox, 'The Compilation', pp. 92–3; id., 'Napier XL and XLII', 9–10.

[139] For a detailed study of the distribution of this construction and its implications, see Mitsu Ide, 'The Distribution of *Beon/Wesan Geþuht(e)* in Old English Texts', *Bulletin of Kanto Gakuin University* 43 (1985), 81–118.

[140] Dorothy Bethurum (*The Homilies of Wulfstan* (Oxford, 1957), p. 189, apparatus) mistakenly ascribes another omission of *and* to N (which she calls manuscript B) at line 115, from *WHom* 9.113 *And mid ðam unwrencan eallan bið huru se earmscapena man Antecrist eal afylled*. The word *mid* is omitted as she notes, but the manuscript does read *and* (in the form of '7'), as reproduced in Scragg's edition.

[141] As for the earlier conclusion contained in OPX^d, the three versions display no change of substance and little difference in verbal details. But on the whole, X^d is more

Conclusion

The tradition of Judgement Day homilies derived directly or indirectly from Vercelli II ends with the three anonymous works examined in the previous sections. There are no other works that survive which can be shown to have used material from the Vercelli source (in its 'original' or re-used form), apart from isolated brief sentences from it in a few works such as Napier XLII and Tristram III.[142] One of them:

> Napier XLII 202.15 La hwæt, we nu ungesælige syn, þæt we us bet ne warniað wið þone egsan, þe toweard is, and þæt we us ne ondrædað þone toweardan dæg þæs miclan domes. Se is yrmða dæg and ealra earfoða dæg,

conflating as it does two warnings to fear the Last Judgement in Vercelli II and Napier XL,[143] shows how an independent use might have been made of the Vercelli II material, suggesting further ramifications of the tradition in which this eschatological homily was re-used and developed. As they survive, however, this borrowing and others mentioned above are all too fragmentary to enable us to add much of significance to the present examination of the tradition of Judgement Day homilies. Nor does another related anonymous work, Napier XXX, which draws upon extracts from Vercelli XXI. Titled *Be rihtan cristendome*, the homily does not use the eschatological passages in Vercelli XXI going back to Vercelli II,[144] and does not feature in this study of the Vercelli tradition, apart from its role as an individual item of compilation in Chapter II.

---

likely to have its own reading, as in its usage of adverbs (X^d 378.1 *lufian we þone hihstan cyningc*, O/P 189.9 *lufian we georne* . . .; X^d 378.5 *þe Gode ær wel gecwemdan*, O/P 189.15 *ær gecwemdon*), preference for verb forms with the *ge-*prefix (X^d 378.5 *gewitan*, O/P 189.14 *witan*; O/X^d 378.8 *gedælað*, P 190.2 *todælað*), and use of the weak feminine genitive *heofonan* (X^d 378.8; O/P 190.1 *heofena*). This last-mentioned form is also common in manuscripts of Ælfric's *Catholic Homilies*; see Malcolm Godden, *Ælfric's Catholic Homilies: Introduction, Commentary and Glossary*, EETS ss 18 (Oxford, 2000), Glossary s.v. *heofen, heofon, heofonan*; Terry Hoad, 'Old English Weak Genitive Plural *-an*: Towards Establishing the Evidence', *From Anglo-Saxon to Early Middle English*, ed. Godden *et al.*, pp. 108–29, esp. pp. 116–8.

[142] See n. 4.

[143] *VercHom* 2.56, expanded in Napier XL 187.8–9, and *VercHom* 2.36–8 and Napier XL 185.18–19. On this Napier XLII passage and its implications for the relation of the homily to Napier XL, see Scragg, *The Vercelli Homilies*, pp. 50 and 68, note to line 56; Wilcox, 'Napier XL and XLII', 15.

[144] For details of the precise extent of the indebtedness of Napier XXX to Vercelli XXI, see Scragg, *The Vercelli Homilies*, p. 397; id,. 'Napier's "Wulfstan" homily xxx', 198–207.

Still, the Vercelli tradition, extending over more than a hundred years, from the composition of Vercelli II perhaps not much later than the middle of the tenth century until the date of the latest manuscripts of Napier XL (OP, both s. xi 3rd quarter), contains a considerable amount of variation and development in language and substance. The former kind can be seen in the modernization which is apparently at work in some parts of the revised texts, the clearest examples being the replacement of 'poetic' and 'archaic' vocabulary items originally used in Vercelli II and the preference for certain 'modern' word orders and other details of grammar. Stylistically, the three homilies derived from Vercelli II show the wide range that was available to authors of composite homilies of the period who drew sometimes very heavily upon the preceding homiletic materials but felt free to adapt and rewrite them in distinct manners of writing which best suited their own preferences and purposes. Thus, the 'pedantic' compiler of Napier XL adopts terse, controlled prose, while the compilers of Vercelli XXI and Fadda X tend to use more straightforward prose to rewrite the common source, with the latter displaying a distinctive fondness for an enumerative style and the syntactic pattern of the concessive clause which also helps to mould his thinking and writing. The successive compilations based on Vercelli II also saw some change in the substance of the homily, which may be seen as a constant shift away from the mostly apocryphal material provided by Vercelli II to the orthodox understanding of Doomsday, with increasing reference and appeal to the Scriptures and learned authorities in the exegetical tradition. Some of the changes summarized above are evident even within the four versions of Napier XL, as in the complete disuse of the preposition *in* (in its local or temporal sense) in favour of *on* in the X^d version and in the later conclusion in N, where passages on Antichrist are borrowed from an orthodox discussion of the subject by Wulfstan and are used effectively and differently than the way in which the figure is represented in Vercelli II and Fadda X. All these effects of adaptation and revision are witnesses to the important variations and new developments called into being in transmitting and transforming the original material of the Vercelli homily.

The fact that Napier XL in one version combines the material from the Vercelli homily with a substituted concluding passage drawn from Wulfstan's writings is also an important reminder of the wider contexts of Old English eschatological literature of which the Vercelli tradition is a part. This literature forms a large body, both in prose and poetry, of relevant pieces and allusions, of which Kathleen Greenfield and Robert DiNapoli give some specific details.[145] Especially important in it are the homilies of Ælfric and Wulfstan, as Richard K. Emmerson argues, in terms of their 'theological advance over the understanding of Antichrist in the anonymous *Vercelli Homilies*':[146]

---

[145] See the introductory section of this chapter.
[146] Emmerson, *Antichrist*, p. 151.

> This use of the tradition ... is especially evident in Old English sermons and particularly in the works of the two great homilists, Ælfric and Wulfstan. Both were influenced by the monastic reform of the tenth century, and both follow patristic exegetical eschatology. As a result, in comparison with the earlier Old English anonymous homilies, such as those in the Vercelli and Blickling collections, their homilies are theologically conservative. Furthermore, their treatment of Antichrist marks the first full development of the tradition in vernacular literature.[147]

Emmerson goes on to exemplify his point, discussing some of the more developed treatments of Antichrist by the homilists and noting a few distinguishing features in them, which would repay further investigation.[148] Beside the corpus of the two homilists one may also consider other treatments of eschatology than the Vercelli tradition, set out in anonymous homilies. Here we may think, for example, of another homily in Napier's collection—Napier XLII, mentioned above in relation to the Vercelli tradition, which is in the main a translation of Adso's *De ortu et tempore Antichristi* and whose author has been claimed to be identical with the author of Napier XL.[149] Study of these several developments or 'traditions' may contribute significantly to our better understanding of the history of vernacular homilies in Old English.

Another notable composite homily of relevance here is Napier XXIX, whose origin—in part going back to Bede's Latin poem *De die iudicii*—suggests another line of development, distinct from the Vercelli tradition, of the Judgment Day theme in Old English. The homily is, however, totally isolated as an extant witness to whatever tradition might have inspired it and other eschatological homilies of the day, and it may not be amenable to analysis of a historical kind. Instead, its unique choice of sources, which include an Old English poem, positively recommends it to examination from a different point of view. This is the subject of the next chapter.

---

[147] Emmerson, *Antichrist*, p. 150.

[148] For a previous study, see, e.g. Milton McC. Gatch, *Preaching and Theology in Anglo-Saxon England: Ælfric and Wulfstan* (Toronto and Buffalo, 1977). This book has five chapters on 'The Eschatology of Ælfric and Wulfstan' (Part III, pp. 60–116).

[149] See Wilcox, 'Napier XL and XLII', 11–19.

V.
NAPIER XXIX:
A HOMILY WITH A POETIC SOURCE

I

Unlike most of the anonymous homilies discussed in the previous chapters, the twenty-ninth item in Napier's collection of 'Wulfstan' homilies (*HomU* 26; Cameron No. B3.4.26), preserved complete only in Bodleian, Hatton 113, fols. 66r–73r, is a composite homily for which Wulfstan's works did not provide any material. It draws, so far as is known, on at least four works which are very different from one another both in genre and apparently date of composition and which divide the whole work into four easily distinguishable parts: (1) formulas and directions for the use of confessors in Bodleian, Laud Misc. 482 (*Conf* 10.5); (2) the Old English poem *Be Domes Dæge* (also known as *Judgement Day II*), which is itself a translation of Bede's *De die iudicii*; (3) an anonymous homily traditionally known as the Macarius homily, which is derived from a Latin homily on the body and soul; and (4) a penitential homily by Ælfric in his *Lives of Saints* (item XII); the last part also contains a passage which is close to the end of Blickling Homily V.[1] This variety does not mean that the homily is a random collection of

---

[1] For details, see Karl Jost, *Wulfstanstudien* (Bern, 1950), pp. 203–8; M. R. Godden, 'An Old English penitential motif', *ASE* 2 (1973), 221–39, esp. 226; D. G. Scragg, 'The corpus of vernacular homilies and prose saints' lives before Ælfric', *ASE* 8 (1979), 223–77, esp. 254. As Godden notes (226 n. 1), Jost did not identify the source for the first part quite exactly, though his identified source (*Conf* 2.1) is not irrelevant, as we shall see. L. Whitbread ('"Wulfstan" Homilies XXIX, XXX and Some Related Texts', *Anglia* 81 (1963), 347–64) divides the homily into five parts, calling the last part containing a similar passage to the ending of Blickling V the conclusion. Nothing certain is known about the date of these sources except for Ælfric. But Graham D. Caie (*The Old English Poem 'Judgement Day II'* (Cambridge, 2000), p. 10) proposes 'the late tenth century' for *Judgement Day II*, while D. G. Scragg dates the original translation of what is now part of the Macarius homily 'at least as early as the 960s and perhaps yet earlier in the tenth century' (*Dating and Style in Old English Composite Homilies* (Cambridge, 1998), p. 5). The Laud manuscript of *Conf* 10.5 (Bodleian Library, Laud Misc. 482) is dated 's. xi med.' by N. R. Ker (*Catalogue of Manuscripts Containing Anglo-Saxon* (Oxford, 1957), p. 419). For a view

topics with no general theme or purpose. It is predominantly a penitential homily, where 'the major aim . . . is to goad the congregation into penitential mood',[2] sustained by a description of the Last Judgement and an exemplum on a lost soul addressing its body and its fate, and by what Malcolm Godden calls 'a penitential motif' — a sentence to the effect that 'it is better to be shamed for one's sins before one man (the confessor) in this life than to be shamed before God and before all angels and before all men and before all devils at the Last Judgement'—which occurs aptly in the homily (Napier XXIX 136.1–5), 'forming a neat transition from the theme of repentance to the topic of the Last Judgement'.[3]

On the other hand, the many sources of the homily and their distinct contents have often tended to put into a narrow focus one or another aspect of the whole homily according to the particular concerns with which scholars have approached it. The concerns of previous scholars have usually been with the exemplum part and its relation to the Macarius homily or, more often, with the part adapted from the *Judgement Day II* poem. For example, D. R. Letson sees it primarily as 'a poetic homily':

> The homily as a whole is well suited to the poetic insertion, since alliteration and rhyme are used to greater and lesser degrees throughout the prose sermon. Conversely *Judgment Day II* employs typically homiletic exhortatives which are incorporated naturally into the sermon. Bede's *Sis memor illius* . . ., for example, becomes *ic bidde, man, þæt þu gemune* in the poem, and, characteristic of the Old English homily, it appears as *nu, leofan men, uton habban us on mycelum gemynde* in the sermon. The homiletic exhortation is formulaic, and the singular monastic scholar has become an Anglo-Saxon popular congregation.
>
> Besides literal borrowing, the homilist apparently takes thematic cues from the translation of Bede. The opening admonition to confess, for example, parallels Bede's introductory monologue, in which the narrator struggles with the necessity to reveal his wounds to the Physician. Similarly the exemplum and the soul's moralizing address to the body (Napier, pp. 140–42), both of which follow the poetic interpolation, merely amplify identical addresses within the poem. The homilist now brings his discourse full cycle, returning to his plea for the sinful to confess. Only the summary prayer and the final doxology seem not to have been inspired by *Judgment Day II*, though even here there is a likeness, since the poem does conclude with a

---

that a prose translation now lost of Bede's poem existed prior to both the poetic translation and the prose homily and that these latter both used the earlier version as source, see E. G. Stanley, 'Studies in the Prosaic Vocabulary of Old English Verse', *NM* 72 (1971), 385–418, esp. 389–90. Stanley admits, though, that 'it is likely that the compiler of the extant prose homily used only part of the prose text that underlies or went with *JD II*' (390); see also Caie, *The OE Poem*, pp. 23–4.

[2] Caie, *The OE Poem*, p. 24.

[3] Godden, 'Penitential motif', 222 and 226.

prayer and a closing doxology. Napier's 29, therefore, does not merely borrow from the poetic tradition; rather, the content of the homily is formally inspired by it, verbally and thematically.[4]

Letson sees the part drawn from *Judgement Day II* (and its original Latin poem) as of central importance to this 'poetic homily', in a way which calls for closer attention. The importance of this part is indisputable, if only for the fact that it is by far the longest of the four parts of the homily. But to argue, as Letson does, that the Old English poem and the 'poetic tradition' behind it not only provided material for borrowing but inspired virtually the whole homily 'verbally and thematically' is another thing. By doing so, Letson fails to do full justice to the other parts of the homily which have their own sources or close parallels as described above, all of them known at the time he was writing. One might think it possible to argue that the poetic content of the *Judgement Day II* part gave the initial impetus, leading the compiler to turn to the other sources for similar qualities they have. Yet, as we shall see in detail in a later section, comparison with the source text makes it doubtful, for example, whether the compiler did not do more than 'merely amplify identical addresses within the poem' as he adapted the Macarius version of the exemplum on the body and soul. In fact, Letson himself would seem to imply that the rest of the homily is independent of the *Judgement Day II* part, when he assumes that the 'poetic insertion' of *Judgement Day II* was rendered easier by alliteration and rhyme used throughout the homily, meaning apparently that these poetic features existed prior to the insertion. And here is another problem. Letson does not give any detail of the 'greater and lesser degrees' to which he says alliteration and rhyme are used in the homily, but in fact one gets the impression that they are rather scarce. A quick look at the usage of alliterative word pairs, as reported by Christiane Berger,[5] will give some idea. Of the eleven examples found in the homily, only three are not from the *Judgement Day II* part, all occurring in the last part of the homily: Napier XXIX 141.29 *onettan and efstan*, 141.30 *magon and motan* and 142.20 *on worde oððe on weorce*.[6] They are moreover common expressions in homiletic writing rather than idiosyncratic uses of a 'poetic homily', as D. G. Scragg points out.[7] Word pairs themselves (as

---

[4] D. R. Letson, 'The Poetic Content of the Revival Homily', *The Old English Homily and Its Backgrounds*, ed. Paul E. Szarmach and Bernard F. Huppé (Albany, 1978), pp. 139–56, at pp. 144–5. The phrase 'poetic homily' is also Letson's, used of the homily earlier on p. 144.

[5] Christiane Berger, *Altenglische Paarformeln und ihre Varianten* (Frankfurt am Main, 1990), pp. 55–161.

[6] There are a few other alliterative phrases Berger does not mention, such as Napier XXIX 140.3 *hæbbe swa hearde heortan* and 141.9 *stingað hine mid sorhlicum sare* (with two variant phrases).

[7] D. G. Scragg, 'Napier's "Wulfstan" homily xxx: its sources, its relationship to the Vercelli Book and its style', *ASE* 6 (1977), 197–211, at 210. Scragg is referring to the first two pairs.

Berger identifies them) are not frequent in the homily, with two examples in the *Judgement Day II* part and six in the rest, besides those alliterating ones just mentioned. Nor does one find any remarkable use of rhyme in the sections not drawing on the Judgement Day poem, apart from grammatical rhyme (seen in 141.29 above, for example) and a few others which might have been accidental, such as Napier XXIX 135.3 *reaflac and leasunga and mæne aþas and lyblac* and 136.27 *hu feallendlic and hu lænendlic and hu hreohlic.*

All this is not to deny that the homily can be, and is, poetic in appropriate places elsewhere, as much as in the part derived from *Judgement Day II*. But the real problem is, it seems to me, whether the 'poetic content' inspired 'verbally and thematically' by the Old English poem is the single theme that sustains the disparate sources being pieced together into a homily, as Letson seems to claim. Even within the *Judgement Day II* part, it remains to be shown clearly how poetic the poetic material still is after being rendered into a prose homily. To answer these questions requires us to review the homily as a composite whole in full detail, examining the language and style of each part vis-à-vis its source text.

II

We may begin with the Judgement Day section itself (Napier XXIX 136.28 to 140.2). Comparative study has been made in detail of this 'poetic section' of the prose homily and the Old English poem of which it is an adaptation (and the original Latin poem by Bede, where appropriate) by two editors of the poetic text,[8] and also, though briefly, by L. Whitbread.[9] Whitbread's main concern is the poetic text and its Latin source, and from this point of view he concludes that 'all told we may say that Bede himself would have found little objection to the ultimate uses to which his poem was put'.[10] In particular, he lists several main features of the prose adaptation which he describes as 'severely practical':

> His methods of adaptation were severely practical. He omitted or compressed what he found repetitive or subsidiary. He left the verses at line 285 primarily because the succeeding passage, dealing with heaven's delights, was less pertinent to the awe of doomsday with which he was most concerned, but possibly also because of the doxological phrase *wuldor and wurðmynt* 270, just before. He altered the singular forms of address to fit a multiple congregation; compare lines 15, 123, 176. He or his scribe

---

[8] Hans Löhe (ed.), *Be Domes Dæge* (Bonn, 1907), pp. 47–52; Caie, *The OE Poem*, pp. 24–32.

[9] L. Whitbread, 'The Old English Poem *Judgment Day II* and its Latin Source', *Philological Quarterly* 45 (1966), 635–56, esp. 646–7.

[10] Whitbread, 'The OE Poem', 647.

normalised some of the spelling and grammar. He added a few connective comments, replaced some unusual words, coinages and fanciful or forced expressions; compare 95, 97, 101, 109–10, 113–17. He substituted a looser syntax more appropriate to prose style. No drastic change of fact or emphasis is to be seen.[11]

Whitbread's emphasis is on the good reasons for which omission is made here and there and the negligible change that has thus been made in substance of the poem. This aspect of the adaptation is described more comprehensively by Hans Löhe and Graham D. Caie, indicating the lines that are omitted and offering likely explanations for the omissions. Thus, according to Löhe, of 180 lines of *Judgement Day II* (lines 93–272) from which the part of the homily being discussed is drawn, 38 lines are not used, because they are repetitive or are of little use for the purpose of the homily, either in content (as lines 234–44, describing worldly joys and vices) or stylistically (as lines 150–2, which repeat previous lines for poetic embellishment).[12] Nothing of importance is lost in the adaptation.

Similarly, there is very little material added to the poem in the homily, apart from a sentence which is of interest as a possible allusion to the infanticide not uncommon in the homilist's day (Napier XXIX 137.27–8)[13] and 138.17 *Nu we magon sylfe þus to urum lichaman sprecan*, which marks a transition, clarifying the nature of the second person *þu* in the soul's address which immediately follows it.[14] Otherwise, Napier XXIX 139.19 *Đonne beoð ealle agene þing þissere worlde, þæt leof wæs ær, hit byð lað þonne*, is independent of the poem, inserted only to make up rather curtly for its lines 234–44 which are omitted (see above), and the first half of the last sentence of the section (140.1 *Ac þær is ece wuldor and wurðmynt and ece lif betweox heahfæderum and haligum witegum*) might be an echo of *JDay II* 270 *wuldor and wurðmynt*, as Scragg appears to think.[15]

Another aspect of the prose adaptation mentioned by Whitbread has since been given a fuller account by Caie, who gives a detailed list of 'linguistic changes' that were made to the poetic source:

> The homilist made relatively few linguistic changes. The alliteration is retained, although metre is sometimes sacrificed. The homilist has added articles and conjunctions which were omitted in the poetry for metric and

---

[11] Whitbread, 'The OE Poem', 647.

[12] Löhe, *Be Domes Dæge*, p. 48. Here line numberings are all Löhe's.

[13] For discussion of this addition, see Caie, *The OE Poem*, pp. 30–1; Whitbread, 'The OE Poem', 647 n. 20. Caie calls the sentence 'the only addition' the homilist made to his source.

[14] See Caie, *The OE Poem*, p. 120, note to line 176.

[15] Scragg, 'The corpus', 254 n. 4. Citation from the poem in this chapter is made from the ASPR edition: Elliot Van Kirk Dobbie (ed.), *The Anglo-Saxon Minor Poems* (*The Anglo-Saxon Poetic Records*, Vol. VI, New York, 1942), pp. 58–67.

stylistic reasons; singular pronouns become plural, as he addresses a congregation, and much of the poetic vocabulary appears to have been considered out of place. Finally, the prose author modernises spelling and changes the syntax where the poetic expression might have appeared archaic.[16]

Caie then goes on to cite examples of these changes and others which together represent thirteen features of the prose homily as he groups them.[17] These include, besides those mentioned in the quotation above, 'the poetic *Eala*' (*JDay II* 247) replaced with 'the prosaic *Ac*' (Napier XXIX 139.22), addition in the homily of "*ge-*" and "*a-*" prefixes where the poet has none' (e.g. Napier XXIX 138.2 *geypte oððe gecydde*, 137.10 *ahreosað*;[18] *JDay II* 142 *ypte oððe cyðde*, 107 *hreosað*), and 'more double negatives' in the prose than in the poetry (e.g. Napier XXIX 139.2 *Ne byð þær nan stefen gehyred*; *JDay II* 201 *Þær nan stefn styreð*). Preference for the prefixed forms noted here presents an interesting parallel to usage in other late Old English anonymous homilies discussed in earlier chapters;[19] the agreement may be important as evidence for a development in the language of the period, at least before prefixes begin to disappear in the transition period and in Early Middle English.[20] Löhe, too, gives a similar, and in some respects more detailed, account of the language of the prose homily, including its use of prefixed verb forms.[21]

Yet Caie's description, and for that matter Löhe's, detailed though they are, seem to give us little idea of the total effect of the linguistic changes and the overall quality of the adapted prose which would have to be looked into if the homily version is to be considered as a whole — an omission which the way both scholars analyse it in terms of discrete features may help to reinforce. I shall now attempt first to fill the lacunae in these scholars' work by examining some of the features in contexts as they occur singly or together in clauses or larger units of adaptation. For example, we are told, as we saw above, that the prose homily has 'more

---

[16] Caie, *The OE Poem*, p. 27.

[17] Caie, *The OE Poem*, pp. 27–31.

[18] This example is from my own collection. Caie (*The OE Poem*, p. 29) does not cite any example of the *a*-prefix. Nor does he mention the homilist's preference for the *a*- over *ge*-prefix, as seen in Napier XXIX 139.9 *afylde*, *JDay II* 209 *gefylde*.

[19] See Chapters II, p. 33 and IV, p. 69 and n. 141.

[20] For the history of prefixes in Old and Early Middle English, see Risto Hiltunen, *The Decline of the Prefixes and the Beginnings of the English Phrasal Verb* (Turku, 1983), pp. 47–151.

[21] Löhe (*Be Domes Dæge*, p. 52) makes a curious mistake by adding as an example of this last group the alteration *becwylmað* (*JDay II*, his line 206) and *cwylmað* (Napier XXIX 139.5). The form *becwylmað* is a previous editor's reading (J. Rawson Lumby (ed.), *Be Domes Dæge*, EETS os 65 (London, 1876), p. 14, his line 203), but the other editors, including Löhe himself, agree in reading *þe cwylmað*, as in the manuscript. For discussion of the line in which this occurs in the poem, see Bruce Mitchell, *Old English Syntax*, 2 vols. (Oxford, 1985), §3631, and Caie, *The OE Poem*, p. 122 (note to line 205 *butan*).

double negatives'. But Caie does not tell us that this is so because the compiler of our homily adds *ne* at the beginning of a clause or sentence,[22] either as adverb, as in Caie's two examples—Napier XXIX 139.2 (see above) and 138.23 *Ne mæg nan eorðlic man eall areccan* (*JDay II* 187 *Nænig spræc mæg beon, spellum areccan / ænegum on eorðan*)—or, more importantly, as conjunction. Thus the initial *ne* in Napier XXIX 139.6 . . ., *ne hi mid heora nosum ne magon naht elles gestincan* gives the clause closer association with the preceding one than in the poem, where the corresponding line 207 starts with *hy mid nosan ne magon* after a semicolon at the end of the preceding line in standard editions.[23] It should be noted that in Napier XXIX 138.23 above, the initial *ne* has helped to simplify verb structure, reducing two verbs (*beon . . . areccan*) to one (*areccan*). This simplifying pattern, reinforced by a series of coordinated *ne*'s, accounts for one extensive change made in Napier XXIX 139.11 *Ne bið þær leohtes an lytel spearca, þam earmum ænig frofer; ne arfæstnys ne sibb ne hopa ne ænig gladung*, from

> *JDay II* 219   þær leohtes ne leoht   lytel sperca
> earmum ænig,   ne þær arfæstnes
> ne sib ne hopa   ne swige gegladað
> ne þara wependra   worn wihte.

The homilist adds the initial *ne*, while ending the sentence with *ne* with the noun *gladung*, replacing a second verb *ne . . . gegladað* in the poem. This sentence is followed in the homily, first by a portion containing two sentences with initial *ne byð* and two *þær bið/beoð* sentences and then by an unbroken succession of five more clauses (Napier XXIX 139.26–140.1) of the form '*ne* + V + *þær* S$_1$ + *ne* S$_2$ + *ne* S$_3$ . . .' (where S$_1$, S$_2$ . . . are multiple subjects of the single verb). In these latter, the negative pattern itself is taken over from the poem, but the homilist adds three *ne*'s, replacing *oððe . . . oððe . . . oððe* in the poem; and after omitting a second verb, he further inserts *ne* (italicized below) to render the poetic asyndesis into prosaic coordination in:

---

[22] Löhe obviously recognized this when he noted: 'Zuweilen ist in der prosa doppelte negation statt einfacher des gedichtes gesetzt, und es ist ein teil davon dann zum anschluss verwendet' (*Be Domes Dæge*, p. 50). But he does not pursue the point any further. Another lacuna of previous scholarship is seen in the treatment of poeticism which is not uncommonly retained in the homily. Caie only says that 'a number of words and expressions which the homilist may have considered too poetic or unusual have been simplified', and that '[i]n spite of these examples the homilist has retained much of the poetic nature of *Judgement Day II* including most of the alliterations' (*The OE Poem*, pp. 28 and 30). How far in fact the homily remains poetic and under what circumstances needs close investigation; see below.

[23] Dobbie, *The Anglo-Saxon Minor Poems*, p. 64; Caie, *The OE Poem*, p. 96 (lines 207–8). Löhe (*Be Domes Dæge*, p. 26) has a full stop at the end of the line, printed as line 208.

Napier XXIX 139.28 ne byð þær fefor ne adl ne færlic cwyld *ne* nanes liges gebrasll . . . Ne byð þær liget ne laðlic storm *ne* winter ne cyle ne þunor.

JDay II 259 ne bið þær fefur ne adl ne færlic cwyld, / nanes liges gebrasl . . . / ne bið þær liget ne laðlic storm, / winter ne þunerrad ne wiht cealdes.

In this passage describing the joys of heaven in antithesis to the torment of hell, the homilist thus relies heavily on the negative formula to which he reduces all the verbal and rhetorical complications of the original poem as he prosifies it.

The use just described of the conjunction *ne* in place of asyndesis is made in the Judgement Day poem itself: *JDay II* 108 *and seo sunne forswyrcð sona on morgen, / ne se mona næfð nanre mihte wiht*. This in turn is changed to *and* in the homily, probably because the sentence (Napier XXIX 137.11), unlike 139.6 discussed above, is preceded by clauses whose verbs are in the positive. In fact, the use of *and* forms another basic sentence pattern the homilist uses to render the poem into prose. It is used to replace a variety of linking words in the poem, such as *eac (swa)* (*JDay II* 99, 104, 111, replaced in Napier XXIX 137.5, 137.8, 137.12, respectively), *oþþe* (*JDay II* 97, in 137.2), and *Ufenan eall þis eac* (*JDay II* 145, in 138.4 *and eac þonne*). But the homilist uses the conjunction more often to avoid asyndesis in the source, either of words or phrases, e.g. Napier XXIX 137.23 *mihtleas and afæred* (*JDay II* 126 *mihtleas, afæred*) and 138.24 *areccan þa earmlican witu and ða fulan stowa* (*JDay II* 187 *areccan / . . . earmlice witu, / fulle stowa*) or of clauses. A notable case of this last is Napier XXIX 137.8 *eall upheofon bið sweart and gesworcen and swiðe geþuhsod* (*JDay II* 105 . . . *sweart and gesworcen, swiðe geþuxsað*), where the homilist also changes the asyndetic verb in the source into a past participle, thereby making his predicate phrases strictly coordinate in structure.[24] Finally, simple coordination by *and* is extended to replace a subordinate *þæt*-clause, with appropriate changes in verb forms:

Napier XXIX 137.17 and we beoð him þonne færinga beforan brohte æghwanon cumene to his ansyne, and ðær sceal ælc underfon dom be his dædum.

JDay II 119 We beoð færinga him beforan brohte, / æghwanum cumene to his ansyne, / þæt gehwylc underfo / dom be his dædum æt drihtne sylfum.

Against all this, one can only set two examples of other conjunctions the homilist prefers: *oððe* (Napier XXIX 138.18), inserted between two interrogative sentences in *JDay II* 176, and *ac* (139.22) used in place of what Caie calls the poetic *Eala* (*JDay II* 247; see above).

---

[24] On this variety of use to which *and* is put in the homily, see Löhe, *Be Domes Dæge*, p. 50. In one sentence, the homilist does not render an asyndetic clause with *and* but changes it into a phrase, omitting the verb; see Napier XXIX 138.14 (quoted below).

Napier XXIX 137.17 and 138.4 given above show another aspect of the homilist's addition of *and*. The conjunction is accompanied by the adverb *þonne* in both, as it also is by *ðær þonne* in another curious adaptation: Napier XXIX 137.6 *ða beorgas bugað and myltað, and se egeslica sweg ungerydre sæs, and ðær þonne ealra manna mod myclum bið gedrefed*. Here the homilist, by inserting the linking phrase after *sæs*, appears to have reinterpreted the sentence structure of the source (*JDay II* 101 *beorga hliðu bugað and myltað, / and se egeslica sweg ungerydre sæ / eall manna mod miclum gedrefeð*),[25] but the result is not a happy one. As it stands, it is not very clear whether the homilist's *se egeslica sweg* is meant to be a second subject of the preceding verbs *bugað and myltað* (which seems strained, given the meanings of the verbs) or represents broken syntax with no verb of its own between the two *and*'s. What is fairly certain is that *þonne* in this example as well as the other two is not used so much in a purely temporal sense as for rhythmical reasons, reinforcing the sense of continuation which the *and*-coordination involves. This seems to be no less true when the homilist adds *þonne* or *þonne þær* without being prompted by *and*:

> Napier XXIX 138.14 Þær beoð þonne þearfan and ðeodcyningas, earme and eadige ealle afærede (*JDay II* 162 Þær beoð þearfan and þeodcyningas, / earm and eadig, ealle beoð afæred).

> Napier XXIX 137.22 þonne ðær stent ealra hergea mæst heortleas and earh (*JDay II* 125 stent hergea mæst heortleas and earh).

This close association of the adverbs is characteristic of the homilist's prose, occurring further in two sentences (Napier XXIX 137.28, 138.3). Here he adds *þær* to *þonne*, taken over from the poem (*JDay II* 135, 143),[26] but *þær* is apparently not used in its full sense, any more than *þonne*. The adverbial phrase is a mark of the homilist's rewriting and of his prose rhythm.

I have examined above some of the features listed by Löhe and Caie in a new light. New light may also be shed by others which are not discussed by previous scholars but are as important in revealing how the prose homilist is at work in his adaptation of the poetic lines. Of special interest is his treatment of word order. Changes he makes in this area are surprisingly few. But he shows a few clear tendencies where he does. For example, he feels free, as one would expect, to change orders apparently imposed by alliterative verse into what is probably, for him and the prose of his day, something natural and idiomatic. This can be seen

---

[25] Other possible examples of the homilist's 'reinterpretation' will be discussed below. On the masculine form *sæs* (with a feminine adjective) in Napier XXIX 137.6, see Caie, *The OE Poem*, p. 115 (note to line 102); Löhe, *Be Domes Dæge*, p. 77 (note to line 103).

[26] In another sentence, *þær* alone is added in conjunction with the change of the verb from *byð* to *beoð . . . gegearwode*; see Napier XXIX 136.28 (p. 119).

at its clearest in four sentences in which modifiers, both adjectival and adverbial, are rearranged in relation to their head words, as in Napier XXIX 136.28 *uton... ondrædon us þone micclan dom* (*JDay II* 15 *Ic ondræde me eac dom þone miclan*) and 137.25 *þe on foldan weard æfre gefeded* (*JDay II* 131 *þe on foldan weard feded æfre*); the others, 137.21 (*JDay II* 124) and 137.24 (*JDay II* 129), are exactly parallel to these. A special group is formed by examples where *eal* (pronoun or adjective) is the modifier. The word is removed a few words away from the head word in all the examples in the poem, viz. *JDay II* 104, 165 *forðon hi habbað ege ealle ætsomne*, and 135 *Đonne eallum beoð ealra gesweotolude / digle geþancas on þære dægtide* (the second one) — an arrangement probably dictated, at least in the last two examples,[27] by alliteration. The homilist prosifies this, placing *eall* next to the head word (Napier XXIX 137.8, 138.16 for the first two examples, respectively) and supplying the noun *man* as well for the last (137.28 *ealra manna digle geþancas*).

The examples so far given show that changes the homilist makes are mostly not elaborate, occurring within single clauses. It looks as if the homilist is determined to restrict his work of revision almost to what he sees as the minimum necessary for his purpose, working line by line rather than rewriting in sentence units according to meaning. Nor are his changes in word order always towards 'modern' orders. This will be seen in the position of the verb in relation to other major sentence elements. Thus, he has SV in Napier XXIX 138.2 *þæt bið þonne*... (*JDay II* 143 *þonne bið*...) but reverts to *þonne* VS in 137.10 *Đonne ahreosað ealle steorran nyðer* (*JDay II* 107 *Þonne stedelease steorran hreosað*, where SV order is admittedly required for alliteration). He puts the object *deoflum* of *JDay II* 182 (... *witu, / ða deoflum geo drihten geteode*) after the subject but leaves the verb untouched at the clause-final position (Napier XXIX 138.22 ... *drihten geo deoflum geworhte*); he even prefers this position for a verb: 138.19 *ðu þe þeowast ðissere worulde and her on galnysse leofast* (*JDay II* 179 ... *and her glæd leofast on galnysse*). A similar preference for an order which is not 'modern' may be detected in Napier XXIX 137.17 (see p. 114), with its 'separated' construction *him... beforan* (as against *him beforan* in the poem); here the homilist's sense of prose rhythm, reflected in the insertion of *þonne* as argued above, might be the explanation for the change.

One might be inclined to see modernization in two examples in which the homilist uses a preposition (*on* and *þurh*) in place of the poet's case form:

Napier XXIX 139.8 *Ðær beoð þa waniendan weleras afylde ligspiwelum bryne on þam hellican fyre* (*JDay II* 209 *Þær beoð þa wanigendan welras gefylde / ligspiwelum bryne laðlices fyres*),

---

[27] The other example, *JDay II* 104 *Eal bið eac upheofon*, is a short line and lacks alliteration.

> Napier XXIX 139.25 Þær niht ne genimð næfre þurh þystru þæs heofonlican leohtes sciman (*JDay II* 254 Þær niht ne genimð næfre þeostrum / þæs heofenlican leohtes sciman).

The evidence is not unequivocal, however, especially when set against the case forms (Napier XXIX 137.14 (see p. 121), 137.17, 138.5, 139.10 and *ligspiwelum bryne* in 139.8 just quoted) which the homilist takes over from the poetic source. Given the fact that the case form has the instrumental sense in all these examples, the homilist's prepositional phrases, particularly the *on*-phrase in Napier XXIX 139.8, would seem more likely to represent his concern with meaning than mechanical substitution for usage that has become archaic; for the use of the instrumental *þurh* in the other example, the position immediately after *næfre*, perhaps rather unusual for the case form and potentially ambiguous, might possibly be an explanation. It is interesting in this connection to notice that the homilist on occasion exhibits his own choice of preposition, as in Napier XXIX 137.3 *for ærdædum* (*JDay II* 96 *be*), 137.21 *ætforan godes domsetle* (*JDay II* 124 *beforan*), and *on* for *betwyx*, thereby 'reinterpreting' the relationships of the following noun phrases in:

> Napier XXIX 138.29 Ðuss atelic gewrixl þa earmsceapenan men on worulda woruld wendað þærinne on forsworcennesse sweartes þrosmes and ðæs weallendan pices weana to leanes.
>
> *JDay II* 199 . . . betwyx forsworcenum sweartum nihtum / and weallendes pices wean and þrosme.

The homilist's *on* (the second one) goes with *forsworcennesse*, which the two genitive phrases qualify ('in the darkness of the black smoke and seething pitch'), with the expanded phrase *weana to leanes* 'as the reward for evils';[28] the poet had his preposition govern two phrases: 'betwyx . . . nihtum and . . . wean and þrosme' ('amidst . . . nights and the misery and smoke . . .'). The homilist's sense is more practical and prosaic.[29]

Other grammatical changes the homilist makes include addition of the noun *man* (Napier XXIX 137.29; see p. 118) and of *ðe* as reflexive object of *forhttast*

---

[28] The construction 'noun (gen. pl.) + *to* with genitive' into which *wean* of the poem is expanded appears to be the homilist's favoured idiom, which he uses again in Napier XXIX 138.23 in place of 'noun (gen. pl.) + *to* with dative' in *JDay II* 184 (see p. 122); see also BT, s.v. *to* II (5) and Ælfric's *him to gamenes* (*ÆLS* 32.116). For the dative type of construction in prose, see, e.g. *BlHom* 67.11 *heora siges to wyorþmyndum*.

[29] This change of sense might have been consequent partly on the first half of the sentence in the poem (*JDayII* 197–8), which is open to different readings. For details see Caie, *The OE Poem*, pp. 121–2, note to line 198; Dobbie, *The Anglo-Saxon Minor Poems*, p. 180, note to lines 197ff.

in parallel to the following *þe sylfum ondrætst* (138.21; *JDay II* 181); the personal instead of impersonal construction (138.1 *he forsceamode*; *JDay II* 141 *hwæne sceamode*); and two examples with the relative *þe* as the focus of change. In one of these (Napier XXIX 138.25; *JDay II* 190), the homilist omits it, reducing the relative clause to a phrase, while he adds one in 137.3 *and hwylce þa forebeacn beoð, þe Cristes cyme cyþað on eorðan* (*JDay II* 97 *oþþe hwylce forebeacn feran onginnað / and Cristes cyme cyþað on eorðan*). Here again, with the addition of the demonstrative *þa*, the homilist construes the sentence slightly differently, saying 'what will be the portents which testify . . .' rather than 'what portents begin to occur and testify . . .'.

As has been shown above, the homilist occasionally changes sense as he renders the poetic source into prose. Another such case[30] is

> Napier XXIX 138.5 færð þæt fyr ofer eall, ne byð þær nan wiðersteall; ne nan man næfð þæra mihta, þæt ðær ænige wyrne do,

> *JDay II* 147 Færð fyr ofer eall, ne byð þær nan foresteal, / ne him man na ne mæg miht forwyrnan.

The homilist speaks of man's power and not that of the hell-fire—power which no human being can deny the hell-fire (*him man na ne mæg miht forwyrnan*), as the poet elegantly puts it. Whether the homilist was aware of the effect of the change he has introduced in these sentences seems difficult to say with certainty. But one feels inclined to think that he was probably not. It would seem that the effect is a result of his restricted method of adaptation rather than the aim of an independent mind. Here, as usually elsewhere, the homilist is apparently intent on rendering poetic language into plain prose in a way which suggests not so much elegance and precision as convenience—an impression which one also gets from 'loose' syntax in these sentences:

> Napier XXIX 137.29 Eall, þæt seo heorte hearmes geðohte oððe seo tunge to teonan geclypode oððe mannes hand man gefremode on þystrum healum þissere worulde (*JDay II* 139 oþþe mannes hand mancs gefremede).

---

[30] We may have yet another case of 'reinterpretation' in Napier XXIX 138.1 *eall, þæt he forsceamode her on life, þæt he ænigum men geypte oððe gecydde, þæt bið þonne þær eallum open ætsomne unbehelendlice, ðæt man ær her lange hæl*, as compared with *JDay II* 141 *eal þæt . . . / . . . / þonne bið eallum open ætsomne, / gelice alyfed ðæt man lange hæl*. If *gelice alyfed* in the poem means, as is usually thought, 'and likewise (will be) admitted', it implies that two things will be disclosed on the Day of Judgement. The homilist, by replacing the phrase with *unbehelendlice* (only loosely related in meaning but with the same number of syllables; on this point see further below), appears to be speaking of a single kind of thing disclosed, with the opening *eall þæt* recapitulated by the third and fourth *þæt* (demonstrative and relative, respectively) in the sentence.

Napier XXIX 137.23 Þonne bið gebann mycel þyder aboden, eall Adames cynn eorðbugiendra (*JDay II* 129 Þænne bið geban micel, and aboden þider / eal Adames cnosl eorðbuendra).

Löhe's translation—'alles, was . . . eines menschen hand frevelhaftes verübte' and 'Dann ergeht ein großer befehl, und es wird dorthin entboten das ganze geschlecht Adams'[31]—indicates what is loose. In the former sentence, the homilist's *man* 'evil' should be *manes* like *hearmes* (as in the poem) or *to mane* in parallel to *to teonan*; while the latter makes, to say the least, awkward sense, conflating what are two things in the poem ('there will be a great summons' and 'Adam's race will be called thither') into one, by omitting *and* and consequently making *Adames cynn* appositive to *gebann*. Examples such as these of loosened structure (unless they were products of a careless scribe), like the examples of 'reinterpreted' structure, would tell their own tale of the homilist's approach to the poetic source and the quality of the resultant prose as a 'severely practical' rendering, as Whitbread has called it (see p. 110).

Now, as might be expected from this 'practical' method, the homilist does not always take the trouble to make the text sound more like prose but retains, here and there, the poetic lines almost or even exactly as they are, even if they are overlaid with features that might well have been archaic and poetic. Löhe is quite right when he points out the variable success with which the homilist attempts prosification:

> Die änderungen, die der prosaist in bezug auf verbindung und construction der sätze vorgenommen hat, lassen besonders im ersten drittel des übernommenen teiles viel flüchtigkeit erkennen. Später änderte er abgesehen von auslassungen weniger.[32]

The homilist starts with what is perhaps the most drastic change he makes throughout his revision of the poem, developing the immediately preceding homiletic formula *nu, leofan menn, uton don* . . . Furthermore, he conflates two remote sentences in the poem into one, besides making a range of changes in details of wording, including omission of *wile*. It is in this context that two of the features discussed earlier (position of modifier and addition of *þær*; see pp. 116 and 115 n. 26) occur:

> Napier XXIX 136.28 uton don, swa us mycel þearf ys, ondrædon us þone micclan dom and ða micclan wita, þe þær beoð þam earmsceapenan for heora ærdædum gegearwode; and hu egeslice and hu andryslice se heahlica cyningc þær gedemeð anra gehwylcum for ærdædum;

---

[31] Löhe, *Be Domes Dæge*, p. 19. The other editors of the poem and the prose homily are silent on these points of grammar.

[32] Löhe, *Be Domes Dæge*, p. 50.

JDay II 15   Ic ondræde me eac   dom þone miclan

92   Gemyne eac on mode,   hu micel is þæt wite
þe þara earmra byð   for ærdædum,
oþþe hu egeslice   and hu andrysne
heahþrymme cyningc   her wile deman
anra gehwylcum   be ærdædum, . . .

The shift from the personal (*Ic ondræde me*) to homiletic mode (*Uton don . . . ondrædon*) is properly succeeded a little later by a similar adaptation in a linking sentence: Napier XXIX 137.20 *Nu, leofan men, uton habban us on mycelum gemynde, hu . . .* (*JDay II* 123 *Ic bidde, man, þæt þu gemune hu . . .*)—a change which Letson refers to, quite rightly, as 'characteristic of the Old English homily' (see p. 108). Soon after this opening, however, the homilist begins to assume the less sweeping approach in which he continues till the end of his adaptation of the poem—so much so that there are not infrequently, particularly towards the end of the section, as Löhe points out above, sentences which he borrows from the poem almost or even exactly verbatim without tampering with poetic features they contain.

This is the case even with vocabulary items. Notable examples, found amidst the general tendency showing the contrary, are two definitely poetic words that are nevertheless retained in the homily: *dreosað* (Napier XXIX 137.5) and *foldan*[33] in:

Napier XXIX 137.25 þe on foldan wearð æfre gefeded, oððe modor gebær to manlican, oððe þa ðe wæron oððe woldon beon oððe towearde geteald wæron awiht.

JDay II 131   þe on foldan wearð   feded æfre
oððe modar gebær   to manlican,
oþþe þa þe wæron   oððe woldon beon
oþþe towearde   geteald wæron awiht.

The retention of *foldan* may not be by accident. The whole relative period in which it occurs is borrowed verbatim, with all the alliteration kept intact (apart from the reversed word order *æfre gefeded*; see p. 116), despite many points in it, such as the last *oþþe*-clause, which are to all appearance far from natural, idiomatic prose. The homilist does not bother to translate the whole sentence into his

---

[33] For details of the usage of these and thirteen other poetic words in late Old English prose, see Roberta Frank, 'Poetic Words in Late Old English Prose', *From Anglo-Saxon to Early Middle English: Studies Presented to E. G. Stanley*, ed. Malcolm Godden, Douglas Gray, and Terry Hoad (Oxford, 1994), pp. 87–107; *folde* and *(ge)dreosan* are discussed on pp. 96–7 and 102–3, respectively.

own prose, reshaping it and rephrasing it; to do so would have demanded a different method of rewriting than the one he has adopted.

In syntax, we have already seen how the homilist chooses not to abandon those case forms which denote the instrumental sense, as against prepositions of other senses. But a major area of 'poetic syntax' taken over into the homily is word order. Thus, the order VS at the head of a clause, which 'is especially common . . . in the Ælfredian Bede and in some of the poetry',[34] is used in Napier XXIX 137.16 *Sit þonne se mæra heofonlica dema on his heahsettle*, 138.5 and 139.13, as in *JDay II* 117 *Sitt þonne sigelbeorht swegles brytta / on heahsetle*, 147 and 223. It may be added that the subject noun has the appropriate form of the demonstrative *se* added before it in all three, while in the first of these the retained word order contrasts with replacement of the poetic phrase for God in the source, as above.[35]

More revealing is the way the prose homilist retains the order in the poem of adjectives in relation to the nouns or noun phrases they qualify, as seen in:

Napier XXIX 137.14 þonne cumað ealle engla þreatas, stiðe astyrode standað abutan, eall engla werod ecne embtrymmað þone mæran kyning mihte and ðrymme.

JDay II 113 þonne cumað upplice   eoredheapas,
              stiþmægen astyred,   styllað embutan
              eal engla werod,   ecne behlænað,
              ðone mæran metod   mihte and þrymme.

Ecne is separated by the verb from the noun phrase in the homily, just as in the poem, where the adjective may well be used, as Elliot van Kirk Dobbie punctuates the line, as a noun meaning 'the Eternal One' on which *ðone mæran metod* in the next line is a variation. This unusual word order in the homily,[36] it should be noted, is accompanied by heavy asyndesis and case forms in the instrumental sense, also taken over from the poem, whereas again the poetic word

---

[34] Randolph Quirk and C. L. Wrenn, *An Old English Grammar*, 2nd edn. (London, 1957), p. 94. For the use of this word order in the Vercelli Homilies and Blickling Homilies and their later versions, see my article 'Initial Verb-Subject Inversion in Some Late Old English Homilies' (*Studies in the History of Old English Prose* (Tokyo, 2000), pp. 235–62).

[35] For *brytta* and *swegl* as poetic words, see Frank, 'Poetic Words', pp. 93 and 99–100.

[36] Mitchell notes that '[s]eparation [of the qualifying element and its headword] is much more common in the poetry' (*OES*, §1499), with discussion of *Beo* 1474–5 (with a problem similar to the one being discussed) and various other examples and their metrical implications (§§150–7 and §3959). The discussion does not include, though, the type *womma/weana to leane(s)* mentioned before (p. 117) and below (p. 122).

metod is rendered as *kyning*. This contrastive treatment in syntax and vocabulary, illustrating another aspect of the limited scope of the homilist's prosification, is further seen in

> Napier XXIX 138.20 Hwi ne forhttast þu ðe fyrene egesan and þe sylfum ondrætst swiðlice witu, þa drihten geo deoflum geworhte, awyrgedum gastum, womma to leanes?

> *JDay II* 181   Hwi ne forhtas þu   fyrene egsan,
> and þe sylfum ondræd   swiðlice witu,
> ða deoflum geo   drihten geteode,
> awyrgedum gastum,   weana to leane?

In the homily the separated qualifier (*womma . . . leanes*) and poetic variation are allowed to stand while the word *geteode* is replaced with *geworhte*; in the same way, the separated construction *teð . . . manna* is retained beside the prosaic *gnyrrað* (replacing *gryrrað* in *JDay II* 196[37]) in Napier XXIX 138.28 *Hwylon eac þa teð for mycclum cyle manna þær gnyrrað*. Similarly, though with no contrast to a lexical replacement that occurs side by side with it, the 'poetic syntax' is retained in *synnige . . . sawla* (Napier XXIX 139.18 *and ðær synnige eac sawla on lige and on blindum scræfe byrnað and yrnað*, where the homilist in fact makes no change to *JDay II* 230–1 beyond adding the second *and*), and in the asyndesis of three clauses in 138.4–6 (drawn as it is from *JDay II* 145–7). Different from all this is the homilist's treatment of poetic variation in the first line of:

> *JDay II* 159   Þonne fela mægða,   folca unrim,
> heora sinnigan breost   swiðlice beatað
> forhte mid fyste   for fyrenlustum.

He resolves it using a prepositional phrase: Napier XXIX 138.11 *Ðonne of fela þeodum folc ormætlice mycel hyra synnigan breost swyðe beatað* . . . But he still keeps in one sense close to the poem, adopting post-position for the qualifying *ormætlice mycel*, corresponding to *unrim* in *folca unrim* (partitive genitive followed by noun) in the poem, which he rephrases as noun with postposed modifier. Here, as in most of the earlier examples, adaptation is made within a short span, on word or at the most phrase level and seldom going beyond that.

The point just made suggests an explanation for an aspect not previously noticed of the way the homilist changes vocabulary items used in the poem. It has been shown abundantly by Löhe and Caie, and in part illustrated by my examples such as Napier XXIX 137.14 and 138.20 given above, how he replaces poetic

---

[37] The verb *gnyrran* occurs only in prose, though recorded no more than twice, in the homily sentence being discussed and *ProgGl* 1 (Först) 217 *gnyrende*. *Gryrran* is recorded nowhere else in Old English.

expressions by prosaic ones or those that are supposedly so. But there is a further group, small as it is, of changes which do not evidently rely as much on equivalent meaning. For example, in Napier XXIX 138.15 *Ðær hæfð ane lage se earma and se eadiga, forðon hi ealle habbað ege þone mæstan*, the last two words are used in place of *ealle ætsomne* in the poem (*JDay II* 165 *forðon hi habbað ege ealle ætsomne*), not because they are a less poetic expression of the same meaning[38] but, perhaps, because they are useful, so to speak, as a 'line-filler', with roughly the same number of syllables. This last point is brought out more neatly in:

> Napier XXIX 138.9 Þonne nele se wrecenda lig and se deoflica bryne ænine forbugan, buton he æror beo her afeormod and ðonne þyder cume þearle aclænsod (*JDay II* 157 *buton he horwum sy her afeormad, / and þonne þider cume, þearle aclænsad*).

> Napier XXIX 139.2 Ne byð þær nan stefen gehyred, buton stearc and heard wop and wanung for wohdædum (*JDay II* 201 . . . *butan stearcheard / wop and wanung, nawiht elles*).

The homilist's *æror beo* and *for wohdædum* both mean something widely different from the corresponding two word phrases (*horwum sy* and *nawiht elles*) in the poem but are exactly of the same length as these latter. It may be noticed that the replacements are the only changes the homilist makes in the *buton*-clause and *buton*-phrase, apart from a very minor one from *stearcheard* to *stearc and heard* in the latter example. The homilist concentrates almost entirely on words and phrases which he sometimes finds unacceptable for his purpose, without bothering to rewrite the whole clauses in which they occur. His method of adaptation is severely local and practical.

III

If, as I have endeavoured to show, the 'poetic section' of Napier XXIX is characterized by an overall tendency to stay close to the source poem, this 'severely practical' attitude of the homilist to his source is seen even more clearly in a later section (Napier XXIX 141.32–142.9), where the homilist borrows verbatim a portion from Ælfric's *Lives of Saints* (XII *In Caput Ieiunii*, lines 79–87). He just adds an empty phrase *for worulde* at the end of a sentence (Napier XXIX 142.5 *þeah ðe he si welig for worulde*), otherwise using every bit of the passage as it is in the source, including a typically Ælfrician sophistication of condensed apposition (142.2 *syndon gode dagas, na swaþeah manega dagas, ac an*) and equally char-

---

[38] As a matter of fact, the two words do change the meaning of the poetic line, where *ætsomne* of course refers to *hi*, not *ege*. Moreover, they show poetic post-position of the modifier (as in *JDay II* 15; see p. 116).

acteristic repetition of the word *lif* in different senses (141.32 *We sceolon gewilnian symle þæs ecan lifes . . . Ðeah þe hwa wylle her on life habban gode dagas . . .*), or double alliteration linking parallel clauses (142.6 *oððe his freond him ætfeallað, oððe his feoh him ætbyrst*).[39]

This attitude, however, does not seem to reflect a choice the homilist makes as a matter of principle for the whole of his revisory work. If we turn back to the first section of the homily, we find some of the features of the homilist's language noted in the 'poetic section' anticipated there—such as verb forms with a prefix (Napier XXIX 134.22 *gebeorge* and 135.16 *alæton*, in place of simplexes in the source), an instrumental dative case form (134.18 *eallon mægne*, amidst six *mid*-phrases; on this see below), addition of *þær* (135.21, again promoted by *þonne*) and other adverbs, mostly intensifying (134.22 *georne*, 135.9 *huru . . . æfre*, 135.16 *geornlicor*), a sequence of negative clauses (135.8–14,[40] with eight *ne*'s and four *næfre*'s, mostly taken over from the source but rearranged in a symmetrical pattern), and word order which avoids the 'split construction' (135.19 *ys uncuð seo tid and se dæg*, rewriting *Conf* 10.5.38 *is seo tid swiðe uncuð ⁊ se dæg*).[41] But these common features are if anything minor details in the revision for this section of the homily. What is more striking here is the extent to which the homilist chooses to rewrite his source, both in syntax and, occasionally, in contents.

In rewriting formulas and directions for confessors as the initial section of a homily, our homilist has in the first instance to change personal pronouns in accordance with the change in the type of discourse, from one in which three 'roles' are involved (the writer of the document (the covert 'ic'), the confessor ('þu'), and a man whose confession he hears ('he')), to one where a homilist directly

---

[39] For details on Ælfric, see (for apposition) Ann Eljenholm Nichols, 'Methodical Abbreviation: A Study in Aelfric's Friday Homilies for Lent', *The Old English Homily*, ed. Szarmach and Huppé, pp. 157–80, esp. pp. 165ff., and (for repetition and wordplay) John C. Pope (ed.), *Homilies of Ælfric: A Supplementary Collection*. 2 vols. (EETS os 259 and 260. London, 1967–8), Vol. I, pp. 109–11 and James Hurt, *Ælfric* (New York, 1972), pp. 123–4. On apposition, see also such examples as *ÆCHom* i, Praefatio 1 *Ic ælfric munuc ⁊ mæssepreost swa ðeah waccre ponne swilcum hadum gebyrige*, and my paper 'Syntactical Revision in Wulfstan's Rewritings of Ælfric' (*Studies in the History*, pp. 205–20), where I argue for the importance of this feature in Ælfric as against Wulfstan, who often expands it into a clause in rewriting Ælfric's prose.

[40] Part of the relevant sentence reads as in Napier XXIX 135.5 quoted below (the latter half beginning with *eow ys*), corresponding to the source text as it stands in the DOE Corpus: *Conf* 10.5.24 *þe is neodþearf þæt þu riht do ⁊ þæt þe næfre deofol beswican. Ne mote þæt þu læte ænige synne ungeandet . . .* But the Corpus does not seem to have construed the syntax correctly. Its *Ne mote* should be part of the preceding clause (*. . . beswican ne mote*), followed by a *þæt*-clause of purpose or result; the original manuscript has a punctus after *ne mote* (all in lower case), followed by the abbreviation *þ*.

[41] Since this source text has not appeared in a printed edition as yet, I quote from the DOE Corpus, with references to manuscript line, as in the Corpus.

addresses his audience. The homilist makes the necessary adjustments by assuming the persona of the originator of the instructions but at the same time identifying himself with the audience he is addressing. He does make a distinction between 'we' as teachers and 'ge' as those who are being taught where the distinction is clearly intended from the source:

> Napier XXIX 135.5 We halsiað eow and beodað, þæt ge god lufian and him eallunga gehyrsume beon, forðam us ys neod, þæt we eow rihtlice tæcon, and eow ys oferþearf, þæt ge hit rihtlice healdon, and þæt eow næfre se deofol to ðam beswican mote, ne þæt ge næfre huru ne læton ænige synne ungeanded, . . .

Otherwise, the homilist chooses to teach what a man should do as a true Christian in terms of the inclusive 'we' (both you and I) and exhortative *uton*, rather than 'ge' or 'þu' and the imperative, which could have been expected from the mode of speech of the source—a decision which sets his homily distinctly apart from another homiletic piece based on the same material, as Karl Jost points out:

> Ebenso glaube ich, dass die Stellen Wulf. XXIX 135, 5–25 and Wulf. LVI 291, 2–20, die unter sich nur geringfügig abweichen, einer gemeinsamen, sonst unbekannten Quelle entnommen sind. Der Hauptunterschied zwischen den beiden Fassungen ist, dass Wulf. LVI an der gleich von Anhang an eingenommenen Vorstellung einer Einzelunterredung zwischen einem Priester und einem Beichtenden konsequent festhält. Der Priester redet den Beichtenden (290, 13) mit *leofa cild* an und bleibt auch in der mit Wulf. XXIX sonst gleichlautenden Partie bei der Anrede 'du'.[2)]
>
> 2) In Wulf. XXIX spricht der Priester nach Homiletenart von sich als *we*.[42]

Translation into homily mode may not in itself be very innovative. But the homilist goes far beyond that. The very beginning of the homily illustrates this:

> Napier XXIX 134.11 Men ða leofestan, gehyrað, hwæt us halige bec beodað, þæt we for godes lufan and for his ege ure lif rihtlice libban and mid eaðmedum urum drihtne hyron and urne cristendom and ure fulluht wel healdon, þæt ure dæda beon gode gecweme, and we mid eadmedum urum scrifte ure synna andetton and georne betan mid fæstene and mid ælmessan and mid ciriclicre socne and mid geornfulnesse godes beboda and ure lareowa.

---

[42] Jost, *Wulfstanstudien*, p. 205. Jost goes on to assert in the same footnote that the homily form was the original one: 'Ich halte die Predigtform für ursprünglich, die Umsetzung in eine persönliche Ermahnung eines Beichtvaters für sekundär.'

Conf 10.5.4 bide hine þonne ærost for godes lufon ⁊ for his ege þæt he his lif mid rihte libbe ⁊ his drihtne mid eadmedum hyre ⁊ his cristendom ⁊ his fulluht wel gehealde ⁊ his misdæda andette ⁊ his sawle læce georne sece ⁊ his fæsten wel bega ⁊ his cyrcan clænlice sece ⁊ godes beboda georne hlyste ⁊ his larþeowa.

The homilist, perhaps inspired by the first *mid eaðmedum* (in the third line) which he takes over from the source, introduces five more *mid*-phrases (in the last four lines), thereby drastically simplifying the verb structure of the latter half of the sentence, from the five verbs (*andette . . . sece . . . bega . . . sece . . . hlyste*) of the source text to two (*andetton . . . betan*).[43] The revision is made even more thorough by a complete clause (if not of an innovative nature) inserted before all this (*þæt ure dæda beon gode gecweme*) and by a few personal touches in details of wording, such as the order AdvO (*mid eaðmedum urum drihtne*, from the reverse order in the source, succeeded by *mid eadmedum urum scrifte*) and avoidance of *mid rihte* in favour of *rihtlice*.[44]

Use of fewer verbs as noted above may be partly consequent on the nature of the source material which the homilist undertakes to make less formulaic and more like a sermon. So may the change he makes a little later, from a long list of sins as objects of the imperative *forbeod him* (*Conf* 10.5.20) which follows them, to the order VO followed by the explanatory *þæt is*: Napier XXIX 134.23 *utan . . . forbugan geornlice þa synleahtras, þe us forbodene synd, þæt is unrihthæmed and . . . ealle þa unþeawas, þe deoflu on mancynn gebringað*. However, the homilist's intention evidently goes deeper when he adds there two relative clauses and the word *synleahtras*.[45] The first relative clause (*þe us forbodene synd*) rewrites the imperative *forbeod him* of the source, while the second relative clause (*þe deoflu . . . gebringað*, at the end) and the addition of the noun are seen to develop associations with the relevant words—*englas* changed into *deoflum*, and *leahter*, both the homilist's contributions—in the immediately preceding sentences:

Napier XXIX 134.18 And uton eallon mægne us scyldan wið ofermodignesse,[46] forðam þe hy awurpon iu englas of heofonum, and hi wurdon þærrihtes to deoflum forsceapene. Forði is ælcum men oferþearf, þæt

---

[43] The homily sentence as it stands, however, might be defective. Sense requires us to assume an inadvertent omission of a verb to go with the final *mid*-phrase, corresponding to *hlyste* in the source.

[44] The homilist again uses *rihtlice* twice in Napier XXIX 135.7–8 in the passage quoted above (p. 125), where the source text has *riht* as the object of *lære* and *do*.

[45] On the word *synleahter* as *hapax legomenon*, see Jost, *Wulfstanstudien*, p. 204 n. 5.

[46] The form *ofermodignesse* here is glossed by L. H. Dodd (*A Glossary of Wulfstan's Homilies* (New York, 1908), s.v.) as accusative singular. But it should be taken as plural, since it is referred to as *hy* in the next clause.

> he him georne wið þone leahter gebeorge, þe læs þe him beo forwyrned his sawle reste on domes dæg.
>
> *Conf* 10.5.12 ⁊ beod him þæt he hine wið ofermetta healde for þam þan men is swiðe mycel þearf þæt he him beorge þæt ofermetta ne forwyrnon his sawle reste.

The three additions thus allow the homilist at once to remain intelligibly close to his source and to write sustained prose to secure his point with some rhetoric. Within the last-quoted passage, too, the homilist makes several changes. He first puts in new causal clauses (where the reference to the fallen angels is made), an addition of material which has led him to start afresh with *Forði*, and finally he gives a twist, turning the *þæt . . . ne* clause to the *þe læs þe*, accompanied by the change in voice of the verb *forwyrnan* and other details. Far from being a 'practical' reviser as he was in the 'poetic section', here the homilist proves to be a writer of conscious style who is not slow to show his ideas and preferences in wording and selection of material.

If tightly-knit prose is a distinct feature of writing in the part of the homily being discussed, it is seen more concisely and clearly when the homilist comes to rewrite a 'moralizing' passage of the source: *Conf* 10.5.32 *geþenc þæt þu ænne nacodne lichaman on þas woruld brohtest ⁊ þu hine scealt eft ana lætan*. The homilist reshapes the coordinate noun clauses serving as objects of *geþenc* into a noun and a *þæt*-clause with a relative clause in between—a variant of what Bruce Mitchell calls the 'lilies of the field' construction[47]—, thereby focusing upon *þone nacodan lichoman*, a focus which is then reinforced by repetition of the word *nacod* in the *þæt*-clause and further by the associations with that word which have called forth the verb *bewreon* 'to cover' in the following *butan*-clause:

> Napier XXIX 135.14 Utan nu, leofan men, geþencan þone nacodan lichoman, þe we on ðas woruld brohton, þæt we hine sceolon eft ealswa nacodne alæton, butan we þe geornlicor nu us sylfe mid godum dædum bewreon.

The word *nacod* is repeated anaphorically (*ealswa nacodne*) in place of *ana* of the source, while the *butan*-clause has its wording thoroughly reset around its replaced verb. The whole sentence is reconstructed so as to develop the homilist's emphasis, with an effect which might be called almost literary. The distance from the attitude to his source and the resultant language in the 'poetic section' is here again remarkable.

The part of the homily so far discussed is followed, prior to the 'poetic section', by about a page length of text for which no exact source is known.[48] A sentence near its opening (Napier XXIX 136.1–5) has been shown by Godden to be a

---

[47] See *OES*, §2067.
[48] See Jost, *Wulfstanstudien*, pp. 203–5; Godden, 'Penitential motif', 225–6.

version of what he calls a penitential motif (see section I), paralleled in his Group A of seven examples, including three from the pseudo-Egbert *Ordo Confessionis* (*Conf* 2.1).[49] Then come sentences insisting on the importance of learning the *Credo* and *Paternoster*, explaining specific details of the times set for fasting, and finally forbidding tasting the blood of animals and fowls against God's law. Such a variety of fundamentals of Christian faith may not be the homilist's own contribution but is more likely to be drawn from some unknown penitential source.[50]

More importantly, the passage has peculiarities of linguistic usage of its own. This is seen most clearly in the mode of direct address, particularly as adopted a sentence after the penitential motif:

Napier XXIX 136.16 and fæstað eower lenctenfæsten rihtlice to nones ælc man, þe beo ofer .xii. wintre, and ða feower ymbrenu on twelf monðum, þe eow rihtlice asette synd, and ðæra haligra martyra mæsseæfenas, þe for Cristes lufon martyrdom þrowedon and man eallum folce to healicum freolse byt.

The homilist addresses the congregation in the second person imperative (*fæstað*), in contrast not only to the inclusive 'we' and the exhortative *uton* in the opening part of the homily (Napier XXIX 134.11–135.25) but also to the mode assumed in the immediately preceding sentences (Napier XXIX 136.9 *Uton geþencan . . . And gyf hwylc man sy, . . . beo he swyðe geornlice embe . . .*). Moreover, the form *fæstað* is accompanied by *ælc man* as its grammatical subject.[51] How all this has found its way into the homily is difficult to say with certainty. Given the fact that there are no

---

[49] For details, see Godden, 'Penitential motif', 223–7; Jost, *Wulfstanstudien*, pp. 204–5.

[50] It might be noted that like the penitential motif, the sentence immediately following it in the homily (Napier XXIX 136.5–9) has a parallel in some manuscripts of the pseudo-Egbert *Ordo* (*Conf* 2.1.31); see Robert Spindler (ed.), *Das altenglische Bussbuch* (Leipzig, 1934), pp. 171–2, apparatus. Whitbread ('Wulfstan Homilies', 349) appears to suggest Ecclesiastes 12:14 as the source for Napier XXIX at this point. But the verbal correspondence is far from close.

[51] No similar examples are recorded in *OES*, §§887–91 ('second person imperatives'). On the opening clause of Napier XXIX 136.18, Bruce Mitchell (private communication) says: 'I would explain it thus: (a) [from *fæstað* to *nones*] is a non-dependent command with imp. pl. *fæstað* with unexpressed subj[ect] . . . (b) [from *ælc* to *wintre*] is an independent statement limiting those who have to keep this fast, explanatory of *[ge] . . . eower*'. In any event, the sentence is, as he adds, not 'very polished'. Another not 'very polished' point of syntax in Napier XXIX 136.18 is the last paratactic clause (*and man . . . byt*). It must be assumed to be 'an independent observation' explanatory of the *mæsseæfenas* to which the singular *freolse* obviously refers rather loosely, to be translated as 'and all are summoned to the high or noble feast', as Mitchell (private communication) says; though syntax would make us inclined to construe it as part of the *þe*-clause (in which case the relative pronoun would require, quite irregularly, different antecedents for the

examples of this kind elsewhere in the homily, however, one feels tempted to think that they may reinforce the idea of a lost penitential text as the source at this point. The homilist has apparently not, for some reason or another, undertaken to rewrite it as extensively as he could have been expected to do after what he did in the opening part. His attitude to the source again varies from one part of the homily to another, with different effects on the language and style of each part.

IV

The last major section to be discussed, Napier 140.3–141.25, is a version of the Old English vision of Macarius, as related in an anonymous work (*HomU* 55) traditionally called the Macarius Homily after the visionary. The exact relationship between the two versions has long been a matter of dispute. But recent scholarship accepts the view that the Napier XXIX version is an adaptation of the relevant extract from the Macarius Homily rather than an independent translation of a single Latin original, as its initial promulgator asserts:

> Wulf. XXIX 140, 3–141, 25 deckt sich mit Stellen aus der Einleitung der *Ecclesiastical Institutes* [Macarius Homily edited by Thorpe], die ihrerseits teilweise auf eine lateinische Vision zurückgeht. Die wörtlichen Übereinstimmungen zwischen Eccl. Inst. und Wulf. XXIX sind so weitgehend, dass ich nicht an zwei voreinander unabhängige Übersetzungen zu glauben vermag. Der Kompilator von Wulf. XXIX hat einfach den Eccl. Inst. das für ihn Brauchbare entnommen und stilistisch leicht überarbeitet.[52]

D. G. Scragg and Hans Sauer, the latest editor of the Macarius Homily, both concur.[53] Hence my choice of the Macarius version rather than the Latin original

---

two clauses it introduces — *martyra* for the first and *mæsseæfenas* for the second). On *beodan* 'to summon' with dative of person, see *DOE*, s.v. A.8.

[52] Jost, *Wulfstanstudien*, pp. 206–7. On the earlier view that the Napier XXIX version is an independent translation, see Julius Zupitza, 'Zu "Seele und Leib"', *Archiv* 91 (1893), 369–404, esp. 369–78; and Louise Dudley, 'An Early Homily on the "Body and Soul" Theme', *JEGP* 8 (1909), 225–53, esp. 225–39. In its opening, the Macarius Homily in turn is parallel to Vercelli Homily IV; see D. G. Scragg (ed.), *The Vercelli Homilies and Related Texts*, EETS os 300 (Oxford, 1992), pp. 87–9; Whitbread, '"Wulfstan" Homilies', 351. On the very recent evidence that the Macarius Homily represents the earliest version which Vercelli IV expands rather than the other way round, and its implications for dating the relevant homilies, see Scragg, *Dating and Style*, pp. 3–5; Charles D. Wright, 'The Old English "Macarius" Homily, Vercelli Homily IV, and Ephrem Latinus, *De paenitentia*', *Via Crucis: Essays on Early Medieval Sources and Ideas in Memory of J. E. Cross*, ed. Thomas N. Hall (Morgantown, 2002), pp. 210–34.

[53] See Scragg, 'The corpus', 254 and 256 n. 3; Hans Sauer (ed.), *Theodulfi Capitula in England* (Munich, 1978), pp. 93–4.

as the source.[54] On the other hand, it remains to be considered more carefully whether one can dismiss the whole section as cavalierly as Jost does with the brief remark quoted above, for that is all he has to say on it. There is, in fact, reason to doubt that the homilist is always content with very minor changes of style to the source, however useful and convenient he may have found it.

As Julius Zupitza has noted,[55] the Napier XXIX version of the vision differs considerably from the Macarius text, usually in details of wording. Zupitza describes the difference in terms of the Latin original to which the two Old English versions (being, as he assumes, independent translations) are more or less closely related at individual points. From our point of view, the difference is a mixture of familiar features of the homilist's linguistic usage found in the previous sections and new features. The former include prefixed forms of verbs (Napier XXIX 140.6 *alyson* and 141.24 *forswealh*, in place of the simplexes in *MacHom* 24 and 124); dative case forms in the instrumental sense (141.4 and 141.20 (for a *mid*-phrase in *MacHom* 119), both with the noun *stefn*; see the Napier XXIX 140.19 passage (p. 132)); word order *þa* VS rather than *(þa)* SV (e.g. 140.9 *þa geseah he sume earme sawle* (*MacHom* 77 *He geseah sumes mannes sawle*)); and addition of the intensifying *georne* (140.6, and twice more in the homilist's own sentence at 140.18; see n. 61) and of a noun, either as antecedent of a relative pronoun (140.7 *ealle þa þing, þe on hyre syndon* (*MacHom* 25 *ealle þa þe*)) or headword of an adjective (140.29 *þu earma lichama* (*MacHom* 96 *þu earma*)).[56] Of similar importance are features not mentioned before in this study but shared by the previous sections, such as *deofol* as a masculine rather than neuter noun (Napier XXIX 140.19 and 141.4 (*MacHom* 100 *Ðæt deofol*), as earlier at 135.8 and 135.30),[57] and the

---

[54] References to the Macarius version are to Sauer's edition of the homily (*Theodulfi Capitula*, pp. 411–6), with his short title *MacHom* and line numbering.

[55] Zupitza, 'Zu "Seele und Leib"', 375–8.

[56] There are, not unexpectedly, examples which show that the homilist is not always rewriting in the way these examples would point to, such as the unprefixed *læddon* at Napier XXIX 141.23 (*MacHom* 122 *gelæddon*); word orders closer to modern orders (140.17 and 141.2, both with an adverbial phrase moved to a position after the verb, from the pre-verbal position in *MacHom* 85 *and ic symble mid hyre wæs* and 98; and 140.12 *cwæð . . . to hyre* (*MacHom* 81 . . . *hyre to cwæð*)); and omission of the intensifying *symble* (see 140.17 above) and *swiðe* at 141.3 (*MacHom* 99 *þa swiðe swætan*). On omission of *swiðe* in the opening section, see Napier XXIX 135.19 (p. 124).

[57] In the plural, however, the neuter form *deoflu* (nom., acc.) is the homilist's invariable choice (Napier XXIX 135.4, 141.13 and 141.23, the latter two repeating the same form in *MacHom* 112 and 121). Our homilist's practice thus represents what *DOE* (s.v.) describes as the 'more common' usage of the word *deofol*. For a very recent study of details of the morphology and syntax of this word, see E. G. Stanley, 'Old English *þæt deofol; se deofol* or Just *deofol*', *And gladly wolde he lerne and gladly teche: Essays on Medieval English Presented to Professor Matsuji Tajima on His Sixtieth Birthday*, ed. Yoko Iyeiri and Margaret Connolly (Tokyo, 2002), pp. 51–71.

form of address *leofan men* (140.3, against *MacHom* 20 *men þa leofestan*, as always elsewhere in the homily except at its opening 134.11). All these are sure marks of a single homilist working on materials of widely differing natures, adapting them to his purpose and taste, to some extent at least.

On the other hand, the unique material of the section has provided the homilist with opportunities to make changes of the kind he does not elsewhere. Some of these exhibit certain preferences in phraseology. He prefers the periphrasis with *willan* (Napier XXIX 140.13, 140.15) to the simple verb form used in the source (*MacHom* 81, 83);[58] uses 'composite predicates' of the type '*habban/niman* + noun' instead of single verbs (140.21 *niman eardungstowe*, *MacHom* 89 *ingangan* (Latin *ingredi*[59]); 141.17 *ðu næfst þær nane wununge . . . ðu næfst þær nane gemanan*, *MacHom* 116 *þu þær ne most wunian; . . . þe nis lyfed þær to eardianne* (Latin *requiescis . . . habitas*)); and repeats the prepositions *on* (together with *þis*: 140.22 *on þis fulestan and on þis wyrstan lichaman*) and *mid* (141.2). He also repeats *to* where there is none after the verb *geweorðan* in the source, resulting in the 'possessive dative' construction: 141.1 *gewurðan to fulan hræwe and wyrmum to mete* (*MacHom* 96 *geworden þæt fuleste hreaw and wyrma mete*). Most of these changes seem to be purely matters of style, though the first might be taken to be an attempt to reproduce the usage of speech, since it occurs in a devil's words to the soul.

Others may be features of the homilist's prose that have finally found their place as he turned to narrating a story of actions and events in this section. Thus, the homilist apparently avoids the 'expanded form' ('*beon* + present participle'), replacing all the four examples in the source (*MacHom* 86, 91, 92 and 114) except the second, which is used in a relative clause and is taken over as such by him:

Napier XXIX 140.22 . . . on þis fulestan and on þis wyrstan lichaman, þe[60] wæs a nymende earmra manna æhta on unriht.

MacHom 89 '. . . on þisne fulestan and wyrrestan lichoman?' Heo þa locade to hyre lichoman and cwæð: 'Wa þe, þu earma lichoma! Ðu þe wære nimende fremdra manna speda . . .'.

Whether this association in our homilist with subordinate clauses is significant or not—what is, in other words, the nuance of meaning he attaches to this particular instance and how it may differ from the usage in the source—is a problem which demands further analysis. But it might mean, since he rewrites another

---

[58] He has, though, omitted the auxiliary in the 'poetic section' (Napier XXIX 136.28); see section II (p. 119).

[59] Quotation of the Latin text is made from Batiouchkof's edition, as reproduced in Zupitza's parallel texts ('Zu "Seele und Leib"', 370–4). For Batiouchkof's Latin text, see also A. B. Van Os, *Religious Visions: The development of the eschatological elements in mediaeval English religious literature* (Amsterdam, 1932), pp. 279–80.

[60] This is Napier's emendation; the manuscript reads *he*.

example in a parallel relative clause as a simple verb in a main clause and replaces the one example in the main clause with a simple verb, that our homilist liked to give the main plot quick movement; he might have promoted it by presenting the individual actions and events of main clauses plainly without the subtleties of the expanded form. In fact, there is another detail in the homilist's use of verbs which points to the same tendency. In introducing each of the alternate speeches of the Soul and the devil, the Macarius version always has a pair of verbs of saying and related action, usually combining the verb *onginnan*, probably suggested by the Latin original, with the first element of the pair. Our homilist definitely prefers a simplified pattern, invariably with a single verb and/or omitting the verb *onginnan*:

> Napier XXIX 140.19 Seo earme sawul beseah uppan þone deofol and earmlice clypode (*MacHom* 87 . . . heo ongan earmlice cleopian and cwæð; *Latin* dicere cepit) . . . And se deofol hludre stefne clypode and cwæð (*MacHom* 100 . . . ongan þa cleopian and cwæð; *Latin* dixerunt) . . . Hi [the devils] cwædon (*MacHom* 112 Hig hyre andwyrden and cwæden; *Latin* Responderunt demones) . . . Heo [the Soul] ongan þa wependre stefne cweþan (*MacHom* 119 . . . ongan mid micele sare and wope heofian and cwæð; *Latin* cepit . . . dicere) . . .

The homilist in effect quickens the movement of narration and shifts his emphasis onto the speeches themselves. The shifting also occurs within one of the speeches, as rewritten by the homilist. Making the Soul begin to speak as above (140.19), he then makes a continued speech of the Soul out of two separated ones in the source, by suppressing a narrative sentence linking them (*MacHom* 90 *Heo þa locade to hyre lichoman and cwæð*) as the Soul turned from the devils to the Body. Our homilist also introduces his own emphasis by a repeated use of instrumental datives (*se deofol hludre stefne . . . Heo . . . wependre stefne*) to point up the contrast between the devil and the Soul.

The last-mentioned group of simplified verb structures is only one example of simplification, for which our homilist rewrites apparently more often than for addition.[61] Other examples include a rewriting of a whole sentence wherein a

---

[61] There are, for example, only three clauses added by the homilist: Napier XXIX 140.18 *and heo a ful georne hlyste minre lare and georne fyligde*, 140.26 *and forgeate me*, and 141.22 *(wa me earmre, þæt . . .) and þæt ic swa mycele beorhtnesse forlætan sceolde*. This last, apparently a translation of the Latin (*aut quare . . . dereliqui claritatem illam*), might make us wonder if it is still possible to think, as Zupitza and Dudley have done, that the Napier XXIX and Macarius versions of the vision are independent translations of the Latin. So might Napier XXIX 140.14 *Michael se heahencgel . . . wyle þe geniman of us* (L *nobis eripiat*), where the Macarius version has . . . *þe genime raðe*. For full details of the difference between the two versions vis-à-vis the Latin original, see Zupitza, 'Zu "Seele und Leib"', 377–8. However, Batiouchkof's text has been shown not to be the immediate source for

participial phrase is omitted at the end of the vision (Napier XXIX 141.23; see below), condensing of two verb phrases into one (140.4 *þæt he ne mæge him ondrædon þa toweardan witu?*; *MacHom* 21 . . . *wepan þa toweardan witu and him þa ondrædan?*), and replacement of an adverb of denial (140.16 *nese*) for a negative sentence (*MacHom* 84 *Ne þurfe ge eow ondrædan*). The homilist even omits, occasionally, whole clauses and sentences, as in one of the Soul's speeches (see above) and in:

> Napier XXIX 140.5 Hwæt is us la selre, þonne we ealne weg ure synna beton and hi mid ælmessan georne alyson, forðam þe þeos woruld ateorað and ealle þa þing, þe on hyre syndon?

The homilist has simplified the last clauses considerably, where the corresponding causal clause is flanked by *þæt*- and *and*-clauses in the source (*MacHom* 22–7).[62] What is common to these examples of simplification and other features of our homilist's revision, whether the familiar ones or those uniquely found in the section being discussed, is that they are changes on the phrasal or clausal level, made within single clauses. They show the homilist working in a way not unlike the 'practical' method of the 'poetic section'; to that extent, the homilist has retouched his source 'stilistisch leicht', as Jost says (see above).

Yet the homilist does not always confine himself within clauses but occasionally goes beyond to introduce his sense of larger adaptation. A good case in point is a sentence describing the journey of the Soul and the devils:

> Napier XXIX 141.11 Ða deoflu feredon þa earman sawle þa to þystrum; þa geseah heo be þam wege mycele beorhtnyssa; þa axode heo þa deoflu, þe hi læddon, hwæt seo beorhtnys wære.

> *MacHom* 108 Hig genaman þa þa earman sawle mid micle sare and geomorunge, and hi asettan ofer hyra þa sweartestan fyðra. And, mid þi þe hi wæron ferende, seo earme sawl geseah miccle beorohtnesse. Heo axode þa deoflu, hwæt seo beorohtnysse wære.

In his first sentence, our homilist, rewriting the Macarius version drastically, speaks literally of their journeying. This has perhaps made the original temporal clause *mid þi þe hi wæron ferende* redundant for the homilist, who telescopes it

---

the Old English translation; see Zupitza, 'Zu "Seele und Leib"', 375–8, and Dudley, 'An Early Homily', 235–9. The source text which has since been lost might have contained a reading which is represented more closely by the Macarius version in those sentences.

[62] Other examples of simplification include omission of 'unidiomatic' dative pronouns (*MacHom* 94 *ic me wæs blac*; . . . *ic me wæs unrot*; see Napier XXIX 140.26 (p. 134)), and of some adverbs and adverbial phrases such as *on þisse weorolde* (*MacHom* 22 *Hwæt is us la selre on þissere worulde*; see Napier XXIX 140.5 (above)), and *swa* (121) and *swa þeah* (118).

into *þe þam wege*, and then adds the reference to the devils as the relative clause *þe hi læddon*. The result is again a brisk movement of the 'þa . . .; þa . . .' sequence, instead of the delayed movement of clauses which it replaces. Part of this process is paralleled some ten lines later, when the homilist first omits paired present participles but adds *innan þone muð* after *anum fyrenan dracan*, thereby dispensing with an entire clause with a superlative adjective (*se ontynde . . . goman*) immediately following in the source, to move the more quickly to the final moment in the vision:

> Napier XXIX 141.23 Ða deoflu hi ða læddon and bescuton hi anum fyrenan dracan innan þone muð, and he hi þærrihte forswealh and eft aspaw on ða hatostan brynas hellewites.

> MacHom 121 Ða deoflu hig þa gelæddan, and wepende and geomrigende hy hy[63] sealdon suman fyrenan dracan: se ontynde his þa fyrenan and þa scearpestan goman, and he hig swealh, and hig eft aspaw on þa hattestan ligas.

For omission of clauses, see further Napier XXIX 140.9–10 (*MacHom* 77–9) and 140.29–141.2 (*MacHom* 96–7).

But brevity is not the only consideration for the homilist when he makes a change across clause boundaries. Out of an unvaried sequence of *and*-clauses forming three antitheses between Body and Soul in the source, he makes a sharpened contrast by transforming it into two hypotactic sentences of the form 'þonne . . ., þonne . . .', with adverbs and other expanding words thrown in:

> Napier XXIX 140.26 Þonne ðu wære glæd and reod and godes hiwes, þonne wæs ic blac and swyðe unrot; þonne þu smercodest and hloge, þonne weop ic biterlice.

> MacHom 94 and þu þe wære reod, and ic me wæs blac; þu wære glæd, and ic me wæs unrot; þu hloge, and ic weop.

Or he transposes the adjective *earm* from within the *þæt*-clause (*MacHom* 120 *Wa me, þæt ic æfre swa earm* . . .) into the main clause (Napier XXIX 141.21 *Wa me earmre, þæt ic æfre* . . .),[64] perhaps repeating the order used earlier at 140.20 (*MacHom* 88 *Wa me earmre! To hwon sceolde ic æfre* . . .?). These cases suggest an

---

[63] Benjamin Thorpe (*Ancient Laws and Institutes of England*, 2 vols. (London, 1840), Vol. II, p. 398, line 38), and the DOE Corpus following Thorpe, read *hy sealdon suman fyrenan dracan*, with one *hy*. But, as Sauer (*Theodulfi Capitula*, p. 415, apparatus) points out, the manuscript has two *hy*'s.

[64] Here again our homilist is closer than the Macarius homilist to the Latin text (*Heu me miseram* . . .); see n. 61.

attempt, however isolated, on the homilist's part to impart elements of rhetorical elaboration as he deems it best for his purpose, as he was seen more clearly to do in the opening section.

Whether making for rhetorical refinement or easier syntax, the range of what I have called the homilist's 'larger adaptation' makes the whole work of his revision in this 'Macarius section' less superficial than Jost might have led us to believe. What the homilist has produced is an interesting mixture of these larger changes and smaller ones, a product of more or less 'practical' attitudes towards the source, as much as a mixture of features found elsewhere in the homily and those found only in this section.

V

What can we say, then, about the question raised at the beginning of this chapter? Napier XXIX is a homily which, perhaps more than any other single composite homily, has a wide range of sources and has made accordingly numerous changes, large and small, to them to secure its own identity as a homily. The changes naturally include what might well be idiosyncrasies of a single writer working on the several sources to make a continuous homily, such as the instrumental dative and the attempt to introduce rhetorical elements, which both recur in more than one section of the homily.[65] However, there seems to be little that substantiates Letson's claim that Napier XXIX is as a whole a 'poetic homily', inspired primarily by the use of the *Judgement Day II* poem in the second section. There is very little, apart from the examples given earlier (see section I), of alliteration or rhyme elsewhere in the homily; nor is any important part played in the other sections by poeticism, except in the concluding part in the last section, which 'continues as a direct prayer to God, addressed somewhat poetically':[66]

> Napier XXIX 142.21 Heofonan heahcyning and ealles middaneardes alysend, gemiltsa us synfullum, swa swa ðin milda wylla sy, and geunne us, þæt we moton geearnian mid fæstum geleafan and mid fæstenum and mid

---

[65] To the examples of the instrumental dative already given (pp. 117,124,130, and 132) is to be added another in a passage of unknown origin in the first section: Napier XXIX 136.21 *his agenum muðe*. On rhetorical elaboration, see n. 66.

[66] Whitbread, 'Wulfstan Homilies', 351. It may not be coincidence that this concluding sentence is immediately preceded by a portion (Napier XXIX 142.12–21) which contains one of the few repetitive word pairs used elsewhere than in the 'poetic section' (142.20 *on worde oððe on weorce oððe on geðance*) and is rhetorically structured, with repeated uses of each of the two key phrases *to/ongean his (...) willan* and *on/æfter/of þis(s)ere worulde* echoing each other. The sentence in Napier XXIX 142.21 is then followed by a list similar to that in Blickling V of the qualities we do and do not find in heaven (142.26–143.2). On this resemblance, see Whitbread, 'Wulfstan Homilies', 352; Godden, 'Penitential motif', 226.

ælmesdædum and mid oðrum godum weorcum, þæt we moton becuman to þære ecan reste.

But even this, occurring as it does in a passage of unknown origin, might not be our homilist's contribution but that of some unknown author whom he might have followed closely.

On the contrary, Napier XXIX is a product of the varying degrees and varying ways in which adaptation is made in each of the four sections constituting it, reflecting the widely different natures of the sources and, more importantly, the widely different attitudes the homilist shows to them. These attitudes range from the 'severely practical' method of adaptation shown in the section based on the Judgement Day poem (itself quite distinct in kind from the 'prose dilution' in Vercelli XXI; see Chapter IV) to the relative freedom with which he adapts sentences from formulas and instructions for confessors. The resulting homily is a 'Stilgemisch' (mixture of styles), as Jost has aptly called it,[67] with little sign of the consistent style and tone with which Letson seems to credit the work.

This conclusion may throw a new light on the authorship of Napier XXIX. The problem has long been disputed, particularly since Whitbread argued that the homily is by the same homilist as another anonymous composite homily, Napier XXX, discussed in Chapter II.[68] My conclusion above seems to add evidence to Scragg's more recent view denying common authorship for the two homilies largely on the basis of source study,[69] by pointing to Napier XXIX's distinctive method of adaptation and the resulting mixture of styles. Napier XXX is a more homogeneous homily, with a more or less consistent attitude of the compiler to the several sources involved, making the composite work more like a homily of his own, as I argued in Chapter II. My argument there implies another important distinction from Napier XXIX—the use of often alliterating repetitive word pairs for which Napier XXX has such a strong affinity,[70] if not precisely to 'imitate' Wulfstan's manner of using this verbal technique. From a homily of this kind, Napier XXIX shows itself to be set substantially apart both in the general method of adaptation and in specific details of verbal usage, thereby representing a different aspect of the 'personal characteristics' which Angus McIntosh ascribes to a certain group of composite homilies in late Old English.[71]

---

[67] Jost, *Wulfstanstudien*, p. 207.

[68] Whitbread, 'Wulfstan Homilies', 357–64.

[69] Scragg, 'Napier's "Wulfstan" homily xxx', 209–11.

[70] It is partly on the evidence of this stylistic tendency that Scragg calls the Napier XXX homilist a 'Wulfstan imitator' ('Napier's "Wulfstan" homily xxx', 208). On this problem, see Chapter II.

[71] Angus McIntosh, 'Wulfstan's Prose', *PBA* 34 (1948), 109–42, at 126 (see Chapter I, pp. 8–9).

There is still another sense in which Napier XXIX differs clearly from Napier XXX, though this difference may not reveal much about their authorship. Unlike Napier XXX, Napier XXIX draws upon earlier materials which do not include any extracts from Wulfstan's writings but do draw upon a passage from Ælfric's homiletic work. Its verbatim treatment of this short passage contains nothing very remarkable in the use of Ælfric as source. But its use of this source at any rate points to a large problem which has yet to be considered in full detail in this study of Old English composite homilies. The next chapter is devoted to this problem.

VI.

In Die Sancto Pasce and *De Descensu Christi ad Inferos*: Two Easter Homilies Using Ælfrician Material

The present chapter deals with two anonymous Easter Sunday homilies[1] for which *HomS* 27 (Cameron No. B3.2.27) and *HomS* 28 (B3.2.28) are the DOE short titles. They are both preserved only in one manuscript, *HomS* 27 in CCCC 162 (s. xi in.) and *HomS* 28 in Junius 121 (s. xi 3rd quarter),[2] in which they are titled, respectively, *In die sancto pasce* (as the manuscript rubric) and *De descensu Christi ad inferos* (as a note in the margin by a later hand).[3] As these titles suggest, the two homilies derive from distinct traditions of Easter Sunday homilies and show no evidence of connection with each other in textual transmission. What brings them together for discussion here is the fact that they both use a homily of Ælfric as source material for part of the composite work — a feature which indicates another important strand of Old English composite homilies. Moreover, as we shall see, the two homilies use different items in the *Catholic Homilies* and differ remarkably in the way they modify the borrowed passages for their use. To compare these homilies is to examine a facet of the history of the composite homilies in late Anglo-Saxon England not covered by the discussion of the

---

[1] There are two other anonymous Easter homilies that have survived from the Old English period, one of which is known as Blickling Homily VII (*HomS* 26) and is in fact related to the central sections of the *De Descensu* homily. See the section on the *De Descensu* homily below.

[2] For details of the manuscripts, see N. R. Ker, *Catalogue of Manuscripts Containing Anglo-Saxon* (Oxford, 1957), pp. 51–6 and 412–8.

[3] See Ker, *Catalogue*, p. 54; Anna Maria Luiselli Fadda, '"De descensu Christi ad inferos": una inedita omelia anglosassone', *Studi Medievali* 13 (1972), 989–1011, esp. 998, apparatus. K. G. Schaefer and Enid M. Raynes, in their editions of the *De Descensu* homily, say that the marginal note in Junius 121 is 'in a modern hand' ('An Edition of Five Old English Homilies for Palm Sunday, Holy Saturday, and Easter Sunday' (Ph.D. dissertation, Columbia University, 1972), p. 141, apparatus) and 'Unpublished Old English Homilies: Mainly from MSS. CCCC 188, Hatton 114, 115, and Junius 121, together with Vercelli Homily IX' (D.Phil. thesis, Oxford, 1955), p. 72, respectively).

previous chapters, both in terms of language and style and attitudes to the preceding monuments of the genre.

Use of Ælfric's homilies by later homilists is as widespread, perhaps, as that of Wulfstan's writings, judging from the number of relevant manuscript texts that are extant. Mary Swan has shown that there are 26 composite homily texts using material from the *Catholic Homilies*, 18 of them being copied in the tenth or eleventh century and 8 in the twelfth.[4] These composite texts tend, Swan argues, to show 'not simply recopying but rather recontextualisation'[5] — an attitude which goes contrary to Ælfric's famous instructions (stated in the final prayer of the *Catholic Homilies*, Second Series and in the Preface to the *Lives of Saints*) for careful preservation and transmission of his own homilies, because

> his texts are broken down and refashioned to fit the style and concerns of the anonymous homiletic tradition. Certainly, the meanings of his texts are transformed from the careful and complex expositions of biblical and hagiographical narrative and doctrine which he designed to be read in sequence and without interruption from other material, into the convenient, familiar and detachable stock of narrative snippets which compilers find useful to focus and heighten the effect of their composite homilies.[6]

While this conclusion is drawn for the whole corpus of what she calls 'Ælfric/anonymous' composite homilies of which our two Easter homilies are a part, Swan goes on to speak of 'the variety and frequency with which his [Ælfric's] writings are reinscribed'.[7] In particular, she notes 'different degrees' to which Ælfric material is adapted in individual homilies and the 'varied methods of combining C[atholic]H[omilies] and non-Ælfrician material' which are 'evident'[8] in them. Some composite homilies even 'testify to a creative response to Ælfric's work, either for its strong narrative style, thematically organised material or didactic force'.[9] These manifest indications of diversity make one feel that one

---

[4] Mary Swan, 'Ælfric's *Catholic Homilies* in the twelfth century', *Rewriting Old English in the Twelfth Century*, ed. eadem and Elaine M. Treharne (Cambridge, 2000), pp. 62–82, at p. 65 n. 13.

[5] Swan, 'Ælfric's *Catholic Homilies*', p. 63.

[6] Mary Swan, 'Memorialised Readings: Manuscript Evidence for Old English Homily Composition', *Anglo-Saxon Manuscripts and their Heritage*, ed. Phillip Pulsiano and Elaine M. Treharne (Aldershot, 1998), pp. 205–17, at p. 214. See also Swan's Ph.D. thesis on which her articles are based, 'Ælfric as Source: The Exploitation of Ælfric's *Catholic Homilies* from the Late Tenth to Twelfth Centuries' (University of Leeds, 1993), especially Chapter V (pp. 324–33); quotation from this is made below in the final section.

[7] Swan, 'Memorialised Readings', p. 214.

[8] Swan, 'Ælfric as Source', p. 331.

[9] Swan, 'Ælfric as Source', p. 329. This is said of three 'Ælfric/anonymous composite homilies', viz. Cotton Cleopatra B. xiii, article 6 (a variant text of Vercelli XIX, on the story

wants, and needs, to know in more detail about the methods and practices of the individual homilies.[10] It is also important from the viewpoint of this study to see how such individual uses of Ælfric material are a mirror of, and mirrored in, the narrative technique and general style of the other parts of each specific composite, including those which are probably original to the compilers. The following sections are an attempt to do this with reference to the two Easter Sunday homilies.

In Die Sancto Pasce

Our first text, *In Die Sancto Pasce* (*HomS* 27), is an Easter homily which is not based on a lection of the Bible assigned for the day. On the contrary, it is a concatenation of five major themes — the Earthly Paradise, the Evils of the Sixth Day, the Sunday List, the Harrowing of Hell, and the Last Judgement, as Clare A. Lees calls them[11] —, which are thus given 'an orderly treatment'[12] according to the Christian history of mankind but which lack, in that treatment, a consistent narrative or exegesis that would weld them into a continuous development of a single dominant subject. It is as if the homilist has selected the themes which, though they are not all associated particularly clearly with Easter, he finds useful to dwell upon on this particular occasion, with little evident attempt on his part to integrate them. In Lees's words:

> The accumulation of such a number of themes and motifs, the attraction to lists, and the treatment of the extracts from Ælfric, together with the bridging passages between the major themes, suggests an indiscriminate

---

of Jonah) and Lambeth Palace 489, articles 5 and 6. Of these homilies, Malcolm Godden points out that the latter two are 'mainly prescriptive and admonitory', but that '[c]omposite homilies made up mainly of narrative, such as the one on Jonah . . ., are rare, and I do not know of any composite homily which could be described as explanatory or exegetical' ('Old English composite homilies from Winchester', *ASE* 4 (1975), 57–65, at 64–5).

[10] See Joyce Hill, 'Reform and Resistance: Preaching Styles in Late Anglo-Saxon England', *De l'Homélie au Sermon: Histoire de la Prédication Médiévale*, ed. Jacqueline Hamesse and Xavier Hermand (Louvain-la-Neuve, 1993), pp. 15–46, esp. p. 40. Swan describes each 'Ælfric/anonymous composite homily' in detail in her dissertation, and what she has said there on the two Easter homilies will be acknowledged as appropriate in the discussion below.

[11] Clare A. Lees, 'Theme and Echo in an Anonymous Old English Homily for Easter', *Traditio* 42 (1986), 115–42, at 125. Schaefer ('An Edition', p. 168) perceives five different themes, calling them the marvels of God's creation, a contrast between events of the ill-fated sixth day and those of the glorious Lord's Day, the wonder of the Eucharist, the need for alms-giving, and the coming of the Day of Judgement.

[12] Schaefer, 'An Edition', p. 168.

and unsophisticated selection of material. The homily is a mass of information loosely based on Easter without any clear message for its audience.[13]

Nor are 'bridging' passages and phrases numerous or always effective. Lees notes two methods the homilist uses to link the major themes, reference to Easter and reference to penitence, of which the first seems to work more successfully.[14] The reference occurs at the end of the Evils of the Sixth Day and Sunday List sections:

> *HomS* 27.28 and on þam sixtan dæge þeostru wæron gewordene ofer eorðan . . . and stanas wurdon tobrocene and eorðbyrgenna wurdon opene on gewitnysse ures Drihtnes, þæs þe nu todæg of deaðe aras on þisne drihtenlican Easter dæg. Þæt is þonne wurðung-dæg and gebletsod dæg . . .[15]

> *HomS* 27.67 And on þone drihtenlican dæg þære Eastrena ure Drihten aras of deaðe, and þurh þa rode his þrowunge þæs ecan lifes ærest he gecydde, se ðe nu todæg us generede of Adames gylte. And nu todæg Crist eode on helware . . .

In this way the reference makes an easy transition into the next theme, with *nu todæg* in both places. This linking phrase is further used three times in the Harrowing of Hell section (lines 76, 78, 80) and once in the Last Judgement section (line 153), as well as at the beginning of the homily (line 2), as a persistent reminder of the day the homily is now being delivered. However, such linking is an exception rather than the rule in the homily. One wonders if the resultant accumulation of 'a mass of information' might be suggestive of the way its anonymous part was composed. D. G. Scragg assumes composition of much of the anonymous part to be 'no later than the tenth century',[16] and our homilist himself speaks at the very beginning of 'ðisum bocum' as his sources (though

---

[13] Lees, 'Theme and Echo', 142.

[14] Lees, 'Theme and Echo', 141.

[15] Citation from *HomS* 27 is made from Lees's edition ('Theme and Echo', 117–23), by line number, except that I have not reproduced its editorial square brackets indicating supplied words or parts of words not on the manuscript. The homily has also been edited by Schaefer, 'An Edition', pp. 174–84. Schaefer's edition, however, incorporating as it does 'all corrections which make grammatical sense' made either by 'the main hand or a slightly later one' (p. 172), sometimes seems to complicate the reading. The DOE Corpus text, said to be based on this edition, in fact differs from it (as it stands in my xerox copy of the original dissertation, obtained from UMI Dissertation Services) in several ways, including the system of punctuation and its failure to distinguish the original text and later corrections.

[16] D. G. Scragg, 'The corpus of vernacular homilies and prose saints' lives before Ælfric', *ASE* 8 (1979), 223–77, at 242 n. 3. The assumption is based on the date of the manuscript (s. xi in.) and the style and language of the homily which Scragg thinks 'are typical of many early pieces'.

without even hinting at what these books are).[17] However, no direct source is known to exist, apart from Ælfric's homily which our homilist uses in discussing the Eucharist. Given that there are instead analogues and traditions similar to the themes and motifs of our homily that are found in Latin and Irish as well as vernacular literatures,[18] the lack of evidence might mean, as Swan appears to assume,[19] that the homilist worked directly from those popular traditional elements, freely varying and rearranging them, rather than from any written source. Examination of the prose of the homily may help to clarify the problem.

Something of the quality of the homilist's prose may be illustrated by the opening passage (as the homily now stands, with one leaf missing after the initial few lines), which 'assumes a kind of pulpit cadence the momentum of which seems to override some of the grammatical and logical inconsistencies of the text':[20]

> *HomS* 27.6 . . . and þæt he mihte libban buton geswince and buton deaðe wunian, and anra gehwilc on tælmete mihte wunian and libban swilce he þrittig wintre wære, and symble habban leoht buton þeostrum and dæg buton nihte. And efne swa þa tida on hærfæst mid wæstmum and mid blostmum beoð gefylleda, swa him wæron ealle god gesealde oððe æt nextan he forheold Godes bebodu swa him Drihten ne bebead. Ac þurh unwisdom he gesyngode beforan Gode and þa æfter þam nænige hreowe he ne dyde þæs gyltes. Swa hit is awriten on halgum bocum, 'Se ðe synne deð and þa ne beteð se bið þære synne þeow' oð ðæt he hi eft gebeteð Gode to willan.
>
> Swa þonne, men ða leofestan, æfter þam þeowdome Drihten God wæs ariend and helpend menniscum cynne. And swa swa on ðam sixtan dæge Adam gesceapen wæs, and on þam sixtan dæge he gesyngode æfter þan.

The inconsistencies are to be observed particularly clearly in the use of *swa swa* and *swa* which dominate the entire passage. Grammatically, *swa . . . ne* (as in the manuscript) in the sixth line (*he forheold Godes bebodu swa him Drihten ne bebead*, meaning literally 'as God did not command him') is irregular; Lees omits *ne*. But *ne bebead* might well be 'a lax substitution for *forbead*', suggesting 'a kind of colloquial understatement', as K. G. Schaefer thinks, paraphrasing the *swa*-clause as 'as God commanded him not to'.[21] More blatant perhaps is the inconsistency of the *swa swa* in the last line but one. It is evidently a conjunction introducing a subordinate clause of manner but lacks a proper main clause, which would have

---

[17] See Lees, 'Theme and Echo', 124, note to lines 3ff.; Schaefer, 'An Edition', p. 168.
[18] For details, see Lees, 'Theme and Echo', 125–38.
[19] Swan, 'Ælfric as Source', p. 101. See also Lees, 'Theme and Echo', 127–8, 133 and 135. On the other hand, Lees adds that the question whether the three speeches in the Harrowing of Hell section are written by the homilist himself or borrowed from a lost source 'must remain unresolved' (135).
[20] Schaefer, 'An Edition', p. 185, note to his lines 3ff.
[21] Schaefer, 'An Edition', p. 185, note to his lines 11–12.

run something like 'swa on þam sixtan dæge gesyngode he ...', rather than 'and on þam sixtan dæge he gesyngode' as it stands in the manuscript. It looks as if the homilist lost sight of the syntax of the complex sentence, continuing instead in a compound sentence.[22] This may be what the corrector attempted to improve, though only unsuccessfully, for he added *and* ('ʒ') (incorporated into the text by Lees) before the *swa swa* and also *he* (not incorporated into the text) before the second *on þam sixtan dæge*, omitting the original *he* before *gesyngode*, but left the ungrammatical *and* in question as it is; the loose syntax has remained.

It is interesting to observe that this loose syntax occurs in what Schaefer refers to as 'a non sequitur after the sentence [*Swa þonne . . . cynne.*]'.[23] In fact, the non sequitur seems to originate with this latter sentence itself, where the initial adverb *swa* is not logically consistent. Unlike the other uses of *swa* and *swa swa* in the passage, it has no modal sense, since it has no statement about God's mercy and help to man to refer back to in the preceding sentences. It is apparently used, at what both Lees and Schaefer print as the beginning of a new paragraph, rather loosely, together with the empty word *þonne*, as a sentence connective,[24] not unlike ModE *so* in a sentence like 'So, that is what I mean', in the sense defined by *OED* as 'As an introductory particle, without a preceding statement (but freq[uently] implying one)' (s.v. *So* 10b.) — a sense in which our homilist appears to use the word again later in:

> *HomS* 27.90 þæt is Crist sylfa, se ðe of heofonum astah on eorðan, and hine geeadmedde menniscum hiwe to onfonne, and þurh his þrowunge eall mancyn alysde. And swa manna gehwilcum gedafenat to arisanne of his gyltum.

The use is not otherwise unknown in Old English.[25] But given that the usage is dated in *OED* only from the eighteenth century, our homilist's apparent examples might belong to colloquialism of his day, like *swa . . . ne bebead* mentioned above.

---

[22] Of course, our homilist is not alone in producing this kind of 'ungrammatical' sentence. For similar examples of anacoluthic *and* after a *þeah*-clause in Old English anonymous homilies, see the passage from 'the anchorite and devil story' in Vercelli IV and its different versions, discussed in Chapters II (pp. 27–8) and IV (pp. 85–6).

[23] Schaefer, 'An Edition', p. 186, note to his lines 17ff.

[24] This may be compared with another time the homilist uses the same phraseology in *HomS* 27.86 *Swa þonne, men ða leofestan, helware wæron be Drihtnes tocyme*. Here *swa* is strictly modal, meaning 'in such a state [as described immediately above]', as Schaefer translates it ('An Edition', p. 188, note to his line 80). See also *HomS* 27.133 *Forðan þonne, men ða leofestan, micel neadþearf us is . . .* (starting a new paragraph in Lees's edition).

[25] See Eston Everett Ericson, *The Use of* Swa *in Old English* (Göttingen and Baltimore, 1932), p. 19, where the use in question is referred to as 'a mere transitional link between clauses or at the head of a sentence' and 'approximat[ing] "and"'. However, *swa* in *HomS* 27.90 might enhance the contrast between the two *of*-phrases it compares — Christ's

So might another use of *swa* typical of the homilist, which is seen in *HomS* 27.82 *and hi þa swa cwædon . . . and eac hi swa cwædon . . .* Introducing as it does a biblical quotation each time, the *swa* obviously means 'in this way; thus; as follows'—a sense which *OED* dates only from *a* 1250 (s.v. 2c). In fact, a later hand wrote in the word *ðus* above another comparable example of *swa*: *HomS* 27.147 *Þonne andswarað him ure Drihten and swa cwyð* (followed by a quotation from Matthew). All these details may be another aspect of the prose which allows grammatical and logical inconsistencies.

After the opening passage on the Earthly Paradise, the rest of the major themes are dealt with one by one, with little integration into a unified structure of homiletic discourse, as shown earlier. Nor does the homilist show much refinement and sophistication in recounting the themes and the several motifs that they contain—plainness is the gist of his prose. This may be seen in the opening passage itself along with its inconsistencies, but more clearly in purely narrative sections. Thus, the Evils of the Sixth Day and Sunday List sections are framed into a list of events which is accumulative and heavily paratactic, of the form: 'On this day X happened. And on this day Y happened. And . . .'. The lists are interspersed with extended accounts of particular motifs or events which the homilist chooses to dwell upon. But even these accounts are heavily paratactic, with 'and' repeated to pile up the sentences that constitute them, as in this passage from the Evils of the Sixth Day section:

> *HomS* 27.20 And on þam sixtan dæge Cain acwealde Abel his broðor. And on þam sixtan dæge Sodoma burh and Gomorra Godes englas bærndon for Godes yrre mid fyres lige. And on þam sixtan dæge Iacobes suna, hi endleofone, becipton heora twelftan broðor Ioseph ęgiptum on þeowdom wið þrittigum scillingum. And on þam sixtan dæge se unlæda Iudas becypte urne Hælend. And on þam sixtan dæge Petrus se apostol wiðsoc urum Drihtne þriwa, and eft sona he gelyfde. And on ðam sixtan dæge ure Drihten wæs on rode ahangen.

The passage goes on with three more *and*-clauses with a relative clause coming at the end (*HomS* 27.28–31; see p. 142), and is further succeeded a little later by an extended account of John's vision of the Apocalypse (lines 48–65), where the biblical account is selected and adapted into a central motif in the Sunday List in the same way.[26]

One thing that deserves special attention in this narrative style is the comparatively frequent—at any rate more frequent than in the *De Descensu* homily to be discussed later—use of the verbal periphrasis '*beon* + present participle',

---

coming down from heaven ('of heofonum astah') and man's rising from his sins ('to arisanne of his gyltum').

[26] For analysis of this passage, see Lees, 'Theme and Echo', 131; Schaefer, 'An Edition', pp. 187–8.

known as the expanded form. There are four examples, with two of them in rather telling contexts:

> *HomS* 27.79 Be þyses dæges leohte micelnysse nu todæg wæron wundrigende þa hiwscipas on helle, forðan hi næfre ær ne gesawon swa fæger leoht swa hi þa gesawon, and hi þa swa cwædon, 'Hwæt la is þes wuldres Cyning buton hit si se ælmihtiga God?'[27] and eac hi swa cwædon, . . .

> *HomS* 27.138 Þy us þonne gedafenað þæt we ondrædon þa andweardnysse Godes and his engla. And hu he andswarigende byð þam arleasum gastum, and þus cwæþende, 'Gaþ fram me ge awyrgde on þæt ece fyr . . .'. And he þonne cwyð ure Drihten to ðam arleasum, . . .

In both passages the expanded form marks, as it turns out, the beginning of an account of a particular event, in clear contrast to the simple verb forms (*cwædon . . . cwædon* in the first passage; and, in the second, *cwyð*, followed by a further exchange with *cweðað/cwyð* and *andswarað*) that follow it as the account is gradually developed. These might be examples of the use to mark 'a time-frame' for other actions.[28] So might, in a different grammatical context, a third example in *HomS* 27.151 *we us sculun ondrædan þysne andweardan cwyde þe Drihten þonne cwyð þonne he demende byð lifigendum and forðgewitenum*.[29] Distinguished from all these is the other example, which is the second in a series of verbs: *HomS* 27.162 *And on ðam dæge ealle deade arisað, and æfter þam hi beoð standende and andettenne heora dæda beforan þam hehstan Cristes heahsetle*. It is more difficult to say with certainty what nuance the expanded form is meant to convey here, though it is not unlikely to refer to 'a continuing process . . . being contrasted with a general truth'[30] and serves, to that extent, for vivid description. It may also be noted that all the four examples except the first occur in the Last Judgement section. But it would seem doubtful that the homilist has seen them in terms of rhetorical language appropriate to a proper treatment of that theme.

---

[27] Here I follow Schaefer rather than Lees, who reads 'Hwæt la! is þes wuldres Cyning . . .?' The Latin (Psalms 23:8) has *quis est iste rex gloriae?*

[28] For this use of the expanded form, see Bruce Mitchell, *Old English Syntax*, 2 vols. (Oxford, 1985), §685; id., 'Some Problems Involving Old English Periphrases with *Beon/Wesan* and the Present Participle', *NM* 77 (1976), 478–91, esp. 478–83; Gerhard Nickel, *Die Expanded Form im Altenglischen* (Neumünster, 1966), pp. 256–7.

[29] In fact, Mitchell's definition covers this type of context for the expanded form: 'Sometimes, in both the present and the past, it seems to refer to a specific moment, sometimes to a continuing process, either serving as the frame for another action . . .' (*OES*, §685).

[30] *OES*, §685.

But there are places in the homily, very occasional though they are, where the homilist does rise to rhetorical writing. Thus, the opening passage on the Earthly Paradise (see above) depends for its effect in part upon chiasmus (*libban buton geswince and buton deaðe wunian*) and parallelism (*habban leoht buton þeostrum and dæg buton nihte*)[31] as well as a word pair (*wunian and libban*), all in close succession in one sentence and keyed to each other by a few shared words. Word pairs are used elsewhere sporadically, as in lines 32 *bodedon and sædon*, 71 *tobræc and towearp*,[32] 134 *clænsien and gemedemien* and 160 *awriten and gecweden*, but most effectively in the Last Judgement section leading to the conventional end of the homily based on the Doxology:

> *HomS* 27.166 And þonne æfter þan ure Drihten God he geladað and gecigð ealle his gedefan and gecorenan on þæt ece lif and on þa ecan gefean, and þus him to clypað . . . And þonne þa halgan mid heahsittendum and mid englum, and mid heahfæderum, and mid þam halgan apostolum, and mid eallum halgum wuniað on ðære ecan and on ðære langsuman sibbe and blisse þæs singalan dreames. He þonne Drihten wile þæt ealle men hale and gesunde sin and he nele þæt ænig forweorðe, ac ealle he wile gelædan and gelaþian on þæs ecan lifes gefean þæra þe her willað rihtlice and clænlice æfter boca bebodum libban. Þær he nu mid þam clænum and þam rihtwisum leofað and rixað mid Fæder and mid Suna on annysse Haliges Gastes a on ecnysse buton ælcum ende. Amen.

The word pairs have their effect heightened by occasional alliteration and rhyme and further by the *mid*-phrases which are apparently controlled rhythmically rather than logically; tautological repetition of the word *halig* (*And þonne þa halgan . . . mid eallum halgum wuniað*) might be another case of the 'pulpit cadence' in favour of which the homilist seems ready to sacrifice logical consistency. However, such highly rhythmical and rhetorical passages are exceptional in the homily.

After the Harrowing of Hell comes the section on 'the wonders of the Eucharist' as Schaefer calls it, again with no bridging explanation for this transition; the section begins simply with the conjunctional phrase *Eac swilce*. It is in this manner that the homilist now turns to Ælfric's homily for an extract for some thirty lines after a brief introduction and a biblical quotation from John 6:57 (*HomS* 27.98 *Se man se ðe þigeð minne lichaman and drincð min þæt halige blod, se wunað on me and ic beo on him*). The extract, beginning with a quotation

---

[31] For analogues from which the homilist might have derived these formulaic phrases, see Lees, 'Theme and Echo', 127.

[32] This word pair may be compared with *(ge/to)bræc and (ge)fylde*, which is a hallmark of the Blickling and Vercelli versions of the Life of St Martin. For details, see Hiroshi Ogawa, *Studies in the History of Old English Prose* (Tokyo, 2000), pp. 18 and 24 n. 43.

of Matthew 26:26–27,[33] is taken from the *Catholic Homilies*, Second Series, item XV (*Sermo de Sacrificio in Die Pascae*), with considerable alteration. The homilist's method is seen typically as he rewrites Ælfric's explanation of the mystery of the Eucharist through an elaborate analogy with baptism in:

> *ÆCHom* ii. 15.107 Hæðen cild bið gefullod. ac hit ne bret na his hiw wið-utan. ðeah ðe hit beo wiðinnan awend; Hit bið gebroht synfull þurh adames forgægednysse to ðam fantfæte. ac hit bið aðwogen fram eallum synnum wiðinnan. þeah ðe hit wiðutan his hiw ne awende;[34]

Central to Ælfric's elaboration is the contrast between unchanged outward appearance and inward conversion, which he repeats through two sentences which are syntactically parallel ('. . . , ac . . ., þeah ðe . . .') but are, perhaps deliberately, balanced chiastically, so to speak, in terms of the 'changed' and 'unchanged' ('Hæðen cild "changed", ac "unchanged", þeah ðe "changed"', but 'Hit "unchanged", ac "changed", þeah ðe "unchanged"'). This chiastic arrangement has inevitably brought with it reversed distribution of *wiputan* and *wipinnan*, but syntactically again the two words remain parallel in that they both occur finally in the *ac*-clause but medially in the *þeah ðe*-clause, indicating Ælfric's conscious hand that runs through the passage. All this is apparently not appreciated by our homilist, who destroys Ælfric's rhetoric and prose rhythm by simplifying the extended analogy into one sentence and the complex structure of three clauses ('. . ., ac . . ., þeah ðe . . .') into ordinary coordinate clauses ('. . ., ac . . .'):

> *HomS* 27.113 Hæðen cild þe man fullað ne bryt hyt na his hiw wiðutan, ac hit bið swa ðeah wiðinnan awend and aþwogen on þam fante fram eallum synnum.

With Ælfric's two sentences collapsed into one, the homilist's *ac*-clause has two past participles coordinated, drawn together from the original two sentences. It

---

[33] In his edition of the *Catholic Homilies*, Benjamin Thorpe renders Ælfric's Old English translation *Drincað ealle of þisum* (Matt 26:27 *bibite ex hoc omnes*) incorrectly as 'Drink all of this' (*The Homilies of the Anglo-Saxon Church: The First Part, Containing the Sermones Catholici, or Homilies of Ælfric*, 2 vols. (London, 1844–46; rpt. New York, 1971), Vol. II, p. 267).

[34] Citation from the *Catholic Homilies* is made here from Malcolm Godden (ed.), *Ælfric's Catholic Homilies, The Second Series* (EETS ss 5, London, 1979), and, later in the next section, from Peter Clemoes (ed.), *Ælfric's Catholic Homilies, The First Series* (EETS ss 17, Oxford, 1997). Swan notes about Ælfric's baptism passage that the homilist 'continues to reproduce most of the substance of the Godden text, but begins by showing alterations of sentence structure, possibly in an attempt at simplification' and he 'goes on to shorten the Ælfric text as represented by Godden by omitting reinforcing and descriptive phrases' ('Ælfric as Source', p. 102). But she gives no further details about how the homilist does all this.

may be noted that the *ac*-clause has acquired the adverb *swa ðeah*. But the phrase does not make up for the lost *þeah ðe*-clause so much as reinforce the contrast between the 'changed' and 'unchanged' as he reformulates it in simplified terms. The homilist has simplified the Ælfric homily at the cost of losing its 'sophisticated and carefully modulated discussion'[35] of the subject.

The homilist's insensitivity to Ælfric's careful treatment of the subject is also seen when he rewrites (lines 115–8) another analogy with the water of the baptism font which Ælfric introduces immediately following the one just examined. Ælfric writes:

> *ÆCHom* ii. 15.111 Eac swilce þæt halige fantwæter þe is gehaten lifes wylspring. is gelic on hiwe oðrum wæterum. and is underþeod brosnunge. ac þæs halgan gastes miht genealæhð þam brosniendlicum wætere. ðurh sacerda bletsunge. and hit mæg siððan lichaman and sawle aðwean fram eallum synnum. ðurh gastlicere mihte;

The homilist omits, from the opening portion of this, the relative clause (*þe is... wylspring*)[36] and the *and*-clause (*and... brosnunge*), both of which are obviously essential for Ælfric's explanation of the nature of baptism. Reference to the physical corruptibility of water is again omitted from the following *ac*-clause (rewritten by the homilist as 'ac þurh þæs sacerdes bletsunge genealæcð þæs Halgan Gastes miht', with inversion[37]) and from a passage which the homilist subsequently entirely omits (see below). Even the small word *mæg* (*mæg... aðwean*) in the last clause might well be an example of Ælfric's deliberate etymologizing repetition in association with the word *miht* used both before and after it.[38] But the homilist has casually (so one would think) abandoned it in favour of the simple verb form *aþwyhþ*.

Not only does our homilist simplify Ælfric's sentences but he also edits out a long stretch of sentences Ælfric gives to theological argument. He does this twice, skipping over, after his line 108, sixteen lines (in Malcolm Godden's edition) on the nature of bread and wine signifying the true nature of Christ and, after line 118, forty-two lines on the physical and spiritual natures of the housel, thereby suggesting, as Lees points out, 'an imperfect understanding of Ælfric's

---

[35] Lees, 'Theme and Echo', 139.
[36] See Lees, 'Theme and Echo', 140.
[37] Alternatively, one could possibly take *þæs Halgan Gastes miht* as a rare accusative object of *genealæcan* (see BT s.v.), with the subject (*þæt halige fantwæter*) supplied from the preceding clause. But this is unlikely.
[38] For Ælfric's use of this rhetorical device, see John C. Pope (ed.), *Homilies of Ælfric: A Supplementary Collection*, 2 vols. (EETS os 259 and 260, London, 1967–68), Vol. I, pp. 109–10; James Hurt, *Ælfric* (New York, 1972), pp. 123–5; Joyce Hill, 'Ælfric's use of etymologies', *ASE* 17 (1988), 35–44.

homily' and 'an indiscriminate approach to source material'.[39] Moreover, when he resumes, he goes back on both occasions directly to Ælfric's text, continuing from where he has left off without any bridging phrase. The one change he makes then after the first omission at line 109 is the substitution of the pronoun *heora* for Ælfric's *sacerda* (*ÆCHom* ii. 15.102 *se hlaf and þæt win ðe beoð ðurh sacerda mæssan gehalgode*), probably in order to refer back to the apostles' 'æftergengan' (line 107), and thereby to link his resumed adaptation to the source text, but, without the intervening sixteen lines, it only helps to create a considerable degree of repetition in what are now consecutive sentences:

> *HomS* 27.106 Eac swilce heora [the apostles'] æftergengan . . . be Cristes hæse halgiað hlaf and win to husle on his naman mid þære apostolican bletsunge. Soðlice se hlaf and þæt win þe beoð þurh heora mæssan gehalgode, . . .

On the other hand, the homilist adds the phrase 'Eac we rædað þæt' (line 127) to begin the second exemplum on the mystery of the Eucharist (where Ælfric uses the introductory phrase only for the first exemplum) and also inserts the words *þa* (line 124), probably a conjunction correlative to *þa* in the next line, and *sona* (line 125), while replacing Ælfric's *ða* 'then' by *sona* (line 132) in narrating the exempla. But in the narrative he again omits (line 122) a relative clause from the source sentence (*ÆCHom* ii. 15.161 *Ða gesawon hi licgan an cild on ðam weofode þe se mæssepreost æt mæssode*), despite the power of the mass Ælfric seems to emphasize through it. These personal touches show our homilist's emphasis very clearly; he uses the Ælfric text for the clear story and dramatic narrative content it contains, rather than for its elaborate treatment of theological issues, as Swan has pointed out.[40]

Other changes in wording our homilist makes to the Ælfric homily include the initial *swa* characteristic of him in *Swa is eac þæt halige fantwæter* . . . (line 115) in place of *Eac swilce* . . ., the paratactic *and þus cwæð* (line 101) in place of the Ælfrician appositive participle *þus cweðende*,[41] and the simple relative *þæt* (line 103) in place of *þæt ðe* (*ÆCHom* ii. 15.80 *þis is min blod. þæt ðe bið for manegum agoten. on synna forgifenysse*). This last might be another example of the homilist's failure to appreciate Ælfric's rhetorical language, for Ælfric often uses the compound relative pronoun in exegesis as against factual statements, as he appears to do

---

[39] Lees, 'Theme and Echo', 140. See also Schaefer, 'An Edition', p. 171.

[40] Swan, 'Ælfric as Source', p. 104. See also Schaefer, 'An Edition', p. 171.

[41] On Ælfric's frequent use of this type of appositive participle, see Morgan Callaway, Jr., 'The Appositive Participle in Anglo-Saxon', *PMLA* 16 (1901), 141–360, esp. 285–8 and 345–6; Paul Theodor Kühn, *Die Syntax der Verbums in Ælfrics 'Heiligenleben'* (Leipzig diss., 1889), pp. 37–8; Harvey A. Minkoff, 'Ælfric's Theory of Translation and the Styles of the *Heptateuch* and *Homilies*' (Ph.D. dissertation, City University of New York, 1970), pp. 166–70; *OES*, §1436.

here as against *ÆCHom* ii. 15.87 *se hlaf þe bið of corne gegearcod . . . oððe þæt win ðe bið of manegum berium awrungen* (in a passage omitted by our homilist).[42] Finally, the homilist has *tweonigendum mode* (line 129) replacing Ælfric's *mid twynigendum mode* (*ÆCHom* ii. 15.169). But what this change precisely means is difficult to say; the instrumental dative case form is not used elsewhere by the homilist.

I have referred earlier to the casualness with which our homilist rewrites extracts from the Ælfric homily. It is a quality which may, on one hand, have much in common with 'the grammatical and logical inconsistencies' which were seen to characterize the prose of the opening passage. On the other hand, it seems to make itself felt as clearly in the treatment of biblical material on which he often draws in developing each of the five major themes. He gives quotations from the Scriptures which are on the whole much freer than is usually the case in Old English anonymous homilies. For example, he adds explanatory words, in *HomS* 27.140 *Gað fram me ge awyrgde on þæt ece fyr, on hellewite, and on þone ecan ungefean* (Matthew 25:41 *discedite a me maledicti in ignem aeternum*)[43] and in two further quotations—*HomS* 27.14 (see the long quotation on p. 143, for John 8:34 *omnis qui facit peccatum servus est peccati*) and 98 (see p. 147, for John 6:57 *Qui manducat meam carnem et bibit meum sanguinem in me manet et ego in illo*);[44] the added words in the latter two (*and þa ne beteð*, and *þæt halige*) were probably suggested by his own wording in the sentences which have led to those quotations (lines 13 *nænige hreowe he ne dyde* and 97 *his þæt gebletsode blod*, respectively). A different kind of free rendering is shown in:

> *HomS* 27.77 Þam mannum on þam lande eardigendum under þæs deaðes sceade micel leoht nu todæg him wæs upcumen. And þæt folc þe þa on helle on þystrum sæt micel leoht hi þa gesawon (Isaiah 9:2 *populus qui ambulabat in tenebris vidit lucem magnam habitantibus in regione umbrae mortis lux orta est eis*).

Here the details are closely rendered, including the 'recapitulatory' personal pronoun (*þam mannum . . . him*). But the order of the pair of sentences is reversed

---

[42] A better example will be an alternation of *se þe* and *þe* in *ÆCHom* i. 2.42–67: *ure hælend godes sunu efenece ⁊ gelic his fæder: se ðe mid him wæs æfre buton angynne: . . . witodlice on swa micelre sibbe wæs crist acenned: Se ðe is ure sib: . . . he wæs acenned on ðæs caseres dagum þe wæs octauianus gehaten: . . . Se nama gedafenað þam heofenlicum cyninge criste þe on his timan acenned wæs: Se ðe his heofonlice rice geihte . . . ⁊ þone hryre þe se feallenda deoful on engla werode gewanode. mid menniscum gecynde eft gefylde; . . . he getacnode crist se ðe is soð yrfenuma þæs ecan fæder.* I hope to discuss this distinction between simple and compound relative pronouns in Ælfric in future.

[43] Quotation from the Vulgate is made from Robertus Weber (ed.), *Biblia Sacra Iuxta Vulgatam Versionem* (3rd edn.; Stuttgart, 1983).

[44] For these quotations, see Lees, 'Theme and Echo', 137 and 139; Schaefer, 'An Edition', pp. 182, 186 and 179, apparatus.

from the arrangement in the biblical Latin. Similarly, *HomS* 27.140 based on Matthew 25:41 (see above) is combined with a subordinate *þær*-clause (line 142) derived from Matthew 25:30, which in turn combines two phrases taken from distinct sentences of the verse: 142 *þær is toða gristbitung and þa singalan þystru* (Matthew 25:30 . . . *eicite in tenebras exteriores illic erit fletus et stridor dentium*). These examples suggest that the homilist is sometimes working from memory, as Lees believes.[45]

The homilist's method of treating biblical material is perhaps seen at its clearest in an extended passage in the Last Judgement section. In what immediately follows the Lord's first speech in *HomS* 27.140–3 (see above), the homilist goes on to quote the exchange of words between the Lord and the unrighteous in Matthew 25:41–45, but even more casually than before. He abridges their speech twice, saying only 'and ic wæs nacod þa ne wruge ge me mid eowrum hræglum' (line 145) for verse 43 (*hospes eram et non collexistis me nudus et non operuistis me infirmus et in carcere et non visitastis me*) and *swa pearfiendne* (line 148) to refer collectively to the various occasions of Christ in need in verse 44 (*esurientem aut sitientem aut hospitem aut nudum aut infirmum vel in carcere*); expands the wording of the Bible (e.g. line 147 *þa unrihtwisan men* (Matthew 25:44 *ipsi*) and 148 *minum þam earmestum þe ic eow to sende* (25:45 *uni de minoribus his*)); replaces, as in the extract from the Ælfric homily, the participial construction with a clause (147 *Ponne cweðað* (25:44 *dicentes*), 148 *and swa cwyð* (25:45 *dicens*)); and finally adds the concluding sentence 'Soð ic eow secge, ne can ic eow' (line 150), drawn, perhaps by memory, from Matthew 25:12. The homilist gives all this account of the damned before he deals with the saved, thereby reversing the treatment in the Bible.[46]

The freedom that the homilist shows in biblical quotation obviously comes, in part at least, from the fact that he does not usually quote the biblical Latin before

---

[45] Lees, 'Theme and Echo', 125. See also Schaefer, 'An Edition', p. 171. Ælfric seems to contribute his share of this method of working with biblical material when he quotes from Genesis in his *De Initio Creaturae*, saying *ÆCHom* i. 1.190 *god . . . asende ren of heofonum feowertig daga togædere. ⁊ geopenode þærtogenes ealle wylspryngas ⁊ wæterpeotan of þære miclan nywelnesse* (Genesis 7:11 *rupti sunt omnes fontes abyssi magnae et cataractae caeli apertae sunt*). Ælfric does not appear to distinguish clearly *fontes* (his *wylspryngas*) and *cataractae* (his *wæterpeotan*), making them refer together to the abyss (his *þære miclan nywelnesse*); cf. Ælfric's close translation of the verse in the Old English Heptateuch. For further discussion on memory as a method of homiletic writing by Ælfric as well as anonymous writers, see J. E. Cross, 'Ælfric—Mainly on Memory and Creative Method in Two *Catholic Homilies*', *Studia Neophilologica* 41 (1969), 135–55; id., 'The Literate Anglo-Saxon—On Sources and Disseminations', *PBA* 58 (1972), 67–100, esp. 92–3; Swan, 'Memorialised Readings', *passim*; Swan, 'Ælfric's *Catholic Homilies*', *passim*; Loredana Teresi, 'Mnemonic transmission of Old English texts in the post-Conquest period', *Rewriting Old English*, ed. Swan and Treharne, pp. 98–116.

[46] See Lees, 'Theme and Echo', 137.

he translates it, as in all the examples above. Where he does just for once, in *HomS* 27.168, as 'a fitting conclusion to the homily',[47] his Latin text (*Uenite benedicti Patris mei percipite regnum quod uobis paratum est ab origine mundi*) differs from the Vulgate (Matthew 25:34 *venite benedicti Patris mei possidete paratum vobis regnum a constitutione mundi*). Nor does his translation of the sentence agree with the accepted one, reading 'Cumað ge gebletsode and onfoð mines Fæder rice . . .', and not 'Cumað ge gebletsode mines Fæder and . . .', as in the West-Saxon Gospels and Ælfric's Dominica I in Quadragesima (*ÆCHom* ii. 7.145). Our homilist's treatment might not have been entirely an inaccuracy, since there is evidence to suggest that it is based on a Latin text current in his days beside the Vulgate.[48] One feels inclined all the same to ask if the homilist understood Latin rather indifferently—an impression which one also gets from *HomS* 27.154 *swa hit on þam godspelle awriten is*, '*Drihten cymð swa se þeof cymð þonne he stelan wile*', where, quite apart from the *þonne*-clause which is the homilist's addition, '[t]here is some confusion in the text of the Biblical translation here. According to I Thess. 5:2 it is the *day* of the Lord that will come like a thief in the night and not God himself'.[49] Lees detects a similar confusion on the homilist's part of two verses from Revelation as he deals with John's vision in the Sunday List section.[50]

There remains one passage which seems to show another aspect of the homilist's language in biblical quotation. For details of John's vision as he retells it in the Sunday List section, the homilist draws mostly upon Chapters 1 and 21 of Revelation[51] and says towards the end of the vision:

> *HomS* 27.59 And on ðone drihtenlican dæg Iohannes geseah metan þa burh þa heofonlican Hierusalem mid gyldenre rode. And þa wæron on ðære byrig twelf gatu of ðam .xii. gimstanum geworhte þurh synderlice þing,

---

[47] Lees, 'Theme and Echo', 137.

[48] The same Latin text of Matthew 25:34 is used in one manuscript of Ælfric's Quadragesima homily; see Godden, *Catholic Homilies, The Second Series*, p. 65, apparatus. Remarking in the textual notes that in some manuscripts of Ælfric's homily, *gebletsode mines fæder* is altered to *gebletsode to mines fæder (rice)*, Godden reminds us of a further aspect of the Latin biblical text in question in Old English: 'the difficulty caused by this expression [*gebletsode mines fæder*], evident here in the manuscripts of the DEF group, is also apparent in M at Pope XI 409, where the same alterations have been made' (p. 353).

[49] Schaefer, 'An Edition', p. 190, note to his line 149. As Schaefer goes on to note, the confusion is set right in the next sentence: *HomS* 27.156 *Swa ungecyþed he byð æghwilcum men ge se dæg ge seo niht swa him byð þæs þeofes cyme*.

[50] Lees, 'Theme and Echo', 131. See further Schaefer, 'An Edition', p. 187, note to his lines 39–42 (which he thinks 'seem paradoxical . . . Perhaps the difficulty arose because the author has confused Sunday (as a day of rest) with the seventh day (originally Saturday)') and p. 188, note to his line 57.

[51] For details, see Lees, 'Theme and Echo', 118–9.

and seo strætlanu is on ðære byrig of clænum golde geworht. Seo leng and seo widnys and seo hehþo syndon gelice twelf mila ælces þinges.

This is an abridged translation of several verses from Chapter 21 which he has rearranged, but the phrase *purh synderlice þing* in the second sentence renders, accurately and perhaps too literally,[52] the biblical Latin: Revelation 21:21 *et duodecim portae duodecim margaritae sunt per singulas*. It is not easy to assess this evidence of 'literal translation' in the light of what was seen to be the homilist's usual method. What is of real interest here is the word *þing* added as a 'prop word' to the adjective *synderlice*, apparently to translate the Latin *singulas*, acc. pl. of *singuli* 'one to each, separate, single' used as a substantive. If that is the case, the use may be a very early example of what is defined in *OED* as: 'In unemphatic use: mostly with adj. or other defining word or phrase (the two together corresponding to the absol. use of a neuter adj. in Latin or Greek)' (s.v. *Thing* 7a); it may be the earliest known example used with a pure adjective, all the *OED*'s examples before the end of the fourteenth century being with such defining words as *all* and *any* or a numeral. To the extent that it is, it may reflect a colloquialism of the day which the homilist introduced in his prose. So may a second use, at the end of the above quotation, of the word *þing* in *ælces þinges* meaning 'in every respect', which the first use has obviously prompted as the homilist added this redundant phrase in his translation. This evidence of colloquial language, if this is indeed what the two examples of *þing* are, would reinforce what we have seen earlier in some details of his language (such as *swa* in the sense 'thus, as follows' and *ne bebead* as litotes for 'forbead') and the generally casual writing which is seen in the homily.

De Descensu Christi Ad Inferos

If *In Die Sancto Pasce* is a homily which 'lacks a consistent narrative or a consistent exegetical commentary',[53] our second anonymous Easter homily *De Descensu Christi ad Inferos* (*HomS* 28) differs sharply from it in having both these.[54] It is

---

[52] Latin *per singulas* is translated in the Wycliffite Bible (Earlier Version) as 'by ech' and the Rheims Bible as 'one to euery one'. But none of the other major English translations (Tyndale, the Authorized Version, and the New English Bible) gives literal translation of the Latin phrase.

[53] Lees, 'Theme and Echo', 125.

[54] Citation from this homily is made from Fadda's edition ('De descensu Christi', 998–1010), with reference to line number, but without the editorial angle brackets indicating supplied forms; I have also corrected a few printing errors in the edited text. Schaefer's edition ('An Edition', pp. 141–55) suffers from the same problem as his edition of *HomS* 27 (see n. 15). The DOE Corpus text, again said to be based on Schaefer's edition, turns out to be on occasion even more inexplicable in reading, e.g. *And beswac*

a dramatic account of the Harrowing of Hell, while it has its homiletic design sustained by consistent exegetical remarks it introduces as it goes on, including a passage which is taken from a different Ælfric homily and given accordingly different treatment than in the other Easter homily. This basic contrast is reinforced by several distinctive features the homily shows in language and style, though their origin remains partly a problem. In the Harrowing scene of the middle section (lines 79–160) to which a Blickling homily provides a related version, those features are often likely, as we shall see, to be derived from a Latin work which our homilist (and the Blickling homilist) might have used as source material.[55] For the rest of the homily (apart from the excerpt from Ælfric), no related text is known to exist, and one may safely assume with Swan[56] that it was written by the homilist himself. We shall also argue that details of language and style in the Harrowing of Hell section are very much of a piece with the rest of the homily, suggesting the degree to which the homilist has adapted the source here.

The homily is a consistent narrative of the Harrowing of Hell. It is entirely devoted, as the homilist announces at the start (lines 2–4), to the account of how Christ descended into hell and bound the devil and led all the elect out of there, surrounded by a detailed account of the roles played by the devil and Christ in man's history leading to the Harrowing (lines 5–78) and the Ascension scene at the end (lines 196–202). More importantly, it shows the unity of a single homily, with its parts welded into and echoing each other both in wording and narrative structure, as Jackson J. Campbell aptly summarizes:

> Admittedly the homilist has no sophistication of style to speak of, and his Latin was possibly a little shaky, but he does put together a coherent structure which never loses sight of his primary theme. He keeps in view the dramatic scene of hell and the action there during virtually all of the homily, and his first-person exhortations and elaborations are closely connected to ideas developed by the dramatic story. His introduction of the fall of Adam at the beginning gives good background not only for the specific material about Adam and Eve in hell, but also for the extended meaning that the events of the Harrowing are a paradigm for the salvation of all fallen

---

weard . . . (line 46), *þa syððan hi wæron ealle gesceafta underþeod* (60), and *Ac ic wene is wen þæt* . . . (88, where *ic wene* in fact is a 'tremulous' gloss given above the line; see Schaefer, 'An Edition', p. 146).

[55] The source of the middle section and its relationship to Blickling Homily VII has long been a problem; see n. 79. For the Blickling version, citation is made below from Richard Morris's edition: *The Blickling Homilies*, EETS os 58, 63, and 73 (London, 1874–80; repr. as one volume, 1967). I had completed all the chapters of this book before Richard J. Kelly's new edition (*The Blickling Homilies: Edition and Translation* (London and New York, 2003)) came to my attention.

[56] See Mary Swan, 'Old English Made New: One Catholic Homily and its Reuses', *LSE* 28 (1997), 1–18, at 6–7. See also Schaefer, 'An Edition', p. 138.

men. He obviously used several sources, but he welds them together satisfactorily, if not brilliantly, into an optimistic homily.[57]

The motif of the fall of Adam is only one of the many details of what Campbell calls 'a coherent structure'. One may further note, for example, how the homilist moves from one section into another to achieve a continuous narrative. Towards the end of the opening 'background' section leading into the central account of the Harrowing of Hell, he narrates the Crucifixion of Christ, ending with: *HomS* 28.60 *and he ða freo astah fram þam nyðerlican witum, syððan he hæfde geondfaren þa ðystru and þa gemæro*.[58] Through this hypotactic arrangement and the pluperfect tense reinforcing it, the homilist prepares himself and us not only for the Hell scene now about to come but also for the Ascension which is the ultimate destination of his narrative. He never loses sight of this narrative order but takes the opportunity to record his sense of it throughout the subsequent narrative, reiterating the emphasis on the Ascension and the temporal relationship which highlights it, when he summarizes the Harrowing and then, after a long exegetical commentary, moves on to the last narrative scene:

> *HomS* 28.161 Þa astah se Hælend of þære helle and he hæfde þær gebunden and genyðerad deaðes ordfruman, and he ða hrædlice ða gehergadan mid him gelædde of deaðes gryne, and he sealde mannum ða gife þæs ecan lifes, and he þa ðone ealdan feond nyðer gefylled hæfde.... (196) Mid þam ðe engla weorod and heahengla werod gesegon þone Hælend astigan mid unarimendre mænigu on heofona rices heannysse, þa cwædan hi: 'Hwæt is þes wuldres cyning?'

Then comes finally a short concluding remark, where the homilist says: 'Blissige nu eall manncynn . . . and blissian huru þa ðe his æriste glyfað and weorðiað' (lines 203–4), bringing to the fore the primary theme of his narrative as an Easter homily, just as he did when he began the homily.

Another example of anticipation through which the first section is closely linked to the rest of the homily is the exegetical remark made there about the Crucifixion. After the devil's first speech in hell in which he boasts of the plot against Christ, the homilist adds that Christ was then crucified but the devil was misled into thinking himself victorious because he could not see Christ's divinity (lines 36–8). But, the homilist continues, the devil was soon conquered, not so much by force as with right:

---

[57] Jackson J. Campbell, 'To Hell and Back: Latin Tradition and Literary Use of the "Descensus ad Inferos" in Old English', *Viator* 13 (1982), 107–58, at 141.

[58] A corrector added the words *[h]elle grundes* at the end of the sentence; Schaefer incorporates them in his text.

> *HomS* 28.43 Þa hrædlice se ealda feond, þe Adam on neorxna wonge mid facne and mid his leasungum forlærde and beswac, wearð mid ecum bendum gebunden and mid ecum geniðerungum geniðerad fram þam æfteran Adame, þæt is ure Drihten Crist. Næs he na swa mid mægne ofercumen, swa swa he mid rihte gehyned wæs and afylled into cwicsusles geniðerunge.

By these remarks the homilist makes a central point to which he comes back later in appealing to the simile of the devil as fish swallowing the bait but not seeing the hook and the idea of the devil forfeiting his right over mankind,[59] both developed in a passage from Ælfric's *Dominica Palmarum* (*Catholic Homilies*, First Series, item XIV), and used virtually verbatim. Swan, with a slightly different emphasis, sees this 'devil-as-fish simile' of the Ælfrician passage as linked rather with the first section through the latter's 'devil/lion and devil/dragon similes'.[60] Whichever of the two is the more important link, they put it beyond any reasonable doubt that use is not made of the Ælfrician passage indiscriminately but as a result of careful thought by the homilist about the structure and wording of his homily. It should also be noted that in the second exegetical remark above the homilist refers to the devil as 'mid ecum bendum gebunden and mid ecum geniðerungum geniðerad' (with alliteration and etymological repetition). The phrase is distinctly the homilist's own (as opposed, for example, to 'gebunden mid isenum racenteagum' in *In Die Sancto Pasce*, line 85), and is repeated in varied forms at lines 69, 85, and 202,[61] providing a case of coherence achieved at the hands of one homilist in the details of the language of the homily.

The extract from the Ælfric homily has been the primary interest for most of the scholars who have discussed the anonymous *De Descensu* homily. But they have scarcely paid attention to the extract in relation to the other parts of the homily which have called it forth, as described above. Nor has its use been analyzed closely enough. Two things demand notice here. First, Schaefer says that 'our passage is identical to the text in Thorpe's edition [of the *Catholic Homilies*]',[62] but this identity is not quite exact. The homilist in one place (line 168) changes word order—from Ælfric's *wurdon we* to *we wurdon*, missing a possible fine flourish of rhetoric in the source; Ælfric might have meant the VS order preceded by *þurh his . . . deaðe* as chiasmus to SV followed by *to cristes cweale* in the previous sentence:

---

[59] See Campbell, 'To Hell and Back', 138.

[60] Swan, 'Old English Made New', 7.

[61] The example in line 69 (the first sentence of *HomS* 28.68 (p. 159)) is without a preposition for the first hemistich. Schaefer supplies *in* ('An Edition', line 71), but the preposition should be *mid* as in the other examples of this formulaic phrase. See also related phrases such as 'þone deofol geband' (line 3) and 'hæfde . . . gebunden and genyðerad' (line 161, quoted in full above (p. 156)).

[62] Schaefer, 'An Edition', p. 165, note to his lines 172–184.

ÆCHom i.14.169 He hit forwyrhte þa ða he tihte þ folc to cristes cweale þæs ælmihtigan godes; ⁊ þa þurh his unsceððian deaðe wurdon we alysede: fram þam ecan deaðe. . . .

On the other hand, the homilist follows the source perhaps too closely when he opens the passage, just as Ælfric does, saying 'We habbað oft gesæd and gyt secgað', for here Ælfric was, as Godden shows, 'possibly . . . referring to his own preaching rather than written texts'.[63] Whether or not our homilist was conscious of this implication but ignored it one cannot say. But the faithful use here, as generally elsewhere in the extract, at any rate emphasizes the homilist's attitude to his Ælfrician source, which is distinct from that of the *In Die Sancto Pasce* homily. The use of the particular passage from the *Dominica Palmarum*, as against the two exempla in the latter, itself emphasizes exegesis as a central feature of the homily which makes it unique among the anonymous homilies of the period, when there seems to be no other 'composite homily which could be described as explanatory or exegetical'.[64]

In addition to the extract from the Ælfric homily just discussed, there are half a dozen biblical references on which exegetical remarks are based,[65] interspersed throughout the account of the Harrowing of Hell. The homilist's method of exegesis is generally elaborate and effective.[66] For example, in a passage (lines 182–7) explaining how Christ did not lead out all the people he met in hell, based on 'O mors, ero mors tua, morsus tuus ero, inferne' (Hosea 13:14), he exploits the word *helle bite* as gloss for *morsus*, developing it into the phrase 'dæl genam and . . . dæl forlet' and finally explaining that phrase with: 'Ðæt wæs þonne þæt he þær geleafulra manna sawla onfeng and sinfulle þær forlet'.[67] No less elaborate

---

[63] Malcolm Godden, *Ælfric's Catholic Homilies: Introduction, Commentary and Glossary*, EETS ss 18 (Oxford, 2000), p. 117.

[64] See Godden, 'OE composite homilies', 65, where he says that he does not know of any such composite homily; see n. 9.

[65] For details, see Schaefer, 'An Edition', pp. 133–4.

[66] He is perhaps less successful in explaining the sentence 'Næs he na swa mid mægne ofercumen, swa swa he mid rihte gehyned wæs' (line 47; see p. 157). Schaefer is rather uncharitable on this passage: 'This passage has as its core a subtle and effective bit of exegesis, but the argument has been blunted if not totally obscured by the author of this version. . . . This passage . . ., placed where it is and stated as cryptically as it is, must have been as baffling to its audience as the Modern English translation seems now' ('An Edition', pp. 157–8, note to his lines 50–54).

[67] For a similar use of the Hosea text in pseudo-Augustine 160, see Schaefer, 'An Edition', p. 166, note to his lines 191–197. Campbell ('To Hell and Back', 140) argues that our homilist cannot be following the Latin homily for the explanation, since the language differs so much in the two homilies.

is the exegesis using 'the devil/lion and devil/dragon similes', based on Psalms 91:13, which is 'reasonably and clearly presented', as Schaefer puts it:[68]

> *HomS* 28.68 Þa he þone ealdor ealles wrohtes and þone ordfruman ælces yfeles ecere nyðerunge geniðerod and mid ecum bendum gebunden hæfde, þa wæs gefylled þæt gefyrn worulde be Criste gesungen wæs and gewitegod: *Super aspidem et basiliscum ambulabis et conculcabis leonem et draconem*, þæt is, 'Ðu tredst leon and dræcan'.
>
> Geherað we nu þæt ðam deofle ægðer þyssa naman wel geðwæreð. Seo leo bið cyng and ealdor ealra reðra wilddeora, swa þonne se deofol bið ealdor and wealdend ealra yfelra manna. Se draca mid his þam geættredan orðe geswencð menn, swa se deofol mid his ungeleafan blæde ealles mancynnes staðel afyrsode and awyrde, and of þam stealle þæræ godcundlican fægernysse awearp and aweg adraf.

The force of this clear explanation comes in part from the immediately preceding passage (lines 62–7), where another commentary is given on an event of the Harrowing in exactly parallel terms, consisting of a 'þa . . ., þa . . .' period, followed by a biblical quotation in Latin (Psalms 91:7), which is then explained as 'Þæt is . . .'.

Another indication of the homilist's method is given by a passage where he explains the Crucifixion as instigated by the devil just before he turns to the central account of the Harrowing. He begins: *HomS* 28.53 *and þa wæron ealle þing underþeod urum Drihtne Hælende Criste, se ðe be him sylfum mycele ær sang and þus cwæð: Si exaltatus fuero a terra omnia traham ad me ipsum*, and then, 'inject[ing] a bit of exegesis',[69] translates the biblical Latin (John 12:32) as: *Þæt is on englisc: 'Gif þæt gelimpð þæt ic beo on rode up ahafen, þonne teo ic ealle þing to me'*, with an addition of two words (*on rode*) which makes his subsequent explanation the more pointed: *Ealle þing he to him teah, ða þa he on rode gefæstnod wæs, and he his gast to God Fæder asende. Þa him wæron ealle gesceafta underþeod*. The addition does not mean that the homilist, unlike the *In Die Sancto Pasce* homilist, is casual in his biblical references. On the contrary, he is a translator careful enough to begin the *gif*-clause with *þæt gelimpð*, to render the future perfect tense of the Latin verb *fuero*. He is also careful enough to cite the biblical Latin as well here as elsewhere, which he translates reasonably and clearly, if not always perfectly.[70]

---

[68] Schaefer, 'An Edition', p. 159, note to his lines 73ff.

[69] Schaefer, 'An Edition', p. 158, note to his line 58.

[70] See Campbell, 'To Hell and Back', 139 n. 80, in which he mentions the homilist's phrase 'þes stranga middaneard' (line 82) as an example of his imperfect understanding of the Latin. Schaefer, detecting a textual corruption in lines 65–7, also notes that the homilist 'incorrectly translated' the text of Psalms 91:7 ('An Edition', pp. 158–9, note to his lines 68–70) and makes a similar observation on p. 133.

In the passages discussed above our homilist follows the method of traditional exegesis. What is more characteristic of him is theological exposition couched in dramatic direct speech, which I would argue is a different kind of exegetical commentary in the homily. This appears first in the devil's speech to his companions in hell, referring to John the Baptist through a Gospel passage (Matthew 11:11 and Luke 7:28):

> *HomS* 28.20 Ða cwæð he to his geferan: 'Geseoð nu, þis is þæs sawl, be ðam wæs cweden þæt betweox were and wife ne arise nan mærra wer, þonne Iohannes wære se Fulluhtere. . . .'

Schaefer says: 'Placing this speech in the mouth of the devil is a fanciful treatment of Christ's words'.[71] I would rather say a characteristic treatment. The homilist starts speaking as the devil but soon switches, perhaps without realizing that he does, into the persona of homilist commenting on the devil; his voices as narrator and commentator are fused into one in this portion of the speech, as they are in an earlier sentence where the narrative *Ða þuhte ðam deofle* . . . changes imperceptibly into the homilist's comment *oð þæt Crist com and us alysde*: *HomS* 28.10 *Ða þuhte ðam deofle þæt he ahte ealles middaneardes geweald, forðam næs nan mann on ðisum life swa halig ne swa mære þæt he ne sceolde to helle faran swa hraðe swa he of þisum life ferde, oð þæt Crist com and us alysde*. One might think, alternatively, that in the boast against John the devil is made to assume a sarcastic tone which reference to Christ's words as above would enhance. Sarcasm, however, hardly makes sense in the light of the devil's subsequent words (lines 30–2), where he refers to himself as intending to incite the Jews to 'charge falsely' (*onleogan*) and 'to calumniate maliciously' (*forwregan niðfullice*) Christ. These words, which the devil would never have used himself to his own dishonour, obviously indicate the homilist's faith in Christian history, turning the whole sentence in which they occur into an interpretive commentary in disguise. Placed beside this and the sentence in line 10, Christ's quoted words, too, may be seen more definitely as explanation or exegesis—'dramatic exegesis', so to speak, since it is exegesis given through the devil's dramatic voice, echoing the homilist's own earlier use, in a narrative sentence, of Christ's speech about John (lines 16–7).

Use of dramatic direct speech continues into the central section dealing with the Harrowing of Hell, and so does 'dramatic exegesis' in the sense just explained. It is this time the speech of the devil's companions in hell through which the homilist gives his commentary. Frightened at the great light, they are apprehensive:

> *HomS* 28.86 Ac is wen þæt ðis is se ylca be þam ure ealdor nu hwene ær sæde, þæt he ðurh his deað ealles middaneardes anweald onfenge; and gif hit ðes is, þonne is ures cempan cwyde on wyðerweardnysse gecyrred mid

---

[71] Schaefer, 'An Edition', p. 156, note to his lines 20–22.

ðy þe him wæs geðuht þæt he mihte hine oferswyðan. Þa wæs he him sylf fram þysum oferswyðed and gefylled.

Comparison with the Blickling Homily version of the scene demonstrates our homilist's emphasis. He has a sequence of sentences (*and gif hit ðes is . . .* to end) that has no equivalent in the other version, in which he focuses on the devil's fate with repeated *he* and related forms. The sentences are already present in much the same language in pseudo-Augustine 160, and hence might well have been so in a related lost Latin homily which our homilist and the Blickling homilist probably used;[72] on this see below. But our homilist is no mere slavish imitator. He adds pronouns (*hine oferswyðan . . . fram þysum oferswyðed and gefylled*), stressing the reversed positions of Christ and the devil. The damned souls then go on to accuse their leader of failure to bring about what he has promised:

> *HomS* 28.93 Gehyr nu, ure ealdor: þa ðu þine welan ðe þu on þam ærestan men begeate ðurh forhogodnysse Godes beboda, nu ðu þæt forlure þurh rode treow. Geseoh nu þæt eall ðin blis þe losade mid þam ðe þu Crist on rode ahenge; ac ne mihtest ðu næfre geseon, ne ðe gifeðe næs, þa forwyrde þines rices.[73] Ðu hine on deað gelæddest butan ælcere scylde, and þu ðær gylt beheolde þar þu næfre nænne ne fundest. For hwon dorstest þu him æfre æthrinan?[74]

Throughout this passage *þu* is the grammatical subject, sharpening the focus on the devil as the accused, even more so than in the Blickling version.[75] Yet the passage does not voice the personal resentment of the lost souls so much as the homilist's own denunciation of the devil. This is perhaps implied in the preceding sentence where the second person *ðe* is the indirect object of *foregehete* ('you promised to yourself', line 91), indicating our homilist's preoccupation with the devil, rather than his companions', which is emphasized by the first person dative in both the Blickling ('þu us . . . gehete' (*BlHom* 85.19)) and Latin ('nobis . . . promittebas') versions. The passage quoted above brings this implied viewpoint

---

[72] For the text of the relevant parts of the Latin homily (now represented by pseudo-Augustine 160 and, for a later portion, by the Book of Cerne), see Schaefer, 'An Edition', pp. 160–4; citation from the Latin text is made from these pages. In the light of the Latin text (*Sed si iste est, in contrarium est nostri præliatoris versa sententia: et dum sibi vincere visus est ipse potius victus atque prostratus est*), the *mid ðy*-clause of the Old English homily should perhaps be read as subordinate to the following *þa wæs . . .* Schaefer (his lines 90–3), like Fadda, construes it as dependent on the preceding clause.

[73] Here I have changed Fadda's text (*ac ne mihtest ðu næfre geseon ne ðe gifeðe næs. Þa for wyrde þines rices ðu hine on deað gelæddest . . .*) in favour of the reading of Schaefer (his lines 101–2) and Raynes ('Unpublished OE Homilies', p. 78, lines 9–10).

[74] Fadda mistranscribes the word *hwon* as *whon* here and in lines 50 and 92.

[75] The Blickling version uses third person subjects (*he, monige earfoðe*) together with *þu*.

to the fore by the use of 'exegetical' words such as *ne . . . gifeðe* 'not granted by fate (that is, by God)' and *butan ælcere scylde* '(led to death) without any sin' and, most decisively and effectively, by the last sentence ('For hwon . . . æthrinan?'). The sentence again echoes Christ's words which the homilist has quoted in an earlier exegetical passage on the devil's fate: *HomS* 28.47 *Næs he na swa mid mægne ofercumen, swa swa he mid rihte gehyned wæs . . . Swa se Hælend sylf be þam cwæð: 'Hwæt gemettest þu yfeles on me? For hwon hrine ðu on me?'* These are all our homilist's own innovations, with no equivalents in the Latin homily (as represented by pseudo-Augustine 160) from which he is making 'an abridgement' at this point.[76] The Blickling version of the passage (*BlHom* 85.29–87.2) has reference to Christ being crucified without any sin (*læddest þu þeosne freone & unscyldigne*) but lacks the other exegetical elements. The Blickling version then has a sentence describing the breaking of the gates of Hell. This our homilist omits, skipping over these narrative details and moving directly to the speech of the good souls which ensues. His exegetical tone seems to linger on in this speech, where the souls say to Christ: *HomS* 28.105 *Alys nu forðferede and þa ðe on helle gehæfte synd.* The plea sounds more homiletic and universal than the one in the Blickling version, with its contextually bound *us* (*BlHom* 87.13 *Ales us nu of deofles onwalde & of helle hæftnede*).[77]

---

[76] Schaefer, 'An Edition', p. 160, note to his lines 81–104.

[77] For a similar 'exegetical' use of direct speech in the Harrowing of Hell material, see what Campbell has to say on the prayers of Adam and Eve in the fragmentary *Oratio* of the Book of Cerne: 'These speeches of Adam and Eve are a clever pastiche of phrases from the psalms, quite well adapted to the new speakers and the new situation. David's phrase, "ne derelinquas in inferno animam meam," smoothly fits into Adam's speech, and Eve's speech might almost be a newly discovered penitential psalm' ('To Hell and Back', 133). An example of a phrase from the Psalms is 'conparatus sum iumentis insipientibus. et nunc similis factus sum illis' (48:13 and 48:21), which is rendered closely in Eve's speech (lines 138–9), as pointed out by Fadda ('De descensu Christi', 1006, apparatus). Other phrases from the Psalms are identified by Raynes, 'Unpublished OE Homilies', pp. 137–42. At this point, as often elsewhere, both 'the Blickling VII text and Junius 121 seem to be based on this same Latin text [represented by the Book of Cerne fragment]' and 'Junius 121 translates more closely than Blickling VII', as Schaefer notes ('An Edition', p. 164). But whether or not our Junius 121 homilist was conscious of the 'pastiche of phrases from the psalms' and had his method of 'dramatic exegesis' suggested by it we cannot say. Its origin apart, it is to be noted that his use of direct speech for 'dramatic exegesis' is in marked contrast to Ælfric's use of discourse in some of his Lives of Saints, where, as Ruth Waterhouse has demonstrated, Ælfric distorts, through the use of indirect speech, what is referred to in both the Latin source and the preceding Old English versions as 'our religion' into 'his shameful gods', for example: 'This slanting of the indirect speech away from what the character would actually have said in the context of the story to an interpretive and affective comment on what such a speech would imply has the double function of weakening the dramatic effectiveness of the character who is morally

As can be seen in this discussion, the Harrowing of Hell section provides us with an unusual opportunity to examine the language and style of the homily, in comparison with the Blickling Homily version of the Harrowing[78] and with the Latin text which seems to underlie both Old English versions, though the textual relationship seems to be far from a simple one of immediate dependence of one of them on another. It is generally accepted that the two Old English versions are independent translations of a Latin text (now lost) which is very close to, and in part the same as, that of pseudo-Augustine 160 (for lines 79–99 of our homily) and the fragmentary *Oratio* of the Book of Cerne (for lines 100–152).[79] One cannot think in terms of changes made in one of the two Old English texts to the other. But one can make comparison, and can also consider the results of the comparison in terms of the source material which is now represented closely, if not exactly, in the two Latin texts just mentioned. We are concerned here with differences between the two Old English versions and whatever they may tell of our homilist's use of language, rather than the textual history of the Old English Harrowing of Hell literature.

It has been pointed out that our homily often 'translates more closely than Blickling VII'.[80] Perhaps the best illustration is the prayer of the good souls in hell to Christ (lines 103–21) and the subsequent ones of Adam and Eve (lines 124–35 and 136–57), in which direct appeal to Christ to be merciful and forget their sins is the central motif, uniting the whole scene closely, with insistent use of the words *mildheortnys* (lines 109, 112, 124, 129, 141) and *(ge)miltsian/milts* (lines 124, 125, 131).[81] Our homilist takes over verbatim all this insistence from

---

"bad" and of directing the audience to condemn him for his wicked beliefs and action' ('Ælfric's use of discourse in some saints' lives', *ASE* 5 (1976), 83–103, at 84). This contrast again suggests a variety of personal styles of Old English homilists, in which direct/indirect speech is put to effective use in their different ways.

[78] For a discussion of the Blickling version of the Harrowing of Hell, see Marcia A. Dalbey, 'Patterns of Preaching in the Blickling Easter Homily', *American Benedictine Review* 24 (1973), 478–92, esp. 483–6.

[79] See Schaefer, 'An Edition', pp. 130–3 and 159–64. Campbell ('To Hell and Back', 138–41) concurs in the main, but thinks that '[i]t is probable that J[unius 121] was translated from a version of sermon 160 different from that which Blickling VII used' (139). See also Swan, 'Old English Made New', 6; Fadda, 'De descensu Christi', 990–2; Raynes, 'Unpublished OE Homilies', pp. clxxxi-cci, esp. p. cxcvii; Max Förster, 'Altenglische Predigtquellen. I', *Archiv* 116 (1906), 301–14, esp. 301–7. For the earlier views that our homily is an adaptation of the Blickling version and that the two descend from a common source and are not independent translations, see, respectively, Pope, *Homilies of Ælfric*, Vol. I, p. 73 n. 2, and Scragg, 'The corpus', 255.

[80] Schaefer, 'An Edition', p. 164, note to his lines 137–141.

[81] The word *milts* occurs in 'and on þare menigu þinra miltsa adilga mine unrihtwisnyssa' (line 125), as Fadda correctly punctuates it. Schaefer's reading (his line 130, Gemiltsa me, min Drihten, on þinre þære miclan mildherotnysse ⁊ on þare menigu þinra miltsa.

the Latin text (as represented by the Book of Cerne), translating its *misericordia* and *miserere/miseratio* directly as above. He might well have continued to do so (lines 150, 153, 156), even after the Book of Cerne text breaks off, in the rest of Eve's speech made in the same vein and in Abraham's words, which conclude the scene with yet another reference to Christ's *mildheortnys* (line 159). The Blickling homilist, on the other hand, has no relevant sentences in the speech of the good souls nor any reference to Christ's mercy in Abraham's words; in this latter he emphasizes Christ as conqueror of death instead: *BlHom* 89.30 *We ondettaþ þe, Drihten, & þe hergeaþ; forþon þe þu us alesdest from deaþes fruman*. With the same slanting, the Blickling text reads at one place in the speech of the good souls entirely differently from our homily, which again translates the Latin directly:

> *HomS* 28.119 Drihten, þu ðe tobræce ure bendas, þe we heriað and lofiað and þanciað, þæt ðu us ne dydest æfter urum synnum, ne us ne gulde æfter urum unrihtwisnyssum.

> *BlHom* 87.22 Astig nu, Drihten Hælend Crist, up, nu þu hafast helle bereafod, & þæs deaþes aldor on þyssum witum gebundenne. Gecyþ nu middangearde blisse þæt on þinum upstige geblissian & gehyhton ealle þine gecorenan.

The different emphases which thus distinguish the two Old English versions might be suggestive, as Campbell thinks,[82] of different source texts of a Latin homily rather than different degrees of dependence on a Latin text. But the question is of secondary importance for our concern here. What is important for us is to notice that our homilist was probably conscious of the *misericordia* theme that runs through the Latin text he follows closely, for he reinforces it by the use of the word *milde* which he introduces independently of his Latin text, first, prior to the appearance of the Latin *misericordia*, in *HomS* 28.107 . . . *þæt ðu þinne ðone mildan ansyne us fram ne acyrre*,[83] and then in 132 *Bletsie, min sawl, Drihten . . . Se is milde geworden minum unrihtwisnyssum*, where the Blickling

---

Adilga . . .) misses direct translation at this point from the Latin (*miserere mei in magna misericordia tua. et in multitudine miserationum tuarum dele iniquitatem meam*, based on Psalms 50: 3). For another feature of Eve's prayer to Christ, both in *HomS* 28 and Blickling VII, based on her motherhood of Mary, see Mary Clayton, *The Cult of the Virgin Mary in Anglo-Saxon England* (Cambridge, 1990), pp. 255–6.

[82] See n. 79. Campbell is led to think so by comparison of the speech of the good souls in the two Old English texts, noting that 'this idea ['sy þin mildheortnys ofer us . . .', as in our homily, line 109] occurs only in the Cerne text and not in sermon 160 or in Blickling VII' ('To Hell and Back', 139).

[83] Here it is the Blickling text that corresponds to the Book of Cerne text closely: *BlHom* 87.15 *þonne þu to þinum uplican rice cyrre* (Latin *cum fueris reuersurus ad superos*).

homilist's *arfæst* translates the Latin *propitius* more closely. Our homilist is no mere slavish translator.

The homilist also often follows closely the discourse structure of the Latin text which tends to be rhetorical. Thus, he keeps the rhetorical balance of the Latin in *HomS* 28.103 *Nu ðu to us come, middaneardes Alysend, and nu þu to us come, þone we . . ., and nu ðu to us come, þu ðe . . . sealdest* (Latin *Adueinsti redemptor mundi. Aduenisti quem . . . Aduenisti donans . . .*),[84] 132 *Bletsie, min sawl, Drihten . . . Se is milde . . ., se gehælde . . ., se alysde . . ., se gefylde . . .* (Latin *Benedic anima mea dominum . . . Qui . . . qui . . . Qui . . . qui . . .*, rendered with consistent *þu* by the Blickling homilist), and 139 *Ac ne gemun ðu, min Drihten, þa gyltas mines geogeðhades and minre dysinysse, and ne acyr ðu . . ., and ne ahyld þu . . .* (Latin *Sed tu domine delicta iuuentutis et insipientiae meae ne memineris. Ne auertas . . . et ne declines . . .*);[85] see also *Gehyr nu . . . Geseoh nu . . .* (lines 93–6).[86] Other examples of a similar kind occur in that part of Eve's speech for which the Book of Cerne text is deficient, but these, too, might reflect the rhetorical structure of the Latin text now apparently lost. For example, Eve's words 'Þu wast mine gyltas and mine dysinyssa' (line 145) echo line 139 (see above), and the description of Christ and Eve after the latter's speech (*HomS* 28.153 *And þa wæs se Hælend sona mid mycelre mildheortnysse astyrod and hy ða hrædlice alysde of þæs wites bendum; and heo ða geornlice onleat to þæs Hælendes cneowum and þus cwæð*) closely parallels the previous one after Adam's speech (lines 131–2); while a succession of imperatives (*HomS* 28.150 *Geara me, forðanþe ðu . . . Miltsa me, forðanþe ðu . . . Alys me, forðanþe ðu . . .*) again shows a rhetorical balance which is lost in the Blickling text (*BlHom* 89.23 *& min Scyppend miltsa me, & genere me of þysses deaþes bendum*). Even in

---

[84] The Latin text has another *Aduenisti* sentence between the last two in the Old English text.

[85] The Latin makes suspect the Blickling text of the first clause of the corresponding sentence, which Morris reads as *BlHom* 89.10 *Ac þu Drihten scyld minre iugoþe & min, onunwisdomes ne wes þu gemyndig*, with the translation: 'But thou Lord, shield of my youth and of me, be not mindful of my folly'. Kelly (*The Blickling Homilies*, pp. 90–1) reads the same way, with a similar translation, as does Michael Swanton (*Anglo-Saxon Prose* (London, 1975), p. 66). But there would appear to be errors in the Blickling text, including *scyld* for *scylda* (gen. pl. of *scyld* 'guilt, sin', not *scield* 'shield, protector'), a complement of *gemyndig* parallel to *onunwisdomes*, rendering closely the Latin *delicta iuuentutis et insipientiae meae ne memineris*. In its turn, the form *onunwisdomes* might well be a ghost word, as Bosworth-Toller, Supplement, suggests with respect to the main entry for the word in the Dictionary which is based solely on the Blickling passage being discussed: 'Probably this word should be rejected, for the passage in which it occurs seems corrupt' (BTS, s.v.). The Supplement goes on to conjecture, with a question mark, a reading which is different from mine and might have been more natural for the editor to whom the Latin source was obviously not known: 'Þu, Drihten, forgif þa scylde minre iugoþe, and mines unwisdomes ne wes þu gemyndig'.

[86] On this example, see Schaefer, 'An Edition', p. 161, note to his lines 97–100.

details of syntax, the homilist sometimes shows 'Latinisms', as in *nelle þu* (line 107, for Latin *Noli*) and *wæs geðuht* (line 89 (p. 161), for Latin *visus est*).[87]

Yet direct translation is not entirely the characteristic of our homilist's language in the Harrowing of Hell section. It was seen above that he can be independent of his Latin text in his choice of adjectives. So he is in a certain group of sentences from the speeches of Adam and Eve, as in line 139 (see above), where he, unlike the Blickling homilist (see n. 85), follows the negative pattern but otherwise arranges the words in the order VSO in accordance with the usual Old English pattern. Similarly, he prefers in the rest of the group not to follow the Latin word order, putting the subject at the clause-initial position: *HomS* 28.125 *forðon ic þe anum gesyngade and ic yfele dyde beforan ðe* (Latin *quia tibi soli peccaui et malum coram te feci*, rendered literally as *BlHom* 87.29 *forþon þe anum ic gesyngade, & mycel yfel beforan þe ic gedyde*) and 136 *Drihten, þu eart rihtwis, and þin dom is riht, forþon ic mid gewyrhtum ðas witu prowige* (Latin *Iustus es domine et rectum iudicium tuum. quia merito hæc patior*, rendered as *BlHom* 89.6 *Soþfæst eart þu, Drihten, & rihte syndon þine domas; forþon þe mid gewyrhtum ic þas prowige*);[88] it is again the Blickling homilist who imitates the Latin word order. The distinction between the two Old English homilists comes out neatly in:

> *HomS* 28.127 Alys nu mine bendas forðonþe þine handa me geworhtan and me gehiwodon; and ne forlet ðu on helle mine sawle, ac þine mildheortnysse on me gecyð and me gelæd of þyses cwearternes huse and of þyses deaðes[89] sceade,

as compared with:

> *BlHom* 87.31 Sec nu þinne þeow, Drihten, forþon þe þine handa me geworhtan & geheowodan; ne forlæt þu mine saule mid hellwarum; ac do on me þine mildheor[t]nesse, & alæd me ut of þyssum bendum, & of þyses carcernes huse, & of deaþes scuan.

---

[87] On the first construction as 'a clear case of Latin influence', see *OES*, §917. On the second, see *OES*, §§1049–51, and Mitsu Ide, 'The Distribution of *Beon/Wesan Gepuht(e)* in Old English Texts', *Bulletin of Kanto Gakuin University* 43 (1985), 81–118, where the author shows that the construction frequently corresponds to Latin *videri* and occasionally to *visum est*. The author also shows that it is most frequent in Ælfric's works and is rare in anonymous homilies.

[88] In this sentence and two others (*HomS* 28.142, 155), our homilist places the vocative *(min) Drihten* initially, while the Blickling homilist places it after the initial (C)VS; the Latin text, available only for the first of the three, shows that the Blickling homilist is here again closer to it. But our homilist's usage varies; see line 139 (see p. 165).

[89] Fadda's text (line 130) has a wrong form *deaðed*.

The latter's consistent imperative order V(S)O might as well be an imitation of the Latin (*resolue uincula mea . . . ne derelinquas . . . animam meam. Sed fac mecum misericordiam et educ uinctum . . .*) as an instance of the Old English pattern for that sentence type. On the other hand, our homilist deviates from that normal order (and the Latin) in the last two clauses, for whatever effects he might have thought to secure. Given, for example, the importance of Christ's mercy throughout the speeches of Adam and Eve, it might be that he placed the object *þine mildheortnysse* before the verb for emphasis and, consequent on that, *me* before *gelæd* for contrast, though it is difficult to be certain of this. Another group of sentences shows our homilist preferring sentence-initial position for the adverb *þa*, whether with following VS or SV (lines 123, 131, 153, 158), and *þa gyt* (lines 122, 136), in clear contrast to the Blickling homilist who never fails to place these words immediately after the subject which comes initially in the corresponding sentences (*BlHom* 87.26, 35, 89.24, 28; 87.25, 89.5). In these cases, our homilist often agrees with the Latin (with initial *tunc* and *adhuc*), but the evidence of the Latin text is not complete. His word order here is at any rate as idiomatic Old English as the Blickling homilist's.

If our homilist's word order points to independence from the Latin text in favour of natural and idiomatic Old English prose, some other details of his style confirm this direction. Particularly noteworthy are expressions that are expansive as compared with the Blickling homilist's. These include a clause instead of an appositive phrase (*HomS* 28.149 *Ara me . . ., þeah ic wære ungesæligast ealra wifa*, beside *BlHom* 89.22 *ara me ungesæligost ealra wifa*),[90] and *and*-coordination instead of a single clause (*HomS* 28.142 *min lif gewat on sare and mine gear on geomerunge synd geendode*, beside *BlHom* 89.14 *on sare & on geomrunga min lif & mine gear syndon fornumene*) or instead of a relative clause (*HomS* 28.126 *Ic dwolade swa swa þæt unwise sceap and forweard and losade*, beside *BlHom* 87.30 *Ic gedwolede swa swa þæt sceap þæt forwearþ*); related to this latter is coordination of clauses with the same subject (*HomS* 28.131 *Ða Drihten Adame gemiltsade and hine of þam bendum alysde*) where the Blickling text has coordinate clauses with different subjects (*BlHom* 87.35 *Drihten Hælend þa wæs miltsigende Adame, & raþe his bendas wæron onlysde*), rendering more closely the Latin ablative absolute (*domino miserante adam e uinculis resolutus . . .*) on that score. By these grammatical choices our homilist strengthens the flow and makes his point more simply and clearly. These cases are parallelled by a few others in which our homilist tends to be concise and succinct in wording, using *ec ofer þæt* (line 85) instead of *nis no þæt an þæt . . .* (*BlHom* 85.15) and avoiding repetition and redundancy (e.g. *HomS* 28.143 *Drihten, þu wast þæt ic eom gedrorenlic dust*, as compared with *BlHom* 89.15 *Drihten, þu wast mine geheowunga, þæt ic eom dust & axe*)—a tendency which is best seen in the cry of horror-stricken lost souls at seeing a great light: *HomS* 28.83 *Syððan he wæs*

---

[90] The other examples are *HomS* 28.81 and 28.132 beside *BlHom* 85.9 and 87.36. For yet another example of apposition in the Blickling text (*BlHom* 89.13 *ic earm to þe cleopie*), our homilist (line 142) has no equivalent word.

us underþeod, næfre ær he us þyllic gafol ne gegeald, ne us næfre ær þyllic lac hyder ne onsende. Hwæt is ðes...? The plainness of language and its effectiveness at this particular point is the more obvious in comparison with the other version, where the Blickling homilist takes almost double the length in a rather clumsy sequence of five clauses *... &...; ne... þæt..., ne...* (*BlHom* 85.11–14).[91] It may also be the same tendency that accounts for the difference between our homilist and the Blickling homilist in rendering the Latin *lacrimabili uoce et obsecratione saluatorem deposcunt dicentes* in the description of the good souls:

> *HomS* 28.101 þa þe wæron gehæfte on hell, wependre stemne and mid micele halsunge þone Hælend bædon and þus cwædon:

> *BlHom* 87.6 þa sona instæpes seo unarimedlice menigo haligra saula þe ær gehæftnede wæron to þæm Hælende onluton, & mid wependre halsunga hine bædon, & þus cwædon.

Our homilist is closer to the Latin, using two verbs and lacking the verb *onluton* 'bowed, bent down' which the other homilist adds here. It is remarkable, however, that our homilist in his turn uses (though in slightly different phrases) the word *onlutan* or *alutan* at three places, including two (lines 117 and 154, where the Blickling text has no equivalent) to describe the actions of the good souls and Eve after their respective prayers, thereby making the wording in Eve's case closely parallel to the description of Adam (line 132). Moreover, he adds the intensive *geornlice* together with the *onlutan/alutan*-phrase on both these occasions; his use of the verb phrase may be rhetorical as well as descriptive.

This last point takes us back to rhetorical aspects of our homilist's language. It was shown earlier that he often moulds his paragraphs upon the rhetoric of the Latin text he follows closely. Just as this 'Latinate rhetoric' is translated into what proves, in details of wording, to be natural, idiomatic Old English prose, so it is reinforced by the homilist's own stock of rhetorical devices of which the use of *onlutan/alutan* and *geornlice* mentioned above may be examples. Details of this stock are given by Fadda, who describes it in terms of nine 'verbal figures'—word pairs, alliteration, homoeoteleuton and homoeoptoton, paronomasia, etymological association, anaphora, parallelism, antithetical parallelism, and parallelism with variation.[92] With the single exception of this last (see below), Fadda's examples are all taken from the sections of the homily other than the Latin-based narrative of the Harrowing of Hell, emphasizing the importance

---

[91] Max Förster has proposed an emendation for this passage of the Blickling text, saying: 'Aus dem Altenglischen läßt sich hier zwar zur Not ein Sinn herauslesen, aber nur ein sehr matter und von der Quelle ganz abweichender' ('Zu den Blickling Homilies', *Archiv* 91 (1892), 179–206, at 183).

[92] Fadda, 'De descensu Christi', 995–6.

of these rhetorical figures for the homilist's own prose. But he does employ many of them in the Harrowing of Hell section. Most important are word pairs, which are almost as frequent here as in the other sections. To some fifteen examples in the latter category,[93] the Harrowing section adds some eleven. Some of them are probably translations of the Latin, e.g. *me geworhtan and me gehiwodon* (line 128; Latin *fecerunt me et plasmauerunt me*) and *seo ben and seo halsung* (line 115; Latin *postulatio et obsecratio*; cf. *BlHom* 87.17 *þeos ben*), but others are derived from the Latin only partly, as in *clypedon and þus cwædon* (line 118; Latin *clamantes*) and *forwearð and losade* (line 127; Latin *perierat*; cf. *BlHom* 87.31 *forwearþ*). The homilist also has a rapid succession of three word pairs at a point in Eve's prayer where the Book of Cerne text has broken off: *HomS* 28.144 *hu mæg ic hit ðonne acuman ænigra þinga oððe aberan? Þu wast mine gyltas and mine dysinyssa and hi næran beforan ðe ahydde ne bemiðene.* The last of the three occurs in the earlier section (line 37, *ahydde and bemað*),[94] and the homilist might well be expanding the Latin text here too, at any rate partly.

There are other rhetorical figures shared by the Harrowing of Hell section. Alliteration, for example, is used in *HomS* 28.88 *is ures cempan cwyde on wyðerweardnysse gecyrred* and for two crucial ideas of the Harrowing story: 'Christ's mercy', as in 124 *on þinre þære miclan mildheortnysse; and on þare menigu þinra miltsa* and 156 *þin mildheortnyss is micel*, and 'captivity in hell' in 101 *gehæfte on helle*, repeated in reversed order in 106. Other examples include etymological association in 85 *mid bendum gebundenne* (said of the devil in hell, as several times in the earlier section; see p. 157); parallelism with variation in 102 *wependre stemne and mid micele halsunge* (beside 123 *geomeriendlicre and earmlicre stemne* and, from the earlier section, 15 *mid his agenan muðe*);[95] and parallelism characteristic of the descriptions of Adam's and Eve's actions after their prayers (see above). Two other features not noted by Fadda may be included here. One is the expanded form, which occurs descriptively in the later section (*HomS* 28.193 *be Godes rice sprecende wæs*) but may be affective, if not rhetorical, where it occurs in the lost souls' complaint to their leader: *HomS* 28.90 *Eala ure ealdor, is ðis se he þæs deaðe þu a fægniende*[96] *wære . . . ?* This affective use may be seen more easily when

---

[93] Some of these are given by Fadda, 'De descensu Christi', 995.

[94] Raynes argues that the use of this word pair 'suggests that the homilist may have been using a glossed copy of the Psalms with alternative glosses' ('Unpublished OE Homilies', p. 141).

[95] Whether or not alteration between a case form and a prepositional phrase in the instrumental sense is purely a matter of rhetoric remains a problem. The three sentences show that our homilist uses the case form with the noun *stemn* but otherwise the *mid*- phrase. The Blickling homilist shows the same distribution (*BlHom* 87.8, 87.26).

[96] Fadda reads *afægniende*, but no such single form of the verb is otherwise recognized in Old English. I follow Schaefer and Raynes in reading *a* as an adverb; *DOE*, too, cites the sentence in question with this word division (s.v. *fægnian, fagnian* 1.b.iv).

one notes that our homilist does not use the expanded form where the Blickling homilist does to describe Christ's actions after the prayers of Adam and Eve, saying *Drihten Hælend þa wæs miltsigende Adame* (*BlHom* 87.35, and 89.25 with *Euan* in place of *Adame*). The other feature is grammatical recapitulation,[97] by which the homilist seems to reinforce the organization of his sense and paragraph, in the Harrowing of Hell section:

> *HomS* 28.108 Ðu ðe þines wuldres tacen on hrodere gecyddest, Drihten, sy þin mildheortnys ofer us, swa swa we aa fæstlice on ðe gehihtað, forðon mid þe is lifes will, and on ðinum leohte we leoht geseoð.

> *HomS* 28.119 Drihten, þu ðe tobræce ure bendas, þe we heriað and lofiað and þanciað, þæt ðu us ne dydest æfter urum synnum, . . .

and later in an exegetical passage:

> *HomS* 28.177 Ne wene nu æfre ænig mann þæt Drihten Crist ealle þa of helle gelædde þe he ðær gemette; ac þa ane ða þe heora lif her on worulde rihtlice leofedan, þa he ðanon gelædde. And he þær forlet morðwyrhtan and dyrne forligras and rihtes geleafan wiþersacan and þeofas and gitseras; and þa ðe heora yfeldæda betan nellað, þa he næfre þanon alyseð.

Just as it focuses, in the first two examples, on the contrast between glory in heaven and mercy on earth ('Ðu ðe þines wuldres tacen . . ., . . . þin mildheortnys . . .') and between Christ and the saved ('þu ðe . . ., þe we . . .'), so recapitulation emphasizes the distinction between the chosen good and the bad in the last example. Schaefer's reading for this last (his lines 185–90), with a period instead of a comma between the last *þa* and *nellað*, destroys the logical plan the homilist presents in it, which depends partly on the paired verbs ('leofedan . . . gelædde', and 'nellað . . . alyseð') in the preterite and present tenses.[98]

Our homilist's own rhetorical figures are thus no stylistic embellishments but are geared to the contents and contexts of his sentences which have called them forth. Altogether, these features, many of them common to the sections supposedly written by the homilist himself and the Latin-based section, suggest a conscious style in which he has made a consistent homily out of different sources. And it is this individual style which carefully moulds narrative and exegesis and dramatic direct speech and narrative statements, welding the various sources they come from into a unity characteristic of its user.

---

[97] For this term, see *OES*, §§1447–8.
[98] Raynes ('Unpublished OE Homilies', p. 84) reads in the same way as Fadda.

Conclusion

Despite the shared feature of being an Easter homily with an Ælfrician passage incorporated into it, *In Die Sancto Pasce* and *De Descensu Christi ad Inferos* differ from each other substantially in a number of ways. The former is built around several themes that are associated loosely with Easter Sunday, with little effective linking between them; the other is a homily devoted to a consistent narrative of the Harrowing of Hell interspersed with consistent exegetical commentaries. The difference is accompanied by predictable variation in language and style. The narrative of the Harrowing of Hell is executed carefully in a style which welds different sources and different modes of discourse into a unity and is at times almost literary, as in what has been described as its 'dramatic exegesis' and its treatment of the central theme of the merciful Christ in the middle section. The homilist owes some of this literary merit to the Latin text he generally follows closely, but he has added his own innovations, thereby enhancing the rhetorical language which he seems to value in the Latin. The *In Die Sancto Pasce* homilist, on the other hand, is unpretentious and can be even casual in thought and wording. This distinction also makes itself felt clearly in the ways the two homilists make biblical references. Here again, the *De Descensu* homilist shows on the whole a better treatment. He gives the Latin biblical text before he translates it into Old English, and his translation is generally reasonable, if not always perfect — a careful treatment obviously called for by the nature of his homily, which is exegetical as well as narrative.

The different natures of the two homilies also called forth dissimilar passages for incorporation, excerpted from different items of Ælfric's *Catholic Homilies* — one consisting mainly of exempla on the mystery of the Eucharist and the other an exegetical commentary using 'the devil as fish' simile. The excerpts are accordingly given different treatments, particularly in the degrees to which change is made to them in precise wording. On the whole, the *In Die Sancto Pasce* homilist seems to be less appreciative of Ælfric's careful writing and subtleties of thought and expression. The two homilists are good illustrations of the varied methods of combining Ælfric's homilies and non-Ælfrician material into composite homilies of which Mary Swan has spoken.[99]

Yet the two homilies agree in one respect. By making an excerpt from the original context of the Ælfric homily, they are both against the original author's instructions to be careful in transmission of his works to preserve their integrity. And they are not alone in this breach. Observations have been made of 'a consistently free use of *C[atholic]H[omilies]* excerpts from the late tenth to the second

---

[99] See p. 140.

half of the twelfth century', as Swan says,[100] and Swan concludes her study of this process with these words:

> The evidence for the breadth of transmission and exploitation of the *CH* has been known for some time, but the texts I have analysed provide a significant supplementary body of evidence for the breakdown of Ælfric's desired pattern of transmission, and for the lack of response to or respect for the finer points of his ideals throughout the church.... Some of these questions can never be authoritatively answered, but the clearest point to emerge from my study of the use of the *CH* in Ælfric/anonymous texts is the tension between Ælfric's self-image and representation of the Reform as expressed in his work, and what can be deduced of the real reactions, interpretations and practical needs of the wider Anglo-Saxon church.[101]

This 'tension' continues well into the twelfth century, as Swan has shown in detail in another study.[102] The two composite homilies examined in this chapter, both preserved in eleventh-century manuscripts, are products of the period which saw all this development and are important witnesses to the changing attitudes with which homiletic literature continued to be produced in late Old English to early Middle English.

---

[100] Swan, 'Ælfric as Source', p. 325.
[101] Swan, 'Ælfric as Source', pp. 332–3. See also Hill, 'Reform and Resistance', pp. 40–1.
[102] Swan, 'Ælfric's *Catholic Homilies*', *passim*.

VII.
Conclusion

In the preceding chapters I have discussed eight Old English composite homilies (and three other variant texts of one of them). The selection of these particular homilies and the order in which they are discussed reflect the problems which gradually unfolded themselves as my interest developed in reading the relevant works of the genre, starting with Napier XXX. The selection and order might, in this sense, not be definitive. On the other hand, however, selection was made with a view to having all important groups of relevant Old English works represented, so that some are taken from Wulfstan composite homilies, some from Ælfrician ones, and some others from the anonymous group; some of the selected homilies also have a strong case for inclusion by virtue of the lines of affiliation they share. Taken together, the eight homilies form a sufficiently extensive and representative sample of the practices of compilers in the period, to allow us to draw some conclusions about the language and style and other aspects of the history of the homilies of late Anglo-Saxon England.

The eight compilations form, together with relevant source works, a large network of homiletic literature, as it were, in which they not only draw upon those earlier materials, approaching them with different attitudes and rewriting them in their own ways and for their own purposes; some of them, in their turn, are also drawn upon to be developed into new composite homilies. A notable example of this process—continuous layers of use and re-use—is Vercelli XXI, derived in part from Vercelli II, being developed into Napier XXX, which is in turn used for the composition of Bazire and Cross 7 and (as I argued) Napier LVIII (see Chapters II and III). Sometimes, within this network of intertextuality, several compilers turn for sources to identical homiletic works, as in the case just mentioned of Napier XXX used in two later compilations, or even to identical passages from the same works, as in the case of a passage from Napier XXIV (probably by Wulfstan) popular enough to be used in four later compilations (see Chapters II and III) and, more importantly, the 'metrical' and related passages from the eschatological Vercelli II which are adapted for use in Vercelli XXI, Napier XL (in its four variant texts) and Fadda X, together constituting what was described in this study as the Vercelli tradition of Judgement Day homilies (see Chapters III and IV). Analysis of such parallel passages helps to identify the stages of development of a work and/or the relationship between the manuscripts which transmit the work. The results of my analysis in this respect have confirmed what previous scholars have assumed or concluded in almost all cases. There are, however, three details which do not appear to agree with previous conclusions exactly. One of them, about the 'popular' passage from Napier XXIV mentioned above, points strongly to a textual relationship—in particular, of the Napier LVIII version of the passage to the others—which is different from the one that has previously been claimed; see Chapter III. The other two may not perhaps be as decisive, but there is a possibility, albeit slight, that they cast some doubt on what has been generally accepted: one, the evidence of two readings (one of them an apparent error) shared by MSS NX^d against OP of Napier XL, might argue if anything against the stemma usually assumed for those manuscripts (see Chapter IV), and the other shows Napier XXIX to be closer in two sentences to the underlying Latin text than the Macarius homily of which it is commonly held to be an adaptation (see Chapter V). How the evidence of these details in the texts can be reconciled with previous assumptions about the relevant homilies and whether in fact they might lead to a reconsideration of these assumptions remains to be made clear by future work.

What has emerged most clearly from my selection of homilies are the diverse prose styles in which the eight compilers adapt and rewrite the source texts they draw upon. Thus, Napier XXX with its conscious but often straightforward style, not hampered by unclarity of syntax or sense, and Napier XL written in terse, controlled prose with precise syntax, both have a strong affinity for rhythmical word pairs, and are as sharply distinct from the fussy additions and prolix expansions characteristic of the prose of Napier LVIII, as the narrative prose, well thought-out and at times becoming almost literary, of *HomS* 28 is from the casual writing, allowing occasional logical and grammatical inconsistencies, of *HomS* 27; distinct from them all are Vercelli XXI's style, which tends towards unadorned and straightforward expression, and the style of the Fadda X compiler, for whom enumeration and a certain syntactic pattern have almost become a habit of mind moulding his sentence structures. All these distinct manners of writing confirm, first and foremost, what Angus McIntosh has very aptly pointed out as the homilists' 'own personal characteristics' to be found among the alleged school of 'Wulfstan imitators'.[1] Neither Napier XXX, Napier XL, nor Napier LVIII, all drawing more or less upon Wulfstan's writings, is the work of a mere 'Wulfstan imitator', any more than any of the other five homilies is written in imitation of any influential writer, known or anonymous.

Particularly revealing in this respect are parallel passages in different homilies drawing on identical sources, as, for example, the 'metrical passage' and the surrounding portions of Vercelli II, shared by at least two of Napier XL, Vercelli XXI, and Fadda X (where the first homily is generally more sensitive to grammar

---

[1] Angus McIntosh, 'Wulfstan's Prose', *PBA* 34 (1948), 109–42, at 126; see Chapter I.

and meaning, while the other two often content themselves with a relatively easy and simple way out in revising their sources; see Chapters III and IV); the versions of a passage from the anchorite and devil story, as preserved in Napier XXX and Fadda X (and two more manuscripts), where Napier XXX shows a clearer syntax and is more readable than Fadda X, which relies very heavily upon its favoured 'þeah . . . , hwæþere' pattern (see Chapters II and IV); and the versions of the Harrowing of Hell narrative in *HomS* 28 and Blickling Homily VII (studied for comparison of this Harrowing section only), both probably based on a Latin text but working with different emphases, show a more literary treatment of the narrative by the former (see Chapter VI). The variant texts in the extant four manuscripts of Napier XL, too, are obviously often very instructive in specific details of this kind of stylistic diversity. Somewhat distinct from all these examples of parallel passages but equally revealing is the comparison of different poetic sources used in two of my homilies. One of them is a 'prose dilution' of probably two poems made in the straightforward prose of Vercelli XXI and the other is a 'severely practical' prosification of a Judgement Day poem, made in Napier XXIX (see Chapters IV and V). It should be added that this last treatment by Napier XXIX, retaining some of the poetic diction and poetic syntax of the source, speaks only for one aspect of this homily, which uses different methods of adapting its sources, ranging from the 'practical' treatment in the poetic section just mentioned to a fairly drastic adaptation in the opening section. In this, Napier XXIX is the one case of mixed styles in my selection of composite homilies, which otherwise show generally, each in its own way, a consistent attitude to their sources and a consistent method and prose style in rewriting them. All this demonstrates clearly that whether written in a consistent style or not, the composite homilies I have studied are all products of compilation, not of imitation, made by individual minds with their own designs and purposes, though perhaps with variable success.

Along with these 'personal characteristics' of the compilers, my examination has also revealed certain features which the eight composite homilies share as a genre in the general area of language and style. In terms of the traditional distinction, for example, they are almost invariably *sermones*, i.e. general addresses on moral and hortatory themes, which may be delivered at various times of the year rather than on specific days of the liturgical calendar, and consequently lack the structure characteristic of the other subgenre (*homiliae*, typically represented by Ælfric's homilies), with the pericope for the day followed by exegesis in the form of verse-by-verse commentary on that biblical text. This lack of consistent form is shared even by one of the Easter homilies in my corpus, *HomS* 27. Titled *In Die Sancto Pasce*, it in fact puts together rather loosely five major themes which are not associated particularly clearly with Easter, without developing them into a consistent narrative or exegesis. There is one which deviates from this general shape in my corpus, the other Easter homily, *HomS* 28, which is a consistent narrative of the Harrowing of Hell with exegetical commentaries interspersed throughout it. However, *HomS* 28 is obviously a real exception in the genre of the period generally, where, as Malcolm Godden observes, '[c]omposite homilies made up mainly of narrative . . . are rare, and I do not know of any composite homily which could be described as explanatory or exegetical'[2] (see Chapter VI). As we shall see, this absence of narrative and exegetical elements common to composite homilies may be a feature of their method of compilation itself, and the unique position of *HomS* 28 as exegetical composite homily may be one of the things that allowed it to rise to the level of achievement it does in comparison with the rest of my eight homilies.

It is perhaps inevitable that these composite homilies constructed as *sermones* should usually turn to a certain range or stock of passages that are useful and manageable enough to lend themselves to compilation. The best example from this stock is the description of the terror of hell in Vercelli II, which is used in three of my eight homilies (Napier XL, Vercelli XXI, and Fadda X; see Chapters III and IV). It is a generalizing description with universal force, not invested with any specific circumstantial detail, which can be easily detached from its original textual context and inserted into any other comparable texts. So are injunctions and exhortations (typically those beginning with *uton* 'let us') from Wulftan's homilies (used in Napier XXX, Napier XL, and Napier LVIII; see Chapters II and III) and Vercelli II (used in Napier XL, Vercelli XXI, and Fadda X; see Chapters III and IV). Similarly usable descriptions of manageable length can take the form of enumeration and listing, as in Napier XL (the CCCC 419 version, using Wulfstan's list of vices and virtues; see Chapter IV) and Fadda X (taking over lists of three kinds of death and life and other lists from Vercelli IX; see Chapter IV); this last homily in fact relies on itemized lists as a structuring principle. To all these cases, Godden's remark on his two Winchester composite homilies (one of them discussed in Chapter II) applies:

> Like a number of his contemporaries, the Winchester compiler has picked out from the work of Ælfric and Wulfstan and others appropriate passages of injunction and warning and discarded the rest—the explanation and interpretation and narrative. The passages are skilfully woven together on a rather superficial level by inserting frequent connectives and using verbal associations, but there is rather less concern with an underlying thread of thought or argument. There is, though, a certain amount of independence in organizing the material.[3]

HomS 27 is again revealing. The compiler does lift from Ælfric's homily passages including two exempla on the mystery of the Eucharist but pares them down to a

---

[2] M. R. Godden, 'Old English composite homilies from Winchester', *ASE* 4 (1975), 57–65, at 64–5.

[3] Godden, 'OE composite homilies', 65.

form he finds appropriate for a dramatic story rather than for the elaborate theological discussion the original author had developed. On the other hand, *HomS* 28 uses his own exegetical passage from the *Catholic Homilies* in a more significant way, integrating Ælfric's 'devil-as-fish' simile with an earlier section of the homily where he anticipates the subsequent narrative. *HomS* 28 stands apart here again (see Chapter VI).

The two general traits—*sermones* as a subgenre and certain stock passages relied on—which my eight homilies have in common may be features of composite homilies as a whole 'individually designed for preaching use (in contrast to the more general, quasi-literary role that might be assumed for the work of Ælfric and Wulfstan)'.[4] The distinction may also explain why the eight homilies, and many others in the genre, are generally written in prose styles which are neither as elegant and rich in rhetorical elaboration as Ælfric's nor as impassioned and forceful as Wulfstan's. There is rather a certain workmanlike quality to them, as witness the practical treatment the Napier XXIX compiler gives in prosifying his poetic source (see Chapter V). This pragmatic quality is understandable since the compilers' main concern is to give a new form to the 'decontextualised' passages by finding appropriate adaptations in verbal details as they rewrite them. On 'decontextualisation' from Ælfric's and Wulfstan's homilies, see further below.

All this does not mean, however, that my eight homilies, and others in the genre, are invariably uninspired products of compilers whose workmanlike approach makes them interesting only for the details of changes they make to earlier works. They can rise to the level of literary achievement not unworthy of Ælfric and Wulfstan, as the Easter homily *HomS* 28 certainly does (see Chapter VI). Its chief strength lies in its structure, with consistent exegetical commentaries developed in the context of the consistent Harrowing of Hell narrative. Drawing on Ælfrician and Latin materials, it welds them into a unity, with Ælfric's exegesis on the devil linked to an earlier section and the subsequent Latin-based narrative. A unique exegetical composite homily, it is often couched in rhetorical language, partly owing to the underlying Latin homily, but the compiler is not a mere translator but renders the story in readable vernacular prose not hampered by slavish imitation of Latin sentences, developing his own emphases, as in his treatment of the mercy of Christ. Even the use of direct speech for 'dramatic exegesis', illogical though it would seem to modern readers, shows that the compiler shifts his point of view to present his message more effectively. Another candidate for our special attention is probably Napier XXX (see Chapter II). Though perhaps not as illustrious as *HomS* 28, it is still worthy of attention, not least by virtue of the tripartite structure which the deployment of appropriate styles sustains and also because it enables us to watch an Old English compiler at work, as he grows gradually more confident in adapting and compiling his source

---

[4] Malcolm Godden, 'Review of Hiroshi Ogawa, *Studies in the History of Old English Prose*', *Studies in English Literature* (Tokyo), English Number 42 (2001), 111–7, at 116.

texts. Its popularity among its original audience as well as modern scholars is a clear indication of the quality it has achieved. And the rest of my eight composite homilies are, of course, at the very least no unreflective 'scissors and paste' jobs but intelligent products of individual minds who have worked with their own design and purpose and in their own prose styles.

I have so far summarized the eight homilies as a single group. The period, however, in which they were written covers roughly a century in terms of the date of the relevant manuscripts. This fairly long span of time in late Anglo-Saxon England might also be expected to have seen developments in the history of vernacular homilies, both in their language and substance. The diverse prose styles of my eight homilies themselves might reflect, in some cases at least, such historical changes of the language as much as the personal characteristics of their compilers, though it is difficult to isolate the two elements from each other. However, the eight composite homilies do contain examples of variation where we can speak more definitely of historical change. In language, for example, the available evidence points to modernization of source language as an important feature of some homilies, notably Napier XXX and Vercelli XXI. Rewriting their respective source materials, which are probably at least half a century earlier, from the Vercelli Homilies, the two homilies update some vocabulary items, replacing poetic words with prosaic ones and apparently archaic words with more common ones. They also provide examples of modernization of syntax, effecting alteration of the wording in the source texts into patterns which later became regular forms of expression in word order and the use of auxiliary verbs (see Chapters II and IV). These changes are found in some other homilies, though there the examples are not without conflicting indications and are more difficult to assess. Another area of syntax which is seen to give witness to historical development in my corpus of homilies is the use of prepositions, from the Anglian *in* to late West-Saxon *on*—a change which is particularly well documented in the four versions of Napier XL and is found to be completed in the language of one of them (the one preserved in Hatton 114, s. xi 3rd quarter). Far less unequivocal is the evidence of variation shown by the prefixed verb forms (particularly *ge-* and *a-*forms) and their simplex equivalents. The former are clearly preferred in some homilies, like Vercelli XXI and Napier XXIX. Whether, however, this is of any historical significance, representing at least a stage prior to the ultimate decline of prefixes in the language, remains a problem; we shall have to learn a lot more about the changing usage in the period before we are able to give a definite answer to this question.

It is more difficult to discern whatever changes of historical significance are represented in the contents of my eight homilies. The few later adaptations that do point to such changes are made in one version of Napier XL, preserved in MS N (CCCC 419, s. xi[1]). This variant text seems to show a rather considerable shift from the apocryphal contents of the Vercelli source to the orthodox teaching of eschatology—a changing focus of preaching which it manifests in the substitution of a Wulfstanian conclusion (introducing Antichrist as a prominent figure and based in part on Alcuin) for the one the homily had in its apparently original version, and also in its appeal to 'the holy books' and to learned authorities to authenticate its own statements; this last aspect may further be detected, in specific details of wording, in the biblical reference uniquely made in Vercelli XXI to the four angels blowing four trumpets at the four corners of the earth before the Doom, probably based on Revelation 7:1 as opposed to a vaguer description given by Vercelli II. This new reliance may also underlie, in a more general way, some other homilies in my corpus, such as Napier XXIX (derived in one part ultimately from Bede's Latin Judgement Day poem) and the Easter homilies (*HomS* 27 and *HomS* 28), as they draw heavily on biblical quotations and references and Latin writings of earlier Church authorities.

The last-mentioned two homilies, on the other hand, have broken away in one respect from the orthodoxy aimed at by earlier authorities—in their case, Ælfric upon whose works they draw. Acting against Ælfric's injunction to preserve the integrity of his homilies which are carefully designed to promote his ultimate aim of orthodox teaching, the two homilies use passages from his *Catholic Homilies* in a way which he would not have approved of, by 'decontextualizing' them from their original intended use. The resultant 'tension between Ælfric's self-image ... and what can be deduced of the real reactions' (to use Mary Swan's phrase)[5] continues well into the twelfth century, as Swan has recently shown in a collection of studies of this century.[6] This period lies beyond the scope of my present study. Seen in this perspective, however, the two Easter homilies (and other composite homilies of the period making similar use of Ælfrician material) might themselves be viewed as looking forward towards a new age in the history of homiletic literature in medieval England.

I have spoken earlier of prose styles as personal characteristics of the individual writers of my eight homilies as opposed to historical developments of the language. But one may also speak of the preaching style of the period generally. And here is perhaps another sense in which our period was to prove a transition to a new one, and that is in the use of word pairs as a feature of the tradition of Old English homiletic prose. Most, if not all, of my selection of eight composite

---

[5] Mary Swan, 'Ælfric as Source: The Exploitation of Ælfric's *Catholic Homilies* from the Late Tenth to Twelfth Centuries' (Ph.D. thesis, University of Leeds, 1993), p. 333; see Chapter VI.

[6] Mary Swan, 'Ælfric's *Catholic Homilies* in the twelfth century', *Rewriting Old English in the Twelfth Century*, ed. eadem and Elaine M. Treharne (Cambridge, 2000), pp. 62–82. Swan says, for example: 'None of the surviving twelfth-century re-uses of *Catholic Homilies* material names Ælfric as the author of its source material. It is clearly because of their usefulness and adaptability rather than because of knowledge of the identity of their author that the *Catholic Homilies* have become absorbed as a principal element in a rich repository of vernacular materials available to twelfth-century homily composers' (p. 81).

homilies clearly show this element of rhythmical style continuing to be an important feature of the prose, as witness Napier XXX and Napier XL (in all the four versions). However, in the latest work in the corpus of what Jonathan Wilcox calls the Wulfstan tradition[7]— Warner XLII (preserved in the manuscript dated s. xii med.)[8]—, one notes a rewriting of the original Wulfstan passage from the *Sermo Lupi* which seems to suggest that a change is beginning to make itself felt in that tradition:

> Warner XLII 133.26 Nu is æighwanen heof ⁊ wop, ⁊ orefcwealm mycel for folces synnen, ⁊ wæstmes, æigðer gea on wude gea on felde, ne synd swa gode, swa heo iu wæron, ac yfeleð swyðe eall eorðe wæstme, ⁊ unrihtwisnysse mycele wexeð wide geond wurlde, ⁊ sibbe tolysnysse ⁊ tælnysse, ⁊ se þincð nu wærrest ⁊ geapest, þe oðerne mæig beswican, ⁊ his æhte him of anymen. Eac man swereð man mare þone he scolde, þy hit is þe wyrse wide on eorðe, ⁊ beo þan we mugen understanden, þæt hit is neh domesdæge. Ne spareð nu se fæder þan sune, ne nan mann oðren, ac ælc man winð ongean oðren, ⁊ Godes lage ne gemeð, swa swa me scolde. Beo þan we mugen ongyten, þæt þiss wurld is aweigweard ⁊ swyðe neh þan ænde þysser wurlde.

The passage, as rewritten here, still retains some word pairs, but the intensity with which they occur in the original passage, Wulfstan's Homily XX (MSS EI), lines 8–68, particularly in

> *WHom* 20.55 Ne dohte hit nu lange inne ne ute, ac wæs here ⁊ hunger, bryne ⁊ blodgyte, on gewelhwylcan ende oft ⁊ gelome. And us stalu ⁊ cwalu, stric ⁊ steorfa, orfcwealm ⁊ uncoþu, hol ⁊ hete ⁊ rypera reaflac derede swyþe þearle; ⁊ us ungylda swyþe gedrehtan, ⁊ us unwedera foroft weoldan unwæstma

has been lost. Thus, the word *orefcwealm* is taken over, but not together with the framework of alliterative pairs of synonyms in which it was originally used (*orfcwealm ⁊ uncoþu*). Again, Wulfstan's last clause, consisting of five words linked tightly by double alliteration (*us un-... un-..., and ...-wedera... weoldan... -wæstma*) is paraphrased into three clauses (⁊ *wæstmes... wæstme*, in the second and third lines) which are explanatory and verge on verbosity and which lack any hint of the parallelism Wulfstan had achieved, both in sentence structure and assonance, between the last clause and the immediately preceding one (⁊ *us*

---

[7] Jonathan Wilcox, 'The Dissemination of Wulfstan's Homilies: The Wulfstan Tradition in Eleventh-Century Vernacular Preaching', *England in the Eleventh Century*, ed. Carola Hicks (Stamford, 1992), pp. 199–217.

[8] R. D.-N. Warner (ed.), *Early English Homilies from the Twelfth-Century MS. Vespasian D. xiv*, EETS os 152 (Oxford, 1917), pp. 129–34.

ungylda swype gedrehtan). Such changing emphasis may be seen in a wider context as part of the 'modernized' language which Wilcox finds in Warner XLII.[9] To that degree, the work, though not my eight homilies themselves, may perhaps illustrate a historical aspect of our problem, bringing us to the end of one period.[10]

These changes and signs of changes taken together point to the emergence of a new milieu for vernacular homiletic literature in which Old English homilies continued to be copied and rewritten and new homilies were produced, but with an apparent 'change in taste'[11] having overtaken the genre in the meantime — a new period in which Ælfric's homilies continued to be picked up and put to new 'decontextualized' uses (see above) and Wulfstan 'did not play a major part in the preaching life' any longer:

> Those few homilies and passages [by Wulfstan] that were re-used tend more towards the general and enduringly doctrinal than the political and historically grounded that characterises most of his works. . . . This is no adverse criticism: the joy of Wulfstan's homilies derives precisely from their rhetoric of historical specificity that made them of limited value a century or two later. By the later period, unlike at the time of their composition, it may have seemed to sermon compilers that Wulfstan, with his rhetorically heightened style, was just crying wolf.[12]

It is also a period in which the production of homilies included those made at Rochester with innovations which show 'an increasing focus on the training of the unlettered clergy', as Mary P. Richards has shown with respect to the Vespasian homilies and related ones.[13] The three recent pioneering studies quoted

---

[9] Wilcox, 'The Dissemination', p. 213.

[10] Another point of interest in the rhythmical prose of homilies is the use of rhyme, employed occasionally in my eight homilies, as in Napier XL and Napier XXIX (see Chapters III and V). This question remains to be investigated more extensively. For the moment I can add one example of interest, found in a Wulfstanian composite homily not examined for this study: Napier XLIII 209.17 *ðær is benda bite and dynta dyne, þær is wyrma slite and ealra wædla gripe*. Wulfstan's original lacks a corresponding sentence here, and even the entire corpus of his homilies can produce, as far as I am aware, nothing like this complexity of alliteration and rhyme combined except once in *WHom* 5.25 *mid mænigfealdan mane ⁊ mid felafealdan facne*. For Ælfric's occasional use of rhyme, see Malcolm Godden's Commentary to the Life of St Cuthbert in the *Catholic Homilies*, Second Series, line 73 (*Ælfric's Catholic Homilies: Introduction, Commentary and Glossary*, EETS ss 18 (Oxford, 2000), p. 419).

[11] Ian A. Gordon, *The Movement of English Prose* (London, 1966), p. 43.

[12] Jonathan Wilcox, 'Wulfstan and the twelfth century', *Rewriting Old English*, ed. Swan and Treharne, pp. 83–97, at pp. 96–7.

[13] Mary P. Richards, 'Innovations in Ælfrician Homiletic Manuscripts at Rochester', *Annuale Mediaevale* 19 (1979), 13–26, at 14. Richards notes, for example: 'There are clear indications that the Vespasian homilies have been edited and glossed for oral

above[14] strongly suggest both the importance of this period of the homiletic tradition and the work that still remains to be done in understanding the history of the genre in Old to Middle English. That eventual understanding may reinforce the results of my present study, emphasizing the position of late Anglo-Saxon England as simultaneously a frame of study in its own right and a vital moment of transition in the history of the vernacular homily in medieval England.

---

delivery to an unlettered, unsophisticated audience. . . . Even the simplest Latin words and phrases have been glossed — *angeli*, for example, as *boden*. The changing state of English must have offered additional difficulties in teaching the unlettered, for frequently one English word is glossed by another: *hap* for *werod*, *peigne* for *geferena*, and so forth. The format of the MS as well suggests a teaching text, for the extent of the pieces is readily apparent. . . . Considerations of length as well as clarity surely would have influenced the selection and presentation of material to the young students' (24). See also the same author's article, 'MS Cotton Vespasian A. XXII: The Vespasian Homilies', *Manuscripta* 22 (1978), 97–103.

[14] For some other recent studies, see *Rewriting Old English*, ed. Swan and Treharne.

Appendix
Napier XL (Hatton 114)

The following is a transcription made from the microfilm of Napier XL as preserved in Oxford, Bodleian Library, Hatton 114 (MS O), fols. 1r-4v, of which no complete printed edition yet exists.[1] No attempt is made here to edit the text, but only to reproduce it as precisely as possible as it stands in the manuscript, including punctuation and capitalization (as far as these can be made out with reasonable clarity on the microfilm and its printouts), except that the original manuscript lining has been disregarded in favour of a layout as running text and the abbreviations (apart from the Tironian nota) have been silently expanded; accent marks have also not been reproduced. The primary aim of my transcription is thus not so much to present a readable text in a modern format, as to provide the complete manuscript text in order to facilitate comparison with the other versions of the Napier XL homily, particularly for the purposes of Chapters III and IV of this study.

Unlike the CCCC 419 and Cotton Cleopatra B. xiii versions, this Hatton version of Napier XL is untitled in the manuscript, though it has the title 'de die iudicii' added vertically in the margin.[2] Apart from the superscript marks and glosses entered by the 'tremulous' hand,[3] there are a few additions made to the text, of a word or words above the relevant word (at lines 17, 33 (in a later hand),[4] 69 and 70), and an addition of the inflectional ending *-e* (at line 94) above the original *-on*, which is grammatically incorrect and appears on the microfilm to have been somewhat decoloured; these cases are indicated below by the signs ` ´ and ‹ ›, respectively.[5]

---

[1] The Hatton text has been collated for the editions of the other versions of the homily, and is in part edited as a parallel text to one of these by D. G. Scragg; see Chapter IV, n. 91.

[2] Scragg calls the hand of this added title 'early modern' (*The Vercelli Homilies and Related Texts*. EETS os 300 (Oxford, 1992), p. 53, apparatus). Christine Franzen (*The Tremulous Hand of Worcester: A Study of Old English in the Thirteenth Century* (Oxford, 1991), p. 36) ascribes the title to the tremulous scribe.

[3] On these, see Franzen, *The Tremulous Hand*, pp. 23, 34-8, *et passim*.

[4] See Scragg, *The Vercelli Homilies*, p. 57, apparatus.

[5] On the other hand, there is an empty space for about two characters between *to* and *truwianne* (line 86). What would appear to be traces of erased letters are dimly seen on the microfilm, but they are illegible. Scragg reads *ge* (*The Vercelli Homilies*, p. 61, line 102 of his collated text).

Leofan men utan don swa us mycel þearf is beon swyðe gemyndige ure 1r
agenre þearfe. ⁊ geþencan gelome hu læne þis lif is. ⁊ hu egeslic se dom is
þe ealle men to sculan on ðam micclan domdæge. þonne god demeð manna
gehwilcum be ærran gewyrhtan. Ðæs dæges weorc bið swyðe egesfull eallum
gesceaftum swa se apostol cwæþ. In quo omnis creatura congemescit. In þam 5
dæge heofone ⁊ eorðe cwaciað ⁊ heofiað ⁊ ealle þa þing þe on him syndon.
In þam dæge þa hleoðriendan ligettas forgleddriað þone blodgemencgedan
middangeard. ⁊ þæt mancynn þe nu is in idelum gylpe. ⁊ on synlustum ⁊ in
þam wohgestreonum goldes ⁊ seolfres beswicen. ⁊ ðæs him noht ne ondrædað.
ac him orsorh lætað. Ac in þam dæge þæt earme mancynn. ⁊ þæt synfulle ofer 10
him sylfum heofiað ⁊ wepað ⁊ waniað. ⁊ hi þonne swyðe forhtiað. forðan þe
hi ær noldon heora synna gebetan. ⁊ in þam dæge on þam fyrenan wylme. sæ
forhwyrfeð. ⁊ eorðe mid hyre dunum. ⁊ heofonas mid heora tunglum. ⁊ eall
forsyngod mancynn. þonne / forswelgeð seo fyrenlust heora ærran gewyrhta. 1v
⁊ unrihtwise deman ⁊ gerefan. ⁊ ealle þa wohgeornan woruldrican mid heora 15
golde ⁊ seolfre. ⁊ godwebbum ⁊ eallum ungestreonum þonne forwurþað. On
þam dæge singað þa byman of ðam feower sceatum 'halfum' middangeardes.
⁊ ðonne ealle men ariseð of deaðe. ⁊ swa hwæt mancynnes swa eorðe ær
forswealh. oððe fyr forbærnde. ⁊ sæ besencte. ⁊ wilde deor frætan. ⁊ fugelas
tobæran. eall þy dæge ariseð. In þam dæge ure drihten cymeð in his þam 20
micclan mægenþrymme mid þam .ix. endebyrdnessum heofonwaruː þæt bið
mærlic ⁊ wundorlic mægenþrym. ⁊ ðonne bið he þam synfullum swyðe wrað
æteowed. ⁊ þam soðfæstum he bið bliðe gesewen. ⁊ þonne þa iudeas magon
swutele geseon. þone þe hi ær ahengon ⁊ acwealdon. ⁊ se soðfæsta dema
þonne demeð anra gehwylcum æfter his gewyrhtum swa swa we leorniað on 25
halgum gewritum. Reddet deus unicuique: secundum opera sua. þæt is on ure
geþeode. He forgylt þonne anra gehwylcum. æfter his agenum gewyrhtum
/ ⁊ in þam dæge ures drihtnes ansyn bið swa we ær sædon reðe ⁊ egesfull 2r
þam synfullum gesewen. ⁊ he bið bliðe ⁊ milde þam soðfæstum æteowed. þæt
is þam þe him to ðære swyðran healfe þonne beoð gelædde. Ða fyrenfullan 30
witodlice him beoð þonne on dæg on þære wynstran healfe gehwyrfede. ⁊
he þonne hrædlice to heom cweð. Faraþ ge awyrgedan on þæt ece fyr. þe
wæs deoflum geearwod ⁊ his gegengum 'uel englum' eallum. La hwæt þonne
þam synfullum þinceð. þæt nan wiht ne sy. þæs hates. ne þæs cealdes. ne þæs
heardes. ne þæs hnesces. ne þæs wraðes. ne þæs wynsumes. ne þæs eaþes. 35
ne þæs earfoðes. ne þæs leofes. ne þæs laðes. þæt hy þonne mihte fram ures
drihtnes lufan asceadan. gyf hi þonne þæs wealdon mihton ⁊ ða ungesæligan
yrmingas. nellað nu þæt geþencan. ne his willan be suman dæle wyrcan. nu
hy eaðe magon. Eala hwæt þæt is ofer eall gemet to smeagenne ⁊ to sorgianne.
⁊ on mycelre care to cweþanne. þæt ða earman synfullan sceolon þonne sare 40
aswæman fram ansyne / ures drihtnes. ⁊ ealra haligraː ⁊ fram wlite ⁊ fram 2v
wuldre heofona rices. ⁊ ðanon gewitan in þa ecan tintregu hellewites. La hwæt
manna mod syndon earmlice aþystrode. ⁊ adysgode. ⁊ gedwealde. þæt hi æfre

scylen lætan þæt deadberende deofol. mid ungemætere costnunge hy to ðan
gedwellan. þæt hy swa mycle synna fremmen swa swa hi nu doð. ⁊ nellað þæs
willan gewyrcan þe hi of eorðan lame geworhte ⁊ mid his gaste geliffæste. ⁊
him ece lif begeat. La hwæt þence we þæt we us ne ondrædað þone toweardan
dæg þæs micclan domes. Se is yrmða dæg. ⁊ ealra earfoða dæg. In þam dæge
us bið æteowed. seo geopenung heofona. ⁊ engla þrym. ⁊ helwihta hryre. ⁊
eorðan forwyrd. treowleasra gewinn. ⁊ tungla gefeall. Đunorrada hlynn. ⁊ se
þeostra þrosm. Þæra lyfta leoma. ⁊ þæra ligeta blæst. þa graniendan gesceaft.
⁊ ðæra gasta gefeoht. þa grimman gesihð. ⁊ ða godcundan miht. se hata
scur. ⁊ helwara hream. þara beorga geberst. ⁊ ðara bymena sang. se brada
bryne ofer ealle / woruld. ⁊ se bitera dæg. se micla cwealm. ⁊ ðæra manna
man. seo sare sorh. ⁊ þæra sawla gedal. se sara sið. ⁊ se sorhfulla dæg. þæt
brade bealo. ⁊ se byrnenda grund. þæt bitere wite. ⁊ se blodiga stream. feonda
fyrhto. ⁊ se fyrena regn. hæðenra granung. ⁊ reafera wanung. Heofonwaru
fulmægen. ⁊ heora hlafordes þrym. þæt ongrislice gemot. ⁊ seo egesfulle fyrd.
se reða waldend. ⁊ se rihta dom. ure synna edwit. ⁊ ðæra feonda gestal. þa
blacan ⁊wlita. ⁊ þæt bifiende wered. se forhta cyrm. ⁊ ðara folca wop. þæra
feonda grimnes. ⁊ se hluda heof. þæt sarige mancynn. ⁊ se synniga heap. seo
graniende neowelnes. ⁊ seo forgleddrede hell. þara wyrma ongripa. ⁊ ðara
sorhwita mæst. se niðfulla here. ⁊ se teonfulla dæg. On þam dæge us bið eall
þyllic egesa æteowed. ⁊ ða synfullan þonne woldon gewiscean georne gif hi
mihton. þæt heo næfre acennede næron fram fæder ne fram meder. ⁊ him
þæt þonne wære leofre. þonne eall middaneard. to æhte geseald. La hwæt
we nu ungesælige syn. þæt we us bet / ne warniað. ⁊ þæt we ne ondrædað us
þe swyðor þe we dæghwamlice geseoð ætforan urum eagum. ure þa nehstan
'freond' feallan ⁊ sweltan. ⁊ ðonne sona þam lichoman bið. laðlic legerbed
gegyred. ⁊ in ðære cealdan foldan 'eorðan' gebrosnoð. ⁊ þæt lic þær to fulnesse
gewurþeð. ⁊ ðam wælslitendum wyrmum weorðeþ to æte. Đonne bið sorhlic
sar. ⁊ earmlic gedal. lichaman. ⁊ sawle. ⁊ gyf þonne seo sawul huru slidan
sceal. in þa ecan witu. mid þam werigan ⁊ awyrgedan gaste. ⁊ ðær þonne mid
deoflum drohtoð habban in morðre ⁊ on mane in susle ⁊ on sare. in wean. ⁊
on wyrmslitum. betweonan deadum ⁊ deoflum. in bryne. ⁊ on biternesse in
bealwe ⁊ on bradum lige. in yrmðum ⁊ on earfoðum. on swiltcwale ⁊ in sarum
sorgum. in fyrenum bryne ⁊ on fulnesse. in toða gristbitum. ⁊ in tintregum in
angmodnesse earmra sawle. On cyle. ⁊ in wanunge. in hungre ⁊ in þurste. on
hæte. ⁊ in earfoðnesse. in neowlum attre. ⁊ in ecere forwyrde. in arleasnesse. ⁊
in mysenlicum wita cynne. on muðe. ⁊ on fæðme þæs deaðberendan dracan. se
is deofol nemned. / Eala leofan men utan warnian us swyðe georne ⁊ beorgan
wið þæne egesan. ⁊ utan geornlice yfeles geswican. ⁊ ðurh godes fultum to
gode don þæne dæl þe we don magan. Utan man ⁊ morðor æghwar forbugan.
⁊ ealle fracoddæda swyðe ascunian. ⁊ utan don swa ic lære. utan god lufian
inweardre heortan. eallum mode. ⁊ eallum mægene. ⁊ godes lage healdan. ⁊
utan gecnawan hu læne ⁊ hu lyðre þis lif is on to truwianne. ⁊ hu oft hit wyrð

raþost forloren. ⁊ forlæten þonne hit wære leofost gehealden. Ðeos woruld
is sorhfull. ⁊ fram dæge to dæge a swa leng swa wyrse. forðam þe heo is on
ofstum. ⁊ hit nealæcað þam ende. ⁊ ðy heo nære wyrðe þæt hyg ænig man ne
lufode ealles to swyðe. Ac lufian we georne þone hyhstan cyning. ⁊ þæt uplice   90
rice. ⁊ ondrædon we us symle þone toweardon dom þe we ealle to sculon. On
ðam dome ure drihten sylf eowað us sona his blodigan sidan. ⁊ his þyrlan
handa. ⁊ ða sylfan rode þe he on ahangen wæs. ⁊ wile þonne æt us witan hu we
him þæt geleanodon þæt he for us geþrowod‹e›. Wel þam þonne þe gode ær ge/   4v
cwemdon swa swa hy sceoldon. Hi þonne syððan eac. ece eadlean þurh godes   95
gyfe. þanonforð habbað betweoh englum ⁊ heahenglum aa to worulde on
heofona rice. Ðær næfre leofe ne gedælað ne laðe ne gemetað. ac þær halige
heapas symle wuniað. on wlite ⁊ on wuldre ⁊ on wynsumnesse. Ðær bið mærð
⁊ myrhð ⁊ ece blis mid gode sylfum ⁊ mid his halgum in ealra worulda woruld
a butan ende. amen.   100

Bibliography

Adams, Arthur, *The Syntax of the Temporal Clause in Old English Prose*. Yale Studies in English 32 (New York, 1907).
Amos, Ashley Crandell and Antonette diPaolo Healey, 'The Dictionary of Old English: The Letter "D"', *Problems of Old English Lexicography. Studies in Memory of Angus Cameron*, ed. Alfred Bammesberger (Regensburg, 1985), pp. 13–38.
Bammesberger, Alfred (ed.), *Problems of Old English Lexicography: Studies in Memory of Angus Cameron*. Eichstätter Beiträge 15 (Regensburg, 1985).
Bately, Janet (ed.), *Anonymous Old English Homilies: A Preliminary Bibliography of Source Studies* (Binghamton, New York, 1993).
Bazire, Joyce and James E. Cross (eds.), *Eleven Old English Rogationtide Homilies*. Toronto Old English Series 7 (Toronto, 1982; 2nd edition, King's College London Medieval Studies IV. London, 1989).
Becher, Richard, *Wulfstans Homilien* (Leipzig diss., 1910).
Belfour, A. O. (ed.), *Twelfth-Century Homilies in MS. Bodley 343. Part I, Text and Translation*. EETS os 137 (London, 1909).
Berger, Christiane, *Altenglische Paarformeln und ihre Varianten*. Münster Monographs on English Literature 13 (Frankfurt am Main, 1990).
Bessinger, J. B., Jr. and Philip H. Smith, Jr. (eds.), *A Concordance to the Anglo-Saxon Poetic Records* (Ithaca and London, 1978).
Bethurum, Dorothy (ed.), *The Homilies of Wulfstan* (Oxford, 1957).
———. 'Wulfstan', *Continuations and Beginnings: Studies in Old English Literature*, ed. Eric Gerald Stanley (London, 1966), pp. 210–46.
Biggs, Frederick M., Thomas D. Hill, and Paul E. Szarmach, with the assistance of Karen Hammond (eds.), *Souces of Anglo-Saxon Literary Culture: A Trial Version*. Medieval and Renaissance Texts and Studies 74 (Binghamton, New York, 1990).
Blockley, Mary, *Aspects of Old English Poetic Syntax: Where Clauses Begin* (Urbana and Chicago, 2001).
Bosworth, Joseph and T. Northcote Toller, *An Anglo-Saxon Dictionary* (Oxford, 1898); with *Supplement*, by Toller (Oxford, 1921) and *Enlarged Addenda and Corrigenda*, by Alistair Campbell (Oxford, 1972).
Brunner, Karl, *Die englische Sprache: Ihre geschichtliche Entwicklung*. 2 vols. (Tübingen, 1960–62).

———. *Altenglische Grammatik nach der Angelsächsischen Grammatik von Eduard Sievers*. 3rd, revised edition (Tübingen, 1965).

Caie, Graham D. (ed.), *The Old English Poem* Judgement Day II: *A Critical Edition with Editions of* De Die Iudicii *and the Hatton 113 Homily* Be Domes Dæge. Anglo-Saxon Texts 2 (Cambridge, 2000).

Callaway, Morgan, Jr., 'The Appositive Participle in Anglo-Saxon', *PMLA* 16 (1901), 141–360.

Cameron, Angus, Ashley Crandell Amos, Sharon Butler, and Antonette diPaolo Healey, *The Dictionary of Old English Corpus in Electronic Form* (Toronto, 1981; now available as TEI-P3 conformant version, 2000 Release, on CD-ROM).

Cameron, Angus, Ashley Crandell Amos, Sharon Butler, and Antonette diPaolo Healey (eds.), *The Dictionary of Old English* (Toronto, 1986–; now A to F available on CD-ROM, 2003).

Campbell, Alistair, *Old English Grammar* (Oxford, 1959).

Campbell, Jackson J., 'To Hell and Back: Latin Tradition and Literary Use of the "Descensus ad Inferos" in Old English', *Viator* 13 (1982), 107–58.

Cassidy, F. G. and Richard N. Ringler, *Bright's Old English Grammar and Reader*. 3rd edition (New York, 1971).

Clayton, Mary, *The Cult of the Virgin Mary in Anglo-Saxon England*. Cambridge Studies in Anglo-Saxon England 2 (Cambridge, 1990).

Clemoes, Peter (ed.), *Ælfric's Catholic Homilies. The First Series*. EETS ss 17 (Oxford, 1997).

Cross, James E., 'Ælfric—Mainly on Memory and Creative Method in Two Catholic Homilies', *Studia Neophilologica* 41 (1969), 135–55.

———. 'The Literate Anglo-Saxon—On Sources and Disseminations', *PBA* 58 (1972), 67–100.

———. 'A Doomsday Passage in an Old English Sermon for Lent', *Anglia* 100 (1982), 103–8.

———. *Cambridge Pembroke College MS. 25: A Carolingian Sermonary Used by Anglo-Saxon Preachers*. King's College London Medieval Studies I (London, 1987).

Dalbey, Marcia A., 'Patterns of Preaching in The Blickling Easter Homily', *American Benedictine Review* 24 (1973), 478–92.

———. 'Themes and Techniques in the Blickling Lenten Homilies', *The Old English Homily and Its Backgrounds*, ed. Paul E. Szarmach and Bernard F. Huppé (Albany, New York, 1978), pp. 221–39.

DiNapoli, Robert, *An Index of Theme and Image to the Homilies of the Anglo-Saxon Church: Comprising the Homilies of Ælfric, Wulfstan, and the Blickling and Vercelli Codices* (Hockwold cum Wilton, Norfolk, 1995).

Dobbie, Elliot Van Kirk (ed.), *The Anglo-Saxon Minor Poems*. The Anglo-Saxon Poetic Records, Vol. VI (New York, 1942).

Dobyns, Mabel Falberg, 'Wulfstan's Vocabulary: A Glossary of the "Homilies" with Commentary' (Ph. D. dissertation, University of Illinois at Urbana-Champaign, 1973).

Dodd, Loring Holmes, *A Glossary of Wulfstan's Homilies*. Yale Studies in English 35 (New York, 1908; repr. in *Word-Indices to Old English Non-Poetic Texts*. Hamden, Connecticut, 1974).

Dudley, Louise, 'An Early Homily on the "Body and Soul" Theme', *JEGP* 8 (1908), 225–53.

Emmerson, Richard Kenneth, *Antichrist in the Middle Ages: A Study of Medieval Apocalypticism, Art, and Literature* (Manchester, 1981).

Ericson, Eston Everett, *The Use of* Swa *in Old English*. Hesperia 12 (Göttingen and Baltimore, 1932).

Fadda, A. M. Luiselli, '"De Descensu Christi ad Inferos": una inedita omelia anglosassone', *Studi Medievali* 13 (1972), 989–1011.

———. (ed.), *Nuove omelie anglosassoni della Rinascenza benedettina*. Filologia Germanica, Testi e Studi I (Florence, 1977).

Fisiak, Jacek (ed.), *Studies in English Historical Linguistics and Philology: A Festschrift for Akio Oizumi*. Studies in English Medieval Language and Literature 2 (Frankfurt am Main, 2002).

Förster, Max, 'Zu den Blickling Homilies', *Archiv* 91 (1892), 179–206.

———. 'Altenglische Predigtquellen. I', *Archiv* 116 (1906), 301–14.

———. 'Der Vercelli-Codex CXVII nebst Abdruck einiger altenglischer Homilien der Handschrift', *Studien zur englischen Philologie* 50 (1913), 20–179.

———. (ed.), *Die Vercelli-Homilien. I-VIII Homilie*. Bibliothek der angelsächsischen Prosa. XII. Band (Hamburg, 1932; repr. Darmstadt, 1964).

Frank, Roberta, 'Poetic Words in Late Old English Prose', *From Anglo-Saxon to Early Middle English: Studies Presented to E. G. Stanley*, ed. Malcolm Godden, Douglas Gray, and Terry Hoad (Oxford, 1994), pp. 87–107.

Frantzen, Allen J. (ed.), *Speaking Two Languages: Traditional Disciplines and Contemporary Theory in Medieval Studies* (Albany, New York, 1991).

Franzen, Christine, *The Tremulous Hand of Worcester: A Study of Old English in the Thirteenth Century* (Oxford, 1991).

Funke, Otto, 'Studien zur alliterierenden und rhythmisierenden Prosa in der älteren altenglischen Homiletik', *Anglia* 80 (1962), 9–36.

Gatch, Milton McC., 'Eschatology in the Anonymous Old English Homilies', *Traditio* 21 (1965), 117–65.

———. *Preaching and Theology in Anglo-Saxon England: Ælfric and Wulfstan* (Toronto and Buffalo, 1977).

———. 'The Achievement of Aelfric and His Colleagues in European Perspective', *The Old English Homily and Its Backgrounds*, ed. Paul E. Szarmach and Bernard F. Huppé (Albany, New York, 1978), pp. 43–73.

Gneuss, Helmut, 'The origin of Standard Old English and Æthelwold's school at Winchester', *ASE* 1 (1972), 63–83.

Godden, Malcolm R., 'An Old English penitential motif', *ASE* 2 (1973), 221–39.
———. 'Old English composite homilies from Winchester', *ASE* 4 (1975), 57–65.
———. (ed.), *Ælfric's Catholic Homilies. The Second Series*. EETS ss 5 (London, 1979).
———. (ed.), *Ælfric's Catholic Homilies: Introduction, Commentary and Glossary*. EETS ss 18 (Oxford, 2000).
———. 'Review of Hiroshi Ogawa, *Studies in the History of Old English Prose*', *Studies in English Literature* (Tokyo), English Number 42 (2001), 111–7.
Godden, Malcolm, Douglas Gray, and Terry Hoad (eds.), *From Anglo-Saxon to Early Middle English: Studies Presented to E. G. Stanley* (Oxford, 1994).
Gordon, Ian A., *The Movement of English Prose*. English Language Series (London, 1966).
Grau, Gustav, *Quellen und Verwandtschaften der älteren germanischen Darstellung des jüngsten Gerichten*. Studien zur englischen Philologie 31 (Halle, 1908).
Greenfield, Kathleen, 'Changing Emphases in English Vernacular Homiletic Literature, 960–1225', *Journal of Medieval History* 7 (1981), 283–97.
Griffith, M. S., 'Poetic language and the Paris Psalter: the decay of the Old English tradition', *ASE* 20 (1991), 167–86.
Grünberg, M., *The West-Saxon Gospels: A Study of the Gospel of St. Matthew with Text of the Four Gospels* (Amsterdam, 1967).
Hall, John R. Clark (ed.), *A Concise Anglo-Saxon Dictionary*. 4th edition, with a Supplement by Herbert D. Meritt (Cambridge, 1960).
Hall, Thomas N. (ed.), *Via Crucis: Essays on Early Medieval Sources and Ideas in Memory of J. E. Cross* (Morgantown, 2002).
Hamesse, Jacqueline and Xavier Hermand (eds.), *De l'Homélie au Sermon: Histoire de la Prédication Médiévale* (Louvain-la-Neuve, 1993).
Hicks, Carola (ed.), *England in the Eleventh Century* (Stamford, Lincolnshire, 1992).
Hill, Joyce, 'Ælfric's use of etymologies', *ASE* 17 (1988), 35–44.
———. 'Reform and Resistance: Preaching Styles in Late Anglo-Saxon England', *De l'Homélie au Sermon: Histoire de la Prédication Médiévale*, ed. Jacqueline Hamesse and Xavier Hermand (Louvain-la-Neuve, 1993), pp. 15–46.
Hiltunen, Risto, *The Decline of the Prefixes and the Beginnings of the English Phrasal Verb*. Turun Yliopiston Julkaisuja, Ser. B, Tom. 160 (Turku, 1983).
Hoad, Terry, 'Old English Weak Genitive Plural *-an*: Towards Establishing the Evidence', *From Anglo-Saxon to Early Middle English: Studies Presented to E. G. Stanley*, ed. Malcolm Godden, Douglas Gray, and Terry Hoad (Oxford, 1994), pp. 108–29.
Hofstetter, Walter, *Winchester und der spätaltenglische Sprachgebrauch: Untersuchungen zur geographischen und zeitlichen Verbreitung altenglischer Synonyme*. Texte und Untersuchungen zur Englischen Philologie 14 (Munich, 1987).
Holthausen, H., *Altenglisches etymologisches Wörterbuch*. 2nd edition (Heidelberg, 1963).
Hurt, James, *Ælfric*. Twayne's English Authors Series 131 (New York, 1972).

Ide, Mitsu, 'The Distribution of *Beon/Wesan Gepuht(e)* in Old English Texts', *Bulletin of Kanto Gakuin University* 43 (1985), 81–118.

Irvine, Susan, 'Linguistic Peculiarities in Late Copies of Ælfric and their Editorial Implications', *Essays on Anglo-Saxon and Related Themes in Memory of Lynne Grundy*, ed. Jane Roberts and Janet Nelson (London, 2000), pp. 237–57.

Iyeiri, Yoko and Margaret Connolly (eds.), *And gladly wolde he lerne and gladly teche: Essays on Medieval English Presented to Professor Matsuji Tajima on His Sixtieth Birthday* (Tokyo, 2002).

Jordan, Richard, *Eigentümlichkeiten des anglischen Wortschatzes: Eine wortgeographische Untersuchung mit etymologischen Anmerkungen*. Anglistische Forschungen 17 (Heidelberg, 1906).

Jost, Karl, *Wulfstanstudien*. Swiss Studies in English 23 (Bern, 1950).

———. (ed.), *Die 'Institutes of Polity, Civil and Ecclesiastical'*. Swiss Studies in English 47 (Bern, 1959).

Kahlas-Tarkka, Leena, *The Uses and Shades of Meaning of Words for* Every *and* Each *in Old English*. Mémoires de la Société Néophilologique de Helsinki 46 (Helsinki, 1987).

Kelly, Richard J., *The Blickling Homilies: Edition and Translation, with General Introduction, Textual Notes, Tables and Appendices, and Select Bibliography* (London and New York, 2003).

Ker, N. R., *Catalogue of Manuscripts Containing Anglo-Saxon* (Oxford, 1957).

Kienzle, Beverly Mayne (ed.), *Models of Holiness in Medieval Sermons* (Louvain-la-Neuve, 1966).

Kinard, James Pinckney, *A Study of Wulfstan's Homilies* (Johns Hopkins University diss., Baltimore, 1897).

Kivimaa, Kirsti, Þe *and* Þat *as Clause Connectives in Early Middle English with Especial Consideration of the Emergence of the Pleonastic* Þat. Commentationes Humanarum Litterarum 39:1 (Helsinki, 1966).

Korhammer, Michael, with Karl Reichl and Hans Sauer (eds.), *Words, Texts and Manuscripts: Studies in Anglo-Saxon Culture Presented to Helmut Gneuss* (Cambridge, 1992).

Koskenniemi, Inna, *Repetitive Word Pairs in Old and Early Middle English Prose: Expressions of the Type* Whole and Sound *and* Answered and Said, *and Other Parallel Constructions*. Turun Yliopiston Julkaisuja, Ser. B, Tom. 107 (Turku, 1968).

Kühn, Paul Theodor, *Die Syntax der Verbums in Ælfrics "Heiligenleben"* (Leipzig diss., 1889).

Lapidge, Michael and Helmut Gneuss (eds.), *Learning and Literature in Anglo-Saxon England: Studies Presented to Peter Clemoes on the Occasion of His Sixty-Fifth Birthday* (Cambridge, 1985).

Lees, Clare A., 'The Dissemination of Alcuin's *De Virtutibus et Vitiis Liber* in Old English: A Preliminary Survey', *LSE* 16 (1985), 174–89.

———. 'Theme and Echo in an Anonymous Old English Homily for Easter', *Traditio* 42 (1986), 115–42.

———. 'Working with Patristic Sources: Language and Context in Old English Homilies', *Speaking Two Languages: Traditional Disciplines and Contemporary Theory in Medieval Studies*, ed. Allen J. Frantzen (Albany, New York, 1991), pp. 157–80.

Lendinara, Patrizia, '"*frater non redimit, redimet homo . . .*": A Homiletic Motif and its Variants in Old English', *Early Medieval English Texts and Interpretations: Studies Presented to Donald G. Scragg*, ed. Elaine Treharne and Susan Rosser (Tempe, Arizona, 2002), pp. 67–80.

Letson, D. R., 'The Poetic Content of the Revival Homily', *The Old English Homily and Its Backgrounds*, ed. Paul E. Szarmach and Bernard F. Huppé (Albany, New York, 1978), pp. 139–56.

Löhe, Hans, *Be Domes Dæge*. Bonner Beiträge zur Anglistik 22 (Bonn, 1907).

Lumby, J. Rawson, *Be Domes Dæge, De Die Iudicii, An Old English Version of the Latin Poem Ascribed to Bede*. EETS os 65 (London, 1876).

McGinn, Bernard, *Antichrist: Two Thousand Years of the Human Fascination with Evil* (New York, 2000).

McIntosh, Angus, 'Wulfstan's Prose', *PBA* 34 (1948), 109–42.

Minkoff, Harvey A., 'Ælfric's Theory of Translation and the Styles of the *Heptateuch* and *Homilies*' (Ph. D. dissertation, City University of New York, 1970).

———. 'Some Stylistic Consequences of Ælfric's Theory of Translation', *Studies in Philology* 73 (1976), 29–41.

Mitchell, Bruce, 'Some Problems Involving Old English Periphrases with *Beon/Wesan* and the Present Participle', *NM* 77 (1976), 478–91.

———. *Old English Syntax*. 2 vols. (Oxford, 1985).

Morris, Richard (ed.), *The Blickling Homilies*. EETS os 58, 63, and 73 (London, 1874–80; repr. as one volume, 1967).

Mossé, Fernand, *Histoire de la Forme Périphrastique* Être + Participe Présent *en Germanique*. 2 vols. Collection Linguistique Publiée par la Société de Linguistique de Paris 42 and 43 (Paris, 1938).

Murray, J. A. H. *et al.* (eds.), *The Oxford English Dictionary*. Second Edition, Prepared by J. A. Simpson and E. S. C. Weiner (Oxford, 1989).

Napier, Arthur (ed), *Wulfstan: Sammlung der ihm zugeschriebenen Homilien nebst Untersuchungen über ihre Echtheit* (Berlin, 1883; 2nd edition with a bibliographical appendix by Klaus Ostheeren. Dublin and Zurich, 1967).

Nichols, Ann Eljenholm, 'Methodical Abbreviation: A Study in Aelfric's Friday Homilies for Lent', *The Old English Homily and Its Backgrounds*, ed. Paul E. Szarmach and Bernard F. Huppé (Albany, New York, 1978), pp. 157–80.

Nicholson, Lewis E. (ed.), *The Vercelli Book Homilies: Translations from the Anglo-Saxon* (Lanham, Maryland, 1991).

Nickel, Gerhard, *Die Expanded Form im Altenglischen: Vorkommen, Funktionen und Herkunft der Umschreibung* beon/wesan + *Partizip Präsens*. Kieler Beiträge zur Anglistik und Amerikanistik 3 (Neumünster, 1966).

Ogawa, Hiroshi, *Old English Modal Verbs: A Syntactical Study.* Anglistica XXVI (Copenhagen, 1989).

———. *Studies in the History of Old English Prose* (Tokyo, 2000).

———. 'Syntactical Revision in Wulfstan's Rewritings of Ælfric', *Studies in the History of Old English Prose* (Tokyo, 2000), pp. 205–20.

———. 'Initial Verb-Subject Inversion in Some Late Old English Homilies', *Studies in the History of Old English Prose* (Tokyo, 2000), pp. 235–62.

———. 'A "Wulfstan Imitator" at Work: Linguistic Features of Napier XXX', *Studies in the History of Old English Prose* (Tokyo, 2000), pp. 263–85.

———. 'Aspects of "Wulfstan imitators" in Late Old English sermon writing', *Studies in English Historical Linguistics and Philology: A Festschrift for Akio Oizumi*, ed. Jacek Fisiak (Frankfurt am Main, 2002), pp. 389–403.

Ono, Shigeru, *On Early English Syntax and Vocabulary* (Tokyo, 1989).

———. 'The Old English Equivalents of Latin *cognoscere* and *intelligere* — The Dialectal and Temporal Distribution of Vocabulary', *On Early English Syntax and Vocabulary* (Tokyo, 1989), pp. 169–207.

Orchard, A. P. McD., 'Crying wolf: oral style and the *Sermones Lupi*', *ASE* 21 (1992), 239–64.

Peterson, Paul W., 'Dialect Grouping in the Unpublished Vercelli Homilies', *Studies in Philology* 50 (1953), 559–65.

Pope, John C. (ed.), *Homilies of Ælfric: A Supplementary Collection.* 2 vols. EETS os 259 and 260 (London, 1967–68).

Powell, Kathryn and Donald Scragg (eds.), *Apocryphal Texts and Traditions in Anglo-Saxon England*. Publications of the Manchester Centre for Anglo-Saxon Studies 2 (Cambridge, 2003).

Pulsiano, Phillip and Elaine M. Treharne (eds.), *Anglo-Saxon Manuscripts and their Heritage* (Aldershot, 1998).

Quirk, Randolph, *The Concessive Relation in Old English Poetry.* Yale Studies in English 124 (New Haven, 1954; repr. Hamden, Connecticut, 1973).

Quirk, Randolph and C. L. Wrenn, *An Old English Grammar*. Methuen's Old English Library. 2nd edition (London, 1957).

Raynes, Enid M., 'Unpublished Old English Homilies: Mainly from MSS. CCCC 188, Hatton 114, 115, and Junius 121, together with Vercelli Homily IX' (D.Phil. thesis, University of Oxford, 1955).

Richards, Mary P., 'MS Cotton Vespasian A. XXII: The Vespasian Homilies', *Manuscripta* 22 (1978), 97–103.

———. 'Innovations in Ælfrician Homiletic Manuscripts at Rochester', *Annuale Mediaevale* 19 (1979), 13–26.

Roberts, Jane and Christian Kay, with Lynne Grundy, *A Thesaurus of Old English.* 2 vols. King's College London Medieval Studies XI (London, 1995).

Roberts, Jane and Janet Nelson (eds.), *Essays on Anglo-Saxon and Related Themes in Memory of Lynne Grundy*. King's College London Medieval Studies XVII (London, 2000).

Robinson, Fred C., 'The Devil's Account of the Next World', *NM* 73 (1972), 362–71.

———. *The Editing of Old English* (Oxford, 1994).

Sauer, Hans, *Theodulfi Capitula in England*. Texte und Untersuchungen zur Englischen Philologie 8 (Munich, 1978).

Schabram, Hans, *Superbia: Studien zum altenglischen Wortschatz. Teil I: Die dialektale und zeitliche Verbreitung des Wortguts* (Munich, 1965).

Schaefer, K. G., 'An Edition of Five Old English Homilies for Palm Sunday, Holy Saturday, and Easter Sunday' (Ph. D. dissertation, Columbia University, 1972).

Scragg, Donald G., 'The Language of the Vercelli Homilies' (Ph.D. thesis, Manchester University, 1970).

———. 'The compilation of the Vercelli Book', *ASE* 2 (1973), 189–207.

———. 'Napier's "Wulfstan" homily xxx: its sources, its relationship to the Vercelli Book and its style', *ASE* 6 (1977), 197–211.

———. 'The corpus of vernacular homilies and prose saints' lives before Ælfric', *ASE* 8 (1979), 223–77.

———. '"The Devil's Account of the Next World" Revisited', *American Notes and Queries* 24 (1986), 104–10.

———. *The Vercelli Homilies and Related Texts*. EETS os 300 (Oxford, 1992).

———. 'An Old English Homilist of Archbishop Dunstan's Day', *Words, Texts and Manuscripts: Studies in Anglo-Saxon Culture Presented to Helmut Gneuss*, ed. Michael Korhammer, with Karl Reichl and Hans Sauer (Cambridge, 1992), pp. 181–92.

———. *Dating and Style in Old English Composite Homilies*. H. M. Chadwick Memorial Lectures 9 (Cambridge, 1998).

Shearin, Hubert Gibson, *The Expression of Purpose in Old English Prose*. Yale Studies in English 18 (New York, 1903).

Skeat, W. W. (ed.), *Ælfric's Lives of Saints*. EETS os 76, 82, 94, and 114 (London, 1881–1900; repr. in two volumes, 1966).

Spindler, Robert (ed.), *Das altenglische Bussbuch* (Leipzig, 1934).

Stanley, Eric Gerald (ed.), *Continuations and Beginnings: Studies in Old English Literature* (London, 1966).

———. 'Studies in the Prosaic Vocabulary of Old English Verse', *NM* 72 (1971), 385–418.

———. '*The Judgement of the Damned* (from Cambridge, Corpus Christi College 201 and other manuscripts), and the definition of Old English verse', *Learning and Literature in Anglo-Saxon England: Studies Presented to Peter Clemoes on the Occasion of His Sixty-Fifth Birthday*, ed. Michael Lapidge and Helmut Gneuss (Cambridge, 1985), pp. 363–91.

———. 'Old English *þæt deofol; se deofol* or Just *deofol*', *And gladly wolde he lerne and gladly teche: Essays on Medieval English Presented to Professor Matsuji Tajima on His Sixtieth Birthday*, ed. Yoko Iyeiri and Margaret Connolly (Tokyo, 2002), pp. 51–71.

Swan, Mary, 'Ælfric as Source: The Exploitation of Ælfric's *Catholic Homilies* from the Late Tenth to Twelfth Centuries' (Ph.D. thesis, University of Leeds, 1993).

———. 'Holiness Remodelled: Theme and Technique in Old English Composite Homilies', *Models of Holiness in Medieval Sermons*, ed. Beverly Mayne Kienzle (Louvain-la Neuve, 1996), pp. 35–46.

———. 'Old English Made New: One Catholic Homily and its Reuses', *LSE* 28 (1997), 1–18.

———. 'Memorialised Readings: Manuscript Evidence for Old English Homily Composition', *Anglo-Saxon Manuscripts and their Heritage*, ed. Phillip Pulsiano and Elaine M. Treharne (Aldershot, 1998), pp. 205–17.

———. 'Ælfric's *Catholic Homilies* in the twelfth century', *Rewriting Old English in the Twelfth Century*, ed. eadem and Elaine M. Treharne (Cambridge, 2000), pp. 62–82.

Swan, Mary and Elaine M. Treharne (eds.), *Rewriting Old English in the Twelfth Century*. Cambridge Studies in Anglo-Saxon England 30 (Cambridge, 2000).

Swanton, Michael (ed. and trans.), *Anglo-Saxon Prose*. Everyman's University Library (London, 1975).

Szarmach, Paul E., 'The Vercelli Homilies: Style and Structure', *The Old English Homily and Its Backgrounds*, ed. idem and Bernard F. Huppé (Albany, New York, 1978), pp. 241–67.

———. (ed.), *Vercelli Homilies IX-XXIII*. Toronto Old English Series 5 (Toronto, 1981).

Szarmach, Paul E. and Bernard F. Huppé (eds.), *The Old English Homily and Its Backgrounds* (Albany, New York, 1978).

Teresi, Loredana, 'Mnemonic transmission of Old English texts in the post-Conquest period', *Rewriting Old English in the Twelfth Century*, ed. Mary Swan and Elaine M. Treharne (Cambridge, 2000), pp. 98–116.

Thorpe, Benjamin (ed.), *Ancient Laws and Institutes of England*. 2 vols. (London, 1840).

———. (ed.), *The Homilies of the Anglo-Saxon Church. The First Part, Containing the Sermones Catholici, or Homilies of Ælfric*. 2 vols. (London, 1844–46; repr. New York, 1971).

Torkar, Roland, *Eine altenglische Übersetzung von Alcuins* De Virtutibus et Vitiis, *Kap. 20*. Texte und Untersuchungen zur Englischen Philologie 7 (Munich, 1981).

Treharne, Elaine and Susan Rosser (eds.), *Early Medieval English Texts and Interpretations: Studies Presented to Donald G. Scragg*. Medieval and Renaissance Texts and Studies 252 (Tempe, Arizona, 2002).

Tristram, Hildegard L. C. (ed.), 'Vier altenglische Predigten aus der heterodoxen Tradition, mit Kommentar, Übersetzung und Glossar sowie drei weiteren Texten im Anhang' (Freiburg im Breisgau diss., 1970).

———. 'Stock Descriptions of Heaven and Hell in Old English Prose and Poetry', *NM* 79 (1978), 102–13.

Van Os, A. B., *Religious Visions: The Development of the Eschatological Elements in Mediaeval English Religious Literature* (Amsterdam, 1932).

Venezky, Richard L. and Antonette diPaolo Healey, *A Microfiche Concordance to Old English*. Publications of the Dictionary of Old English 1 (Toronto, 1980).

Vleeskruyer, Rudolf (ed.), *The Life of St. Chad: An Old English Homily* (Amsterdam, 1953).

Warner, Rubie D.-N. (ed.), *Early English Homilies from the Twelfth-Century MS. Vespasian D. XIV.* EETS os 152 (London, 1917).

Waterhouse, Ruth, 'Ælfric's use of discourse in some saints' lives', *ASE* 5 (1976), 83–103.

Weber, Robertus (ed.), *Biblia Sacra Iuxta Vulgatam Versionem*. 3rd edition (Stuttgart, 1983).

Whitbread, L., 'Wulfstan Homilies XXIX, XXX and Some Related Texts', *Anglia* 81 (1963), 347–64.

———. 'The Old English Poem *Judgement Day II* and its Latin Source', *Philological Quarterly* 45 (1966), 635–56.

———. 'After Bede: The Influence and Dissemination of his Doomsday Verse', *Archiv* 204 (1968), 250–66.

Whitelock, Dorothy (ed.), *Sermo Lupi ad Anglos*. Methuen's Old English Library. (London, 1939; 2nd edition, 1952; 3rd edition, revised and reset, 1963).

Wilcox, Jonathan, 'The Compilation of Old English Homilies in MSS Cambridge, Corpus Christi College, 419 and 421' (Ph.D. dissertation, University of Cambridge, 1987).

———. 'Napier's "Wulfstan" Homilies XL and XLII: Two Anonymous Works from Winchester?', *JEGP* 90 (1991), 1–19.

———. 'The Dissemination of Wulfstan's Homilies: The Wulfstan Tradition in Eleventh-Century Vernacular Preaching', *England in the Eleventh Century*, ed. Carola Hicks (Stamford, Lincolnshire, 1992), pp. 199–217.

———. 'Wulfstan and the twelfth century', *Rewriting Old English in the Twelfth Century*, ed. Mary Swan and Elaine M. Treharne (Cambridge, 2000), pp. 83–97.

Willard, Rudolph, *Two Apocrypha in Old English Homilies*. Beiträge zur englischen Philologie 30 (Leipzig, 1935).

Wright, Charles D., 'The Old English "Macarius" Homily, Vercelli Homily IV, and Ephrem Latinus, *De paenitentia*', *Via Crucis: Essays on Early Medieval*

Sources and Ideas in Memory of J. E. Cross, ed. Thomas N. Hall (Morgantown, 2002), pp. 210–34.

———. 'More Old English Poetry in Vercelli Homily XXI', *Early Medieval English Texts and Interpretations: Studies Presented to Donald G. Scragg*, ed. Elaine Treharne and Susan Rosser (Tempe, Arizona, 2002), pp. 245–62.

Zupitza, Julius, 'Zu "Seele und Leib"', *Archiv* 91 (1893), 369–404.

Index

A

ac, 26, 46, 71, 90, 98, 102, 112, 114, 148, 149
Adams, Arthur, 53n42
addition, 7, 14, 17, 20n32, 22, 23, 25, 27, 31–32, 33n72, 34, 39, 39n10, 40–42, 49, 49n36, 50, 51–55, 61, 62n73, 66, 70, 73–75, 78, 80, 81, 96n115, 98, 101, 111, 112, 113–14, 115, 115n26, 118, 121, 126–27, 130, 132n61, 144, 150, 151–52, 159, 168
address, mode of, 124–25, 128, 160–62, 162n77
Adso, 105
Ælfric, 1–2, 5, 8, 54n45, 61, 69n28, 100n134, 102, 104–5, 107, 117n28, 124n39, 139–41, 147–51, 149n38, 150n41, 152n45, 153, 153n48, 157–58, 162n77, 166n87, 171–72, 179n6
   Catholic Homilies, 29, 102n141, 140, 177
      1st Series, 8, 54n45, 94n108, 96n114, 124n39, 151n42, 152n45, 157
      2nd Series, 140, 148, 153, 153n48, 181n10
   Lives of Saints, 29, 107, 117n28, 123, 140, 162n77
   Pope XXVII, 15n17, 35n83, 62
Alcuin, 101, 101n135, 179
alliteration, 39–41, 39n11, 47, 49, 49n36, 54, 55n50, 72, 77, 78, 82, 82n75, 84, 90, 108–9, 109n6, 113n22, 116, 120, 124, 135, 136, 147, 157, 168, 180
Amos, Ashley Crandell, 96n114
anaphora, 50, 127, 168,
anchorite and devil story, 27–28, 34, 85, 144n22, 175
and, 24–26, 28, 32, 40–43, 47, 50, 55n50, 70, 76, 84, 85–86, 96, 98–99, 102, 102n140, 114, 114n24, 115, 119, 133, 134, 144, 144n22, 145, 167. *See also* Tironian nota
Andreas, 82n73
Antichrist, 80, 82, 100, 100n134, 102, 104–5, 179
anticipation, 124, 156–57
Apocalypse of Thomas, 75n47
apocalypticism, 81, 100
apocrypha, 75, 101, 104, 178
apo koinou, 24
apposition, 119, 123, 124n39, 150, 150n41, 167, 167n90
archaism, 19–20, 27n51, 66–67, 104
asyndesis, 25, 43, 43n17, 90, 114, 114n24, 122. *See also* coordination; parataxis
attitude to preceding works, compilers', 3, 6, 18, 101, 135, 158, 172, 173
authority, 74–75, 101, 179
authorship, 38n3, 47, 47n29, 70, 136

B

balance, rhetorical, 23, 43, 51, 81, 148, 165
Batiouchkof, Th., 131n59, 132n61
Bazire, Joyce, 29n59
Bazire and Cross 7 (*HomU* 41), 29–33, 30n64, 33n76, 34, 58, 59n59, 173
Becher, Richard, 18n27, 89n92
Bede, 121
   De Die Iudicii, 105, 107, 107n1, 110

Benedictine Office, 91n99
Benedictine Rule, 53n42
Beowulf, 20n33, 121n36
Berger, Christiane, 14n14, 109, 109nn5–6
Bessinger, J. B., Jr., 97n119
Bethurum, Dorothy, 12n6, 14n13, 16n18, 102n140
biblical quotations and references, 39, 56, 88, 101, 145, 151–54, 171
  Gen., 152n45
  Ps., 146n27, 159, 162n77, 169n94
  Eccles., 128n50
  Ezek., 53, 54, 54n45
  Hos., 158, 158n67
  Matt., 39, 145, 148, 148n33, 151–52, 153, 153n48, 160
  Luke, 160
  John, 147, 151, 159
  Rev., 75, 145, 153–54, 179
Biggs, Frederick M., 101n135
Blickling Homilies, 63, 63n3, 105, 121n34, 166n88
  V, 107, 135n66
  VI, 117n28
  VII, 139n1, 155n55, 161, 161n75, 162, 162n77, 163, 163n81, 164, 164nn82–83, 165, 165n85, 166, 167, 167n90, 168–69, 169n95
Blockley, Mary, 76n52
'body and soul' theme, 107, 132, 134
Boethius, OE prose, 68n25
Book of Cerne, 161n72, 162n77, 163, 164, 164n82, 165, 169
Bosworth-Toller (BT(S)), 20, 22, 69, 69n27, 97n119, 117n28, 165n85
Brunner, Karl, 67n20

C

Caie, Graham D., 107n1, 110n8, 111, 111n13, 112, 112n18, 113, 113n22, 115, 117n29, 122
Callaway, Morgan, Jr., 150n41
Campbell, Alistair, 67n20, 96, 97n120
Campbell, Jackson J., 155, 156n57, 158n67, 159n70, 162n77, 163n79, 164, 164n82

case forms, adverbial relationships expressed by, 116–17, 121, 130, 132, 135n65, 169n95. *See also* dative; genitive; instrumental
Cassidy, F. G., 96n114
causal clauses, 127
  forþam/forþan, 31, 46, 133
  nu, 46, 71, 85
challenge constructions 12, 55
changes, made by compilers. *See* additions; expansions; omissions; simplifications
chiasmus, 46, 147, 148, 157
Clayton, Mary, 163n81
Clemoes, Peter, 148n34
colloquialism, 143, 144, 154
composite homilies, definition of, 2. *See also* Kompilationspredigten
concession, clauses of. *See þeah*
Concordance to Old English, A Microfiche, 14, 14n14, 68n25, 82n73
Concordance to the Anglo-Saxon Poetic Records, A, 97n119
condition, clauses of, 21, 28, 43, 44–45, 54, 54n46, 56, 75–76, 82, 84, 159
connective or linking words, 30, 31–32, 50, 144. See also *ac; and*
coordination, 28, 32, 43, 54, 70, 76n52, 113–14, 127, 167. *See also* asyndesis; parataxis
Creed, 78n57
Cross, J. E., 4, 29n59, 75n50, 76n51, 77n56, 152n45

D

Dalbey, Marcia A., 163n78
dative, 17, 32n69, 46, 53, 58, 78, 94, 96, 98, 98n124, 117n28, 124, 130, 131, 132, 133n62, 135, 135n65
De Descensu Christi ad Inferos (*HomS* 28), 139, 145, 154–70, 174–77
demonstrative, 23, 27, 31, 39, 51, 66, 92, 93n106, 94, 94n108, 118, 118n30, 121
deofol, 68, 68n24, 91, 93n106, 116, 126, 130, 130n57

devil, 80, 80n67, 83–84, 85, 100n134, 132–34, 156, 159, 160–62
  'devil-as-fish' simile, 157, 171
  'devil/lion and devil/dragon' similes, 157, 159
  See also anchorite and devil story
dialectal variations, grammatical and lexical, 38n5, 67, 67n20, 82n73, 99, 178
Dictionary of Old English (*DOE*), 12n6, 69n28, 78n57, 94n108, 128n51, 130n57, 169n96
DiNapoli, Robert, 63n3, 104
Dobbie, Elliot Van Kirk, 111n15, 121
Dodd, Loring Holmes, 126n46
DOE Corpus, 14, 68n25, 124nn40–41, 134n63, 142n15, 154n54
doxology, 22, 110, 147
drihten, 8, 20, 53
Dudley, Louise, 129n52, 132n61

E
Earthly Paradise, 141, 145, 147
echo, verbal, 46, 83, 90, 111, 135n66, 160, 162, 165
Emmerson, Richard Kenneth, 80n67, 100n134, 104
empty words and phrases, 16, 123, 144
enumeration, 76, 81, 83, 87, 104, 174. *See also* list(ing)
Ericson, Eston Everett, 144n25
error, 73, 77n54, 93n104, 94, 94n108, 95, 174
eschatology, 7, 79, 103
etymological association, 149, 157, 168, 169
Evils of the Sixth Day, 141, 145
exegesis, 140n9, 150, 155, 156–62, 158, 158n66, 162n77
  'dramatic exegesis', 160–62, 162n77
exemplum, 150, 158, 171
Exhortation to Christian Living, An (*Exhort*), 25, 77n56, 78, 78n57
expanded form, 39, 68, 131–32, 146, 169
expansion, 7, 14–15, 16–17, 40n12, 46, 51–55, 55n50, 62, 62n73, 72, 76–77, 78, 90, 96, 103n143, 117, 152, 167

F
Fadda, A.M. Luiselli, 41n14, 79n61, 139n3, 161nn73–74, 162n77, 163n81, 166n89, 168, 169n93, 169n96
Fadda X (*HomU* 15), 28n54, 39, 64, 65, 79–88, 83n77, 100n134, 104, 173–74
  interporated passage, 81–85
Förster, Max, 40n12, 43, 43n17, 45, 64n8, 70n30, 73n41, 84, 84n81, 85n86, 168n91
formula, 20, 23, 81, 87, 114, 119, 126, 157n61
Formulas and Directions for Confessors (*Conf* 10.5), 107, 107n1, 124, 124n40, 125–27
Frank, Roberta, 20, 69n26, 97, 97n118, 120n33, 121n35
Franzen, Christine, 183nn2–3
Funke, Otto, 41n15

G
Gatch, Milton McC., 63n3, 70n30, 74, 79n65, 105n148
Genesis, OE prose, 152n45
genitive, 16, 17n22, 21–22, 27, 32n69, 66, 68, 102n141, 117n28, 122
gif. *See* condition, clauses of
Gneuss, Helmut, 49n37
Godden, Malcolm R., 2, 2n4, 5, 29nn60–61, 30, 30n64, 31, 31nn67–68, 34n77, 58n56, 61, 61n68, 74, 102n141, 107n1, 108, 127, 135n66, 140n9, 148n34, 153n48, 158nn63–64, 181n10
Gordon, Ian A., 62, 181n11
Greenfield, Kathleen, 60n65, 63, 104
Gregory's Dialogues, OE (*GD*), 66n17, 82n73
Griffith, M. S., 20, 78n57
Grünberg, M., 67n18
gylt, 8, 49, 49n37, 53

H
hælend, 8
Hall, John R. Clark, 68n25, 93n106
Harrowing of Hell, 141–42, 147, 155, 158–70, 162n77, 163n78, 175

Healey, Antonette diPaolo, 14n12, 96n114
Hill, Joyce, 5–6, 141n10, 149n38
Hiltunen, Risto, 33, 112n20
Hofstetter, Walter, 49n37
Holthausen, F., 70n30
homilies:
   anonymous, *see* the individual titles
   Easter, 9, 139, 139n1, 140–41, 154–55, 177
   Judgement Day, Vercelli tradition of, 9, 63, 70, 75, 87, 97, 100–1, 103, 104
   Latin, 3, 65n9, 75–77, 107, 129, 134n64, 155, 158n67, 161, 161n72, 162, 164–65
   'poetic', 9, 108–10, 109n4, 135
   preaching, 61, 177
   quasi-literary, 61, 177
   vernacular tradition, 1, 16, 37, 59–62, 63, 179–81
   See also Ælfric, Wulfstan
homoeoptoton, 168
homoeoteleuton, 73n39, 90, 95, 168
HomU 12.3, 63n4
Hurt, James, 124n39, 149n38
hypotaxis, 26, 134, 156

I

Ide, Mitsu, 102n139, 166n87
imperative, 78, 125–26, 128, 128n51, 165, 167
In Die Sancto Pasce (*HomS* 27), 139–54, 171, 175
infinitive, 44, 48, 55n50, 70, 77
inflection, irregular or uncommon, 68, 92n102, 93n106, 94, 115n25
instrumental, 58, 66, 78, 117, 121, 124, 130, 132, 135n65, 169n95
intensifying adverbs, 16, 51, 58, 124, 130, 130n56, 168
Irvine, Susan, 94n108

J

Jordan, Richard, 67n21
Jost, Karl, 4, 4n11, 8, 12n6, 13, 15nn15–16, 20n32, 28, 38n3, 47, 48, 49n37, 52, 53n43, 54, 57, 58n54, 69, 75n48, 107n1, 125, 126n45, 128n49, 129n52, 130, 133, 136
Judgement Day, 38, 45–46, 67, 78n59, 79
   descriptions, 40–41, 70, 73, 80, 98, 146, 152–3
   theme, 60, 63–64, 141
   See also homilies; *Judgement Day II*
Judgement Day II (*Be Domes Dæg*), 107, 107n1, 108–10, 110–23, 112n21, 113n22, 116n27

K

Kahlas-Tarkka, Leena, 69
Kay, Christian, 78n59
Kelly, Richard J., 155n55, 165n85
Ker, N. R., 5, 11n3, 29n58, 34, 34n80, 48n31, 60, 61, 64n5, 107n1, 139n2
Kinard, James Pinckney, 4, 16n18
Kompilationspredigten, 2. *See also* composite homilies
Kühn, Paul Theodor, 150n41

L

Lambeth 489, items 5 and 6 in MS, 7–8, 34, 58, 59n59, 140n9
Latin, comparison with, 75–76, 77, 77n54, 131, 132, 132n61, 134n64, 153–54, 158, 161–70
   ablative absolute, 167–68
   phrases, 70, 72, 74, 154n52, 166n87
   word order, 77, 165–67
Lees, Clare A., 5, 6n21, 101n135, 141, 142, 142n15, 143, 143n19, 145n26, 146n27, 147n31, 149, 150n39, 151n44, 152, 153, 153n51, 154n53
Letson, D. R., 108–9, 120, 135
'line-filler', 123
list(ing), 71–72, 76–77, 81–82, 101–2, 135n66, 145. *See also* enumeration
locative, endingless, 96
Löhe, Hans, 110n8, 111, 112, 112n21, 113nn22–23, 114n24, 115, 115n25, 119, 120
LS 34 (Seven Sleepers), 15n17
Lumby, J. Rawson, 112n21

M

Macarius homily (*HomU* 55), 16, 107, 129–35, 129n52, 130n54, 174
man, indefinite, 54, 57, 128, 128n51
  men, 19, 46, 47
manuscript context, 9, 61
manuscripts:
  Bodley 340 & 342, 22n38, 87n90
  Bodley 343, 62
  CCCC 162, 139
  CCCC 201 (X^d), 26n48, 40n13, 43n17, 88–101, 88n91, 97n118, 97n121, 174
  CCCC 303, 28, 86n87
  CCCC 419 (N), 43n17, 45, 47, 60–62, 84, 88–102, 88n91, 97n118, 174, 176, 178
  Cotton Cleopatra B. xiii (P), 38, 43n17, 67, 82n72, 88–101, 88n91, 140n9, 174
  Cotton Otho B. x, 29, 29n58, 34, 48, 61
  Cotton Tiberius A. iii, 28, 86
  Cotton Vespasian A. xxii, 181n13
  Cotton Vitellius C. v, 61
  CUL Ii 4.l6, 29, 30n64, 61n68
  Hatton 113, 11, 62, 107
  Hatton 114 (O), 43n17, 82nn73–74, 88–100, 88n91, 174, 178, 183
  Hatton 115, 28, 79, 85
  Junius 121, 18, 18n27, 26n48, 139, 139n3
  Laud Misc. 482 (*Conf* 10.5), 107n1
  Vercelli, Biblioteca Capitorale CXVII, 64n5
manuscript source, 10
McGinn, Bernard, 80n67, 100n134
McIntosh, Angus, 4, 8, 25, 59, 77n56, 136, 174
memory, 10, 10n27, 72, 81, 152, 152n45
men þa leofestan/leofan men, vocative, 19, 119, 131
mercy, Christ's, 163, 163n81, 164–65, 167, 169–70
'metrical' passage. *See* Napier XL
Minkoff, Harvey A., 150n41

Mitchell, Bruce, 21n35, 38n5, 55n49, 66n17, 112n21, 121n36, 127, 128n51, 146nn28–29. *See also* Old English Syntax
modal verbs, 21, 54n46, 76, 131, 178
modernization, 19–22, 33, 65–70, 78, 97, 104, 112, 178
mood, indicative and subjunctive, 44, 55, 58, 66, 93–94
Morris, Richard, 155n55, 165n85

N

Napier, Arthur, 12n6, 24n43, 27n50, 33n72, 38, 82n72, 88n91, 90, 131n60
Napier XXIV (*HomU* 23), 4n15, 11, 31n67, 34, 49nn35–36, 57, 59n59, 173
Napier XXIX (*HomU* 26), 9, 19n29, 105, 107–37, 174–75, 177
  'practical' rendering, 110, 117, 119, 123, 127, 133, 135, 136, 175
  poetic section, 110–23, 135n66, 175
Napier XXX (*HomU* 27), 9, 11–35, 49n36, 58–59, 59n59, 85–86, 103, 103n144, 136, 136n70, 137, 173–78
Napier XXXVII (*HomU* 59), 14, 14n14
Napier XL (*HomU* 32), 7–8, 37–48, 59–60, 64, 68, 70, 71, 73, 82–83, 83n77, 84, 88–102, 173–76, 178
  'metrical' passage, 40, 40n13, 41, 71, 84n80, 95, 99, 173, 174
Napier XLII (*HomU* 34), 63n4, 103, 105
Napier XLIII (*HomU* 35.1), 181n10
Napier XLVI (*HomU* 37), 35n83, 62
Napier XLIX (*HomS* 40.1), 69n27
Napier LVI (*HomU* 45), 125
Napier LVIII (*HomU* 47), 7–8, 9, 29n58, 32n71, 34, 34n79, 48–59, 61–62, 173–74, 176
Napier LIX (*HomU* 48), 14
negation, 84–85, 113–14, 124, 133, 166
  multiple, 32–33, 112–13, 113n22
  ne, 113–14, 124
  ne ondrædan, 45, 45n23, 46, 46n24, 47, 71, 84–85
Nichols, Ann Eljenholm, 124n39
Nickel, Gerhard, 146n28

O

OED, 21, 67n20, 78n59, 144, 154
oferhyged-/ofermodig-, superbia, words in, 13, 20, 20n34, 126n46
Ogawa, Hiroshi, 13n10, 21n35, 21n37, 24n44, 54n46, 121n34, 124n39, 147n32
Old English Syntax (OES), 21n35, 23n42, 38n5, 53nn41–42, 55n49, 67n17, 67n21, 91n98, 94n108, 98n123, 121n36, 127n47, 128n51, 146nn29–30, 150n41, 166n87, 170n97
omission, 23n41, 25, 29–31, 34, 40–42, 46, 50–51, 51n38, 56, 65n10, 66, 71–72, 72n35, 73, 76, 84, 86, 86n88, 92n102, 95, 96, 97n121, 98, 102, 102n140, 110–11, 118, 119, 126n43, 130n56, 132–34, 133n62, 149–50, 162
ondrædan. *See* negation
onginnan, 132
Ono, Shigeru, 15n16
Orchard, A. P. McD., 16n18
Ordo Confessionis, pseudo-Egbert, 128, 128n50

P

parallelism, 21n37, 22, 25, 31–32, 45n23, 53, 90, 147, 148, 159, 165, 168–69, 180
parataxis, 128n51, 145. *See also* asyndesis; coordination
parenthesis, 28, 48, 74
Paris Psalter (PPs), 20, 69n27
paronomasia, 168
participle, 43, 114, 131–32, 148, 150n41, 152. *See also* expanded form
'pedantic adapter', 8, 38–39, 47, 59, 88, 101
penitential motif, 108, 128, 128n50
'personal characteristics', compilers', 9, 136, 174–75
personal pronouns, 44, 52, 57–58, 98n123, 124–25, 150, 161
   possessive, 27, 52, 58, 58n55, 66
   we, 19, 44, 47, 53n44, 77n54, 125, 128, 161–62
   þu/ge, 53n44, 77n54, 111, 124–25, 161–62, 161n75, 165

Peterborough Chronicle (*ChronE*), 14
Peterson, P. W., 67n19, 67n21
poems, OE, prose adaptation of, 9, 77, 77n56, 78, 110, 175
poeticism, 19–20, 68–69, 69n26, 78, 97, 112, 113n22, 120, 120n33, 121n35, 135
Pope, John C., 39n11, 53n41, 62n73, 124n39, 149n38, 163n79
'practical' rendering. *See* Napier XXIX
predicate, composite form of, 131
prefixed verb, 33, 69, 78, 102n141, 112, 112n18, 112n20, 124, 130, 130n56, 178
preposition, 26, 26n49, 27, 38, 38n5, 38n7, 42, 47, 51, 67, 67n21, 68, 72, 72n35, 82, 91–92, 92n102, 99, 99nn129–130, 104, 117, 122, 124, 126n43, 144n25, 147, 157n61, 169n95, 178
Prognostics (*ProgGl*), 122n37
prosaic words, 68–69, 97, 123, 178
'prose dilution', 77, 77n56, 78, 136, 175
prose paragraph, 24, 42
prose rhythm, 25, 32, 72n35, 73, 116, 148
pseudo-Augustine 160, 158n67, 161–63, 161n72, 163n79, 164n82
punctuation, 24, 24n44, 31n68, 43n17, 124n40, 142n15, 170, 183

Q

Quirk, Randolph, 55n49, 121n34

R

Raynes, Enid M., 68n23, 82n73, 139n3, 161n73, 162n77, 169n94, 169n96, 170n98
reader response, 5–6
reanalysis. *See* reinterpretation
recapitulation, 24, 57, 76, 84, 118n30, 151, 170
reinterpretation, 22, 57, 98, 115, 115n25, 117–18, 118n30
relative pronoun/clause, 22–23, 28, 39, 52n39, 54–55, 68, 86, 98, 118, 118n30, 126–27, 128n51, 134, 145, 149, 151n42

Index   *205*

repetition, 82, 124, 127, 147, 149, 157
resumptive. *See* recapitulation
rhetoric, -cal, 23, 44–46, 81, 127, 135n66, 147, 148, 150, 157, 165, 168–69, 177
rhyme, 41, 68, 72, 108–10, 135, 147, 181n10
rhythmical prose. *See* style
Richards, Mary P., 5, 181, 181n13
Ringler, Richard N., 96n114
Roberts, Jane, 78n59
Robinson, Fred C., 27n52, 28n53

S

Sauer, Hans, 129, 130n54, 134n63
Schabram, Hans, 20
Schaefer, K. G., 139n3, 141n11, 142n15, 143–44, 144n24, 145n26, 146n27, 147, 151n44, 153nn49–50, 154n54, 156n58, 157, 158nn65–67, 159, 159nn69–70, 160, 161nn72–73, 162nn76–77, 163nn80–81, 165n86, 169n96, 170
'scissors and paste' works, not, 2, 13
Scragg, D. G., 2, 3n9, 5, 6, 11n3, 12–17, 12n6, 14n11, 15n17, 16n19, 17n22, 18, 18n23, 19, 19n29, 20, 20n34, 23n40, 27nn51–52, 28n53, 29nn57–58, 32n69, 35n83, 38, 38n2, 38n4, 39n8, 40n13, 43, 45, 45nn22–23, 47n30, 59n59, 60, 60n63, 63n4, 64nn5–6, 64n8, 65, 65n9, 66, 66n15, 66n17, 67nn19–21, 68, 69nn28–29, 70, 72n37, 73, 73nn40–43, 74, 75n50, 77n53, 79, 79n60, 80n66, 81n68, 81n70, 82n71, 83, 85, 86n88, 87, 88n91, 89, 90, 91–92, 93n105, 95nn109–110, 97n121, 100n131, 101n136, 103nn143–144, 107n1, 109, 111, 129, 129n52, 136, 136n70, 142, 163n79, 183nn1–2, 183nn4–5
Shearin, Hubert Gibson, 53n42
simplification, 56–57, 72n35, 82, 84–85, 86–87, 113, 113n22, 126, 132, 133, 133n62, 148, 148n34,149
Smith, Philip H., Jr., 97n119
speech, 132–33, 143n19, 156, 160–62, 162n77, 164, 164n82, 165, 167–68

Spindler, Robert, 128n50
'split' construction, 117n28, 121, 121n36, 122, 124. *See also* word order
Stanley, E. G., 40n13, 44n19, 68n23, 68n25, 88n91, 91n96, 93n106, 97n121, 98, 107n1, 130n57
St Père homiliary, 65n9, 75
style, 7–8, 12, 14, 18, 20n34, 22, 25, 32, 57, 59–60, 71–72, 99, 111, 142n16, 167–68, 174
  conscious, 71, 127, 170, 174
  controlled, 59, 88, 96, 174
  straightforward, 26, 72, 75, 77n54, 104, 174
  matter-of-fact, 26, 57
  unskillful, 62
  preaching, 179
  rhythmical, 39–41, 71–72, 147, 174, 181n10
substance, change in, 3, 10, 14, 30, 65, 74–75, 100–2, 104, 111, 148n34, 178–79
Sunday List, 141, 145, 153
Swan, Mary, 5–6, 6n21, 10n27, 140, 140n6, 141n10, 143, 148n34, 150, 152n45, 155, 157, 171–72, 179
Swanton, Michael, 165n85
swa (swā), 24, 50, 53n42, 54, 94, 114, 133n62, 143–45, 144nn24–25, 149, 150
syntax, 'loose' or ungrammatical/broken, 28, 28n55, 43, 48, 70, 77n54, 115, 119, 143, 144, 144n22
Szarmach, Paul E., 2, 66n16, 72, 77n56, 79n64, 81

T

taste, change in, 62, 181
tautology, 53, 98, 147
telescoping, 87, 133
Teresi, Loredana, 10n27, 152n45
þa, 130, 134, 150, 159, 161n72, 167
þær, 32, 42, 73, 115, 115n26, 124, 152
þæt is/sindon, explanatory, 50, 51, 74, 126, 158–59
þeah, 28, 49, 85–87, 133n62, 144n22, 148–49

þeah..., *(þeah)hwæþere*, 85–87, 175
Thesaurus of Old English, A, 78n59
þonne, 24, 32, 39n10, 73, 73n39, 76, 84, 115–16, 124, 134, 153
Thorpe, Benjamin, 134n63, 148n33
Tironian nota, 25n47. See also *and*
Torkar, Roland, 101n135
transposition, 19, 34, 90, 134. *See also* word order
'tremulous hand', 154n54, 183nn2–3
Tristram III (*HomS* 45), 63n4, 103

U
ubi sunt, 23
understatement, 143
updating. *See* modernization
utan/uton, 18, 66, 74, 78, 102, 125, 128, 176

V
van Os, A. B., 131n59
variation, poetic, 121–22
Venezky, Richard L., 14n12
verbosity, 52, 54n45, 55, 180
Vercelli Homilies, 3, 3n9, 12, 18–25, 37–46, 60, 63–105, 63n3, 121n34, 173
  II, 9, 37–46, 41n15, 46n25, 63–105, 65n10, 83n77, 84n80, 96–97, 97n121, 173–74, 176
  IV, 12, 16, 18, 31, 82n75, 129n52, 144n22
  IX, 12, 14, 18, 23, 64, 79, 79n65, 81, 85, 85n86, 86, 86n88, 87
  X, 12, 24, 26n49
  XVIII (Martin), 147n32
  XIX, 69n29, 70, 140n9
  XX, 69n29
  XXI, 9, 12, 25, 63–79, 63n4, 65n10, 69n28, 78n57, 82, 97, 97n118, 97n121, 136, 173–76, 178
Vespasian Homilies, 181
Vleeskruyer, R., 66n17, 67n21
Vulgate, 151n43, 153

W
Wanley, Humfrey, 34, 61

Warner, R. D.-N., 180n8
Warner XLII, 181
Waterhouse, Ruth, 162n77
Weber, Robertus, 151n43
West-Saxon Gospels, 153
Whitbread, L., 107n1, 110–11, 111n13, 119, 128n50, 135n66, 136
Whitelock, Dorothy, 4, 4n13, 16n18, 53n41
Wilcox, Jonathan, 4, 4n15, 12n5, 13n8, 34n78, 38, 38n3, 39, 40n13, 42n16, 46n25, 47, 47n29, 48nn32–33, 49, 49nn35–36, 58, 60n62, 61n68, 61nn71–72, 62n76, 64nn5–7, 75n49, 89, 92–95, 95n111, 96n115, 97n121, 99n129, 100nn131–132, 102n138, 103n143, 105n149
Winchester words, 49
word order, 7, 20–21, 32, 39, 46, 50–51, 66, 77, 78, 91, 95, 98, 104, 115–16, 121, 121n34, 122, 124, 130, 130n56, 134, 148–49, 157, 166, 166n88, 167, 178
word pair, synonymous or repetitive, 12–18, 15n15, 30, 39–41, 49, 57, 72, 78, 99, 102, 109–10, 132, 135n66, 136, 147, 147n32, 168–69, 169n94, 174, 179–80
Wrenn, C. L., 121n34
Wright, Charles D., 77n56, 78n57, 129n52
Wulfstan, -nian, 1, 3–4, 4n15, 7–9, 11–19, 12nn5–6, 14nn13–14, 15n16, 16n18, 20–21, 26–27, 30, 37, 47, 47n30, 48–52, 53, 53nn41–42, 54, 54n46, 55, 55n50, 56–58, 58n55, 60–62, 64n7, 69, 69n28, 80n67, 91, 91nn98–99, 100–2, 100n134, 102n138, 104, 124n39, 136, 173–74, 176–77, 180–81, 181n10
  usages, 8, 12–13, 15–16, 16n18, 17, 20n34, 33, 53n41, 96
  tradition, 4, 8, 181
  Homilies, 63, 181
  II, 47
  III, 100, 102

IV, 16n18
V, 91, 181n10
VI, 7, 8, 11, 15, 18, 19, 27, 49, 49n36, 50, 51–52, 53, 54
VIIIb, 15, 17, 49, 51, 55, 56
VIIIc, 50–51, 51n38, 52, 52n39, 53n42, 55, 56
IX, 100, 100n134, 101–2, 102n140
Xc, 14, 55n48, 100n132
XIII, 7, 11, 30, 48, 61
XIV, 58n55
XX, 48, 180
Institutes of Polity and associated materials, 11, 12n6, 14, 17, 17n22, 18–19, 21, 26–27, 50–52, 55, 56n51
De Vitiis principalibus, De virtutibus, 100
legal writings, 14
'Wulfstan imitators', 4, 8–9, 12–17, 49, 53, 59, 136, 136n70, 174

Z
Zupitza, Julius, 129n52, 130, 131n59, 132n61